Fundamentals of Business Communication

Fundamentals of Business Communication

Kumkum Bhardwaj
Professor & Head
Department of Department of English and Foreign Languages
SRM University
Delhi-NCR Campus, Modi Nagar
Ghaziabad, U.P.

I.K. International Publishing House Pvt. Ltd.
NEW DELHI

Published by
I.K. International Publishing House Pvt. Ltd.
4435–36/7, Ansari Road, Daryaganj
New Delhi-110002 (India)
E-mail:info@ikinternational.com
Website: www.ikbooks.com

ISBN 978-93-85909-71-9

Published by Krishan Makhijani for I.K. International Publishing House Pvt. Ltd., 4435–36/7, Ansari Road, Daryaganj, New Delhi-110002 and Printed by Rekha Printers Pvt. Ltd., Okhla Industrial Area, Phase II, New Delhi–110 020.

PREFACE

Fundamentals of Business Communication serves as a comprehensive, up-to-date introduction to modern business communication that integrates communication theory and practice to give you the foundations needed for success in business. Organizations today are constantly reviewing the form and substance of their messages—both oral and written. Thus, in a world of increasing competition students seem to need more refined skills of communication than was necessary before. They have to be aware of certain norms, techniques and methods to excel. Thus, business communication has become an important area of concern in both university communication and business programs and in management training programs. This comprehensive text, written in simple, direct, and intelligible style will be helpful both as a textbook for engineering and management classes, and a manual for business communication. The organization of the book is as follows:

Unit 1, "Understanding Business Communication", (Chapters 1-6) introduces the reader to communication and organizations. An introduction to communication gives an overview to all the interrelated factors that contribute to good and effective communication essential for those whose day-to-day work so depends on communication skills. In this section, the fundamentals of communication, including meaning and definitions, classification, components and process, objectives, medium, directions, channels, functions and types, and scope have been covered. This section also elaborates what organizations are, significance of communication in business organizations, communication in different situations in business organizations, barriers to communication and how to overcome those barriers, ethics and communication. The other issues brought in here are seven C's of effective communication and communication skills.

Unit 2, "Interpersonal and Group Communication Skills", (Chapters 7-11) covers the major aspects of verbal, both oral and written. Listening, business presentations, group communication skills, meetings, business etiquettes, conflict resolution have been discussed in this section. Listening is basic to almost every form of effective oral interactions in business. Other related cognitive and interpersonal skills also depend on listening ability. This section discusses the need for listening in business, the hearing-listening distinction, types and essential requirements for active listening. It also discusses barriers to effective listening and techniques to improve listening ability. Oral presentations focus on tips for a successful presentation comprising preparing and planning for presentation, audience analysis, guiding principles for the use of visual aids, etc. It also deals with various features of body language, including facial expression, eye contact, gesture, posture and use of space, time, and environment as they dominate the human interactions in all the business situations. Besides, this section also reviews the other major forms of business communication such as group communication, communication with people from different cultures, participation in business meetings, minutes and agendas of meeting, business etiquettes, and conflict resolution.

Unit 3, "Written Communication Skills", (Chapters 12-17) presents a thorough discussion of the various forms of business writing. It is a review of the basic techniques of writing and an introduction to the writing process. Here the emphasis is on clear writing, the effect of words, and applications to messages. Besides, problem solving skills such as creativity, mind mapping and brain storming all are major forms of communication in the business world. As each of these forms of business writing has its own formal structure, acquaintance with these aspects is necessary. This section is meant to acquaint the reader with the especial requirement of each of these forms of communication and to give them the confidence to operate effectively within their sphere of activity. This section also concentrates on all business letters, reports, and proposals. Modern communication devices are exclusively dedicated to modern technological aids for communication that are widely used now.

Unit 4, "Employment Communication", (Chapters 18-19) concentrates on proven and effective written and oral approaches to getting the job you want. Preparing a job application should never be taken lightly or left to the last moment. You must also be able to communicate that information to the person doing the hiring. This section discusses the written part of the job application—the application letter and accompanying resume—and elaborates how to create a favourable impression once you arrive for the group discussion and interview.

Unit 5, "Grammar, Mechanics and Usage", (Chapters 20-25) focuses on all the fundamental rules of English grammar, comprising vocabulary development, parts of speech, syntax, concord, prepositions, articles, prefixes and suffixes mandatory for successful business writing. Language as the basic tool for communication describes how the language of successful business people creates a favourable impression. Effective sentences and paragraphs elaborate techniques and methods of writing sentences and paragraphs that will be effective for business purposes. Punctuation and mechanics of business communication contains rules of punctuation and capitalization which provides the foundation for writing words and sentences correctly. This division explains the basic resources like, sentence end and internal punctuation, rules of order and spacing with punctuation marks, capitalization, and the expression of numbers.

All chapters, organized into **five major units** contain objectives in the beginning of all chapters to enforce learning. Review questions for practice in the end of every chapter make the text learner-centric.

The book has **six appendices**. Appendix 1 contains guide for typing business letters that aims to produce most effective letters possible. Appendix 2 consists of foreign words and phrases used in business communication. Appendix 3 deals with idiomatic verbal expressions which are formed by the combination of appropriate prepositions with verbs. Appendix 4 comprises some of the commonest groups of words that are sometimes confused in communication. Appendix 5 provides a list of common misspellings which if memorized, may save the reader from trouble. Appendix 6 describes distinction between similar expressions, which the students would find useful in performing their day-to-day language tasks.

Keeping in view the syllabi of almost all Indian universities, the entire material included in the book is class-tested based on practical and empirical problems of the students. My endeavour has been to give a good book to those teachers who teach the subject of this wide and wonderful world of business communication and the students who want to develop and improve their communication abilities.

Constructive comments on the book and suggestions for its improvement are gratefully welcome.

Kumkum Bhardwaj
e-mail: authorkumkum@gmail.com

ACKNOWLEDGEMENTS

In accomplishing this book, I would like to extend my sincere thanks to Hon'ble Dr. T.R. Paari Vendhar, Founder and Chancellor, SRM University, Chennai, Hon'ble Prof Prabir K. Bagchi, Vice Chancellor, SRM University, Chennai, Dr. N. Sethuraman, Registrar, SRM University, Chennai, Pof. (Dr) Manoj Kumar Pandey, SRM University, NCR Campus, Modinagar, and Dr. Sanjay Viswanathan, Deputy Registrar, SRM University, NCR Campus, Modinagar under whose patronage I was able to write this book.

I acknowledge the congenial environment shared by my colleagues and faculty members of SRM University at Delhi-NCR Campus.

I would like to express my sense of gratitude to Prof. P.K.Chaturvedi, Dept of Electronics and Communication, SRM University, NCR Campus, Modinagar for his constant encouragement. My gratitude to Dr A.K.Mathur, retired Reader & Head, NAS College, Meerut, goes, more than mere written words.

At the home front, I sincerely acknowledge the support and the encouragement I got from my family members. My very special thanks are due to my husband Ram Mohan who has been a source of inspiration to me throughout my endeavour. My sons, Harshit and Madhur, and daughters-in-law, Hina and Priyanka, share no less credit for providing me congenial atmosphere and keeping my morale high. My grandson Avyaan also needs a special mention for never complaining about my deep involvement in the work and taking away his time.

I would like to thank all, my mother-in-law, father, relatives, friends, and well wishers who have shown sympathetic considerations to me in various ways.

Kumkum Bhardwaj

CONTENTS

Preface *v*
Acknowledgements *viii*

UNIT–1: Understanding Business Communication

1. An Introduction to Communication **3**
1.1 Role of Communication 3
1.2 Meaning and Definition of Communication 5
1.3 Nature of Communication 6
1.4 Communication Process 7
1.5 Levels of Communication 15
1.6 Scope of Communication in Organizations 18
Review Questions 20

2. Directions of Communication **21**
2.1 Formal Communication 22
2.2 Types of Formal Communication 23
2.3 Formal Group Network of Communication 27
2.4 Informal Communication 29
Review Questions 35

3. Media of Communication **36**
3.1 Verbal Communication 37
3.2 Non-Verbal Communication 42
3.3 Stress/Accent 55
Review Questions 59

4. Organizational Communication **61**
4.1 Understanding the Organizations 61
4.2 Significance of Communication in Business Organizations 66
4.3 Communication in different Contexts in Organizations 71
4.4 Purposes of Communication in Organization 73
Review Questions 74

5. Barriers to Communication **75**
5.1 The Principal Barriers in Communication 75
5.2 Overcoming the Barriers 81
5.3 Ethics and Communication 83
5.4 Significance of Ethical Communication in Organizations 85
Review Questions 86

6. Principles of Effective Communication **87**
6.1 Prerequisites of Successful Effective Communication 88
6.2 Principles of Effective Communication: Six Cs of Effective Communication 88
Review Questions 94

UNIT–2: Interpersonal and Group Communication Skills

7. Listening Skills **97**
7.1 The Need for Listening in Business 97
7.2 What is Listening? 98
7.3 The Hearing-Listening Distinction 99
7.4 Listening Process 99
7.5 Types of Listening 100
7.6 Listening in Specific Situations 101
7.7 The Problems of Poor Listening Skills 102
7.8 Keys to Better Listening 105
7.9 Listening is Hard Work 107
Review Questions 107

8. Oral Presentations **108**
8.1 The Role of Business Presentations 108
8.2 Types of Presentations 109
8.3 Other Business Presentations 110
8.4 Process to Creating an Effective Oral Presentation 111
8.5 Use of Body Language 117
8.6 Optimize Your Presentation Environment 120
Review Questions 121

9. Team Presentations **122**
9.1 Why Form Groups/Teams? 123
9.2 Four Phases of Team Development 123
9.3 Conflict Resolution 124
9.4 Positive and Negative Team Behaviour 124
9.5 Characteristics of Successful Groups/Teams 125
9.6 Virtual Teams 126
9.7 The Ethical Dimension of Work-Team Communication 127
Review Questions 127

10. Communication with People from Different Cultures **128**
10.1 What is Culture? 128
10.2 Characteristics of Culture 129
10.3 Selected Dimensions of Culture 130
10.4 Improving Communication with Multicultural Audiences 133
10.5 Making Ethical Decisions Across Borders 135
Review Questions 135

11. Business Meetings **137**
11.1 What is a Meeting? 137
11.2 Purpose of Meetings 138
11.3 Responsibilities of the Chairperson 138
11.4 Planning the Meeting 138
11.5 Conducting the Meeting 140
11.6 Following Up the Meeting 143
11.7 Business Etiquette 144
Review Questions 147

UNIT–3: Written Communication Skills

12. The Process of Writing **151**
12.1 Business Writing Basics 152
12.2 The Five Steps in the Writing Process 152
12.3 Evaluating 159
12.4 The Role of Persuasion in Communicating 160
Review Questions 161

13. Problem Solving Skills **162**
13.1 Types of Problem 162
13.2 Alternative Approaches to Problem Solving 163

13.3 Creativity 163
13.4 Mind Mapping 174
13.5 Brainstorming 185
Review Questions 188

14. Business Correspondence **190**
14.1 Business Letter 190
14.2 Essential Characteristics of a Business Letter 195
14.3 The Layout of a Business Letter 195
14.4 Planning the Business Letter 197
14.5 Parts/Elements of a Business Letter 199
14.6 Some Practical Examples of Business Letters 204
14.7 Offers and Quotations 206
14.8 Orders 212
14.9 Confirmation Letter 214
14.10 Defective Order 214
14.11 Delay in Execution 214
14.12 Replies 215
14.13 Cancellation of an Order 215
14.14 Complaints and Adjustments 219
14.15 Credit Enquiries 226
14.16 Circular Letters 232
14.17 Sales Letters 234
14.18 Bank Correspondence 240
14.19 Letters to the Editor 245
14.20 Public Relations Letters 248
Review Questions 251

15. Business Reports **253**
15.1 Meaning and Definition of Report 253
15.2 General Characteristics of Business Reports 254
15.3 Significance of Business Reports 255
15.4 Types of Report 255
15.5 Structure of a Report 261
15.6 Planning and Preparing Report 267
15.7 Style of Report Writing 269
15.8 Reports are Often a Collaborative Effort 275
15.9 Some Practical Examples of Report Writing 275
Review Questions 287

16. Business Proposals **288**
16.1 Business Proposal 288
16.2 Types of Proposals 289
16.3 Planning the External Proposal 290
16.4 Main Parts of a Proposal 291
16.5 Evaluation/Feasibility of a Proposal 293
16.6 Internal Proposal 294
16.7 Designing a Proposal 295
16.8 Format of Formal Proposals 296
16.9 Revision Checklist for Proposals 296
16.10 Some Practical Examples of Proposal Writing 297
Review Questions 306

17. Modern Communication Devices **308**
17.1 Role of Technology in Communication 308
17.2 Accessing Electronic Information 309
17.3 The Internet 309
17.4 Evaluating the Quality of Electronic Information 310
17.5 Sharing Electronic Information 311
Review Questions 314

UNIT–4: Employment Communication

18. Resume and Job Application Letter **317**
18.1 The Career Search 318
18.2 Preparing Your Resume 320
18.3 Two Different Resume Types 327
18.4 What a Resume Should Look Like? 329
18.5 Resume vs Curriculum Vitae (CV)? 329
18.6 Electronic Resume 330
18.7 Writing Job Application Letters 331
Review Questions 334

19. Interview Skills **335**
19.1 Definition of Interview 336
19.2 Interview Myths 336
19.3 Structured and Unstructured Interviews 337
19.4 The Special Nature of Interviews 338
19.5 Types of Interview 338
19.6 Factors Relevant to All Interviews 341

19.7 The Interviewer's Preparation 342
19.8 The Interviewee's Preparation 344
19.9 Parts of the Interview 346
19.10 The Panel Interview 347
19.11 Useful Interview Questions 347
19.12 Conducting Yourself During the Interview 348
19.13 Communicating after the Interview 349
Review Questions 352

UNIT–5: Grammar, Mechanics, and Usage

20. Language: Basic Tool for Business Communication **355**
20.1 Language as the Basic Tool of Communication 355
20.2 Definition of Language 356
20.3 The Background of Language: A Brief View 356
20.4 Different Forms of English 357
20.5 Language: Characteristics 358
20.6 Appropriate and Effective English 360
20.7 Correct Business English 361
Review Questions 361

21. Grammar: Parts of Speech **363**
21.1 Nouns 363
21.2 Pronoun 368
21.3 Verbs 370
21.4 Adjectives 376
21.5 Adverbs 378
21.6 Prepositions 379
21.7 Conjunctions 381
21.8 Articles and Interjections 382

22. Aids to Correct Writing **383**
22.1 Tense 383
22.2 Formation and Use of the Tenses 384
22.3 Auxiliaries and Modals 391
22.4 Conditionals 393
22.5 Verbals: Infinitives, Gerunds, and Participles 395
22.6 Active and Passive Voice 397
22.7 Concord: Agreement of the Verb with Its Subject 400
22.8 Analysing Words with Prefixes and Suffixes 403

22.9 Prefixes 405
22.10 Suffixes 408

23. Developing Effective Sentences **412**
23.1 Sentence Unity 412
23.2 Forming Coherent Sentences 418
23.3 Forming Clear and Emphatic Sentences 435

24. Developing Effective Paragraphs **441**
24.1 The Need for Clear Paragraphing 441
24.2 Developing Unified, Orderly Paragraphs 442
24.3 Variety in Paragraphing 442
24.4 Methods of Paragraph Development 443
24.5 Strengthening Coherence in Paragraphs 446
24.6 Emphasizing Key Points 448

25. Punctuation and Mechanics of Business Writing **450**
25.1 Sentence-End Punctuation 450
25.2 Internal Punctuation 452
25.3 Capitalization in Business Writing 461
25.4 The Expression of Numbers 466
25.5 Fractions, Decimals, and Percentages 467

Appendices **469**
1. Guidelines for Typing Business Letters 471
2. Foreign Words and Phrases Used in Business Communication 475
3. Idiomatic Expressions with Prepositions 478
4. Confusables 483
5. Commonly Misspelled Words 490
6. Distinction between Similar Expressions 493

Index **499**

UNIT–1
Understanding Business Communication

1

AN INTRODUCTION TO COMMUNICATION

Chapter Objectives

This chapter will enable you to understand:

- Role of communication
- Meaning and definition of communication
- Nature of communication
- Communication process
- Levels of communication
- Scope of communication

Communication is a basic life skill. There are three major ways in which communication is important to you as individuals. First, it is a process that influences how you see yourself, affecting your self-concepts. Second, communication is the process through which you initiate and maintain your relationships with others. Finally, communication is the principal means by which you influence others and the world around you.

1.1 ROLE OF COMMUNICATION

1.1.1 Communication in Life

Communication adds meaning to human life. Your ability to communicate largely determines your happiness. It helps to build relationship by providing the foundation for human interaction and fosters love and understanding. The importance of communication can be appraised from the fact that you are communicating in some form or the other almost every moment of your life. Whether you are walking, talking, playing, sitting or even sleeping a message is being formulated or transmitted. In fact, every aspect of life, whether personal, social, political, business, religious, national, or international, involves communication. The way you speak and write gives other people a picture of yourself. People who speak and write well are seen as educated and intelligent and give a good impression. Those who write and speak poorly are held in lower esteem, rightly or wrongly. Learning to communicate well give people a good impression of you in life, in general as well as in business.

1.1.2 Communication in Business

It is communication which gives life to the organization; so it is rightly known as the life blood of an organization.

Can you imagine a business in which no meetings were held, no telephone calls were made, no presentatons were given, no faxes or voice-mails or pager messages or letters or memos were sent or no body spoke to each other? Of course not. Communication between people is extremely important for a business to run. The better the communication, the better the business will run. Every organization undertakes business with the objective to earn profits. Business is an economic activity undertaken to procure man, machine, material, and money to produce goods and services with the objective to sell them to the customers to earn profits. During the course of this process, a businessman consults sellers, buyers, engineers, an accountant, and other people. He collects information and also exchanges facts. The communication, people use in sending and receiving messages in the field of business through speaking, writing, reading, and learning, is known as business communication.

1.1.3 Various Changes in the Workplace and the Role of Communication

In the present scenario, the workplace has undergone profound changes, such as the emergence of heightened global competition, changing organizational structures, expanded team-based management, innovative communication technologies, new work environment and an increasingly diverse workforce. In this dynamic workplace, you can expect to be a knowledge worker; that is, you will deal with words, figures, and data. The most important foundation skill for knowledge workers is the ability to communicate effectively. The more effective the system of communication, the better is the co-ordination and integration of various human activities in the organization.

1.1.4 Business Communicators: A Valuable Company Asset

Take a look at the classified job advertisements in newspapers. Many job advertisements ask for people who are good communicators. Why? Because good communicators are good for business. They bring business to the company. They have learned good people skills, they know how to encourage others to buy and so they can quite easily sell their company's goods and services. Their messages are clear and simple and do not have to be repeated or questioned for meaning. Good communicators present information well. They are extremely good listeners also. Good communicators, therefore, are very valuable to employers and indeed to companies, and companies are always on the search for people with good communication skills.

1.1.5 Communication Globally

It is the ability of fostering speedy and effective communication around the world that has shrunk the world and made globalization a reality. Many foreign companies have offices in your country and you may well find yourself dealing with American, Japanese, French or Korean staff. You may travel abroad to other countries on business trips. Good communication is extremely important if your business dealings are to succeed.

1.1.6 Why Learn to Communicate Well

In a recent survey of recruiters from companies with more than 50,000 employees, communication skills were cited as one of the more important decisive factors in choosing managers. The survey points out that communication skills, including written and oral presentations, as well as an ability to work with others, are the main factors contributing to job success.

However, one of the neglected areas of human development is communication. In spite of the increasing importance placed on communication skills, many individuals continue to struggle, unable to communicate their thoughts and ideas effectively - whether in verbal or written format. This inability makes it nearly impossible for them to compete effectively in the workplace, and stands in the way of career progression. To paraphrase Peter Drucker, colleges teach the one thing that is perhaps most valuable for the future employees to know. But very few students bother to learn it. This one basic skill is the ability to organize and express ideas in writing and speaking. This ability to express oneself is perhaps the most important of all the skills a person can possess. It is, therefore, necessary to understand the art of communication and apply or modify it in a suitable manner.

1.2 MEANING AND DEFINITION OF COMMUNICATION

The best way to improve communication is to understand what communication is. Communication is never a matter of handling over a bundle of information; it is a matter of creating meaning out of that information, and then sharing that meaning. If the other person cannot understand what you mean, then your attempts to communicate fail.

When businessmen and professionals are asked to define 'communication', they often respond with something like this: "communication is the process of transferring thoughts and ideas from one person to another." On the surface, this definition seems good. It acknowledges that communication is a process and it transfers our ideas from one person to another. However, the definition implies a simple, one way action. A more accurate definition of communication can be found by looking at its original meaning. The Oxford English Dictionary lists the Latin root of 'communicate' as 'communis', which means "to make common to many," or to share. According to this definition, when people communicate they express their ideas and feelings in a way that is understandable (common) to each of them. Each person has a direct effect on the other person and on subsequent communication.

Scholars have been writing about human communication for long. If we examine these definitions carefully, we begin to understand the variety of perspectives from which the human communication act can be viewed. A few of these definitions are reproduced below:

- "Communication is an exchange of facts, ideas, opinions, or emotions, by two or more persons."

  –George Terry

- "Communication may be defined as giving, receiving or exchanging information, opinions, and ideas by writing, speech or visual means so that the material communicated is completely understood by everyone concerned."

–Shirley Taylor

- "Effective communication is the process of passing information and understanding from one person to another. It is essentially a bridge of meaning between people. By using the bridge of meaning a person can safely cross the river of misunderstanding."

–Keith Davis

- "Communication is interchange of thoughts, opinions, or information, by speech, writing, or signs."

–Robert Anderson

- Communication has been defined "as the transfer of information from one person to another, irrespective of whether or not it elicits confidence."

–Koontz and O' Donell

- "Communication is any behaviour that results in an exchange of meaning."

–The American Management Association

- "Communication is a process involving the sorting, selecting, and sending of symbols in such a way as to help a listener perceive and re-create in his own mind the meaning contained in the mind of communication."

–Raymond Ross

Each of the foregoing definition provides insight into the process of human interaction. For the reader, it is important to keep the following ideas in mind:

- **Communication involves the creation of meaning in the listener**

  Since meaning cannot be transferred, the sender attempts to create a meaning in the mind of the listener similar to the meaning in his own mind. It is never possible to create the exact same meaning, because no two humans are alike.
- **Communication involves the transfer of information**

  As communication takes place, one person is trying to pass along information to another. Information is transferred through the use of symbols, which can be verbal or non-verbal or both.
- **Communication involves thousands of potential stimuli**

  A number of stimuli may be involved in the communication process. A stimulus becomes a message when the individual assigns it a meaning.
- **Communication involves a return response**

  As communication is interchange of information, the person who sends the information gets a return response or feedback (positive or negative) from the receiver.

1.3 NATURE OF COMMUNICATION

The analysis of the above definitions implies that communication has the following characteristics, which define the nature of communication. Good communication:

- is a dynamic process.
- is essentially a physical, social and psychological exercise.
- is systematic.
- leads to personal effectiveness.
- helps one to network with other people.
- influences motivation for enhanced performance.
- builds better understanding between the boss and the subordinates.
- creates better interpersonal relations.
- increases listening ability.
- enables employees to appreciate the need for change.
- creates better environment for knowing why there is resistence to change

The ability to communicate effectively, therefore, is a learned behaviour. When we communicate by applying the techniques and the skills, we do build better understanding with people in our environment despite differences amongst us.

1.4 COMMUNICATION PROCESS

Our understanding of what communication is influences how we act and analyze situations. So it is important to work out what communication involves.

Communication is a process or a flow of transmitting and receiving verbal and non-verbal messages. Communication is considered effective when it achieves the reaction or response from the receiver. Simply stated, communication is a two-way process of exchanging ideas or information. The process of communication consists of several components. These components are interrelated to form the model of communication. In fact, the communication model explains the interrelationship between several components which contributes the process of communication.

1.4.1 The Process Models of Communication

One way to understand the principles and process that define the nature of communication is through modelling. A model is a schematic representation of a complex phenomenon. The model makes the phenomenon easier to understand. Communication is also a complex phenomenon. People make communication complex as their attitudes, orientations, perceptions, and ideas get involved in the process of sending and receiving information. The process models of communication are aimed to show how information is transmitted from source to destination and to analyze what can affect the quality of the information during this process. There are many models of communication, main among them are as under.

1.4.1.1 Shannon and Weaver's Model of Communication Process

The Claude Shannon and Warren Weaver's model is one of the earliest attempts at diagramming communication and the first to level the important paths of the communication. Since the model was done originally to describe electronic, as opposed to human communication, it is a linear model. It seems to suggest that communication is a one-way phenomenon going only from the sender to the receiver. According to this model, the receiver would have no impact on the sender. In reality, the receiver provides a response to the message heard. This response is referred to as feedback and this ability to adjust is the basis of the concept of two-way communication.

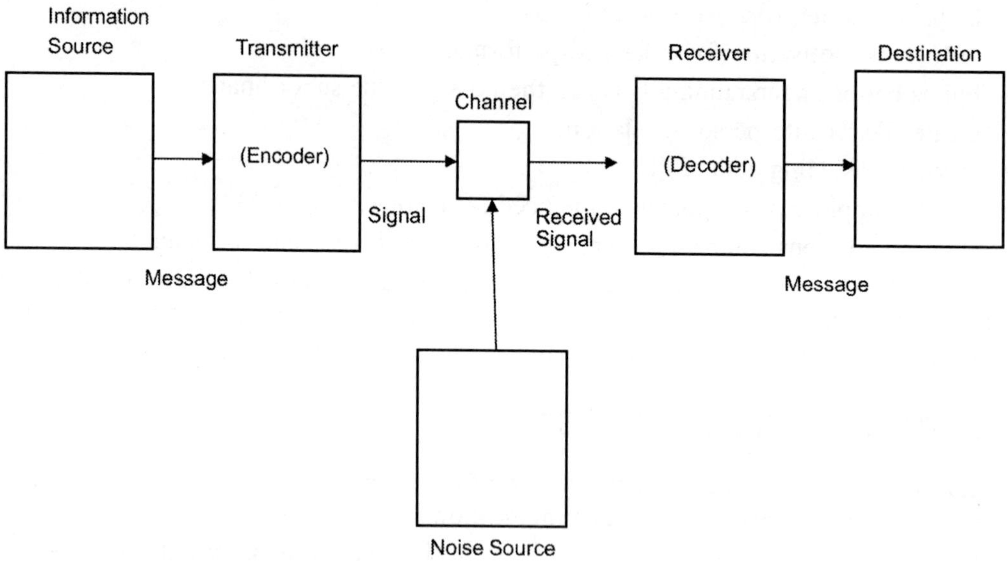

Figure 1.1: Shannon and Weaver's model of communication process.

Thus, the model can be shown as follows:

1. **Information source:** It is the beginning of the process. It represents some purpose as the part of the sender.
2. **Transmitter:** The sender of the message in an encoded form is known as transmitter.
3. **Message:** It is the information passing between the sender and the receiver in the communication process
4. **Channel:** The channel is the medium that transmits the signal from the transmitter to the receiver.
5. **Noise source:** This model recognizes the potential of noise in distorting the message.
6. **Receiver:** The receiver is the person to whom the information is sent. He decodes the information.
7. **Destination:** Destination is the end of the communication process.

The significance of the Shannon and Weaver's model is that it shows all the essential parts of the communication process.

1.4.1.2 Murphy's Model of Communication Process

Murphy's model of communication process is propounded by three writers–H. A. Murphy, H. W. Hildbrandt, and J.P. Thomas. According to this model, there are six components of communication process. They are:

1. **Context:** Every message, whether oral or written, begins with context. Context includes country, culture, organization, external and internal causes of action.
2. **Sender-encoder:** The sender-encoder uses symbols, usually words, that express the message and create the desired response.
3. **Message:** The message is the core idea the sender wishes to communicate. It consists of both visual (written or spoken) symbols and non-verbal symbols.
4. **Medium:** The medium is the channel through which a message is communicated. It can be printed word, electronic mail, sound, or gesture.
5. **Receiver-decoder:** The receiver or listener or reader is the person who receives the message and decodes it. He is also called the decoder.
6. **Feedback:** Sender needs feedback in order to determine the success or failure of the communication. The receiver decodes the message and provides feedback. Feedback can be oral or written. It can be an action such as receiving in the mail an item you ordered.

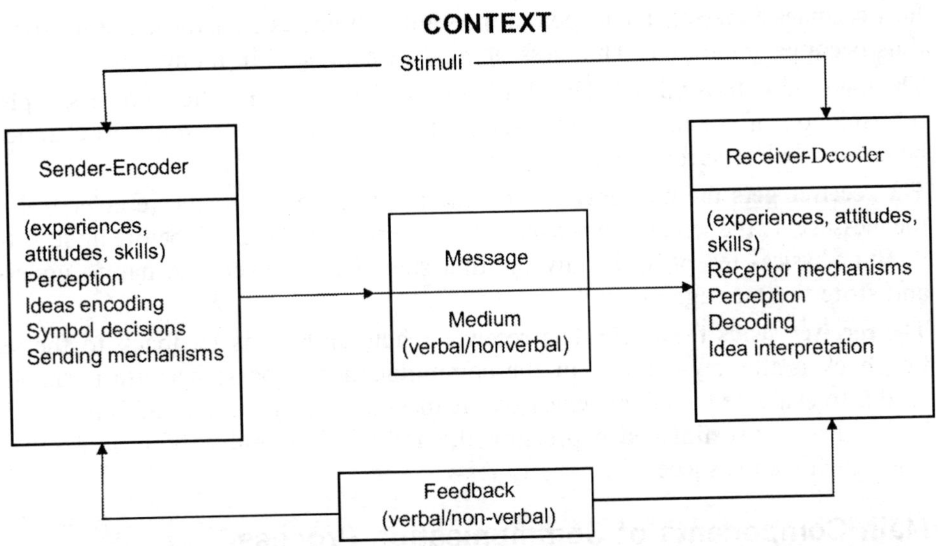

Figure 1.2: Murphy's model of communication process.

In short, the model described above represents what happens in communication. A context exists in which a sender chooses a message to communicate. The sender must also choose the medium for the message. A receiver decodes the message and provides feedback.

1.4.1.3 Thill and Bovee's Model of Communication Process

Thill and Bovee have developed the following model of communication. According to them business communication is more than a single act. It is chain of events consisting of five phases linking sender and receiver.

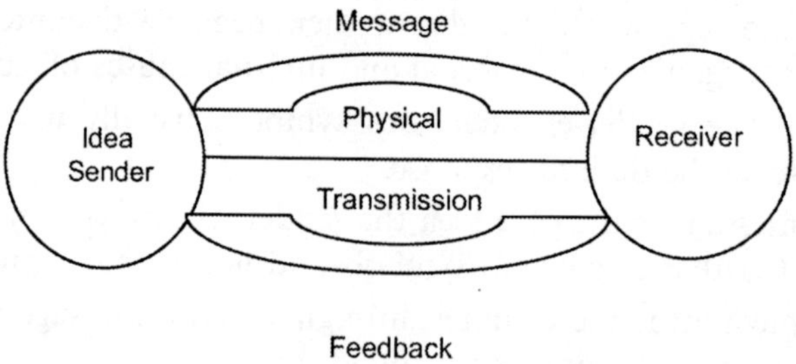

Figure 1.3: Thill and Bovee model of communication process.

The diagram depicts that the communication process is made up of following parts:

1. **Idea:** The process of communication begins when the sender has an idea. In the process of conceiving an idea about the real world, the sender leaves out many things and assumes many others. This means that the idea in the mind of the sender is a simplification of the real world.
2. **Idea becomes a message:** The idea in the sender's mind is transformed into words and thus becomes a message. The message may be expressed in many ways.
3. **The message is transmitted:** The third step in the communication process is physical transmission of the message from sender to receiver. The transmission channel may be non-verbal or verbal, spoken or written.
4. **The receiver gets the message:** For communication to occur, the receiver has to get the message. If the sender sends a letter, the receiver has to read it before understanding it. But physical reception is only the first step. The receiver also has to understand and store the message mentally.
5. **The receiver sends feedback:** The receiver reacts and sends feedback to the sender. Feedback is the key element in the communication process because it enables the sender to evaluate the effectiveness of the message. Then the process is repeated until both parties have finished expressing themselves. Communication is effective only when each step is successful.

1.4.2 Main Components of Communication Process

As you can see each model has a number of important components. Each part of the communication process provides a unique function in any exchange. The models show the relationship between these components of communication. Using all of the models presented, let us examine some of the important elements in the communication process:

1. **Idea:** The idea is the simplification and abstraction of reality filtered through the individual mind. Every message, whether oral or written, begins with an idea. Every idea refers to some context. Context is a broad field that includes external and internal events. Every business organization has its own convention for processing and communicating information. This is the internal aspect of context. Another aspect of context is the external action that prompts you to communicate your idea, the source of this action may be a letter, memo, fax, telephone call, or e-mail.

2. **Sender:** The sender is the originator or source of a message. This is the person who initiates the communication by thinking an idea to communicate to the receiver. Sender is sometimes referred to as the source, the communicator, or the encoder. The sender must have a clear picture in his mind about what he wants to communicate. Messages originate from a variety of sources, at all levels, both inside and outside an organization. For example, a customer making a complaint to a customer care service representative is the sender, i.e., the originator of the message, to the customer care service representative.
3. **Message:** The message is information, verbal (oral/written) or non-verbal, which is to be sent from one person to another. In other words, the message is what the sender says and does during a communication process. The message exists in the mind of the sender. In fact, information is what we create inside our heads as we understand. Information is always in our minds and is the shape of our thinking. The shape of information is constantly changing, evolving as we think, and is dynamic. The most important characteristic of a message as an element of communication is that it is organized, structured and selective. The message can be expressed in different ways depending on the subject, purpose, audience, personal style and cultural background of the sender.
4. **Encoding:** The method by which a message is expressed is called encoding. Before the idea or message is sent to the receiver, the sender needs to encode it in an appropriate code keeping in mind the receiver's ability to understand and interpret them correctly. Thus, encoding is the act of putting an idea into a code so that it becomes perceptible to the receiver.

   This can be done using a verbal code (language, whether spoken, written or sign language) or a non-verbal code (a code without words or language). The sender chooses a code that will make the message accessible to the receiver. It is quite common to encode a message in more than one code. For example, language and body language are used when the sender says 'come' and beckons with his or her hand at the same time.
5. **Code:** A code is a set of symbols which, when combined and used according to the rules agreed upon by the users, conveys meaning. The most commonly used code in the business and technical world is 'language'.

   The set of symbols used in language is alphabet. The letters of the alphabet are combined according to rules to form words, the words are combined according to rules to form sentences, and so meaning is conveyed. The following examples show how easy it is to combine the same four symbols according to agreed upon rules to create meaning.

   TAME
   MATE
   TEAM
   MEAT

The same four letters when combined in a haphazard way no longer create or convey meaning.

ETAM

MTAE

TAEM

AEMT

When using a code to convey meaning, it is essential that you follow the rules. However, language is not the only code to communicate. The clothes we wear, and how we wear them, also convey meaning. For example, whether a man wears a coat and tie to a particular function or not is determined by the 'dress code'. Other codes include body language, colour, and pictures. Any language, both spoken and written, is referred to as non-verbal codes. Both verbal and non-verbal codes can convey the same idea. The effectiveness of the message will depend greatly on the correct choice of the code. For example, when communicating to illiterate people on how to vote, or take medication, a written message will be unsuccessful. Pictures will be needed.

Verbal	Non-verbal
Danger	 Toxic
No Smoking	
No U Turn	

Figure 1.4: Codes for different audience.

6. **Purpose:** People communicate for a reason. Sometimes the sender's reason may be different from the receiver's. Conflict of purpose can create a barrier to communication. Our purpose in communicating at any given time is probably deeply rooted in our psychological state. Occasionally we may not even be consciously aware of our reason for wanting to communicate.
7. **Medium:** The method by which a message is transmitted by a sender to the receiver is called medium. The message must be conveyed to the receiver in a concrete form.

This is achieved through using a medium. Examples of media commonly used in business and professional communication include the telephone, e-mail, meetings, faxes, letters, memos, interviews, and conversations.

Written and Spoken Media

Language	
Written media	Spoken media
Letter	Lecture
E-mail	Telephone
Newspaper	Radio
Fax	Conversation
Road Sign	Meeting
Notice	TV
Book	Interview

8. **Channel:** The channel is the medium which facilitates the sender to convey the message to the receiver. The medium of communication can be the language (written or oral), picture, actions, signals or objects, etc. It is selected by the source, who must determine which channel is formal and which one is informal. Further, the written medium can be in the form of letters, memos, reports, circulars, notices, and so on. Similarly, the oral medium can be in the form of a dialogue, a face-to-face discussion, a telephonic conversation, a conference, and so on. The channel can also be visuals, such as posters, pictures, hoardings, films, and advertisements.

   Thus, there is a difference between medium and channel. In written communication, letter is a medium and postal or courier service is channel. In oral communication, if a message is circulated by telephone, then oral message is a medium and telephone is a channel.
9. **Receiver:** The receiver is the person to whom the sender directs the message. The receiver receives the message, decodes it and acts on it. He understands, interprets, and tries to perceive the total meaning of the message as transmitted by the sender. Everyone in the organization can send and receive the message. The customer care service representative is the receiver of the customer's complaint. However, the customer care service representative in turn reports the complaint to people in the organization—the manager of the customer care service department, the manager of the department where the product was sold to the customer, and co-workers in other departments.
10. **Decoding:** Decoding is the act of translating symbols of communication into their ordinary meaning. Decoding is the mental process by which the receiver draws meanings, from the words, symbols, or pictures of the message. As the receiver decodes or understands the message, he is called a decoder also.

11. **Feedback:** Finally, the receiver completes the chain of communication by responding to the message. There is always feedback to communication. The transmission of the receiver's response to the sender is called feedback. Initially, communication theorists viewed feedback in a very mechanical way. For example, a smile from our customer care service representative could indicate acceptance of, and appreciation for the customer's complaint. Feedback tells us whether the message was properly received and whether the purpose and goal were realized.

    In the process, the sender may get both the positive and negative responses from the receiver, but since he has got some feedback, the communication process is complete. However, the communication is effective only when the message has been understood by the receiver and the sender gets the desired response from the receiver. Therefore, there should be cooperation between the sender and the receiver.

    In face-to-face communication, feedback will be direct. Both sender and receiver give constant feedback as they exchange messages. Feedback on written communication is not often as direct. However, feedback is more likely to come from the result of the message.

12. **Communication environment:** Communication takes place in a well-defined set-up. This is called the communication environment. A classroom, for example, is the communication environment where a teacher delivers lectures to his students.

1.4.3 Noise

Noise is defined as the physical and mental influences that either disrupt or lead to the misinterpretation of messages. In its wider sense, noise includes many factors that exist at the level of the sender as well as that of the receiver. There are three types of noise that can affect a message:

1. **Physical noise** may emanate from the environment, for example, loud talking from the next room, opening or closing of doors, sudden announcements over a loudspeaker that disrupts a conversation.
2. **Semantic noise** refers to differences people have for the meaning of words. Semantic noise includes misheard or misunderstood terms, gender bias (such as saying 'he' when referring to all managers or 'she' when referring to all childcare givers), the perception of racial undertones (such as a fear or anxiety expressed as something 'dark'), in-house or professional jargon, or culturally derived metaphors.
3. **Hierarchical noise** refers to the shading in meaning, we attribute to a message based on a person's rank or status with an organization. For example, a customer may insist on complaining to the customer care service representative's supervisor than to the customer care service representative, even though the manager will refer the message back down the chain of command.

1.5 LEVELS OF COMMUNICATION

Communication is not simply a matter of face-to-face exchange of information. In organizations people participate in a number of different levels of communication. It can be classified according to the number of receivers or participants to whom the message is communicated. These are briefly discussed below. In Chapter 4 communication in different contents in organization will again be discussed.

1.5.1 Organizational Communication

An organization, as is defined by Fielding is, 'consisting of groups of people who work together to reach specific goals.' (Effective Communication in Organizations, 1997) Organizational communication involves communication within an organization such as a school, a university, a business, or a government department. In an organization the individuals have to communicate with each other and share information if they are to reach shared goals.

How the organization is managed affects the communication with the organization. Organizational communication would be particularly concerned with a flow of information–upward, downward, and horizontal. It would also be concerned with the effects of managerial styles, leadership and motivation on communication. Effective communication within a business helps to ensure efficiency for customers. This type of communication covers many types of spoken and written messages. The direction in which the message travels between the sender and the receiver within an organization is referred to as a 'channel'.

1.5.2 Group Communication

Group communication refers to the communication that takes place among people who work together with a common goal. In any organization there are various types of small groups, either formal (for example, a meeting) or informal (for example, study or tutorial groups). Group members all need to subscribe to the same value and norms that are developed within that group if they are to work together effectively. In the best groups every member is encouraged to communicate to his or her full potential. A positive atmosphere of climate is established so that people work well together.

Group communication can be among small or large groups, like an organization, club or classroom, in which all individuals retain their individual identity. In an organization a large number of employees are involved in a number of different activities. With a proper networking system in these organizations, communication takes place even without direct contact between employees. This type of communication can be further divided into:

1.5.2.1 Internal-operational Communication

1. Internal-operational communication takes place within an organization during the process of work. In an organization planning, production, sales, stores, advertising, financing, accounts, welfare, etc. are handled by different departments. The employees of these departments communicate with one another as well as with the management to maintain coordination among them. It includes the orders and instructions that

supervisors give workers, as well as oral exchange among workers about work matters. It also includes reports, proposals, e-mail messages, and so on.

2. Large organizations have a number of branches within the country and even abroad. In such cases, when the organization has more than one branch at various locations, nationally or internationally, the communication through various means is dissipated from one end to the other. In this way the central organization maintains a thorough and up-to-date knowledge of the various activities at the branch offices, also keeps the branch offices well acquainted with the activities at the centre through internal operational communication.
3. Interpersonal communication promotes understanding and cooperation among members of the same organization. If there exists effective communication between the management and the employees, it helps to bring about an atmosphere of mutual trust and confidence. This mutual understanding is very much beneficial to both the parties.

1.5.2.2 External-operational Communication

The work related communication that a business does with people and groups outside the organization (suppliers, customers, service companies, stockholders, government, and the general public) is external operational communication. This form of communication includes all the efforts of business in direct selling such as descriptive brochures, telephone calls, follow-up service calls, and so on. It also includes the advertising that the business does to improve its public relations, etc.

1.5.2.3 Personal Communication

Personal communication is the exchange of information and feelings in which employees engage whenever they come together without official purpose in an organization. Although not a part of operational plan of business, personal communication can have a significant effect on success of any business operation. The nature of personal communication or conversation in a workplace affects the attitude of a worker, which then affects his/her performance. Besides, personal communication also has an emotive function in an organization. In other words, it permits the expression of feeling and satisfaction of social needs.

1.5.3 Mass Communication

Mass communication occurs when the message is sent to large groups of people via mass media (for example, by radio, television, film, newspaper, magazine, computer, telecommunication, etc.) simultaneously and effectively. Organizations that advertise in the newspaper or the radio or television, or issue press releases are involved in this type of communication. Mass communication is involved with large audience, frequent reproduction of messages and rapid distribution of messages.

This kind of communication is largely impersonal as the participants are unknown to each other. In this process, each person becomes a faceless individual with almost no opportunity for personal response or feedback. Therefore, the restricted opportunity for feedback is the most serious barrier to effective mass communication. Mass communication is more persuasive in nature than any other form of communication.

1.5.4 Interpersonal Communication

A great deal of communication in organizations is interpersonal. Interpersonal communication is the sharing of information between two persons. They use common language to transmit message either through oral communication or written communication. In this form of communication direct and immediate feedback is possible. Non-verbal communication plays a major role in the interpretation of message.

Interpersonal communication can be formal (an interview) or informal (interaction between two friends). The success of communication depends on a variety of factors, such as the psychology of the two persons involved, the relationship between them, the situation in which the communication takes place, the surrounding environment, and the cultural context. Interpersonal communication accounts for most informal everyday communication, transactions, including personal and intimate relationships, as well as many business situations.

1.5.5 Public Communication

Public communication refers to public speaking in organizations. This type of communication is formal in nature and occurs in public rather than private places. One person gives a lecture, talk or oral report to a small or large group. Public communication is usually one-way communication and the audience does not participate.

In this type of communication the speaker is concerned with effective analysis of the audience's need, appearance, good preparation, an effective style of delivery, effective nonverbal communication and the audience's response to the speech.

1.5.6 Intrapersonal Communication

This is the most basic level of communication. Intrapersonal communication is the way we talk to ourselves, i.e., without speaking out the words aloud. The message enters the body via the five senses. The thought processes generated and the decision to take action are the result of communication taking place within the individual. Intrapersonal communication forms the basis of all communication.

This type of communication is important in the formation of an individual's self-image. If we give ourselves constant negative messages, we are likely to develop a negative self-image. This will affect our interpersonal communication, as well as positive self-image. We will often show our self-images by our nonverbal behaviour. Other people will interrupt this behaviour and then communicate with us accordingly. Examples are soliloquies or asides in dramatic words.

1.5.7 Extrapersonal Communication

Extrapersonal communication takes place between humans and animals, plants, and objects. We need to learn how animals communicate. When a pet dog wags its tail and a parrot responds to our greeting, these are the examples of extrapersonal communication. Communication also involves machines, for example, computers. Humans use computers to improve communication between them.

1.6 SCOPE OF COMMUNICATION IN ORGANIZATIONS

A business organization is a system. There are two ways of operating and communicating in this system. One is operation of internal links of people, processes and core competencies in the organization. Second is operation of external links of customers, supply chain vendors, and other external vendors of community, media, civic organizations and government.

Thus, the scope of business communication in organizations is very wide and comprehensive, which can be understood under two broad dimensions: internal and external. Internal communication focuses on employees and management interactions for the core processes of people, plans, policies, and operations motivating for action implementation. The external communication is associated with business development in which there is trust, cooperation, collaboration, innovation, and commitment.

1.6.1 Internal Dimension

Internal communication is mostly interpersonal, this channel is used both for formal and informal interactions. It is both vertical and horizontal interpersonal communication encompassing employees' interaction and management interaction within the different business divisions and facilities of an organization. There is technology support to interpersonal communication also. People at all level communicate with each other by telephones, e-mails, Internet, formal presentations, and other question hours to clarify their doubts, and also through informal interpersonal interactions. The informal interpersonal communication is facilitated in staff lounges, lunch rooms, cafeterias, around the vending machines and water coolers. People interact and exchange information and views informally even when they are walking through the office corridors. These social operating machines help to get to know the office happenings, informally exchanging both positive and negative views about people and products, and sharing new ideas and knowledge effortlessly and inadvertently.

Employee and management interaction focuses on building and upgrading the capabilities of the organization and its employees, surfacing the business reality and accountability, finding realistic solutions and implementing them. Some salient communication channels including organization culture facilitate the communication process. The characteristics of the communicator are important in this process. Further, appraisals, as communication tools, help in getting the right person for the right job.

1.6.2 External Dimension

External dimension of communication is associated with business development through the visibility of the organization and its products and services. This could be facilitated through communicating with external links to the corporate business such as supply chain for the product components, distributors, wholesalers, and retailers, consumers, business competitors, public relations, business focused conferences, product marketing and sales through its positioning in the market and product campaigns, community, media, and civic bodies.

Market Information System (MIS) is organized flow of information among external links. The concept is that the flow of information is continuing, interactive with people and procedures to take market decisions.

The scope of business communication (internal and external) in organizations can be expanded to include:

1. **Influence:** The main objective of communication is to influence people. The communicator communicates to create a good environment with the right attitude and pleasant working relationships. All these are examples of influencing.
2. **Facilitating change:** The effectiveness of a change introduced in an organization depends to a large extent on the clarity and impulsiveness of the communication. Communication between the managers and the employees helps in recognizing the difficulties in the planned change and in taking corrective actions.
3. **Decision-making:** Communication to a great extent helps in decision-making. For coming to a conclusion, several kinds of communication are needed, e.g., exchange of information, views and available alternatives, etc.
4. **Information sharing:** The prime objective of communication is to transmit information from a source to target individuals or groups. Various types of information are transmitted in the organization. Some of them are - policies, rules and regulations, vision, mission and the changes and the developments in the organization, etc. There may be a need for the fast diffusion of some of the information in an organization, e.g., special rewards and awards given, settlements with the union and major changes in the organization.
5. **Feedback:** There is a need to give the feedback to the employees on their performance or achievements so that they can align their efforts in the same vector as that of organization. If we cannot relate back to where the company's objectives are and how the employees are going to help the organization and if we cannot make it substantially for our people to translate the vision into personal achievements, we are not going to have internally motivated improvements. Therefore, the feedback mechanism in any organization is an important aspect of communication.
6. **Control:** The management information system (MIS) is one of the tools for an effective monitoring and control mechanism in the organization. The information is transmitted to ensure that the plans are being executed in accordance to the planned schedules and communication ensures for reviewing its efficacy for adhering and ensuring timely corrective and preventive actions.
7. **Problem solving:** In many cases, the communication is aimed to solving problems. The communication between management and the unions on some issues is aimed at finding suitable solution. Many group discussions/meetings are held and brainstorming done to understand the root cause of an issue/problem and evolve a consensus. A typical approach of Define the problem, Measure, Analyze, Improve and Control (DMAIC) is applied as a problem solving approach in a process and is known as six sigma approach.
8. **Gate keeping:** The communication helps to build linkage of the organization with the outside world. The organization can use its environment to increase its effectiveness.
9. **Group building:** Communication helps in building relationships. If the communication breakdowns, the group may disintegrate. The communication provides the necessary cushion for the proper functioning of the groups and keeps groups intact.

REVIEW QUESTIONS

1. Attempt a suitable definition of term 'communication' and elaborate your definition.
2. What is the significance of communication for an individual and for an organization?
3. What is the importance of business communication as a two-way process? Discuss the role of each constituent element.
4. What are the essential elements in communication process? Identify them and describe the role of each.
5. Three models of the communication process were described in the chapter. Choose one model and defend it as best demonstrating the nature of communication.
6. What is 'noise'? What is its effect on the communication process? Explain message and feedback in the communication process.
7. Describe different levels of communication in an organization. Give examples of each within an organization and when communicating with people outside the organization.
8. The scope of communication in an organization is very wide and comprehensive. Discuss.
9. What is the role of effective communication within and outside the organization?
10. What factors influence good communication?
11. Read the newspaper advertisement below and answer the questions that follow:

The Eco Times
Don't be a drip, turn off the tap
Save water, save lives

Brought to you by the Dept. of EFL, SRM University Modinagar

For more information on how to save water, visit our website
www.srmtvaluecell.co.in

Identify the following:

(a) Sender
(b) Medium
(c) Audience
(d) Two different codes
(e) Message
(f) Feedback medium
(g) An example of delayed feedback
(h) Context

2
DIRECTIONS OF COMMUNICATION

Chapter Objectives

This chapter will enable you to understand:

- Formal communication
- Types of formal communication
  - Horizontal
  - Vertical
  - Diagonal
- Formal group network of communication
- Informal communication
  - Grapevine
  - Rumour
  - Consensus
- Difference between formal communication and informal communication

Communication is multidimensional. That is, communication occurs in a variety of ways in an organization. The effectiveness of communication system depends upon the extent to which the necessary information reaches the concerned person at the right time. There are various directions or channels in which communication flows. Every organization creates a network or channel for information to pass through its different levels of authority and functional heads and units. The flow of communication follows the structure of organization. In practice, the information passes through the organizational pyramid as shown below:

In an organization, all communication can be divided into two categories, namely:

- Formal communication
- Informal communication

Communication, whether formal or informal, is all about understanding. Our aim should be to communicate a message successfully so that it is received without any misunderstanding.

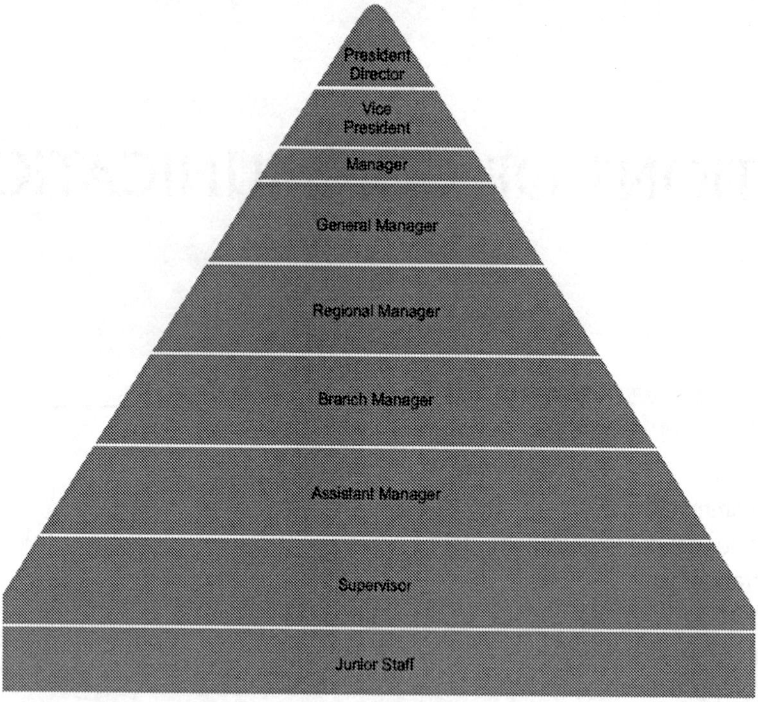

Figure 2.1: Organization pyramid.

2.1 FORMAL COMMUNICATION

Formal communication refers to the communication within an organization that is officially sanctioned. Formal communication follows the official hierarchy and it flows through formal channels. It is a deliberate effort normally created by managers in an organization to control individuals and group behaviour and to achieve the organization's goals. This makes possible for the information to reach the desired place without any hindrance at a little cost and in a proper way. It is also known as 'through proper channel communication'.

2.1.1 Characteristics of Formal Communication

Following are the chief characteristics of formal communication:

1. **Written and oral:** Formal communication can both be written and oral. Daily works are handled through oral communication, while the policy matter requires written communication.
2. **Formal relations:** This communication is adopted among those employees where formal relations have been established by the organization. The sender and the receiver have some sort of organizational relations.
3. **Prescribed path:** The formal communication has to pass through a definite channel while moving from one person to another. For example, to convey the feelings of a worker to the manager the supervisor's help has to be sought. Here the definite channel will be like this:

Worker ⟶ Supervisor ⟶ Manager

4. **Organizational message:** This channel is concerned with the authorized organizational message only and the personal messages are out of its jurisdiction.
5. **Deliberate efforts:** This channel of communication is not established automatically but efforts have to be made for its creation. It is decided keeping in view the objectives of the organization.

Advantages of formal communication

The formal communication has the following advantages:

1. **Maintenance of authority of the officers:** Formal communication maintains contact relations among the superiors and the subordinates as a result of which the dignity of the line superiors is maintained. Consequently, it is convenient to control the subordinates and fix their responsibilities.
2. **Clearer and effective:** In formal communication, there is a direct contact among the managers and the subordinates. Both understand the capabilities, habits, feelings, etc. of one another. Managers know as to when and under which conditions their subordinates need information. In this way, this communication is capable of making available timely information. Hence, it is clearer and effective.
3. **Orderly flow of information:** The information has to pass through a definite route from one person to another. Hence, the flow of information is systematic.
4. **Easy knowledge of source of information:** In this type of communication, the source of each information can be easily located.

Limitations of formal communication

Following are the disadvantages or limitations of the formal communication:

1. **Overload of work:** In a modern business organization, much information, many messages, and other things have to be communicated under formal communication. They are routed through a definite channel and this consumes much of the time of the superiors and thus some other important works are left unattended.
2. **Description of information:** This method can be a hindrance in the flow of information. Sometimes the distance between the sender and the receiver is so big that the information has to pass through many hands and by the time it reaches the receiver it is distorted.
3. **Overlooking by the officers:** The officers do not pay much attention to the suggestions and complaints of the subordinates. They overlook them taking them to be works of daily routine. If the workers have to convey something to the director, the superiors add something or the other from their own disfiguring reality.

2.2 TYPES OF FORMAL COMMUNICATION

The formal communication flows in the following directions:

- Horizontal (or lateral) communication
- Vertical communication
- Diagonal communication

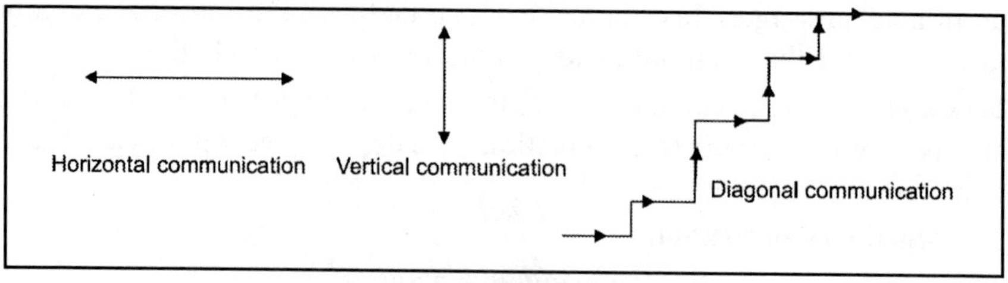

Figure 2.2: Directions of communication.

2.2.1 Horizontal Communication

Horizontal or lateral communication, also known as peer communication, occurs between people of the same level or status in the managerial hierarchy of the organization—sales staff, departmental heads, directors, managers, etc. It is the most frequently used channel of communication. Workers communicating with other workers, clerks exchanging information with one another, supervisors holding a coffee-break session to discuss some organizational problems are all engaged in horizontal communication.

Organizations form divisions on the basis of different functions, such as production, marketing, finance, training and development. All such divisions function independently and yet remain linked with each other through peer-group communication and workflow information. The chain of workflow in an organization can be managed only through horizontal communication between the sections that are directly interlinked.

Importance of horizontal communication

Horizontal communication is often necessary to:

- Save time and help coordinate work assignments
- Share information on plans and activities
- Negotiate differences and develop understanding and interpersonal support among various people of department

Techniques for horizontal communication

- Face-to-face discussions
- Telephonic talks
- Periodical meetings
- Letters, reports, memorandums, etc.

Limitations of horizontal communication

- Intense competition for scares resources
- Lack of trust among coworkers
- Concerns about job security or promotions

2.2.2 Vertical Communication

In an organization there are well-defined lines for passing on communication. Vertical direction can be further divided into downward and upward direction.

2.2.2.1 Downward Communication

This is the flow of communication that flows from people at higher level to those at the lower level in the organizational hierarchy. This kind of communication implies the authoritarian structure of an organization. The Managing Director communicating with the departmental heads, a manager giving a directive to an assistant manager or a supervisor, a foreman instructing a worker, are all engaged in the process of downward communication. A simple policy statement from the top of the organization may grow into a formal plan for operation at lower levels.

Downward communication normally involves both oral and written methods. Downward oral communication takes the form of instructions, speeches, meetings, the telephone and even the grapevine (informal). Downward written communication includes instructions, memoranda, letters, handbooks, pamphlets, policy statements, manuals, electronic news displays, and so on.

Importance of downward communication

This pattern is used by group leaders and managers to:

- give specific directives about some job being entrusted to a subordinate
- explain policies and organizational procedure
- apprise the subordinates of their performance
- give the subordinates information about the rationale of their job so that they understand the significance of their job in relation with the organisational goals

Limitations of downward communication

- A time-consuming process
- Often marred by either under-communication or over-communication
- Often lost or distorted in the course of its journey down the chain of command
- Flow of information through different levels of the organization is time-consuming.

Essentials of effective downward communication

- Managers should be adequately informed
- Managers should be clear about how much to communicate
- Some authority should be delegated to lower levels to shorten the line of communication
- Information should be passed on to the correct person

2.2.2.2 Upward Communication

Upward communication is the flow of information from lower-level employees to upper-level employees in the group or organization. To solve problems and make intelligent decisions management executives depend on lower-level executives to furnish them with accurate and timely report. It also provides the feedback necessary to let supervisors know whether the subordinates received and understood messages that were sent downwards. Finally, upward communication keeps managers aware of how employees feel about their jobs, co-workers, and the organization, in general. Upward communication can take the form of e-mail, memorandum, conferences, reports, suggestion systems, employee surveys, or union publications.

Importance of upward communication

- Provides higher management with the information needed for decision-making.
- Provides the management with the necessary feedback
- Gives the employees an opportunity to be heard, to air their grievances and to offer suggestions.
- Employees offer useful suggestions to promote the welfare of the organization
- Makes the introduction of new schemes easier
- Promotes harmony

Techniques for upward communication

1. **Open-door policy:** The employees are given a feeling that the manager's doors are always open to them. Whenever they like, they can walk into his room, and without any hesitation whatsoever, and talk to him about their problems.
2. **Complaints and suggestion systems:** In an organization, complaints and suggestions boxes are installed at some convenient places. The employees are engaged to drop their complaints or suggestions, if any, into these boxes.
3. **Social gatherings:** Social gatherings are frequently arranged in different departments. Such gatherings have very informal atmosphere in which the employees shed their inhibitions and feel free to talk.
4. **Direct correspondence:** Sometimes the manager may directly write to an employee and ask him to communicate with him. The employees may also write to their higher-ups at their own initiative.
5. **Reports:** Employees may be required to submit reports about the progress of their work at regular intervals.
6. **Counselling:** In some organizations, workers are encouraged to seek the counsil of their superiors on their personal problems. As they feel encouraged to talk about themselves freely, they provide the seniors with valuable information.

Limitations of upward communication

Upward communication is essentially participative in nature and can flourish only in democratic organizational environment.

1. Employees are usually reluctant to express themselves.
2. Employees fear that their criticism may be interpreted as a sign of their personal weakness, and it may adversely reflect on their own efficiency.
3. It is quite often seen that higher ups do not like to be told or even like to hear from their juniors anything against their wishes.
4. The information may be distorted, misunderstood or suppressed.
5. Sometimes workers become too bold, ignore their superiors and directly approach to the topmost authorities with their suggestions or complaints.

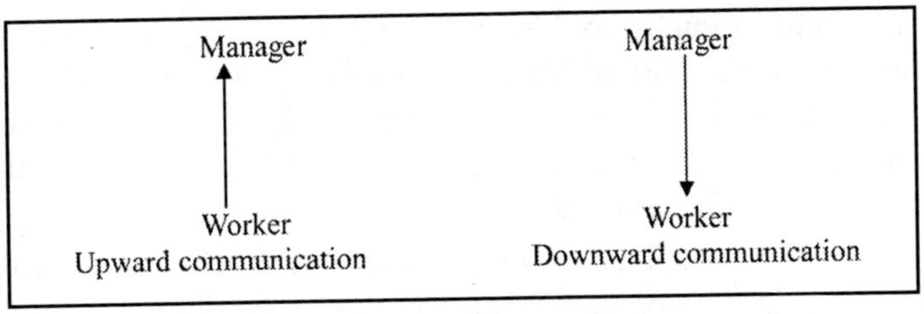

Figure 2.3: Vertical communication.

2.2.3 Diagonal Communication

Diagonal or the cross-channel communication is the exchange of information among employees in different work units who are neither subordinate nor superior to one another. Cross-channel communication is free to move in any direction. This type of communication includes the horizontal flow of information and the vertical flow of information both. Staff specialists use cross-channel communication frequently because their responsibilities typically involve many departments within the organizations. For example, when a supervisor communicates directly with the General Manager, or a Managing Director directly calls a sales manager they are engaged in diagonal communication.

This type of communication is used to speed information flow to improve understanding, and to coordinate activities for the achievement of organizational objectives. Since there is no specific line of command, diagonal communication is also referred to as cross-wise, radial, or circular communication.

2.3 FORMAL GROUP NETWORK OF COMMUNICATION

The three formal small-group networks of communication, combined through vertical and horizontal channels, are the chain, wheel, and all-channel.

1. **The chain communication:** The chain communication refers to the communication between a superior and a subordinate. This type of communication rigidly follows the formal chain of command. All the people in an organization from top to bottom are linked with the help of a scalar chain as has been shown in Figure 2.4, (diagram no. 2), 'A' is placed at the highest rank, 'B' is a subordinate of 'A', 'C' is the sub Figure 2.4, ordinate of 'B', 'D' is the subordinate of 'C', and 'E' is the subordinate of 'D'.
2. **The wheel communication:** In this form of communication all subordinates of a superior talk to one another through this medium. Thus, the wheel communication relies on the leader to act as the central intermediary for the entire group's communication. In Figure 2.4, (diagram no. 2), 'A' is the superior and 'B', 'C', 'D', and 'E' are subordinates. All the four subordinates communicate through the medium of 'A'.
3. **Circular communication:** Circular communication takes place among the members of a group. Every member of a group can communicate with the nearest two members. In Figure 2.4, (diagram no. 3), 'A' can have communication with 'B' and 'E'. Similarly, 'B' can have communication with 'A' and 'C'. The same applies to all the members of the group.

4. **Inverted 'V' communication:** In this form of communication, a subordinate is permitted to communicate with the boss of his boss. In this type of communication the message moves at a rapid speed. In Figure 2.4, (diagram no. 4), 'C' and 'D' are the subordinates of 'B' who in turn is a subordinate of 'A'. Here 'C' and 'D' can talk directly to 'A' who happens to be the boss of 'B'.
5. **Free flow communication:** This form of communication is also called all-channel communication. This type of communication permits all group members to actively communicate with each other. Its special feature is that every member of the group can talk to all the other people in the group. This has been clarified in Figure 2.4, (diagram no. 5). 'A' can talk directly to 'B', 'C', 'D', and 'E'. in the same way 'B' can talk directly to 'A', 'C', 'D', and 'E'. The same applies to all the members of the group. In this case, the communication moves at the rapid pace.

The following diagram illustrates these formal group networks of communication:

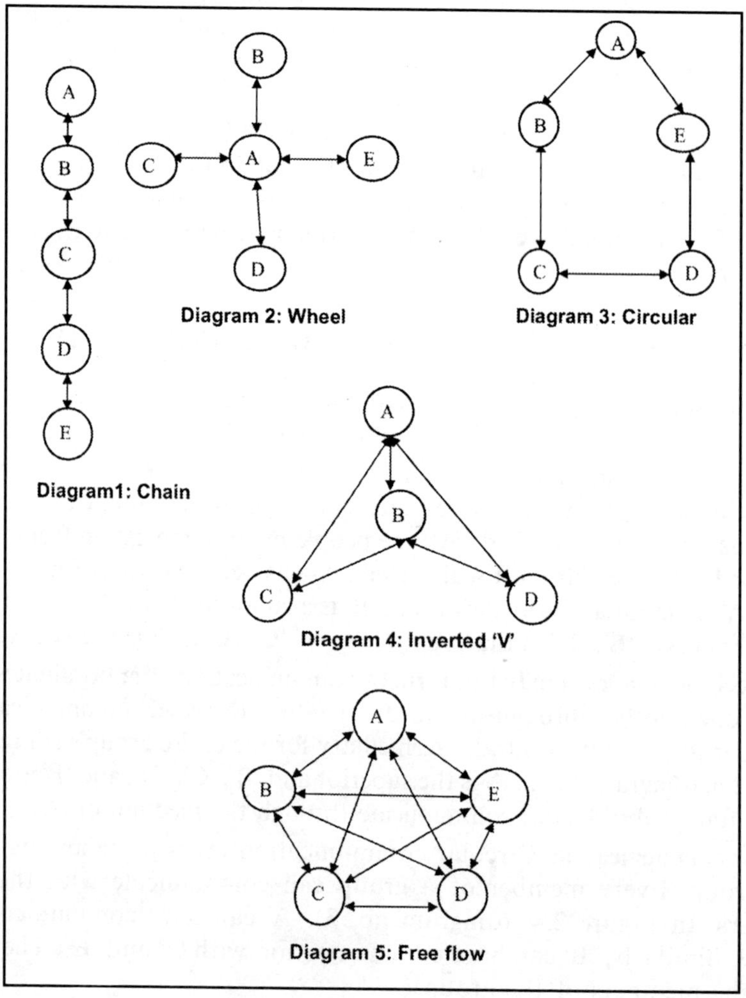

Figure 2.4: Formal network model.

2.4 INFORMAL COMMUNICATION

With the formal channel of communication, every organization side by side has an equally effective channel of communication that is the informal communication network. Informal communication refers to the communication within an organization that is not officially sanctioned. Conceptually the network of formal communication may be adequate to meet the needs of exchanging information within an organization. But in real life, employees feel inadequately informed in a formal system and suspect that the management uses formal channel to conceal rather than reveal the true message. The employees, therefore, modify the formal methods of communication by bringing in an informal communication system.

As the informal communication network is the transmission of information through non-official channels within the organization it is free from all the organizational formalities. In the management language it is called as 'grapevine'. Under it some information passes through many individuals and covers a long distance making its origin obscure. This is exactly like a grapevine where it is difficult to find the beginning and the end. Carpooling to work, waiting to use the photocopier, jogging at noon, eating in the cafeteria, or chatting at a local PTA meet-where workers come together, they are likely to hear and pass on information about possible happenings in the organizations. Employees often say that the grapevine is their most frequent source of information on company plans and performance.

Just as the grapevine has no definite path to grow, so also the informal communication has no definite path and flows in all directions–horizontal, vertical and diagonal.

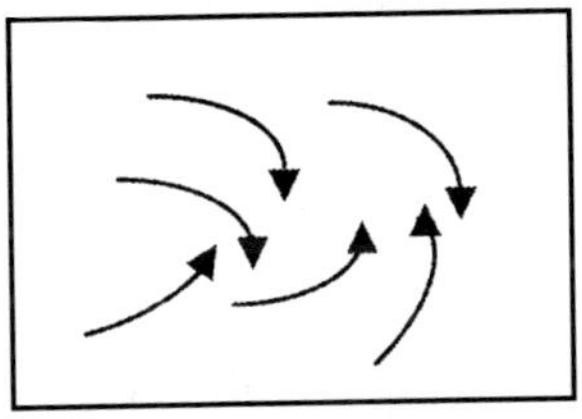

Figure 2.5: Grapevine.

2.4.1 Characteristics of Informal Communication or Grapevine

Informal or grapevine communication has the following characteristics:

1. **An inevitable part of organizational behaviour:** The grapevine is an inevitable part of organizational behaviour. Any attempt to restrict grapevine activity seems to foster employee beliefs that management cannot be trusted. Rather than trying to eliminate the grapevine, competent managers accept its existence and pay attention to it.
2. **Formation through social relations:** This communication is born out of social relations, which means that it is beyond the restrictions of the organizations. No superior-subordinate relationship figures therein. A more sociable superior can gather much information through this channel.
3. **Two types of information:** Through this communication information about the work and the individual can be collected. However, most of the information passed along the grapevine (about 80%) is business related, and most of it (75%–95%) is accurate.

4. **Uncertain path:** Since grapevine is not controlled by management, it follows no definite channel. The grapevine is pervasive. It exists at all level in the organization–from corporate to the assembly line. Like a grapevine it moves in a zigzag manner.
5. **Possibility of rumour and distortion:** Responsibility for the true and false nature of communication does not lie on any individual and, therefore, not much attention is paid to its meaning while communicating. Consequently, the rumours keep floating. However, the management acts promptly to counteract false rumours and uses the formal communication network, including meetings, memos, newsletters, bulletin boards, to ensure that all news–positive and negative–gets out to employees as quickly and as completely as possible.
6. **Quick relay:** Informal communication makes news spread like wild fire. Not only this, people start adding something of their own which sometimes changes the real meaning of the communication.
7. **Most reliable source:** The grapevine is perceived by most employees as more 'reliable source' than formal communication issued by top management. The most important reason is the intense desire to communicate, to talk to share one's feelings and thoughts, or just to gossip or to indulge in small talk.

2.4.2 Factors That Encourage Grapevine Activity

The major factors that may influence the grapevine are:

- Excitement and insecurity
- Involvement of friends and associates
- Recent information
- Procedure that brings people into contact
- Work that allows conversation
- Job that provides information desired by others
- Personality of communicator

2.4.3 Grapevine Network

Grapevine network refers to the various paths through which informal communication is passed through an organization. There is no definite route of grapevine communication for sharing information. In this form of communication, information converges a long way by passing from one person to another person leaving no indication from which point it started. Keith Davis has identified four types of grapevine chains. These are:

1. **Single-strand chain:** In this form of communication a person says something to a person of his confidence who in turn passes on the information to a person of his confidence and in this way a chain starts moving. This creates a sort of chain, which has been shown in Figure 2.6, (diagram no. 1). The signs of cross (X) at the top and bottom of the diagram show that the certain chain can move up and down both ways upto an extent.
2. **Gossip chain:** In this form of communication, a person communicates something to a number of persons during the course of a gossip. A particular person in an

organization knows something specific that happens to be interesting. He tells this thing to all the members of his group and some other people also. Normally such information is not related to the job. Gossip chain has been shown in Figure 2.6, (diagram no. 2). In this diagram, 'A' is passing on his information to B, C, D, E, F, G, H, I, etc.

3. **Probability chain:** In this type of chain, a person remains indifferent about the fact as to whom he should pass on the information. There are numerous people around him. He passes on the information randomly to somebody around him. Those who get the information also have many people around them. They also pass on the information randomly to somebody else. In this way the chain moves.

   Figure 2.6, (diagram no. 3) shows that A has four persons around–F, B, D, and J, but he passes on the information to F and D only. He has not deliberately chosen F and D, but it happens as a matter of chance. The same is the position of F and D. F is passing on the information to K and G while D is passing on the information to H and I. This chain will continue moving in this manner.

4. **Cluster chain:** In this type of chain a person tells something to a few selected individuals, and then some of these individuals further pass it on to another set of selected individuals. In this way the chain moves on. The cluster chain is the dominant grapevine pattern in an organization. Most of informal communication takes place through this chain.

   Cluster chain has been shown in Figure 2.6, (diagram no. 4). This figure makes it clear that A passes on the information received to B, C, and D. B and C do not tell it to anybody else, but D tells it to E, F, and G. Similarly, E and F do not pass it on to anybody else, but G passes it on to H and I. In this way, this chain moves on.

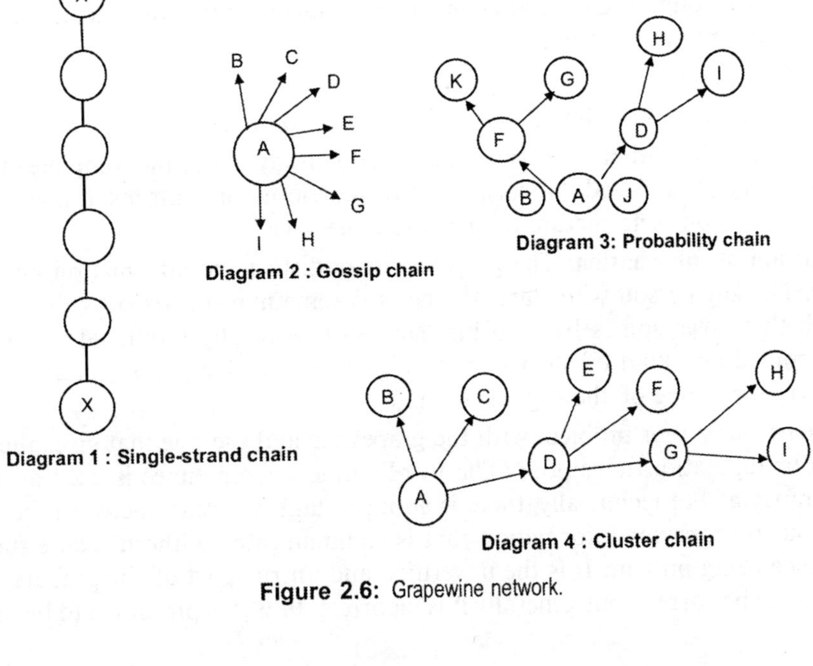

Figure 2.6: Grapewine network.

Advantages of grapevine

Researchers generally agree that the grapevine often functions in a beneficial manner.

1. **Uniting force:** The grapevine brings together workforce in matters of common interest, thus keeping the organization intact as a social entity. Everybody wants good relations with the high officers at the place of his work. Such relations give satisfaction to the employees and they feel proud. But this can be possible only with the help of the informal communication.
2. **Better human relations:** Informal communication saves the employees from tension. Freedom from tension helps the establishment of better human relations. This also affects favourably the formal communication.
3. **True environment:** Informal communication is done in a free environment. Free environment means that there is no pressure of any office–big or small. The attached reactions of the employees can easily be collected.
4. **Quick transmission of information:** The grapevine transmits information at a remarkably fast speed. It spreads like wildfire and its effect is equally great on the people.
5. **Creation of ideas:** There are many problems which cannot be solved with the help of formal communication.

   Informal communication through sharing of ideas and views through grapevine generates ideas that often prove of value to the decision-makers and planners of goals and schemes.
6. **Feedback:** Through the Informal communication or grapevine the top officials of an organization get the feedback regarding their policies, decisions, memos, etc. besides, the feedback reaches them much faster through the informal channel than through the formal channel.
7. **Supplement to other channels:** As all information cannot be transmitted to the employees through the official channels, the grapevine functions as a supplementary channel of communication.

Limitations of grapevine

The defects or limitations of the informal communication are as under:

1. **Incomplete information:** The grapevine does not always carry the complete information. As it is very often based on whispers in the corridors or canteens, it may not give the receiver the complete picture of the whole message.
2. **Distortion of information:** The grapevine may distort the information and dilute the issue. The key person who starts the news is sometime surprised by the final form in which that news comes back to him/her. As it is totally unofficial and informal, it may spread any kind of stories about highly responsible people, even at the risk of spoiling the image of the organization.
3. **Rumour:** The major problem with the grapevine–and the one that gives the grapevine its poor reputation–is rumour. The word 'rumour' sometimes is used as a synonym for grapevine but technically, there is an important difference between the two terms. Rumour is grapevine information that is communicated without secure standards of evidence being present. It is the unverified and untrue part of the grapevine. It could by chance be correct, but generally it is incorrect, thus it is presumed to be undesirable.

Characteristics of rumour

1. **Interest and ambiguity leads to rumour:** Rumour is primarily a result of both interest and ambiguity in situation. If a subject is unimportant or has no interest to a person, then that person has no cause to pass along a rumour about it.
2. **Details are lost:** Since rumour largely depends on ambiguity and the interest that each presumes it tends to change as it passes from person to person. Its general theme usually can be maintained, but not its details.
3. **Subject to filtering:** Rumour is subject to filtering, by which it is reduced to a few basic details that can be remembered and passed on to others. Generally, people choose details in the rumour to list their own interest and view of the world.
4. **Elaboration:** People also add new details, often making the story worse, in order to include their own strong feelings and reasoning. This process is called elaborating. For example, Maria, a factory worker, heard a rumour that an employee in other department had been injured. When she passed the rumour to someone else, she elaborated by saying that the injury probably was caused by the supervisor's poor machine maintenance. Apparently she made this elaboration because she did not like the supervisor, and she felt that if someone was injured, it must have been the supervisor's fault.

Control of rumour

Since rumour generally is incorrect, a major outbreak of it can prove very disastrous for an organization. It spreads information by word of mouth and sometimes a false situation gets created at the workplace through rumour mongering. As a consequence, the management is confronted with a wave of prejudice, emotions, and a situation of ambiguity and uncertainty of issues. Rumour should be dealt firmly and consistently, but how and what to attack must be known.

Following are the ways to control rumour:

1. Remove its causes in order to prevent it.
2. Apply efforts primarily to serious rumours.
3. Refute rumour with facts.
4. Deal with rumours as soon as possible.
5. Emphasize face-to-face supply of facts, confirmed in writing if necessary.
6. Provide facts from reliable sources.
7. Refrain from repeating rumour while refuting it.
8. Listen to all rumours in order to understand what they may mean.

2.4.4 Consensus

Consensus is the process of arriving at agreement through consultation. In an organization when the president or the vice-president is to be elected, or a board meeting is held, it is felt that keeping in view the dignity of these high offices, the decision should be at through consensus. The chief executive plays a very significant role in enabling all the members to arrive at a consensus. Unanimous decisions help to project a good image of the organization.

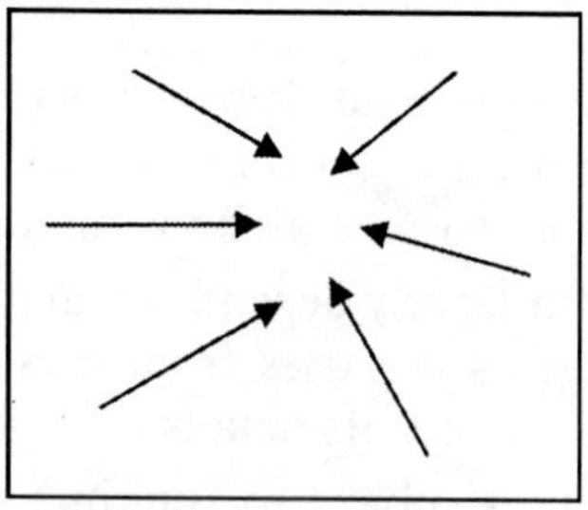

Figure 2.7: Consensus.

Advantages of consensus

- Consensus decisions are easy to accept
- Promotes unity and harmony in the organization
- Prevents unnecessary and undesirable conflicts and splits

Limitations of consensus

- Dissent is often stifled in the name of consensus
- May degenerate into a process of mutual accommodation
- May project false image of the management

Comparison between Formal Communication and Informal Communication

	Basis of difference	Formal communication	Informal communication
1.	Formation	It is born out of formal organizational relations.	It is born out of social relations.
2.	Path	The message has to pass through a definite path while moving from one person to another.	It follows no definite path.
3.	Speed of relay	Its speed to relay the message is slow as it has to follow a definite path.	Its speed to relay the message is fast as it is not supported to follow a definite path.
4.	Identity of the source of message	The source of the message is known.	The source of the message may not be identified.
5.	Media	It is generally written.	It is generally oral.
6.	Mutual relations	The sender and the receiver has some sort of organizational relations.	The sender and the receiver has some sort of personal relations.
7.	Distortion of information	The probability of distortion of information is very less.	The probability of distortion of information is very high.
8.	Authenticity	Formal communication is fully authentic.	Informal communication may not be authentic.
9.	Rigidity	It is rigid.	It is flexible.

It is clear from the above description that both the types of communications have their merits and limitations. On the one hand, formal communication is helpful in attaining the objectives of the organizations very easily, but on the other hand, the informal communication is also important if used properly. In brief, informal communication is complementary to formal communication.

REVIEW QUESTIONS

1. What are the various channels of communication? Write detailed notes on the importance, advantage, and limitations of any two of them.
2. Distinguish between the formal and informal channels of communication? Why is it necessary for an organization to have an informal channel of communication?
3. What are the various types of formal communication? What are examples of each within an organization?
4. Discuss the relative merits and limitations of upward communication.
5. What are the main objectives of downward communication? How can downward communication be made effective?
6. Write a note on the following formal group network of communication:
   (a) Horizontal communication
   (b) Diagonal communication
   (c) Rumour
   (d) Consensus
7. What do you understand by grapevine? What is its importance in an organization? How can its harmful effects be controlled?
8. Briefly discuss the works and utility of the consensus process for an organization.
9. Why does an organization need multiple channels of communication?
10. How does a communication networks help information flow in an organization? What kind of communication networks would you recommend for an organization suffering from poor communication?
11. Identify the different ways you speak and behave in the presence of the following:
    (a) Parents
    (b) Siblings
    (c) Teacher or instructor
    (d) Senior citizen
    (e) Doctor
    (f) Officer
    (g) Police
    (h) Stranger

3
MEDIA OF COMMUNICATION

Chapter Objectives

This chapter will enable you to understand:

- Verbal communication
  - Oral communication
  - Written communication
- Non-verbal communication
  - Body language (Kinesics)
  - Space language (Proxemics)
  - Time language (Chronemics)
  - Smell (Olfactics)
  - Colours (Chromatics)
  - Objective language (Artifacts)
  - Aspects of the voice (Paralanguage)
- Stress/Accent
  - Word stress
  - Sentence stress
- Importance of Non-verbal communication

Media of communication refers to the means of delivering and receiving information. As we know communication is a process in which a communicator or sender transmits a message/ information to the receiver through the mutually understood set of symbols. This mutually understood set of symbols or media of communication is the means or medium through which the sender encodes his message and the receiver decodes it with effectiveness. For humans the most commonly and effectively used medium is language. In an organization a manager passes information to employees working at different levels orally and in writing also. He receives the replies in the same manner, there is the another aspect of communication—the non-verbal aspect. The various media of communication used in an organization are:

1. Verbal communication
   - Oral communication
   - Written communication
2. Non-verbal communication

We make conscious efforts in the use or choice of words. The non-verbal communication is less deliberate and conscious. But, compared to verbal communication it is very much more subtle and instructive. Whatever be the media of communication it should maintain the clarity of facts, opinion and inputs. The communication of information must be well worded, properly fixed and transmitted in decent manner.

3.1 VERBAL COMMUNICATION

Verbal communication means communicating with words. Verbal communication thus includes spoken words (for example, interviews, meetings, lectures, conversations) and written words (letters, books, posters, classnotes). The most commonly and effectively used medium of verbal communication is language. Language is a powerful code that conveys meaning symbolically. Every language selects some symbols for its selected sounds. For example, in English, the sound 'k' has the symbol of/k/for it while the Hindi sound has the symbol /क / for it. These symbols form the alphabet of the language and join in different combinations to form meaningful words.

According to Encyclopedia Britannica, 'language is a system of conventionally spoken and written symbols by means of which human beings, as members of a social group and participants in its culture communicate.' Language allows us to manipulate our surroundings, influence other people, create new responsibilities, and think in complex ways that are not possible in a non-verbal code.

To succeed in communication in the business and professional spheres, you need to know how to use language effectively. Verbal communication can further be divided into two parts: **oral** and **written communication**.

3.1.1 Oral Communication

Oral communication refers to the spoken words in the communication process. The spoken word is one of the most versatile modes of communication. In oral communication, both the parties, the sender and receiver, exchange their views through speech, either in a face-to-face communication meeting of two people or in a manager's presentation to a large audience. It can be formal or informal, and it can be planned or accidental. The conversation on the telephone or the wireless is also oral communication.

Oral communication is vital to human relationships in every business organizations as well as any other social organization. The employees disclose their feelings to one another, they exchange their views, and share each other's knowledge and experiences. For example, a manager attends meetings, asks questions of colleagues, makes presentations, appraises performance, handles customer complaints, or gives instructions. From conversations and meetings to training sessions, oral communication is ideal when a lot of information needs to be exchanged between the sender and the receiver. The whole cycle can be completed quickly, information is exchanged freely, and other tasks can be performed during the exchange.

The success of the business organization depends to a large extent on managing the formal and informal oral communication.

3.1.1.1 Forms of Oral Communication

Forms of oral communication include:

- Face-to face conversation
- Personal instructions
- Conversation over the telephone
- Radio broadcasts
- Lectures
- Interviews
- Group discussion
- Meetings
- Conferences and seminars
- Announcements and speeches over the public address system
- Social and cultural affairs

3.1.1.2 Characteristics of Effective Oral Communication

1. **Clear pronunciation:** Clear pronunciation is the first important prerequisite of effective oral communication. The words should be pronounced clearly and correctly.
2. **Brevity:** People take pleasure in talking, so oral communication tends to suffer from over communication. It is, therefore, important to keep the message as simple and brief as possible. Repetition and vague words and roundabout ways of expression should be avoided. However, the brevity should not be achieved at the cost of clarity and completeness.
3. **Precision:** Precision can make oral communication very effective. Instead of saying, "We shall reach to your office early tomorrow", it is preferable to specify the time and say, "We shall reach to your office tomorrow by nine o'clock."
4. **Conviction:** Conviction comes from sincerity of approach, careful thinking and planning. Lack of conviction causes lack of confidence. Careful analysis of the message while formulating it promotes the speaker's conviction in what he says.
5. **Logical sequence:** Logically arranged ideas make the message forceful.
6. **Appropriate word choice:** Words have different meanings for different people. It is, therefore, important to be careful in the choice of words.
7. **Avoiding hackneyed phrases and clichés:** Use of hackneyed phrases and clichés like 'I see', 'In fact', 'Actually', 'What I mean', etc. interrupt the flow of oral communication.
8. **Natural voice:** Natural and pleasing voice without affectation makes our speech impressive. According to research, these are the most annoying voice qualities, listed in decreased order of annoyance:
   - Whining, complaining, or nagging tone 44%
   - High-pitched, squeaky voice 16%
   - Mumbling 11%

- Talking very fast 5%
- Weak, wimpy voice 4%
- Flat, monotonous tone 4%

(Source: Kathleen Driscoll, "Your Voice can Make or Break You", Democrat and Chronicle, 1993, p. 10B)

9. **Self-confidence:** If the communicator lacks self-confidence, it is likely that he will not be able to impress the message on the listener. He must have a sufficient knowledge of the subject on which he has to talk. Adequate planning, preparation, and organization of the message helps the speaker to raise his morale and self-confidence.
10. **Listening:** For oral communication to be effective, listening is also required. An oral presentation cannot achieve its goal if the intended audience does not have effective listening skills. Some researches have found that nearly 60% of all communication problems in business are caused by poor listening. (Source: Robert L. Montgomery, Listening Made Easy: How to Improve Listening on the Job, at Home, and in the Community, American Management Association, New York, 1981, p. 6)

Advantages of oral communication

The chief advantages of oral communication are the following:

1. **Immediate feedback:** The principal advantage of oral communication is that it makes possible speedy interchange with immediate feedback. The immediate feedback not only lets the communicator to know the kind of response from the receiver but it also helps him to modify his in such a way that it becomes readily and favourably acceptable to the receiver.
2. **On-the-spot improvement or clarification:** The communicator can clarify or describe certain ideals in his message which are not properly understood by the receiver or which might leave some doubts in his mind. The receiver also can ask questions and clarify points on the spot.
3. **Economical in terms of money and time:** Oral communication is not as costly a process as that of the written correspondence, especially when the message is to be communicated within the organization. Besides, when immediate action is required, oral communication is the best media. The written message takes comparatively longer time because it may require consulting, dictating, drafting, typing, posting, etc. which the oral communication does not require.
4. **Persuasion and control:** The oral directives and instructions are the most effective tool of persuasion and control. The communicator can use non-verbal clues to influence the attitude, feelings, and opinions of the receiver.
5. **Friendly relations:** Oral communication is less formal than the written communication. Informal talks can help in building friendships and personal relations between the communicator and the receiver.
6. **Effective in communicating with group:** Oral communication is a convenient and reliable media for communicating in committees, conferences, and meetings where a number of people come together for discussion.

7. **Tone and style:** The communicator can use pauses, emphasis and voice tone to stress certain points. The tone of the voice gives the listener an idea about the feeling associated with the word.

Limitations of oral communication

The limitations or disadvantages of oral communication are:

1. **Retaining the message:** It is found that people tend to have trouble in recalling correctly the main ideas and the factual details which are communicated to them orally. He may even forget the major part of the message after a long time.
2. **Future reference:** The oral message cannot be referred back in future if they are not tape-recorded. As compared to written messages, oral messages do not constitute permanent record. Therefore, it has little or no value for legal procedures.
3. **Speaker's preparedness:** Oral communication cannot be good and effective if the communicator is not a good speaker. He requires to be lively, enthusiastic, vital, and keenly interested in the subject.
4. **Not suitable for lengthy message:** Lengthy messages that constitute minute details are not suitable for oral communication.
5. **Distortion:** The oral message cannot be clearly heard or understood by the receiver. Thus, oral message is more likely to be received in a distorted meaning by the receiver due to his misunderstanding and misinterpretation of it.
6. **Presence of both the parties:** In oral communication it is essential for the sender and the receiver to be present face to face.

Utility of oral communication

Oral communication is useful in the following directions:

1. When the information has to be kept a secret.
2. When it is not possible to give a written form to the information.
3. When some message is to be given to a large group of people.
4. When the receiver is illiterate.

3.1.2 Written Communication

When the information is exchanged in the written form, it is called written communication. Although written communication is a slower, more measured exchange of information, it is crucial to the modern organization. Today, the business houses require a team of specialists and each of them is trained, experienced and most qualified person to carry out his specific assignment. They may be research people, purchasing agents, scientists, technicians, personnel people, sales executives, accountants, psycho-analysts, tax-consultants, physicians, etc. These specialists and experts have to communicate their ideas to one another and also to the management. They assist the management in decision- making process. Their findings, advice, and instructions are vital to business success. This flow of information which helps to operate the business is necessary to be maintained through written communication.

3.1.2.1 Forms of Written Communication

Forms of written communication include

- Instructions
- Memoranda
- Bulletins
- Magazines and Journals
- Correspondence
- Hand books
- Posters and Pamphlets
- Policy statements
- Telegrams
- Reports, Proposals, and Questionnaires
- Policy Manuals

3.1.2.2 Characteristics of Effective Written Communication

1. **A creative activity:** Written communication is essentially a creative activity which requires conscious and creative efforts.
2. **Time factor:** In written communication time factor is involved. It takes quite some time for the message to reach the receiver.
3. **One-cycle event:** Written communication has fewer cycles than face-to-face oral communication. Most written communication is a one-cycle event.

Advantages of written communication

The chief advantages of written communication are the following:

1. **Permanent record for reference:** Some documents with regard to some special facts have to be kept for future references. This is possible only through written communication. It forms a basis for new policy decisions and also for the fresh measures for the development and expansion of the business.
2. **Legal evidence:** Written messages provide tangible evidence of the agreements signed between the two parties. It also gives a proof of the stages in which the transaction was carried out.
3. **Accurate and precise:** Usually, the written messages are organized more carefully than the oral messages. A sender sends the information after careful consideration because of the written proof it carries with it. There is no fear of anything being left out in such a system.
4. **Suitable for lengthy and complicated message:** Howsoever lengthy the message may be, it can be clearly communicated with the help of written communication. The receiver can read it repeatedly till he properly understands it.
5. **Less expensive method:** Messages which are to be sent to distant places and there is no urgency involved, can be sent at a little expense through this method. But if the message is to be sent to a distant place quickly, this method is not useful.

6. **Communication at different places:** When messages have to be sent to different places, written communication proves to be more useful.
7. **Time saving:** Under the written communication, there is no open conversation with a big human group. Hence, time is not lost in useless talks.
8. **Presence of both the parties not necessary:** In this system it is not necessary that the receiver should be present before the sender.

Limitations of written communication

The limitations or disadvantages of oral communication are as under:

1. **Unfit for uneducated persons:** The written communication has no significance for the uneducated persons. There are millions of illiterate people who cannot understand this media. They can only be made to understand orally.
2. **Lack of secrecy:** Because of the written proof, nothing can remain secret in written communication.
3. **A costly and time-consuming process:** In an organization, a number of people get involved in the process of collecting information, consulting, drafting, typing, and posting the messages. It makes the letter very expensive. Secondly, the oral message reaches almost instantaneously on the telephone. If because of the organizational constraints it is essential to send less important facts in writing it shall be the wastage of time, labour and money.
4. **Delayed feedback:** Some difficulty is felt when the reactions of the receiver are not known immediately. It also becomes difficult to bring an immediate change in the message.
5. **Formalism:** Usually, the written communication is more formal and rigid than the oral communication.

Utility of written communication

Written communication can be useful in the following situations:

1. When the message is of permanent nature
2. When the receiver happens to be at different and distant place.
3. When the message is extensive.
4. When it is essential that the message stated contain figures and diagrams.
5. When it is almost impossible to make the message understandable orally.

3.2 NON-VERBAL COMMUNICATION

Non-verbal communication means communication that takes place without the use of words. Communication needs not be verbal in order to convey a message. Just as language uses sets of symbols to convey meaning, your body, consciously as well as unconsciously, carries messages, attitudes, moods, warmth, indifference, feelings, and so on. For example, an efficient manager can quickly get the feedback with the help of facial expression. Often a warm handshake or a hug conveys intimacy much more than words. Similarly, loss of eye contact, yawning or slumping in the chair can express boredom or loss of interest. In fact, non-verbal communication accounts for a larger part of the total message than do the words you send or receive. It communicates feelings of likings and disliking and reinforces the feelings expressed through verbal media.

Understanding non-verbal communication is essential because over 50 percent of a message's impact comes from body movements. Albert Mehrabian (1981) has found that the total impact of a message breaks down like this:

- 7 percent — verbal (words)
- 38 percent — vocal (volume, pitch, rhythm, tone of voice)
- 55 percent — visual (body language)

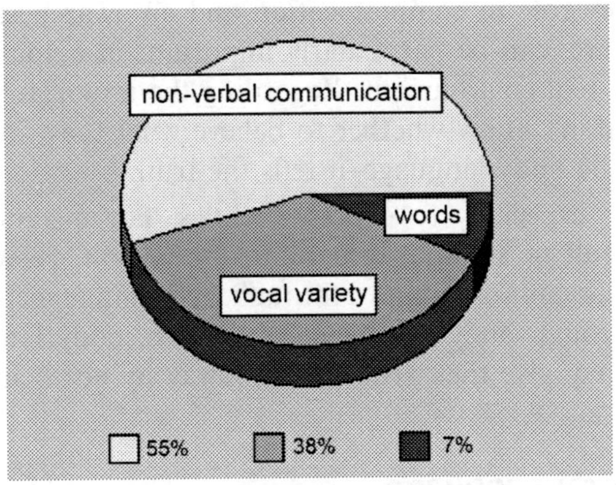

Figure 3.1

3.2.1 Forms of Non-verbal Communication

Following are the five major forms of non-verbal communication:

1. Kinesics (body language)
    - Facial expression
    - Oculesics (eye contact)
    - Postures (position of the body, stance)
    - Gestures (physical movements of head, arms, legs, hands, torso and head)
    - Breathing
    - Haptics (touch)
2. Proxemics (use of space to signal privacy or attraction)
3. Chronemics (use of time, waiting, pausing)
4. Olfactics (smell)
5. Chromatics (colours)
6. Artifacts (objective language)
7. Paralanguage (aspects of the voice)

As you become aware of your non-verbal cues, you will discover that your body language provides a wealth of information about your unconscious feelings and attitudes. Non-verbal cues usually occur in congruent clusters–groups of gestures and movements that have roughly the same meaning and agree with the meaning of the words that accompany them. Awareness of incongruence in your own non-verbal messages can make you a much more effective communicator. For instance, in an awkward social situation you might notice that your arms are folded and your fingers are wrapped tightly around your biceps. You realize that you are nervous and defensive. With this increased awareness of your internal state, you can move to reduce your tension rather than just continue tensing up.

3.2.1.1 Kinesics (Body Language)

Body language plays a key role in communication and an awareness of it and how it can vary from culture to culture, can be particularly important in helping you to develop your ability to understand in a real environment. Regarding the importance of body language, it is said that when people don't know whether to believe what they are hearing or what they are seeing, they go with the body language–it tells the truth.

Body language is used especially to express feelings. For instance, if you do not like someone, it is often difficult to say that directly to the person. However, you can make it clear either intentionally or unintentionally through body language. It is difficult to lie or cover up your feelings through body language. Very often, body language is unintentional and involuntary. People may give their true feelings away by not being aware of their body language.

3.2.1.2 Features of Body Language

Body language is made up of a whole range of features many of which we combine together without ever thinking about what it is we are doing or what we are expressing.

The features of body language are

- Facial expression
- Eye contact
- Gestures
- Posture
- Breathing
- Haptics

Facial expression: Facial expression is one of the most obvious and flexible forms of communication. Facial expressions usually communicate emotions and can easily convey mood, attitude, understanding, confusion and a whole range of other things. A smile, frown, raised eyebrow, corners of lips, the cheeks, yawn, and sneer all convey information. In fact, every facial muscle is an instrument of communication.

Face can be divided into four parts: (1) upper face, which includes eyebrows and forehead; (2) middle face, which includes the eyes, eyelids and foot of the nose; (3) the lower face, which includes mouth and chin; and (4) the sides of the face including cheeks. There are eight basic facial expressions generally associated with happiness, surprise, fear, anger, sadness, bewilderment, astonishment and contentment which are universally found in all cultures. All this is possible because of the proper coordination of the facial features. We can easily mark all the signals sent through these parts of the face by others and observe our own expressions by looking at ourselves in a mirror. For example, the eyes tend to reveal happiness or sadness, and even surprise. The half-closed eyes indicate boredom. An up-curved mouth reveals happiness, and a down-curved mouth indicates unhappiness. The smile can communicate friendliness and cooperation. The lower face, brows, and forehead can also reveal anger.

Thus, the expressions tell the attitudes of the communicator. In 'The Expression of Emotions in Man and Animals', Charles Darwin says that most of the human expressions and facial movements are instinctive, spontaneous, and are, to a large extent, beyond our control. Researchers have discovered that facial expressions continually change during interaction and are monitored constantly by the recipient.

Eye contact: Eye contact, known as 'oculesics', is a direct and powerful form of non-verbal communication. Eyes are very expressive and their gaze can be used to put someone at ease or to give an uncomfortable stare. The eyes, along with the eyebrows, eyelids and the size of pupils convey our innermost feelings.

Good eye contact communicates both personal confidence and respect for your audience. In addition, good eye contact helps your audience feel more relaxed and builds confidence in your speaking, knowledge, and ability. Gaze is used extensively to regulate and monitor interactions. When we look at somebody's face we focus primarily on his eyes and try to understand what he means. Thus, looking at people and meeting their eyes are the first step toward striking up friendship and making positive impressions. Avoiding eye contact with someone as you approach indicates an unwillingness to engage with that person.

Maintaining an eye contact during a conversation indicates that the receiver is listening. You have probably experienced how difficult it is to continue a conversation when the receiver avoids eye contact. In this way gaze is used to regulate interaction. The listener is able to indicate with gaze that he or she wants to speak. The speaker can also use gaze to indicate that he or she has finished speaking and requires an answer.

Eye contact with audiences conveys candour and openness. In presentation, the best advice is to make short frequent glances. Maintaining eye contact when presenting, gives an impression that you are confident and honest. The goal is always to use your eyes in a relaxed way so that you never make others feel uncomfortable. Make eye contact with different people for about 2-3 seconds as if you are talking to them personally. This will keep them all involved. Someone who wants to enter or interject in a conversation will catch the eye of the person speaking to indicate that they want to interrupt, and equally someone who no longer wants to listen will avoid eye contact.

Gestures: Gestures–the physical movements of head, arms, hands, legs, and feet–all play very important role in conveying meaning without using words. Different finger, thumb or hand gestures can convey a range of meanings in different cultures, from insults to approval or even attraction. Shaking hands, touching, holding, embracing, pushing, or patting on the back all convey messages. They reflect an element of intimacy or a feeling of (or lack of) attraction.

Head: People bend their head low (depending upon the situation) to indicate modesty, politeness or difference. They nod their head sideways or back and forth to convey the intended meaning more eloquently than words. Holding a head high is a sign of honour, self-respect, confidence, and integrity.

Arms and hands: People scratch their heads in puzzlement, touch their noses in doubt, rub their necks in anger or frustration, tug on their ears when they want to interrupt, wring their hands in grief, and rub their hands in anticipation. They will put their hands on their knees to indicate readiness or on their lips to show impatience, lock their hands behind their back as a signal of self-control or as a statement of superiority, stick their hands into their pockets to hide their meaning. They clench their fists and sometimes pound their fists on a table as a sign of anger or tension. They will extend their arms out in front of them with palms up to indicate sincerity, as if to say "how should I know?" or "I just couldn't help it." They will cross their arms in front of their chest when feeling defensive or unwilling to communicate openly. They will use their arm and hands to create non-verbal emblems that translates directly into words or phrases such as 'peace' or 'up your'.

Legs and feet: When you sit with your legs uncrossed and slightly apart, you communicate openness. When you straddle a chair, you are indicating dominance. When you put one leg over the arm of a chair you are suggesting indifference. Sitting with one ankle over the other knee or sitting with ankles crossed can be a sign of resistance. Sitting with one leg crossed over other and swinging or kicking it back and forth is often a sign of boredom, anger, or frustration. Agreement is most likely when all limbs are uncrossed. The direction in which the legs and feet are pointed is often the direction in which the individual feels most interested.

It is important to note that gestures are not used individually but in relation to another person, and acquire meaning at particular times. A particular gesture or expression may have different meaning in different contexts. Covering your mouth as you watch a truck smash into the back of a parked car communicates your horror. But you may use the same gesture during a tedious lecture to express your boredom.

Body communication is largely learned. Gestures are passed from one generation to the next without any special training. Many gestures are restricted to a specific peer group, others are typical of a particular region or culture and some body movements are universal.

'Open' and 'Closed' gestures: Our gestures often times tell something about us that we are not able or willing to communicate verbally. 'Open' gestures show that a person is ready and willing to communicate, 'closed' are present when there may be something standing in the way of honest, complete communication.

'Open' and 'closed' gestures

Open Gesture	*Closed Gesture*
open hands	hand covering mouth
palms up	making fists
unbuttoning jacket	peering over top of glasses
spontaneous eye contact	glancing at exit
smile	frown
leaning forward	leaning back
relaxed	rigid
hands away from face	looking at floor
standing straight	moving away
feet apart	legs crossed, shaking foot
shoulders squared	fidgeting

uncrossed legs	locked ankles
welcoming handshake	folded arms
patting	open palm tapping
rubbing palms together	hand wringing
affirmative head nods	head lowered
eye contact	lack of eye contact
calm use of facial movements	staring or eyes closed
body positioned toward other	rocking

Posture: A person communicates numerous messages by the way he walks, talks, stands and sits. Leaning forward or backward, standing or sitting erect, slouching or bending sideways—all these postures convey a whole range of attitudes, from interest or the lack of it, to degrees of respect or subordination.

Good posture portrays confidence. Slumped posture can be a sign of feeling 'low' fatigue, a sense of inferiority. Erect posture is generally associated with higher spirits, receptiveness, and friendliness, and more openness than slumped posture. Leaning forward tends to suggest openness and interest. A tense rigid posture tends to be a sign of defensiveness, while a relaxed posture indicates openness. Some postures like looking down, slouching, bending head or biting one's nail, etc., reveal anxiety, nervousness and the feeling of insecurity in the person. Sitting squarely in a chair, feet on the floor and shoulders straight indicates that the person is confident and in charge. Speakers often use posture to punctuate what they are saying, shifting forward in their seat or leaning in towards their interlocutor to punctuate an important point, or slumping back to indicate that they have finished making a point.

Breathing: Breathing is another indicator of feelings and attitudes. Rapid breathing can be associated with excitement, fear, irritability, extreme joy, or anxiety. A pattern of holding your breath alternatively with short grasp for air, is a sign of anxiety or built-up tension. Shallow breathing in the upper chest often indicates thinking that is cut off from feelings. Deep breathing into the stomach is more likely to be associated with feelings and action.

In the course of everyday events, you can pause at times to notice how you are breathing and feeling. Experiment with varying your breathing pattern. For instance, if your breathing is shallow and you are feeling tired or depressed, try breathing more rapidly and deeply for a few minutes and observe what happens. If your breathing is very rapid and you feel anxious or annoyed, try slow, deep breaths for a few minutes. Changing how you breathe will often change how you feel.

Haptics (Touch): Haptics is the study of how physical contact or touch is used to communicate the ideas and feelings. Touching is a bonding gesture and essential for psychological well-being. Intimacy, sociability, and connectivity are expressed by touching. Touching pattern changes according to the degree of familiarity, status and the familiarity context. As relationships become more intimate, mutual gazes and touch frequency increase, while in interpersonal distance decreases. Different cultures adhere to different touching rules. For example, the Americans interpret positive or negative feelings from the quality of the touch through a shakehand. A limp shakehand indicates lack of interest or friendship for them.

Researchers distinguish between high, moderate and low contact cultures. High contact cultures prefer direct high contact, face each other, touch and kiss frequently and speak in a rather loud voice. Examples are countries like France, Italy, Russia, and Latin America. Lower contact cultures like the Chinese, Japanese use little touching, prefer indirect eye gazes and speak in a lower tone. Our society could be classified as a moderate contact cultures like USA, Canada, and Australia.

3.2.1.3 Proxemics or Spatial Relationship

Non-verbal communication involves not only body language but also the space around us, time, vocal cues and our physical environment. Proxemics is the study of what you communicate by the way you use your space. It may sound strange, but space is used to communicate. This space language is crafted by your culture. For example, the fence around the campus indicates where the campus begins. The way you place your belongings on the desk around you in a lecture indicates to others what part of the desk you regard as yours. How far you stand from a person you are talking to indicates something important about your relations and the nature of our communication with him. By using space in this way you indicate territory, and how you respond to others invading your territory are important non-verbal statements.

Territory is similar to personal space. It is a place you have staked out as your own and where you feel safe. In your territory you can relax and not have to worry about constant intrusion. Your territory may be your home, your office, or your favourite chair. People react strongly in defence of their territory when they feel it is being threatened.

Since 'proxemity' means 'nearness', proxemics has come to be regarded as 'personal space language'. Personal space or the imaginary 'bubble' of space around each person is an important non-verbal consideration in communicating. The father of proxemics was Edward T. Hall (1990), an anthropologist who described four distinct zones that people unconsciously use as they interact with others: intimate distance, personal distance, social distance, and public distance. Each person is surrounded by four concentric bubbles of personally defined space. The bubbles are largest in front of people and smallest at their sides and back. Each zone also has a 'close' and 'far' subphase. Generally speaking, the greater the distance between two people interacting, the less intimate their relations.

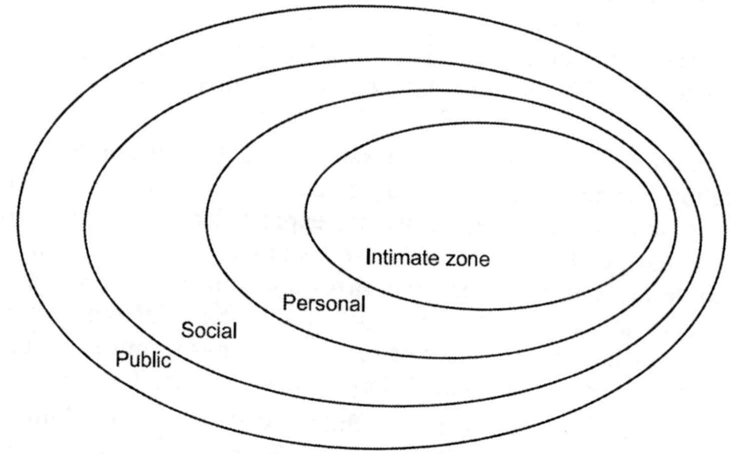

Figure 3.2

1. **Intimate zone (Physical touch or contact to 18 inches):** This zone has a close subphase of actually touching and a far subphase of 6 to 18 inches from the body. Intimate distance is appropriate for lovers, close friends, and children holding on to their parents or each other. Communication through 'physical touch' can create a more direct message than dozens of words; used improperly it can build barriers and cause mistrust. Nonintimates usually feel embarrassed or threatened if circumstances force them to share their space without non-verbal barriers to protect themselves. For example, on a crowded bus or elevator people avoid eye contact and draw away or tense up if touch is unavoidable.
2. **Personal (18 inches to 4 feet):** This zone has a close subphase of 1.5 to 2.5 feet, which is comfortable zone for talking to a party. You can still easily touch your partner, whereas in the far subphase of 2.5 to 4 feet, you can discuss something relatively privately without risking touch.
3. **Social (4 to 12 feet):** This zone has a close subphase of 4 to 12 feet, in which you are most likely to transact such interpersonal business as talking to a client or employee. This surface is often used manipulatively to indicate dominance. A supervisor will stand over a seated employee at this distance as an indication of his or her higher status. The far subphase of 7 to 12 feet is most frequently used for formal business or social interactions. The president of the company will often sit behind a desk at about this much distance from his or her employees, for doing so conveys a superior status even when looking at an employee from a seated position. This distance is also useful for an open office setting, where it allows employees to continue working without feeling rude for not interacting with coworkers nearby.
4. **Public (12 as far as we can see and hear; range of seeing and hearing):** This zone has a close subphase of 12 to 20 feet which is usually used for relatively informal gatherings, such as a teacher working with a classroom of students or a boss talking with a group of employees. The far subphase of 20 feet or greater is reserved for politicians and celebrities.

   In each of these spaces, our communication behaviours differ and convey different meanings. We change the volume and the tone of our voice when someone is 18 inches from us and when he is 12 feet away. For example, consider the volume of your voice when someone is 18 inches from you. Do you shout? Whisper? Now contrast the tone of your voice when someone is 12 feet away. Unquestionably, there is a difference, just because of the distance involved.

   The way people of a group use the space determines their respective places. People who begin conversation and those seated at the front are usually considered leaders of the group. A group of people seated around a table means communication in the form of a conference.

   The four zones vary from culture to culture, and people from different cultures often misinterpret one another for lack of an understanding of their differently defined zones.

   Spatial zones are relatively ignored when people are treated as 'objects'. For example, patients often become non-persons while doctors and nurses discuss their cases in front of them as though they were not there. Similarly, parents might discuss their plans in front of their eleven-year-old boy without asking his opinion on the matter.

Types of space: Proxemics defines three different types of space:

- ***Fixed-feature space***: This comprises things that are immobile, such as walls, room size, the building, its total capacity, places, corners, etc.
- ***Semifixed-feature space***: This comprises movable objects, like mobile furniture. For example, the same furniture can be rearranged for an interview, a group discussion or for an oral presentation.
- ***Informal space***: This comprises the individual space around the body, travels around with it, determining the personal distance among people.

3.2.1.4 Chronemics or Use of Time

Time is a very important factor in all communication. Just as there is a body and space language, there is also a time language. That is, how we give meaning to time communicates to others. It includes how you manage your daily schedule. Do you arrive early for most appointments? Do you prioritize telephone call? Do you prepare agendas for meetings? How you respond to time communicates to others and others' use of time communicates to you? In terms of non-verbal communication, time orientation becomes part of the message we send to and receive from one another.

In business world, time is money for everybody and every successful businessman seems to be very time conscious. Completing the work of a project within a specific recommended time communicates sincerity, hard work, loyalty, and reliability; whereas frequent late coming, and absenteeism may communicate unreliability, laziness, and disinterestedness of the employee. Delay in replying to a business letter, a phone call early in the morning, late entrance in the committee meeting, and innumerable other examples of this kind communicate certain non-verbal messages.

The conception of time and its associations vary from culture to culture. For example, an Indian host may politely invite the British guest to come at any time to his home. But the British guest would misinterpret this 'any time' and would think that the Indian host does not expect him to visit. The British may not pay a visit to the house of the Indian unless he states a specific time for the visit.

3.2.1.5 Olfactics (smell)

Olfactics, the study of the sense of smell, is a part of non-verbal communication. One's culture and sex influence the perception of odours. Smell is a means of forming identity and orientation (landscapes of smell, smell linked memories). In Arab countries, while establishing and maintaining contact olfactics are actively involved. Furthermore, smell can be used as a principle method of organizing time.

3.2.1.6 Chromatics (colours)

Chromatics deals with the way how colours communicate. Colours have a psychological effect. Colours also have a very strong association with moods and attitudes. Some common colour associations are:

Blue : Sincerity, harmony

Green : life, coolness, freshness

Pink : femininity, grace, healthiness
Red : excitement, danger
Yellow : cheerfulness, vigour

3.2.1.7 Artifacts

Artifacts refer to the object language which can either be intentional or non- intentional display of material things. Artifact means any article which is made by employing skill or craft. The artifacts include tool, implements, ornaments, utensils, religious objects, clothes, folk materials, and other art objects. They communicate the owner's cultural economic and social background as well as the style and standard of his living.

Physical appearance, which includes clothing, hair, jewellery, cosmetics, etc., is very meaningfully related to our body language (face, eyes, gestures, and postures, etc.) It is generally said that 'first impression is the last impression' and 'a man is generally recognized by his dress and address.' By address means the way a person speaks to others. No doubt, the speaker's gestures, facial features posture and such would be perceived in relation to attire. A dress may be formal or informal, but it should fit the situation. A person's dress speaks a lot about his attitude to life, to work, to his colleagues and his own feelings. It is not just the dress or clothes that important for any occasion but also shoes, hairstyle, perfume, etc. that convey meaning in non-verbal form.

Every aspect of our surroundings has a symbolic significance in non-verbal communication. For example, everybody is impressed by a tastefully furnished office. It conveys the mood, personality, vision, etc. of an organization. Artists and interior decorators believe that different colours project different meanings.

The preceding details make it clear that meaning can be expressed in two different codes: verbal (written and oral) and non-verbal. Written and oral communication media have favourable and unfavourable characteristics. Consequently, they are often used together that the favourable qualities of each can complement the other, in addition, visual aids may be used to supplement both oral and written communication. Evidence has shown that when a message is repeated through several media, the people receiving it will more accurately comprehend and recall it. For example, a lecture in a management training session may be made more effective when written handouts, transparencies, videotapes, and films are used. However, in selecting the media, one must consider the communicator, the audience, and the situation. The choice of medium is made keeping in mind the capability of the sender, and the receiver, the nature of information and situation.

3.2.1.8 Paralanguage (Aspects of the Voice)

Paralanguage is the vocal component of speech considered apart from the verbal content. While verbal communication consists of the contents of words, paralanguage comprises the way/manner in which the speaker speaks. In other words, paralanguage makes distinction between what is said and how it is said. Is the content of your message contradicted by the attitude with which you are communicating it? Thus, through paralanguage, you unintentionally betray your mood and attitudes. It includes pitch, resonance, articulation, tempo, pause, volume and rhythm.

Paralinguistics is the systematic study of how a speaker verbalizes. As 'para' means 'like', 'paralanguage' literally means 'like language'. The important thing to gain from this is that the voice is important, not just as the conveyor of the message, but as a complement to the message. As a communicator, you should be sensitive to the influence of tone, pitch, and quality of your voice on the interpretation of your message by the receiver. Thus, paralanguage refers to something in addition to language itself.

Voice: In spite of significant strides made by technology, the voice continues to remain the primary tool of communication. The human voice conveys the meaning or message and should not be confused with the words themselves. Thus, the voice heightens the importance of the most difficult element of speech delivery—effective articulation and voice modulation. The clearer the voice, the more effective it will convey the meaning.

The voice tells us so much about the speaker's sex, background, education, training, attitude, and temperament. Any voice which is used for communication has to be first worked on at a physical level to unleash its full natural potential. This stage of voice training aims to create an optimal and healthy voice for broadcasting, singing, acting and speaking.

Speakers differ from each other in terms of voice quality (which is the main reason for our being able to recognize individuals' voices even over the telephone), but they also introduce quite a lot of variation into their voices for particular purpose.

Elements of paralanguage

The seven elements of paralanguage are pitch, resonance, articulation, tempo, pause, volume and rhythm. In order to make our message effective, we need to give our attention to these points.

1. **Pitch:** The pitch of the human voice is continuously variable, and is necessary to make speech effective. As you tighten your vocal cords, you raise the pitch of your voice. Intense feelings of joy, fear, or anger make your voice go up. When you are depressed, tired or calm, the muscles of your vocal cords release. The pitch of your voice goes down. Though your pitch varies in normal conversations, it will move toward the extremes when you are expressing intense feelings. Those who speak in monotones fail to keep the listener's attention.

   Pitch variation can serve different purposes across languages.

   - Pitch variation affects the meaning of a word. This means that one sequence of sounds can have different meanings depending on the tone pattern with which it is produced, i.e., whether it is produced at a continuous high level, a rising or a falling level.
   - In a language such as English, pitch variation can be used to express the intention of the speaker. Your tone of voice and behaviour may show that you are nervous even though you want to appear calm. Similarly, they may show that you are confused even though you want to appear confident. Tone variations in your voice and your corresponding body language may suggest such attitudes as sincerity, trust, respect, hope, or admiration. On the other hand, slight changes in these clues may reveal such attitudes as suspicion, mistrust, dislike or resentment. All of these signals are part of the total context of the message. The listener must consider these signals, as well as the words and sentences themselves, in order to interpret what you are saying.

2. **Resonance:** The shape of your vocal cords and chest determines resonance. Resonance refers to the richness or thinness of your voice. As a man with heavy vocal cords and a large chest is likely to have a deep full voice. A woman with tight, thin vocal cords is apt to have a thin high voice. With some practice, you can control both pitch and resonance as singers and orators regularly do. Deep chest tone communicates firmness and strength. Thin high pitched voices suggest insecurity, weakness, and indecisiveness.
3. **Articulation:** How carefully do you enunciate your words? Do you speak in so relaxed a manner that many of your sounds are slurred together, or do you pronounce each syllable precisely? Different levels of articulation are appropriate in different situations. A slight slur or drawl may add to an atmosphere of comfort and intimacy. But slurred words would be inappropriate in a board meeting, where clear, decisive speech is expected.
4. **Tempo (Speaking Speed):** We speak at different speeds on different occasions and while conveying different parts of message. Speed of speech is measured by the number of words spoken per minute. The tempo or speed at which words are spoken reflects emotions and attitudes. Speech is more interesting to the listener when the speed is varied. Fast talkers convey excitement and can be expressive and persuasive. Speaking too fast, however, can make the listener nervous. Rapid speech can also signal insecurity. A slow, hesitant speaker may give an impression of laziness or indifference. To another listener the slow speaker may sound sincere, thoughtful, and interested.

   The speed at which you speak often reflects the region of the country where you grew up. People from large cities generally tend to speak faster than those from the towns or villages. Fast talkers and slow talkers often feel frustrated when they converse with one another. If the speaker's average speed is too slow, the listener becomes bored, impatient, and often attempts to finish the sentences of slow talkers for them. On the other hand, if the average speed is too fast, the listener does not have enough time to understand the message and may eventually give up trying to communicate.

   As a general rule, we should present the easy parts of a message speedily and the difficult and complicated parts of the information should be conveyed slowly. Easy information, if conveyed at a slower pace, becomes irritating as it is likely to be understood easily. On the other hand, the difficult or highly technical part of the information, if conveyed rapidly, will become difficult to understand. It has also been observed that in a state of anxiety or urgency, we tend to speak fast. When we are relaxed, we speak at a comfortable speed.
5. **Pause:** The speed of speaking is also accompanied by pause. We should not go on speaking without pausing. A pause can be highly effective in emphasizing the upcoming subject and in gaining the listener's attention. However, the pauses should be at the right moments. The incorrect use of pauses or the frequent arbitrary pauses spoil the speech and can create problems. It is, therefore, necessary for a speaker to carefully monitor his pauses as where and when to give a pause in his speech.

   At times pauses are very often inserted with sounds or utterances like, 'ah', 'oh', 'uh', 'um', 'you know', 'actually', 'ok', etc. These pauses are called 'non-fluencies' or 'fillers'. A careful use of these non-fluencies can add to the fluency of the speaker and give him time to relax. But too frequent use of these non-fluencies may irritate the listener.

6. **Volume:** On the positive side, low volume is usually associated with enthusiasm and confidence. On the negative side, it may be associated with aggressiveness, an overinflated ego, or an exaggerated belief in the importance of a message. A person of higher status may raise the volume of his/her voice over that of a subordinate. A loud voice in this case says, "I'm in command. You do what I tell you to do." A soft voice may convey, "Don't attack me, I know my place. I know I'm helpless." In everyday settings, a soft voice is often heard as a sign of trust, worthiness, caring, and understanding. It can also indicate a lack of confidence, a feeling of inferiority, or a sense of that the message is not important. At the same time, an extreme version of the soft voice, a whisper, accentuates communication. A whisper can imply special intimacy, meaning, "This is just between the two of us. It can also convey sadness, fear, or awe.
7. **Rhythm:** Rhythm determines which words will be emphasized in a sentence. In the question, "What time is it?" the emphasis is normally on the word 'time'. If you were to place the emphasis on the word 'what' you would upset the rhythm. Notice the change in meaning as you say vary the rhythm in the following sentence:

   "Am **I** happy!"

   "Am I happy?"

   The sentence changes from some exuberant statement of fact to message of doubt and uncertainty.

   Just as every song has its particular rhythm, so does every language. However, the rhythm patterns are so natural for you that you rarely pay any attention to them. But despite its invisibility, rhythm is extremely important.

Improving your paralanguage: If you do not vary your pitch, resonance, articulation, tempo, volume and rhythm as you speak you would sound like a robot. Others would experience your speaking style as monotonous and tune you out. Monotone does not necessarily mean speaking in a low, droning voice. Some speakers speak in a loud monotone. You must modulate your speaking at whatever volume that you are speaking at, whether loud, medium, or soft.

To assess your own paralanguage and learn what it says about you record your voice as you carry on a normal conversation. Wait at least twenty-four hours before listening to the replay, so you can be more objective. As you listen to the recording, consider the following:

- Does your voice reflect what you want to say?
- Do your voice congruent with the words you speak?
- Is there something about your voice that you dislike?

If you discover something about your paralanguage that you want to change, practice again with a recorder. You can take the help of your friend to get some feedback on your voice quality.

The following vocal exercises are very helpful to improve your paralanguage:

1. **The body vocal stretch:** Your body is the instrument you use to produce your voice. To increase your range of pitch, resonance, and volume, you need to loosen up your body. If you speak too softly, if your resonance is too thin, or if your pitch is unpleasantly high, low or monotonous, this exercise will help you gain greater range.

It will open up your throat and upper chest as well as exercise your vocal cords.

Begin by yawning–widely and loudly. Open your mouth as widely as you can and empty your lungs of air. Then inhale deeply. As you yawn, let your voice travel up and down the tonal scale. After a few minutes, try speaking by yawning.

2. **Voice modulation or waviness:** How loud is loud enough? As a general rule, the loudness of our voice should be adjusted according to the size of our audience. The larger the audience, the louder our voice will be. In fact, we become more convincing by adjusting our volume from loud to soft.

   Modulation in conversational speaking is difficult to detect when you are speaking in front of an audience. If you speak too loudly or too softly, this exercise will help you modulate your volume. It allows you to connect your visual sense with your vocal sense so that you can choose an appropriate volume for each situation.

   Focus your attention on an object near you and say the word 'touch' strongly and precisely. Imagine your voice going out and touching the object. Then look at more distant object and say the word 'touch' louder. Again imagine your voice actually touching that object. Let your eyes find other items in the room to 'touch'. Find out how far away you can touch an object with your voice. With practice, you will be able to sense when the volume of your voice is fully short of or overshooting another person.

3. **Articulation and tempo:** If people have difficulty in understanding you because you speak too rapidly, mumble, or otherwise distort your words, this exercise in articulation is for you. It will help you slow down and enunciate your words in normal, everyday conversation. Recite something you know by heart such as a favourite saying, poem or rhyme, or even your phone number and address. Say it over and over again, out loud. Speak s-l-o-w-l-y. Draw out all the vowel sounds to three or four times their normal duration. Exaggerate all the words so that hard consonants such as p, b, t, and k explode from your lips.

4. **Accent neutralization:** Accent neutralization or accent modification involves a systematic training process focused on modifying speech patterns. It includes a professional speech evaluation followed by working on clarity of speech sounds, pronunciation, intonation and rhythm of speech. Speaking with a noticeable accent may undermine your communication skills both professionally and socially. People may not understand what you are saying and you may have to repeat yourself. Your listeners may pay more attention to your accent than what you are saying. Accent neutralization is also a requirement for certain professions like news anchoring on a national network or call centre work. Accent neutralization helps those, who are proficient with the English language, and speak with a neutral globally understood English accent.

3.3 STRESS/ACCENT

Stress is defined as using more muscular energy while articulating the words. When a word or a syllable in word is produced louder, more lengthy, with higher pitch or with more quality, it will be perceived as stressed. (Roughly speaking, a syllable is part of a word spoken with one jerk of the lower jaw). For the speaker, stressing a word means using more force and making it seem stronger than other words in the same speech, for the listener it means more loudness.

3.3.1 Word Stress

The situation of the strong stresses in words is called word stress. In each word, at least one syllable must be stressed, i.e., must be most prominent/more prominent than other syllables. Take 3 words, for example, photograph, photographer and photographic. Do they sound the same when spoken? No, because one syllable in each word is stressed (stronger than the others).

- PHOtograph
- phoTOgrapher
- photoGRAPHic

This happens in ALL words with 2 or more syllables: TEAcher, JaPAN, CHIna, aBOVE, converSAtion, INteresting, imPORtant, deMAND, etCEtera. Capital letters are an indication of the relative prominence of the syllables in a word. The syllables that are not stressed are called 'weak', 'small' or 'quiet'. Native speakers of English listen for the stressed syllables, not the weak syllables. People tend to judge speakers based on their ability to pronounce words correctly and clearly. If you use word stress in your speech, you will instantly and automatically improve your pronunciation and your comprehension.

Generally speaking, there is no easy formula determining which syllable of polysyllabic English words bears the main stress. Therefore, the learner is advised to learn the stress of each word individually. Every good dictionary indicates the location of word accent; it is necessary to refer to the dictionary to find out the accentual pattern.

3.3.2 Sentence Stress

The manner of giving appropriate degrees of stress to words in sentences is called sentence stress. With sentence stress, some words in a sentence are stressed (loud) and other words are weak (quiet). The stressing of words in sentences varies according to the degrees of emphasis one wishes to give to particular words. There are nearly always some words in a sentence, which are of greater importance than others. The more important words are generally nouns, adjectives, demonstrative pronouns, adverbs and principal verbs. The native speaker of English generally stresses these words in a sentence. Among the unstressed words, we have articles, the prepositions, the helping verbs and the personal pronouns. In the following sentence, for example, do we say every word with the same stress or force? No. The important words in this sentence are WANT and GO.

'We' 'want' to 'go'.

In fact, all words are important which give the hearer a new piece of information. For example: (We make the important words BIG and the unimportant words small.)

- We WANT to GO.
- We WANT to GO to WORK.
- We DON'T WANT to GO to WORK.
- We DON'T WANT to GO to WORK at NIGHT.

3.3.3 Importance of Stress

Word stress is an essential part of the word shape. Stress may change the meaning of the speech. Placing of stress on right syllable is very important in English. Every word has a certain characteristic accentual pattern. No one can learn the pronunciation of an English word without learning its stress. Therefore, it should be very carefully marked either on a word or a sentence. Putting stress on right places is essential for

1. Intelligibility
2. Understanding
3. Comprehension
4. Checking of wrong parts of speech.

Now consider the sentence, "I am not going home with you." Depending on which word receives emphasis, the sentence will have a very different meaning.

- "I' M not going home with you." If the word 'I'm' is emphasized the message is "somebody else might but not me."
- "I am not going HOME with you." When 'home' is emphasized the message is "I might go somewhere with you, but not home."
- "I am not going home with YOU." If the word 'you' is emphasized the message is "I might go home with someone but certainly not with you."

Most Indian speakers of English put stress on wrong syllables. Consequently, their pronunciation becomes unintelligible to the native speaker of English.

3.3.4 Accents in Compound Words

By compound words, we mean words, which are made up of two words. Most compound words (with or without a hyphen) have the main accent on the first element. For example,

GOLDsmith	TEA-party	ANYthing
SCHOOLMaster	PREfix	DAYtime
HAIRbrush	CHURCHyard	BACKbone

There are a few compound words, which have the stress on the second element. They are mostly compound with '-ever' or '-self'. For example,

WhenEVER	YourSELF	ThemSELVES
HowEVER	HerSELF	OurSELVES

3.3.5 Stress-shift

Stress changes its place in different meanings. Words with the same stress do not keep the primary stress on the same syllable. It may vary from syllable to syllable. Stress-shift is quite normal in derivatives. (**Derivative** is a word that has been developed or produced from another word. For example, 'happiness' is a derivative of 'happy').

For example:

• aCAdemy	• acaDEmic	• acadeMIcian
• POlitics	• poLItical	• poliTIcian
• inFErior	• inferiOrity	

3.3.6 Stress Changes According to Function

Stressing syllables or parts of spoken words also changes the meaning. The accentual pattern depends on whether the word is used as a noun, an adjective or a verb. If the word is used as a noun or adjective, the stress falls on the first syllable. And if the word is a verb, the stress comes on the second syllable. For example:

Noun/Adjective	**Verb**
• CONduct	• conDUCT
• DIgest	• diGEST
• OBject	• obJECT
• PREsent	• preSENT
• INcrease	• inCREASE
• SUBject	• SubJECT
• PROgress	• proGRESS
• REcord	• ReCORD

This way of looking language takes us into the area of phonetics that is the 'Science of Speech Sounds'. Though it is not of immediate concern to us, but every educated speaker knows how important it is in conversation to put stress on the word or part of word concerned.

Importance if non-verbal communication

Even without the utterance of words, the language of the body speaks volumes. It is rightly said that you talk with our vocal cords, but you communicate with your facial expressions, your tone of voice, and your whole body. Everything about you, be it outward or subtle, communicates something to somebody else. The words you use, your facial expressions, what you do with your hands, your tone of voice, and your level of eye contact will determine whether people accept or reject you and your message. The manager's view regarding the suggestions of the employees become more clear by his attention and actions rather than his words of encouragement for dropping the suggestions. In this connection, it is important to point out that all bodily movements, postures, gestures, etc. are guided by our thought processes, emotions and feelings, etc.

On the grounds that, 'It's not what you say, it's the way that you say it' non-verbal communication has been a focus of attention for some time in areas such as

- The refinement of presentation skills
- Confidence-building, creativity
- Skills development
- Useful for the deaf
- Can repeat the message the person is making verbally
- Can contradict a message the individual is trying to convey
- Can substitute for a verbal message.

Advantages of non-verbal communication

Following are the chief advantages of non-verbal communication:

1. **Immediate feedback:** Non-verbal communication is the most easily visible aspect of communication. Its quick feedback helps the receiver of the message in decoding the message.

2. **Complements verbal communication:** Non-verbal communication complements verbal communication. Specially in face-to-face communication, no message can be completely sent across without the accompaniment of facial expressions and gestures. It helps in establishing rapport.
3. **Adds intensity to the process:** Non-verbal communication adds intensity to the process of communication. In the absence of any gestures, change of posture, and proper eye contact any face-to-face communication will look ineffective.
4. **Increase in efficiency:** Non-verbal communication goes a long way to improve the overall atmosphere and looks of the organization.

Limitations of non-verbal communication

The limitations or the disadvantages of non-verbal communication are the following:

1. **Cannot be taken seriously:** Words, spoken or written, can be taken seriously, but non-verbal communication cannot always be taken seriously.
2. **Misinterpreted:** People belonging to different cultural backgrounds send out different body signals. They are, therefore, liable to be misinterpreted.
3. **Requires extra care:** Non-verbal communication requires extra care in getting the right message. It becomes ineffective if the listener is ineffective.
4. **Ineffective in large gatherings:** Non-verbal communication is effective in face-to-face situation among two people or a small number but it is ineffective in a large gathering.
5. **Useful only for small messages:** Use of non-verbal communication is useful only for small messages.

Non-verbal tips for improved communication

- Make yourself comfortable with the other. Avoid being too close or too far away physically. (Within two feet is a comfortable range.)
- Be relaxed and attentive. To gain acceptance lean slightly toward the other. Avoid slouching or sitting rigidly.
- Maintain frequent eye contact. Avoid staring, glaring, or looking away.
- Give non-verbal communication while the other is talking, such as a simple nod of approval.
- Keep gestures smooth and unobtrusive. Don't let them compete for attention with your words. Avoid letting your gestures reveal emotional frustration.
- Your rate of speech should be average or a bit slower. Avoid sounding impatient or hesitant. Control the tone of your voice. Avoid sounding cold and harsh.
- Maintain a clearly audible voice—neither too loud nor too soft.
- Your feet and legs should be unobtrusive. Avoid using them as a barrier.
- Smile when appropriate; look pleasant and genuine.
- Stay alert through long conversations. Closing eyes and yawning usually blocks communication.

REVIEW QUESTIONS

1. What are the advantages and disadvantages of written and oral communication? Which do you prefer: written or oral? Under what circumstances?

2. Define communication. Discuss the significance of non-verbal communication.
3. What do you mean by 'kinesics' or body language? Discuss the various types of non-verbal communication.
4. Do you think that pitch variation is necessary to make speech effective? Describe in detail.
5. What do you mean by the saying, "the face is the index of the heart."? Write a short note on Facial expression.
6. What is the significance of pauses in a public speaking?
7. Write a note on the importance of stress in oral communication.
8. Is it correct to say, 'voice acts as a complement to the message'? Justify your viewpoint by describing various aspects of the voice (paralanguage).
9. 'Communication is the sum of all things one person does when he wants to create understanding in the mind of another through gestures.' Discuss and elaborate the statement.
10. Discuss the advantages and limitations of body language.
    (a) Gestures
    (b) Appearance
    (c) Use of space and time in non-verbal communication
    (d) Techniques of making non-verbal communication effective
    (e) Speed variation in speech
    (f) Eye contact for small and large groups
    (g) Accent neutralization
    (h) Voice modulation
11. Decide which medium would be the most appropriate in each of the following situations. Provide at least two reasons why your choice of medium is the best.
    (a) You have a wage proposal to negotiate with striking employees.
    (b) You have secondhand textbooks to sell to other students.
    (c) You have a summary of company's activities to give to your staff for their information.
12. Stand in front of a mirror or practice it with your partner. Using only expressions and posture, try to indicate the following attitude:
    (a) Openness to what a speaker is saying
    (b) Lack of interest
    (c) Interest
    (d) Antagonism
    (e) Unwillingness to listen
    (f) Skepticism
    (g) Agreement
    (h) Worry
    (i) Boredom
    (j) Thoughtfulness
    (k) Intellectual excitement

4
ORGANIZATIONAL COMMUNICATION

Chapter Objectives

This chapter will enable you to understand:

- Organization
- Significance of communication in business organizations
- Communication in different contexts in organizations
- Purposes of communication in organizations
- Barriers to communication and how to overcome them
- Ethics and communication

Organizations are unique. In almost every social encounter, we are influenced by one or more organizations. In fact, organizations enable us to achieve many of our goals. The success of any business or organization to a large extent depends on efficient and effective communication. This chapter will deal more specifically with communication in the organizational setting.

4.1 UNDERSTANDING THE ORGANIZATIONS

Following are some of the most important characteristics of the organizations:

4.1.1 Organizations are Dynamic

Like human beings, organizations are dynamic. They are ongoing, ever changing, constantly forced to meet new challenges. They are continually adapting to rapidly varying conditions in their environments. There are four important ways in which organization must remain dynamic.

1. **Changing markets:** Organizations must be dynamic enough to meet changing markets. Since most organizations market some type of product or service, they must be sensitive

to their potential customers' changing attitudes and predispositions. If there is no market for the organization's product, the organization will not survive.

2. **Changing economy:** As all organizations need financial resources to remain in business, economic conditions are a crucial influence on the operation of the organization. Organizations must pay attention to almost every facet of the economy. The availability of money for expansion, resources to use as raw material, and the cost of labour all pay an important role in the development of the organization. To be able to exist, the organization must be prepared to pay whatever it takes to stay in operation. The organizations, therefore, must remain dynamic to adjust to changing financial conditions.
3. **Changing social conditions:** Since all organizations depend on human talents and initiative, they must remain dynamic enough to adjust to changing social conditions. If social conditions change, the organization must change too.
4. **Changing technologies:** Changes in technology change the nature of work. For an organization to be successful, it must be able to accomplish a particular job. This job is called its task. The methods that an organization uses to accomplish its task are called technologies. Technologies change drastically over very brief periods of time. Research and development department works hard to keep organizations informed of new technologies. In modern times the adoption of new technologies such as computers, telecommunication systems, robotics, and flexible manufacturing operations have a profound impact on the organizations that adopt them. In order to learn about, acquire, and implement them, the organizations must remain dynamic.

4.1.2 Organizations are Informed

All organizations need information within the organization and between the organization and its environment to survive. It is by exchanging information that one part of an organization learns about the duties and activities of another part. Without exchanging information, organizations do not have the know-how to change raw materials into final products. It is equally important for the organization to acquire information that exists in the environment and transmit it internally.

4.1.3 Organizations are Purposeful

Organizations are groups of people who associate together for a common purpose. This is what distinguishes organizations from other social phenomena. Most organizations exist to do a particular thing. For example, educational organizations exist to train young people. Service organizations exist to provide a service to those who need it.

Organizations can said to be purposeful to the extent that (1) all members of the organization share the same goal for that organization; (2) everyone agrees as to which behaviours will best help to achieve that goal; (3) everyone is motivated to behave consistently with the goal. If members disagree about the appropriateness of the goal or the most feasible method for achieving it, problems will arise.

4.1.4 Organizations are Structured

In order to accomplish their objectives, organizations normally establish rules, codes, and hierarchical relationships. The rules, codes, and relationships become the organization's structure. Every organization has structure. Some have rigidly defined and complex structure; others have loose or simple ones. Structure enables the organization to standardize work procedures and to specialize the task associated with the production process.

4.1.5 Organizations have Certain Things in Common

All organizations have certain things in common. Four of these common attributes are human resources, know-how, energy, and environment.

1. **Human resources:** All organizations are made up of people. It is people who guide, manage direct, and cause within organizations. People provide the impetus that give organizations new ideas, new programs, and new directions. Actually people are the organizations. Decision- making is one area in which organizations depend on human resources for survival. In recent years, some organizations have developed sophisticated techniques–computer programs, management information systems, and simulations–to help them in the process of decision making. But mechanical techniques can only provide the necessary information. It is still individuals, or group of individuals, who have the final responsibility for making decisions. Besides, normally organizations grow through the development of new technical specialities and markets and the development of human talents. It is sound management practice to try to sustain these talents. Communication skills play an important role in the development and growth of human resources.
2. **Know-how:** Organizations transform raw materials (inputs) into products (outputs). This ability is called know-how. It is one attribute that can be used to distinguish among organizations. Most organizations spend large sums of money to develop and refine their existing know-how through various types of research and development (R&D) programmes. As organizations expand their know-how, they increased their chances of success.
3. **Energy:** Organizations, like people need energy to function effectively. This energy is supplied by their members. As we know that organizations are always changing, this does not mean that the change is always random. There may be an element of random change, but normally change will be controlled and planned. Organizations that can control energy can sometimes initiate change before they are forced to do so by existing conditions. These organizations are said to be proactive, able to control their own destiny.
4. **Responsiveness:** As conditions change, the organizations must be able to project a complete, coordinated, appropriate response. It must have the energy to provide this response. The more dynamic and controlled the response, the greater the likelihood of successful change. When an organization cannot coordinate its response to changing conditions.

5. **Environment:** An organization's environment represents anything outside the organization itself. We can define the environment as composed of those institutions or forces that are outside the organization and potentially affect the organization's performance. The organization may be diagrammed as a series of arrows inside a circle. But operating outside the circle are political, economic, natural, and technological pressures. These external variables constitute the environment. They influence what goes on inside the organization.

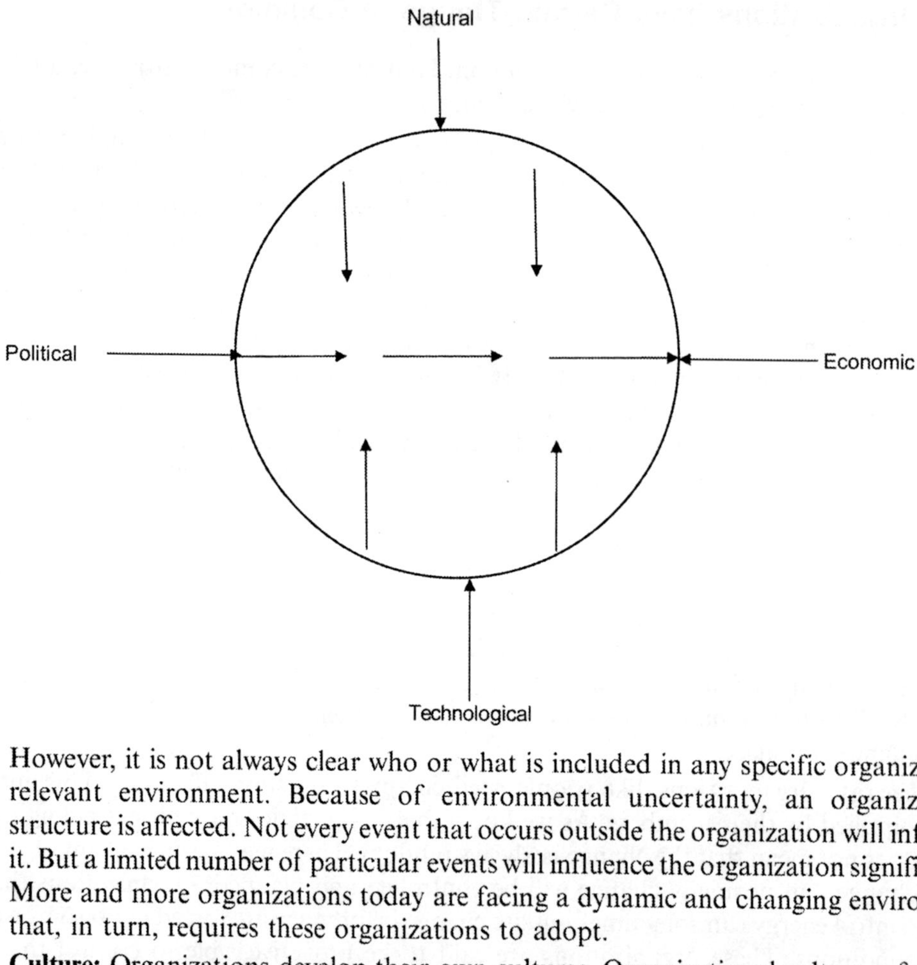

However, it is not always clear who or what is included in any specific organization's relevant environment. Because of environmental uncertainty, an organization's structure is affected. Not every event that occurs outside the organization will influence it. But a limited number of particular events will influence the organization significantly. More and more organizations today are facing a dynamic and changing environment that, in turn, requires these organizations to adopt.

6. **Culture:** Organizations develop their own cultures. Organizational culture refers to a system of shared meaning held by members that distinguishes the organization from other organization. Culture is transmitted to employees to a number of forms. Stories, anecdotes, rituals, material symbols, and social histories of an organization constitute its culture. We are exposed to a company's culture when we go to work for it. Others who have already working there tell us how to function, "who to watch out for," and "the lowdown on the really nice things about working here." These are all cultural phenomena.

4.1.6 Organizations Undertake a Variety of Functions

All business organizations undertake a variety of tasks or functions to operate effectively within their areas of business. In each of these functions, the interpersonal communication skills of the individual members play an important role. Let us consider some of the important tasks that organizations do.

1. **Organizations acquire things:** All organizations tend to acquire things. Most often organizations acquire many things that are worthwhile and a few things that are not. These things may be buildings, land, factories, and financial holdings. They may be files, records, guidelines, and written materials. They may even be such intelligible as history, reputation, image, and community regard. Occasionally, an organization will acquire things it does not need, such as unnecessary regulations and meaningless rules. Organizations sometimes acquire things that would rather avoid at all costs, such as a bad community image. Some organizations acquire things that are very valuable, such as a young, committed workforce, a clean factory, or a reputation as a progressive firm.

   The members' task is to help the organization determine which things are going to be valuable and which things should be avoided as potential hazards. This is primarily a communication activity. Communication among people who are gaining information about things in the environment and within the organization helps the organization to determine which things should be acquired.

2. **Organizations produce things:** The main function of an organization is to produce things. The 'thing' is the product of the organization. All organizations have products. For example, General Motors produces cars. But the Junior League takes young women and 'makes' them into committed public service volunteers in their communities. The Boys' Club also has a product. It attempts to take young men and produces well-structured, healthy adults. A hospital takes in sick people and discharge people who are well.

   Thus, the organizations consist of things modifying the condition of raw material, as is shown in the following diagram. Industrial engineers and management experts spend much time attempting to refine and modify these processes to produce a product rapidly and cheaply.

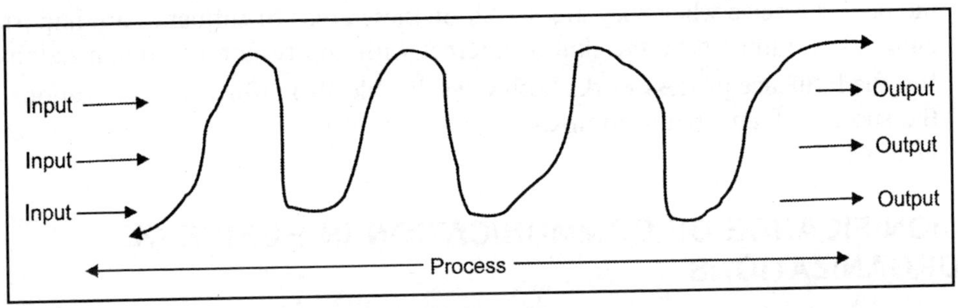

Figure 4.1: Simple sytem of organizations.

The effective production process depends on accurate information. People must obtain and transmit information to keep the improvements coming. Managers must become aware of new products or processes that could help them in bringing the changes for improvements. Information about these things must also be transmitted within the organization. The success of the production processes, then, depends on good communication skills. Without good communicators, the organization could not continue to produce a good product.

3. **Organizations develop responsibilities and duties:** As organizations acquire and avoid things, they begin to develop responsibilities and duties. With minor exceptions most organizations attempt to operate within some kind of ethical standard. This means that an organization must live up to the standards, it has established for itself as well as to the standards of society. These standards provide the organization with a special set of responsibilities, which may or may not be related to the product it makes.

   Certain responsibilities are mandated by law, such as, "Don't pollute", "Provide safe condition for workers".

   Often a particular organization will be judged by how well it has fulfilled its responsibilities to the community rather than by the quality of its product.

4. **Organizations affect and are affected by people:** Organizations affect and are affected by people. It is people who guide, manage, direct, and cause growth within organizations. People provide the impetus that gives organizations new ideas , new programmes, and new directions. Actually, people are the organization.

   On the other hand, people, both customers and members, are affected by the organization. Most of us will spend about 50 to 60 per cent of our adult working time as members of organizations. Under normal circumstances, we will lend to take on the special characteristics of these organizations. If we work in a bank, we will probably grow increasingly concerned about detail and finances. If we work in a grocery store, we will probably become sensitive to people's food-buying habits and the way in which they spend money. Thus, we begin to manifest those psychological and social tendencies which are associated with our job.

   Organizations influence people in still other ways. Television organizations influence what they watch. Newspaper organizations influence what they read. Construction organizations influence where they live. Hospital organizations influence the treatment the people receive when they are ill. All of these areas of influence are important to all of us. We must have the skill to interact with and respond to organizations.

   But the influence process works both ways. People also influence organizations. Thus, the success of an organization can be a function of the quality and abilities to its members.

4.2 SIGNIFICANCE OF COMMUNICATION IN BUSINESS ORGANIZATIONS

Communication in organizations takes many forms. The following discussion views it from three major perspectives. Each perspective represents one aspect of communication in the organization.

4.2.1 Macro Approaches

In a macro approach, organization is viewed as a global or total structure interacting with other organizations in its environment.

All the following tasks are macro activities, that is, they are jobs that must be done by the entire organization.

4.2.1.1 Processing Information from Environment

To exist, an organization must develop information from its environment. They take raw informational inputs from outside the organization and transmit these inputs from outside the organization. Processing information means being attuned to what is happening in the environment, transferring the relevant information to decision points within the organization, and then formulating an appropriate response to the informational input. Later the information will be used in some of the tasks, e.g., goal setting and identification.

Getting information from the environment is primarily a communication activity. People are the vehicle through which information is processed and transmitted within the organization. The individual assigns particular significance to what is going on outside and then sends messages about the significance to other individuals within the organization.

4.2.1.2 Identification

An organization uses the information processed from the environment to reach some kind of negotiated agreement with its potential and existing customers. This process of accommodating customers is called identification. Here the term 'customer' means institutions, other organizations, or people for whom an organization produces its goods and services. These are the organization's customers. Each potential customer makes this identification in his or her own way. Whether the customer is large or small, identification almost always involves communication. Therefore, most organizations attempt to identify with customers by using a variety of techniques. Most of these techniques involve some kind of intentional communication behaviour. Organizations that do not reach an accommodation with potential customers run the risk of having no customers – a calamitous state for any organization.

4.2.1.3 Interaction with Other Organizations

No organization operates in a vacuum. The products of common consumption are available in the market in many brands and the customers are free to buy any of them. Every organization is influenced by the activities of other organizations in its field. Organizations must monitor these activities to determine what influence they will have on them. If a competitor puts out a product that does the same job as yours, but does it better and cheaper, your operation will be in trouble. In other words, organizations who want to survive in this world of free competition, should know their competitors, the quality and the prices of their products, the discounts, terms and conditions of sales, the policies of advertising, government laws, etc. If they are not able to communicate better in this respect, their business will not be satisfactory. Most of the time organizations use simpler communication techniques – reading pamphlets, brochures, trade magazines, and talking with specialists in the field – to keep track of their competitors.

4.2.1.4 Goal Setting

Of all the macro activities that require communication, goal setting is probably the most important. A goal is the place an organization wants to be after a given period of time. The organization should not begin to establish goals until it has processed relevant information from the environment, identified with potential customers, and done enough interaction with other organizations to clarify its purpose. The information generated through all this interaction can then be used in goal settings. To set goals, organizations must develop information about internal and external forces. Internal forces include the conditions of human resources and of the manufacturing process. External forces include customers attitude, availability of raw materials, status of governmental regulations, and behaviour of competitors. This information is then used to formulate goals that the organization can realistically expect to achieve.

Traditionally, high-level managers do most of the goal formulation in organizations. Lower-level managers then implement policies for reaching those goals. Even under this relatively conservative view of management, goal-setting communication plays a significant role, people at the top of a hierarchy depend on those at the bottom for information that must be plugged into the goal-setting formula.

4.2.2 Micro Approaches

Micro approaches focus heavily on the important units or subunits of the organization. Several aspects of communications are also required at this level.

4.2.2.1 Group Membership

Within an organization, there are numerous social groups formed on the basis of mutual interest. The large size of business houses have their branches and sub-branches which are further divided into functional departments. Thus, organizations are really many groups of groups. Groups in organizations can have various purposes. The group's purpose may support the goals of organization. The mutual interests are safeguarded by various activities of planning by the managements. In any group effective communication system must be present if the group is to internalize its objectives. When the participants in a task group are informed about the overall objectives of the group, are comfortable with each other, see the immediate or long-term benefits to themselves of working hard, and can provide some degree of leadership, they will usually support the organization's goals.

4.2.2.2 Orientation and Training

Communication is the vehicle through which people are oriented to and trained for the specific jobs in the organization. People learn about the job from reading about it, having someone tell them how to do it. For appraising employees, performance standards must be properly and clearly communicated, so that the employee understands what he needs to do, and can draw lessons from the feedback. All of these require communication to bring someone else up to date about what is going on in the unit. This task can be accomplished by the leadership of the unit, as well as by the rest of the members.

4.2.2.3 Member involvement

Organizations believe that they need to persuade members to contribute to the goals of the organization. Participation, cooperation and team work of the management and employees can yield best results because of their common commitment to goals that encourage better performance. Whether it is the pep talk at the beginning of the year by the corporation executive officer or the "worker of the month" column in the employee newsletter, many techniques are still used to encourage the members to contribute. Much of the communication directed downward from upper management is intended to generate member involvement. Participative managers communicate with their employees. They ask for the opinions, views, suggestions and recommendations of the employees in the decision-making process so that they work together as a team. In its most negative form, member involvement in the tasks of an organization is achieved by having the boss stand over a subordinate and yell, "Get to work you M ......"

4.2.2.4 Establishment of climate

Organizations, departments, units, subunits of all sorts and workgroups all have climates. Climates are established by the behaviour of leaders, the behaviour of peers, and the behaviour of the organization. Sometimes certain physical conditions, such as an overcrowded work area or a very warm office, can contribute to climate. These climates are sometimes perceived similarly by all of the members and sometimes not. By and large, climate is determined by the communication behaviour of the leader toward the group.

4.2.2.5 Supervision and direction

Supervising and controlling others is the task of a few members of organizations. Organizations are designed to enable a few people who move to the top of the hierarchy to supervise the behaviour of many people who fall below them in that hierarchy. Supervision is activated through communication. In fact, effective supervision and effective communication go hand-in-hand. When the objectives of the organization are made clear to the employees, the employees are motivated to work in that direction. Therefore, the employees and the management should develop the link of communication for better mutual understanding and encourage each other to achieve their self-interests.

4.2.2.6 Functionalization

The division of work into different kinds of duties can be called functionalization. For example, the difference between an office supervisor and an operator's assembly or machine shop supervisor is a functional one. This functionalization is found in most of the business organizations today. Functionalization leads to specialization. There are specialists who acquire a vast knowledge and experience in their limited subject. This specialized knowledge, training and experience will be useless if it is not communicated. The accountants, engineers, scientists, and the experts of many kinds must be able to communicate their knowledge to the management and the employees. The organization may get benefit by the advice, suggestions and information provided by these experts.

4.2.2.7 Satisfaction

Job satisfaction is a very complex area people enjoy their jobs for many reasons. However, there is little evidence to suggest that good organizational communication will produce satisfied workers, or that satisfied workers will necessarily be productive workers.

When people are unhappy with some aspect of their work situation, they are said to experience job dissatisfaction. Two important causes of job dissatisfaction are related to communication. First, the worker may think that he or she does not have adequate information to do the job. Second, interpersonal relations among members of a unit may be poor. The two causes of jobs dissatisfaction identified above can be reduced by communication. We feel satisfied when we like our co-workers and seem to have established good communication relationships with them.

4.2.3 Individual Approaches

Individual approaches focus on the communication behaviour of the individual in the organization. Individual communication takes many forms.

1. **Talking to workgroups:** Workgroups are central to the effective operation of the organization. Therefore, one must develop the skill to interact with them. Talking to workgroups can be done by a member, a supervisor, or outsider who is not a member.
2. **Attending and interacting at meetings:** Meetings are a way of life in most organizations, so one needs skill at interacting in meetings. This skill consists of being able to provide information when it is called for, to persuade others to accept a proposal, and to lead the meeting when necessary.
3. **Writing manuals:** Organizations produce reams of printed and written materials. Some of these are distributed inside the organization, some outside. Each piece of written copy is produced by those who have developed unique skill and knowledge in their fields.
4. **Drafting a letter:** The task of developing a manual normally allows some latitude in terms of time. This means that the writing style can be polished and refined. Letters, on the other hand, are usually written under the pressure of a deadline, and the same luxury of refinement is not possible. Drafting letters is an important communication task.
5. **Making a sales contact:** Marketing the company's product is an important communication responsibility. Most sales contacts are one-on-one situations where the representative must be articulate and responsive to the needs of the potential customer.
6. **Arguing for a proposal:** In organizations, important decisions are made in small meetings where people argue out the opposing sides of a question before choosing a particular course of action. People in organizations must make a case for their proposal, be it a budget increase or a new programme. To succeed, they need skill in persuasion.
7. **Working in a quality circle:** Many of today's organizations group their employees into small groups. The groups are charged with the mission of making suggestions and offering ideas about how to improve the product of the workplace. Contributions made by the team members are utilized by the organization to cut cost and reduce

waste. The ability to contribute in these quality circles is becoming an important communication skill for today's organizational members.

Thus, effective communication is vital to every part of business. Conducting meetings, arguing for a position, participating in group discussion, making presentations, writing letters and reports, and listening to others are among the most vital things than members of an organization do. Communication is also essential for explaining disciplinary rules and procedures while ensuring their proper implementation. It is also required for fostering effective participative and collaborative work culture in the organization, because communication is so important in organizations, organizations want and need people with good communication skills.

4.3 COMMUNICATION IN DIFFERENT CONTEXTS IN ORGANIZATIONS

The communication process occurs in three major types of situations. Communication may be dyadic, involving a one-to-one situation. It may take place in a small group, or it may take the form of a public (one-to-many) speech. In addition to organizations function within the context of an external environment.

4.3.1 One-to-One (Dyadic)

Dyadic communication refers to talk between two participants. A casual conversation with a friend, a job interview, a conference with your teacher, and a meeting with a physician are all examples of dyadic communication. In dyadic communication both participants are free to create and send messages. There is typically a fairly rapid exchange of messages. Although one person may talk more than the other, and in a few special circumstances one participant may do all of the talking, typically the amount of time each participant talk is about equal. And regardless of how much each person talks, non-verbal messages are also being conveyed through facial expressions, eye movement, posture, gestures, physical distance between participants, and so on.

4.3.2 Group

Group communication takes place among a fairly small number of participants who interact both verbally and non-verbally. You are participating in group communication when you are working on a class project with other students, when you are carrying on a conversation with a group of friends, and when you meet with the other officers of your club or organization. In each case every one typically has a chance to talk, although each person probably talks less than he or she would if involved in a dyadic situation. As in dyadic communication messages are exchanged fairly rapidly. Notice, however, how the addition of participants complicates the situation. When we have several participants who bring different experiences, interests, knowledge, goals, and general background to the situation and all of whom are influencing one another. Just think about how much more different it is to keep a group like this focused on a common topic of talk. Typically, it is also harder to get a chance to be heard, simply because there are more people trying to talk. Often these are competing or different goals. This is not to say that in dynamic communication there are never competing goals but simply that with an increasing number of participants, the chances for competing goals goes up, and the difficulty associated with everyone trying to achieve their goals also increases.

4.3.3 One-to-Many (Public)

Public communication refers to a situation in which one person does most or all of the talking to one or more others. A speech is an example of public communication. So is a sales presentation, a sermon by a preacher, and an oral report you make about a project. The crucial difference between this situation and dyadic and group situations is that one person has responsibility for most of the talking, if not all of it. Of course, there are times when the listeners have the opportunity to ask questions, but these questions are directed to the speaker, who then has the responsibility of answering them. Essentially, in public communication, if the speaker did not show up, either nothing would happen or another speaker would fill the void. The speaker controls the communication by deciding what is to be talked about and what is not to be discussed.

That does not mean that the listeners do not communicate. The listeners' reactions may be observed and interpreted by the speaker. In fact, a good speaker will attempt to adjust to the responses of the listeners. For instance, a good speaker will look for signs that the audience members are confused or bored or uncomfortable and will alter the speech to accommodate to that audience. That does not mean that the speaker says whatever the listeners want to hear, but it means that the speaker changes the way ideas are presented to suit the audience better.

4.3.4 External Environment

Organizations function within the context of an external environment. This environment consists of customers, suppliers, the general public, government departments and the country as a whole. Companies will undertake advertising or public relations campaigns to communicate with these people. They will also arrange meetings and write letters.

4.3.4.1 Communication Activities in Different Contexts

All these contexts will demand a large number of communication activities. The following table summarizes these activities:

4.3.5 Contexts in Organizations, Communication Activities, and Types of Messages

(Source: Michael Fielding; Effective Communication in Organizations; 2006; pg.12)

Contexts			
One to one	Group	One to many	External environment
Manager to Manager	Group of Managers	Department	Customers
Manager to Subordinate	Managers and Staff	Whole Company	Potential Customers General Public Local Pressure Groups

Communication Activities in Different Contexts			
Discussion	Discussion	Union Meetings	Advertising
Problem Solving	Decision Making	Deciding on Long Terms	Public Relations
Making Policy	Problem Solving	Strategies	Briefing
Interviewing	Resolving Conflict	Briefing	Analysing
Instructing	Instructing	Managing Directions & all	Customers' needs
Briefing	Briefing	Staff/Shareholders'	
	Brainstorming	Meetings	

4.4 PURPOSES OF COMMUNICATION IN ORGANIZATION

Defining the purposes of communication, K. O. Locker says, "Effective communication is a process by which information is transmitted between individuals and organizations with the purpose to inform, to request, or persuade, and to build goodwill. It is clear, complete, and saves the reader's time and helps in achieving its goal."

When we communicate, we have an aim in mind. The communicator should be clear about the purpose of his communication so that his message will be effective. An awareness of purposes helps the communicator to tailor the message, -especially written ones, -to meet his purpose.

Communication in the business is always purposeful. Having a clearly defined purpose–the result that you want from your message–ensures that your message has a clear focus, and that you do not wander off the point. Try to make sure that you are as clear as possible about all the purposes of your document or talk, and that you address all of them in the way you design your communication. Examples might be a wish to provide or ask for information, or to advise, warn, or motivate the audience regarding a particular course of action. These various purposes may be grouped as follows:

- **To give information:** For example, that a seminar on communication skills is to be held on 22 July 20....
- **To persuade:** For example, that your XYZ product can fulfil customers' needs.
- **To promote goodwill:** The aim is to create a positive image of yourself and your organization, as in the following example:

Welcome to Swastika Bank

> For your convenience, we provide a number of facilities:
>
> - Saving accounts
> - Current account
> - Credit cards
> - Home loans
> - Internet banking
> - ATM facility
>
> Should you have any queries, pl. call in (telephone number 011-823456) or contact us at our website www.swastikabank.in. We'll be delighted to assist you.

Successful communication is really planned. The message must have a clearly defined purpose, to ensure a clear focus. Usually, writers have a combination of purposes in communicating with one primary or main purpose and one or more secondary purpose(s). For example, in writing to a client to refuse a request, your primary purpose would be to inform the client that the request would be refused, while your secondary purpose would be to maintain goodwill.

Purpose in communicating has an impact as the language you choose for your message. If your purpose is mainly to give or ask for information, select objective (factual) language, taking into account what your audience needs to know. The following message is intended for an audience with little technical knowledge or interest. Purpose is to inform the audience about the features of a particular cell phone that would be of interest to them.

> The Alline S 303, cell phone, which weighs 64 g, offers six hours talk time and 48 hours standby time. The phone is equipped with covers in seven different colours: white, orange, green, yellow, purple, blue, and black. The price is Rs. 4,999.00.

If your purpose is mainly persuasive, you might use subjective (emotional) language in addition to objective language. The following message is intended for a young, fashion-conscious audience, for whom appearance is a priority. The purpose is to persuade readers that a particular cell phone is an essential item for fashion-conscious people.

> The Alline S 303 cell phone comes in seven attractive shades to match your wardrobe–soothing white, funky orange, live green, wicked yellow, sizzling purple, electric blue, and bewitching black-so you can have a new look every day.
>
> Weighing only 64 g, the Alline S 303 won't make your clothes sag or bag, and priced at Rs. 4,999.00, it won't make a hole in your pocket.

Thus, purpose of the message influences the choice of either objective or subjective language. Although most business messages contain mainly objective language, subjective language, based on facts, should be used sparingly in business messages, other than in advertising or promotional messages.

REVIEW QUESTIONS

1. Briefly describe what constitutes an organization. What are its components? How does it operate?
2. All organizations undertake a variety of functions with their areas of business. Discuss.
3. Organizations are at once similar to and different from each other. Why?
4. What role does communication play in the success (or failure) of an organization?
5. Write short notes on the organization's environment and culture? How do these things influence an organization?
6. This chapter indicated that the organization has both human and natural resources. Which do you think are more important to the success of the organization? Why?
7. This chapter has suggested that communication is highly functional and takes any forms. What does this mean?
8. It is generally believed that communication in the business is always purposeful. Briefly describe the various purposes of communication in an organization.

5
BARRIERS TO COMMUNICATION

Chapter Objectives

This chapter will enable you to understand:

- The principal barriers in communication
  - Frame of reference barriers
  - Verbal barriers
  - Non-verbal barriers
- Overcoming the barriers
- Ethics and communication
- Significance of ethical communication in organizations

The primary goal of communication is for the receiver to interpret the message as the sender intended. The information to be communicated should be clear and accurate. Often that goal is not achieved in organizations, but managers frequently cite breakdowns as one of their most important problems. Barriers, as we see, come in many shapes and forms and they are potentially present in all communication and in all of the models, we have so far considered. These barriers can create an impenetrable 'brick wall' that marks effective communication impossible. Understanding how barriers in communication can arise is essential, if we are to suggest ways in which communication might be improved.

5.1 THE PRINCIPAL BARRIERS IN COMMUNICATION

Learning to recognize the following communication barriers will help you overcome them:

1. **Frame of reference barriers:** Some communication problems are related to individual's frame of reference.
2. **Verbal barriers:** Verbal barriers are related to 'what you write or say.' They include
   - Inadequate knowledge
   - Poor vocabulary/semantic gap

- Differences in interpretation
- Language differences
- Inappropriate use of expressions
- Over abstraction
- Ambiguity
- Polarization

3. **Nonverbal barriers:** Some communication problems are related to 'how you communicate.' Nonverbal barriers to communication include:
   - Inappropriate or conflicting signals
   - Differences in perception
   - Inappropriate emotions
   - Distractions

5.1.1 Frame of Reference Barriers

Each person's mind is shaped by his or her unique frame of reference. This frame of reference is the sum of an individual's cultural and educational background, attitudes, values, beliefs, physical attributes, age and, gender. An individual's frame of reference is not static and can change because of experiences over a lifetime.

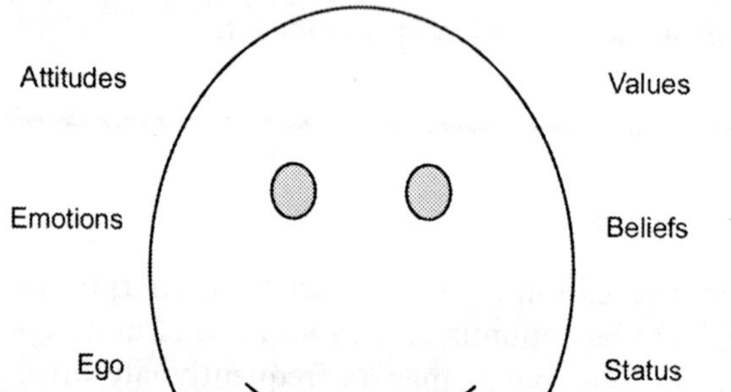

Figure 5.1: Frame of reference.

Aspects of frame of reference

You develop all aspects of your frame of reference through a process of interpersonal communication. These, in turn, affect how you communicate with others, and how you act.

None of these can be directly observed, they can only be inferred from your behaviour. All are learnt from the people with whom you associate. No two people have identical frames of reference. The difference in frames of reference complicates the creation of understanding between people and cause a communication breakdown.

5.1.2 Verbal Barriers

5.1.2.1 Inadequate Knowledge

Before you can even begin to think about how you will communicate an idea, you must, first of all, have sufficient knowledge about the topic to know what you want to say. However, this may not be as simple as it sounds. Sometimes the sender may send information which is not clarified to the receiver.

5.1.2.2 Poor Vocabulary/Semantic Gap

Poor vocabulary makes our message more difficult and less effective. Can you safely use abbreviations like NPV and RRR, or will you have to spell out or perhaps define the terms like 'net present value' or 'required rate of return' appropriately? Thus, poor vocabulary does not allow the communicator to write or speak effectively. It does not allow the receiver to understand the words and the sentences.

5.1.2.3 Differences in Interpretation

Sometimes senders and receivers attribute different meanings to the same word or attribute the same meaning to different words. When this happens, miscommunication can occur.

Every word has both a denotative and a connotative meaning. 'Denotative' refers to the literal, dictionary meaning of a word. 'Connotation' refers to the subjective, emotional meaning that you attach to a word. There are many words of English such as 'light', 'cheap', etc. which can be used with favourable as well as unfavourable connotations. Sometimes the intended meaning of the sender's word is wrongly entered by the receiver by attributing negative meaning to it. For example, the denotative meaning of the word 'plastic' is 'a synthetic material that can be easily moulded into different forms.' The word also has a connotative meaning (sometime negative) for some people–cheap or artificial substitute.

Most of the interpretation problems occur because of the personal reactions engendered by the connotative meaning of a word. Whenever one interprets a symbol, one's own understanding may be different from that of others. The terms aggressive, hard-hitting, workaholic, head-hunter, gay, golden parachute, or wasted can stand for positive, neutral or negative reactions. The problem with such terms is not only that people assign different meanings to the term but also that the term itself might cause such an emotional reaction that the receiver avoids any further communication with the sender. As inferences can give a wrong signal, more information may be sought to clarify doubts.

5.1.2.4 Language Differences

Language use oral or written arbitrary symbols to transmit meaning from one person to another. Every human language has its own vocal symbol system and its own grammatical structures. If the sender and receiver belong to different language groups, their ignorance of each other's language or the lack of common language will be a barrier to communication between them. In an ideal world, all managers should know the language of each culture with which they deal. It is often said that you can buy in your native language anywhere in the world, but you can sell only in the language of the local community.

Most of the correspondence in the international business market is done in English. But communication barriers are seen because of cultural differences. For example, in China, the slogan 'Finger Licking Good' may be translated as 'so good you suck your fingers.' The word 'Nova' (General Motor's Chevrolet is named as 'Nova') sounds like the Spanish phrase 'No Va', which means 'it doesn't go.' Communication difficulties can arise even among native speakers. For example, the Hindi word 'kaka' means 'uncle' in one part of the country but would denote 'small boy' in another part of the country.

5.1.2.5 Inappropriate Use of Expressions

Expressions are groups of words whose intended meanings are different from their literal interpretations. The use of slangs, jargons, and euphemisms is sometimes appropriate and sometimes inappropriate.

- **Slang:** 'Slang' is an expression, often short-lived, that is identified with a specific group of people. Following are some slang terms and their meanings currently popular among youth:

  Barbie – A painstakingly dressed and groomed female

  My bad – My fault

  Mc paper – A quickly or poorly written paper

  Pose – Group of friends

  Teenagers, college students, workers of an organization, immigrants, knowledge professionals, and just every other subgroup all have their own set of slang. Using appropriate slang in everyday speech presents no problem; it conveys precise information and may indicate group membership. Problems arise, however, when the sender uses slang that the receiver does not understand. Slang that sends a negative non-verbal message about the sender can also be a source of problems.
- **Jargon:** 'Jargon' is a technical terminology used with specialized groups. As with slang, the problem is not in using jargon – jargon provides a very precise and efficient way of communicating with those familiar with it. The problem comes either in using jargon with someone who does not understand it or in using jargon in an effort to impress others.
- **Euphemisms:** 'Euphemisms' are inoffensive expressions used in place of words that may offend or suggest something unpleasant. Sensitive writers or speakers use euphemisms occasionally, especially to describe bodily functions. But how can you say, for example, with the same sense and spirit that someone has died?

  Slang, jargon, and euphemisms all have important role to play in business communication so long as they are used with appropriate people and in appropriate contexts. They can, however, prove to be barriers to effective communication when used to impress, when used too often, or when used in appropriate setting.

5.1.2.6 Over Abstraction

An abstract word identifies an idea or a feeling instead of a concrete object. For example, 'communication' is an abstract word whereas 'report' is a concrete word. A concrete word is a word that identifies something that can be seen or touched. Abstract words are necessary in order to communicate about things you cannot see or touch. However, communication problems result when you use too many abstract words or when you use too high a level of abstraction. The higher the level of abstraction, the more difficult it is for the receiver to visualize exactly what the sender has in mind. For example, which sentence communicates more information: 'I acquired an asset at the store' or 'I bought a laser printer at Binary Computers'?

5.1.2.7 Ambiguity

Communication problems result from the overuse of ambiguous terms such as few, some, several, and far away, which have too broad a meaning for use in much business communication.

Similar communication problems occur with the roundabout verbiages. It is a long-winded way of saying the meaningless padding. For example, instead of saying 'in the majority of cases' or 'in a number of instances' you can say 'some' or 'usually'. Similarly, instead of saying 'prior to' you can say 'before'. By omitting such words and phrases, you can save your message from confusion and misunderstanding.

When a message is transmitted through translations, interpretations, explanations, and simplifications, some part of it gets distorted or lost. Then the accuracy of the message is lost.

5.1.2.8 Polarization

At times, some people act as though every situation is divided into two opposite and distinct poles, with no allowance for a middle ground. Of course, there are some true dichotomies. You are either male or female, and your company either will or will not make a profit this year. But most aspects of life involve more than two alternatives.

For example, you might assume that a speaker either is telling the truth or is lying. In fact, what the speaker actually says may be true, but by selectively omitting some important information, he or she may be giving an inaccurate impression. Is the speaker telling the truth or not? Most likely, the answer lies somewhere in between. Skilled communicators avoid inappropriate either/or logic and instead make the effort to search for middle – ground words when such language best describes a situation.

5.1.3 Non-berbal Barriers

5.1.3.1 Inappropriate or Conflicting Signals

A non-verbal message is any message that is not written or spoken. The non-verbal message may accompany a verbal message. Non-verbal messages are more difficult to manipulate than verbal messages. Therefore, when verbal and non-verbal signals conflict, the receiver tends to put more faith in the non-verbal signal.

Many non-verbal messages vary from culture to culture. For example, our sign for 'okay' – forming a circle with our forefingers and thumb – means 'zero' in France, 'money' in Japan and a 'vulgarity' in Brazil. Americans and Canadians consider eye contact important. In Asian and many Latin American countries, however, looking at a partner full in the eye is considered an irritating sight of ill breeding. Similarly, touching behaviour is very culture specific.

Communication competence requires that you communicate non-verbal messages that are consistent with your verbal messages and that are appropriate for the context.

5.1.3.2 Differences in Perception

Every individual has his own 'personal' perception. The experience of the same situation by two individuals brings quite different reactions. Even when they hear the same speech or read the same document, people of different ages, socioeconomic backgrounds, cultures, and so forth often form very different perceptions. Because each person is unique with unique experiences, knowledge and viewpoints, each person forms a different opinion about what he or she reads or hears.

Some people tend automatically to believe certain people and to disrupt other people. If we trust the speaker, we may change our attitudes easily and readily according to whatever the speaker proposes. If we distrust the speaker, everything that he says can motivate no action from us, nor can it bring any change in our attitudes, views and values. The communication barrier thus arises as a result of different selective perceptions of the same object or idea by two or more people.

5.1.3.3 Inappropriate Emotions

Emotions are our feelings about the world around us. Usually, the positive emotions such as joy, love or affection do not interfere with communication, but the negative emotions act as strong barriers to effective communication. Emotionally excited communicator is unable to organize his message properly. In most cases, a moderate level of emotional involvement intensifies the communication and makes it more personal. However, too much emotional involvement can be obstacle to communication. For example, excessive anger can create such an emotionally charged environment that reasonable discussion is not possible. Likewise, prejudice (automatically rejecting certain people or ideas), stereotyping (placing individuals into categories) and boredom all hinder effective communication. Such emotions tend to create a blocked mind that is closed to new ideas, rejecting or ignoring information that is contrary to one's prevailing belief.

5.1.3.4 Distractions

Any environmental or competing element that restricts one's ability to concentrate on the communication task hinders effective communication. Such distractions are called 'noise'. Examples of environmental noise are poor acoustics, extreme temperature, uncomfortable seating, body odour, poor telephone connections, and illegible photocopies. Examples of competing noise are other important business to attend to, too many meetings, and too many reports to read.

Competent communicators make the effort to write and speak clearly and consistently and try to avoid or minimize any verbal or non-verbal barriers that might cause misunderstandings.

5.2 OVERCOMING THE BARRIERS

Barriers can be overcome if sufficient effort is put into the communication process. Basically, to communicate is to share 'information' in its widest sense, with others in an intelligible, participative form through the medium of words – spoken or written, or body gestures, or other symbolic signs.

The sender should be clear about the following 5 W's and 1 H in order to be effective in his communication.

- Who: To whom should the message go
- Why: Why should I communicate
- What: What should I communicate
- When: When should I communicate promptly
- How: How should I communicate that the receiver may understand the message clearly
- Whose: A suitable location which will not interfere with the reception, understanding and acceptance of the message.

The receiver should also be aware about the following, to overcome the different barriers.

- Be attentive to sender.
- Listen actively to the message being sent.
- Ask for clarification and repetition wherever necessary
- Keep checking the receipt of information with sender.

Keith Davis (Keith Davis, 1993) lays down the Rule of Five to guide the receiver to be an effective element of the communication process. "In the communication process, the role of receiver is, I believe, as important as that of sender. There are five receiver steps in the process of communication – Receive, Understand, Accept, Use, and Give a Feedback. Without these steps, being followed by the receiver, no communication process would be complete and successful." Thus, communication is successful when

- The message is properly understood
- The purpose of the sender is fulfilled
- The sender and the receiver of the message remain linked through feedback.

One way of eliminating the barriers to communication is to check continuously during the communication process what the message really is. This action should be taken by the sender and the receiver both.

In addition, both the receiver and sender should realize that the misunderstanding is bound to occur, and they should be alert for all cues to this effect. They can make the communication smooth if they listen attentively and share opinions, feelings and perceptions generated by the message. Thus both parties separately as well as together have to work to remove the barriers and achieve the communication effectiveness.

5.2.1 Additional Measures to Overcome the Barriers

5.2.1.1 Fostering Good Relationships

In organizations, strong relations must be fostered between the employer and employee in order to avoid misunderstandings. They should understand and accept each other's viewpoints in order to facilitate proper communication in the organization.

5.2.1.2 Well-focused Communication

In organization, communication should always be purposeful so that the receiver should not be left to feel that communication had been meaningless or useless.

5.2.1.3 Adequate Knowledge

An adequate knowledge of the subject is essential for effective communication. The sender should know the subject on which he is going to express his thoughts, ideas, and feelings. Similarly, the receiver should also have sufficient knowledge of the subject.

5.2.1.4 Coordination Between the Management and Employees

There should be proper coordination and cooperation between the superiors and subordinates for effective communication.

5.2.1.5 Avoid Jargons

The technical or specialized language should be least used or avoided. However, technical vocabulary may be essential for discussions on technical problems among the group of professionals. But, if such vocabulary is used before the general public or in a letter to a layman, it will not be properly understood. Thus, efforts should be made to use the language commonly understood by the receiver and sender of the message.

5.2.1.6 Accuracy

There should be accuracy in the message to be transmitted between both parties for the communication to improve its effectiveness.

5.2.1.7 Clarity

The message to be transmitted should be clear and complete in every respect. The communicator must be very clear about all the aspects of the idea in his mind and about the purpose for which it is communicated.

5.2.1.8 Organizational Policies

Organization, policies, structure and philosophy must be clear and understood by everyone easily. The organization should have clear cut and simple structure. There should be consistency when messages are passed from a sender to a receiver. One should not introduce a personal view in the message.

Organizational philosophy should be properly communicated to its employees. Wrong information to be transferred to anyone in the organization can be the cause of communication barrier.

5.2.1.9 Minimize Semantic Problems

Proper semantic selection is essential for the accurate replication of ideas on the mind of the receiver. Still there is uncertainty about the exact perception of the message by the decoder, because of the multiple denotative and connotative meanings of symbols used for encoding the contents of information. People use either the same word in different ways or different words in the same way. The use of words not only depends on the given subject but also on the occasion, media, the type of communication received and the conditions under which a person communicates. Thus, the usage of words must be based on their appropriateness in different situations.

5.2.1.10 Proper Communication Media

There is an infinite variety of communication media and the communicator has to select any one or more of them. He has to select the most suitable medium available to him for his set purpose and may even change it and take over another medium which is more effective when the situation changes. The correct choice of medium which is suitable for related encoding and decoding system can help to enhance the effectiveness of the communication process.

If one wants immediate action from the receiver, there is no need to send a lengthy formal report. One can pick up the telephone or go his office to tell him what to do.

5.2.1.11 Right Feedback

As feedback is the receiver's response to the communicator's message, right feedback helps both sender and receiver to measure their understanding and improves their joint commitment towards the task.

Thus, to overcome barrier, the sender should be aware, as to whom, why, where, and what message is to be transmitted and how it is to be transmitted. The receiver should listen to the message attentively. Besides, to communicate effectively, we need to acquire skills to improve existing communication abilities.

5.3 ETHICS AND COMMUNICATION

Each of us has a personal code of ethics or rules of conduct, that might go beyond legal rules to tell us how to act when the law is silent. When composing a business proposal, drafting a sales letter, writing a human resource policy, writing a feasibility report, or recruiting a candidate for a job, we make conscious decisions regarding what information to include and what information to exclude from our messages. For the information that is included, we make ethical choices–moral decisions about how to phrase the language, which words and sentences to use, how much to emphasize each point, and how to organize the message. Such decisions have legal and ethical dimensions–both for the writer and for the organization.

5.3.1 Legal and Ethical Dimensions

5.3.1.1 Defamation

Any false or malicious statement that is communicated to others, and that injures a person's good name or reputation may constitute defamation. Defamation in oral communication is called slander and in written communication or videotape is called libel. The three major conditions for defamation are that

- the statement be false,
- the statement be communicated to others,
- the statement be harmful to a person's good name or reputation.

Telling a person on his face that he is a liar does not constitute defamation unless a third person hears the remarks. Code of business ethics believes that you should use objective language and verifiable information when communicating about others.

5.3.1.2 Invasion of Privacy

An unreasonable intrusion into the private life of another person may constitute an invasion of privacy. Using someone's name or photographs in a sales promotion without the person's permission may be considered an invasion of privacy.

National laws protect the individual's right to privacy. The central government defines 'right to privacy' as the right of individuals to participate in decisions regarding the collection, use, and disclosure of information personally identifiable to that individual. Thus, someone's right to privacy may be violated if his or her records are read by someone not authorized to examine them or who has no compelling business reason for examining them.

Competent communicators ensure that they do not misuse information about others in their communication.

5.3.1.3 Fraud

A deliberate representation of the truth for the purpose of including someone to give up something of value is called fraud. Fraud can occur either when party deliberately conceals some information that he or she is required to reveal. Thus, the statements must involve facts.

Being dishonest will only lead to more lies which can really do damage to your relationship be it personal or official. A fact remains that lies are hard to keep straight unlike the truth because truth does not change, it is constant. However, opinions or arguments or claims about a product should not be exaggerated as this is called sales puffery. Although a puffery does not constitute fraud even if it turns out to be false.

One should recognize that a statement of opinions, even if it is not a fraud, might still be unethical.

5.3.1.4 Misrepresentation

Misrepresentation is a false statement that is made innocently with no intent to deceive the other party. If misrepresentation or fraud is proved, the contract or agreement may be considered invalid and the offended party may collect monetary compensation.

In business communication, one should be aware of the relevant laws and ensure that their oral and written messages are accurate in terms of what is communicated and is nit communicated.

5.3.1.5 *Other Ethical Considerations*

Many organizations have developed their own codes of ethics to govern employee behaviour. Ethics in business communication not only govern what language we use but also how we use language. Communication ethics is a primary concern for most business.

Sometimes being legally right is not sufficient justification for our actions. A message can be true and still be unethical.

When you want to achieve your goals in an ethical manner, ask yourself these questions

- Is this message true?
- Does it exaggerate?
- Does it obscure information that should be communicated?
- Does it promise something that cannot be delivered?
- Does it betray a confidence?
- Does it play unduly on the fears of the reader?
- Does it reflect the wishes of the organization?

Regardless of the size and type of organization, every employee faces ethical questions when communicating orally and in writing.

It is important to practice ethical communication for resolving conflicts as well as everyday interactions. No one likes being talked about behind their back. In choosing what information to convey, he should make conscious decisions–ethical choices about what is right, even when no question of law is involved.

A person who practices ethical communication advocates truthfulness, accuracy and honesty as these foster and maintain the dignity and integrity of communication.

5.4 SIGNIFICANCE OF ETHICAL COMMUNICATION IN ORGANIZATIONS

Ethics are those principles which guide the conduct of individuals. In the organization's context, ethical behaviour implies such decisions which are taken after giving due thought to their impact on the stakeholder and society as a whole. When an organization communicates internally it shapes the values of its employees. Dealing honestly with colleagues and customers develop trust and build stronger relationships. When an organization communicates externally, it influences the perception of the external public. Ethical organizations endure less litigation, less resentment, and less government regulation.

Ethics play a crucial role in communication. Communication has always been of critical importance of the success of organizations. Corporate reputation is one of an organization's most valuable and enduring assets. It plays a central role in the achievement of key business objectives such as creating shareholder value, attracting, retaining and motivating customers, enhancing reputation with all audiences, marshalling stakeholder support on public policy issues, creating consumer preference for products and services, and minimizing the impact of a crisis can have on a company's financial position and business prospects. Questions of right and wrong arise whenever people communicate.

Ethical communication is fundamental to responsible thinking, decision-making, and the development of relationships and communities within and across contexts, cultures, channels, and media. Ethical communication enhances human worth and respect for self and others. In business communication, however, knowing right from wrong does not always mean that doing the right thing is either obvious or easy.

Ethical communication supports diversity of perspective and freedom in all forms: whether self expression, lifestyle and ideas. This aspect of ethical communication is promoting communication that consists of caring and mutual understanding that respects the unique ideas and also characteristics of individuals.

REVIEW QUESTIONS

1. What are the main barriers to business communication? How can they be overcome?
2. Describe the factors responsible for miscommunication for business organizations?
3. What are barriers to effective verbal communication in business organizations?
4. How does language act as a serious barrier to effective communication?
5. What are non-verbal barriers to effective communication in business organizations?
6. How do the personal attitudes and prejudices act as the barriers to effective communication?
7. It is suggested in this chapter that a person who practices ethical communication advocates truthfulness, accuracy, and honesty. What role does the personal code of ethics play in business communication? How one can foster and maintain the dignity and integrity of communication?
8. Briefly describe the significance of ethical communication in organization. How an individual can achieve his goals in an ethical manner?
9. Write short notes on the following:
   (a) Frame of reference barriers
   (b) Differences in interpretation
   (c) Different perceptions
   (d) Noise

6

PRINCIPLES OF EFFECTIVE COMMUNICATION

Chapter Objectives

This chapter will enable you to understand:

- Prerequisites of effective communication
- Seven C's of effective communication
  - ◇ Completeness
  - ◇ Clarity
  - ◇ Conciseness
  - ◇ Concreteness
  - ◇ Candidness
  - ◇ Courtesy
  - ◇ Correctness

Today's world has developed rapidly from an industrial age to an information age. In this age, effective communication is the foundation on which the success of a business largely depends. It extends across all areas of business including managerial, technical, clerical and social positions. However, of the many problems that confront organizations and their managers, communication nearly appears at or close to the top of any list. It is the responsibility of all persons in the organization, managers as well as workers, in working toward a common aim. In fact, a successful businessman should be able to clearly, concisely and eloquently convey information and ideas to the people."

Effective communication, whether written or oral, is a skilled job. It depends on the skill of one who sends messages as well as the skills of one who receives the messages. Communication cycle begins with the generation of an idea in the mind of a person. In order to make our communication effective, we should follow certain scientific principles. These principles provide guidelines for composing written and oral messages. Generally, these principles are called 'seven Cs of effective communication'. They are

(i) Completeness
(ii) Clarity
(iii) Conciseness
(iv) Concreteness
(v) Candidness
(vi) Courtesy
(vii) Correctness

Before discussing the principles (seven Cs) of effective communication, it is desirable to understand the prerequisites of successful effective communication.

6.1 PREREQUISITES OF SUCCESSFUL EFFECTIVE COMMUNICATION

Following are the prerequisites of a successful effective communication:

1. **Perception:** The sender of the communication should be able to predict how his message will be received. He anticipates the reaction of the receiver and shapes the message accordingly. He reads the respond of the receiver correctly and constantly adjusts to remove any misunderstanding.
2. **Precision:** The contents of the message are exact for both the sender and the receiver.
3. **Credibility:** The message of the sender is believable. The receiver has a faith in the substance of the message. He trusts the information transmitted by the sender. The receiver also has faith in the sender's intentions.
4. **Control:** The sender transmits the message in such a form that it is able to manoeuvre the reaction of the receiver in his favour. Depending on the purpose of the sender, he can make the receiver change his mind or take action.
5. **Congeniality:** The sender maintains friendly pleasant relations with the receiver regardless of whether he agrees with him or not. A good communicator commands the respect and goodwill of the receiver. The sender is willing to work with the receiver despite some differences of opinion.

6.2 PRINCIPLES OF EFFECTIVE COMMUNICATION: SIX CS OF EFFECTIVE COMMUNICATION

6.2.1 Completeness

The principle of effective communication is that the message must be complete. A business message is considered complete when it contains all the facts the receiver needs for the feedback. The completion requires inclusion of the following three elements in the business message.

1. **Inclusion of all necessary information:** A complete communication includes all the necessary information required by the receiver for complete understanding. 'Five W' questions–who, what, where, when and why- and any other important points like

'how' also helps to make our message complete. For example, to order some goods make clear 'what' you want, 'when' you need it, to 'whom' and 'where' it is to be sent, and 'how' the payment will be made.

2. **Inclusion of answers to all questions:** A complete business communication includes answers to all possible questions stated and implied. It is essential that your communication (presentations, discussions, or dialogues) should be as far as possible planned and structured. Do not quit anything whenever you are answering an enquiry about your product.
3. **Inclusion of something extra, when desirable:** A complete message includes something more than the answers to customer's specific questions since the customers may not know what they need or their questions may be inadequate.

6.2.2 Clarity

Simple, clear English which is easily understood is what is needed in all business messages. Long, difficult words show disrespect for the reader, and should be avoided. Use simple words which everybody understands, every time.

1. **Clarity in thought:** Clarity is most important in all communications. To ensure that you express yourself clearly, your thoughts should be clear and well organized. You should be clear about three points:

- What is the objective of communication?
- What is to be communicated?
- Which medium will be the most suitable for this purpose?

2. **Clarity of expression:** The receiver learns about the idea in the sender's mind through the coded message. If the encoding is faulty, the message may be misinterpreted. Since most of the messages are transmitted with the help of words, you should be careful about the meanings and organization of words.

- **Use of simple words:** Simple and short words are more effective than long unfamiliar ones. For example,

Pompous (avoid them)	Simple (use them)
acquaint	tell/inform
demonstrate	show
compensate	pay
visualize	see
utilize	use
terminate	end
facilitate	help
eradicate	get rid of
nullify	cancel
supposition	idea

- **Use of single words for long phrases**: A single word is more effective than a long phrase. For example,

Long phrases (avoid them)	Single words (use them)
at all times	always
at a later date	later
at the present time	now
subsequent to	after
prior to	before
despite the fact that	although
to the fullest possible extent	fully
will you be kind enough	please

- **Use of verbs for nouns:** Using verbs in place of noun brings about simplicity and clarity. For example,

Using nouns (difficult)	using verbs (simple)
to a conclusion	conclude
make a decision	decide
submit a proposal	propose
take into consideration	consider
make the announcement	announce

- **Use of double entry:** Phrases with two words conveying the same idea should be avoided. For example,

Double entry	Simple
actual fact	fact
revert back	revert
absolutely complete	complete
my personal opinion	my opinion
11 a.m. in the morning	11 a.m.
during the year 1997	during 1997

- **Use of concrete expression:** Concrete expressions create visual images that are easy to register. Instead of vague, generalized statements, you should give definite facts. We should avoid the words like high, low, soon, quick, easy, several, a few, many, etc.

Vague and general	Concrete and effective
Goods are soon being dispatched	Goods will be dispatch on 2nd July.
This piece of jewellery is inexpensive.	This piece of jewellery costs Rs. 200.
A few students....	5-7 students....

- **Use of active voice:** In ordinary circumstances, it is better to use active voice because they are easier to understand.

Passive (awkward)	Active (elegent)
Your efforts are appreciated by all of us.	All of us appreciate your efforts.
Your report will be discussed by a committee.	A committee will discuss your report.

The results were reported in our July 9 letter.	We reported the results in our July 9 letter.
The policy was enforced by the committee.	The committee enforced the policy.

- **Excessive use of the infinitive:** The use of the infinitive (to-verb) makes the style impersonal and formal.

Action in the infinitive (formal)	Action in the verb (direct)
It is my job to supervise....	I supervise....

- **Use of jargon:** Technical terms that are peculiar to an industry are described as jargon. Thus, Jargon refers to the special language of a trade or a profession. It creates difficulty in understanding and makes the style formal and stiff. The writer should use only those technical terms which the reader is sure to understand.

Formal and stiff	Simple
This is to acknowledge...	Thank you for your...
Would you be good enough	Would you please
Beg to say, beg to inform and oblige	Avoid 'beg'
Under separate cover	Separately

- **Use of ambiguity:** If your message means more than one thing, it is ambiguity. For example,

  "Rajiv told Rohan that he was not being considered for promotion."

  Who is being considered for promotion–Rajiv or Rohan?
- **Use of faulty punctuation:** Punctuation also can cause ambiguity. For example,

  "Go slow, work in progress." Or "Go, slow work in progress."
- **Use of effective sentences**

  In order to get clarity, you should use short sentences of about 16-18 words for middle-level readers. Short sentences communicate better because of mind limitations. Important characteristics to consider are length, unity, coherence, and emphasis. Generally, short sentences make the expression more clear. Unity in the sentence means conveying only one main idea. Coherence means that all the words are correctly arranged in the sentence. Emphasis helps expressing the intended meaning clear.

6.2.3 Conciseness

Another principle of effective communication is conciseness. Conciseness means 'saying something in the fewest possible words without sacrificing the other qualities of effective communication.' In business and professional communication, be brief and be able to say in minimum words. Transmission of maximum information by using a minimum of words should be your aim in communication. In order to achieve conciseness you should include only relevant fact. Repetition should be avoided and there should be proper organization of the message. Vague words and round about ways of expression should be avoided.

Following are the guidelines to achieve conciseness.

1. **Only relevant facts:** An effective concise message should include only relevant material. Quit irrelevant statements, long introductions, unnecessary explanations, excessive adjectives, and propositions

2. **Eliminate vague words and round about ways of expressions:** Some of the guidelines to be followed to write words expressions in a concise manner without changing the meaning are:
   (a) Use single words instead of phrases
   (b) Omit unnecessary details
   (c) Omit 'which' and 'that' clauses whenever possible
   (d) Limit use of passive voice
3. **Avoid needless repetition:** As concise communication saves time and expense for both the sender and the receiver, words and sentences should not be repeated in the effective communication. For example,

Verbosity/Repetition	Simple and short words
In considerable number of cases	Often
In close proximity to	Nearby
Enclosed herewith please find	Enclosed is
The department budget can be observed to be decreasing each new year.	The department budget decreases each new year.
He criticised everyone he came in contact with.	He criticised everyone he met.
If you are not satisfied, return it back to us.	If you are not satisfied, return it to us.
We should plan in advance for the future.	We should plan.
Due to the fact that	Because

6.2.4 Candidness

Candidness, in a way, implies consideration of the other person's interest and his/her need to know things objectively and fairly. In our communication, you must show consideration for the reader. The writer must take into consideration the nature, the post and the mental level of the receiver so that the reader can read it with ease. This can be done in the following ways:

1. **The you-approach:** 'You' attitude is the secret of effective business communication. To make our communication more effective, we must avoid ***I's*** and ***we's*** and have as many ***you's*** as possible. The 'you' attitude can be used effectively in all kinds of business communication letters, proposals reports, etc. In any case, we should not forget the reader's point of view.

We-attitude	**You-attitude**
• We acknowledge your letter of June 15, 20....	• Thank you for your kind letter of June 15, 20...
• I am happy to report....	• You will be happy to learn....
• I want to express my sincere thanks for the good words....	• Thank you for your kind words....
• Our customers will appreciate....	• You will appreciate....
• We are pleased to inform our customers...	• We are pleased to inform you...

• We have four different savings schemes in which our customers can invest their savings.	• You have a choice of four savings schemes in which you can invest your savings.
• We give 20% discount	• You will be enjoying 20% discount
• Anyone visiting our shop knows…	• If you visit our shop you will know…

2. **Gender bias approach:** As the business world is no longer dominated by men, it is important to avoid gender bias. We should use plural forms inclusive of both the genders. It is often possible to use 'the' for his/her.

Write not this	**but this**
• The chairman handled the situation tactfully.	• The chairperson handled the situation tactfully.
• The policeman was duped.	• The police was duped.
• Dear Sir	• Dear Sir/Madam
• Each member cast his vote.	• All the members cast their votes.
• The manager talked to his customers.	• The manager talked to the customers.

3. **The positive, pleasant approach:** Another way to show consideration is to emphasize positive pleasant facts. In a written communication, the reader accepts calmly and coolly all the no, regrets and sorry if they are expressed in a positive manner. An approach with a negative beginning irritates the reader, a positive approach, on the other hand, convinces the reader of the writer's helplessness. In fact, a positive and pleasant approach says 'no' in a sugarcoated manner and retains the customer's goodwill. As a rule, you must try to avoid negative words like, fear, mistake, unpleasant, unwelcome, disagree, etc. you should use positive and pleasing words like, please, thankful, welcome, appreciate, happy, agree, benefit, pleasure, loyal, generous, help, etc. in fact, candidness is a result of integrity and honesty.

Negative	**Positive**
• We regret to inform you that we will not be able to execute your order until…	• Thank you for your order. The goods will be sent to you as soon as….."
• We regret to inform you that we must deny your request for credit.	• For the time being we can serve you only on the cash basis.

6.2.5 Courtesy

The term 'courtesy' implies politeness that grows out of respect and concern for others. Courtesy demands that you should not use words insulting or hurtful to the listener. One should say things with force and assertiveness without being rude. Your tone should reflect your respect for your listener. Courteous attitude win's sympathy, respect and mutual understanding. The following points help to promote courtesy;

- You should answer the queries promptly. You should acknowledge a document the same day it is received.
- Irritating expressions should be omitted. Expressions like 'you forgot', 'you failed', 'your irresponsible approach' are bound to irritate or hurt the reader. For instance, the

message "I can't follow anything written in this letter" is discourteous. A courteous message should read "it is ignorance that I could not understand this letter properly."

- Courtesy demands that the message should be respectful, thoughtful, and appreciative. If you fail to do something, you must apologize sincerely. If someone does favour to you, you must acknowledge it promptly and thank the person.
- Avoid questionable humour.
- When using names treat each gender with respect. Courtesy requires equal treatment of the people regardless of gender or race.

6.2.6 Correctness

The term correctness of the communication does not simply mean proper grammar, punctuation, and spelling. It is used in a wide sense. Correctness means that the facts and figures presented in the communication should be accurate. Accuracy requires checking and double checking to ensure that figures, facts and words used are correct.

The language used in communication should also be correct. Business writing should be formal and informal according to the audience and the purpose. It should be sent at the proper time. Correct communication depends upon authentic facts, date and detail.

Thus, we may conclude that an effective business communication must satisfy all the seven Cs. Some authors have also suggested that besides above mentioned seven Cs an effective communication should also satisfy four Ss. These are shortness, simplicity, strength, and sincerity. However, it may be pointed out that seven Cs are all comprehensive and include the so-called Ss also.

REVIEW QUESTIONS

1. What are the prerequisites of successful effective communication? Discuss.
2. Write a note on the importance of clarity and correctness in an effective communication.
3. Explain seven C's of effective communication?
4. What is effective communication? Discuss the general principles of effective communication?
5. Describe the guidelines to achieve conciseness in an effective business communication?
6. What is meant by completness as a principle of communication? Briefly describe.
7. Why is it important to adapt the message to the needs of the receiver? Explain and illustrate 'You' attitude as the secret of effective business communication.
8. In business communication the positive and gender-bias approaches are as important as you approach. Discuss with examples.

UNIT–2
Interpersonal and Group Communication Skills

7
LISTENING SKILLS

Chapter Objectives

This chapter will enable you to understand:

- The Need for Listening in Business
- What is listening
- The Hearing-Listening Distinction
- Listening Process
- Types of Listening
- Listening in Specific Situations
- The Problems of Poor Listening Skills
- Keys to Better Listening

In contemporary organizations, probably even more of the typical member's time is devoted to listening. Yet few of us know very much about this communication skill. There is wide agreement among experts that we spend more time in organizations practicing listening and that we do not do it particularly well. In fact, people are not trained in effective listening skills because it is assumed that, as listening is natural it does not need to be learnt.

7.1 THE NEED FOR LISTENING IN BUSINESS

Listening is basic to almost every form of effective oral interactions in business. Other related cognitive and interpersonal skills also depend on listening ability. To make effective decisions, employees at all levels of a company must be aware of all information–facts, opinions, feelings–that affects and is affected by these decisions. Some of this information comes from reading letters, memos, reports, and other documents. But far more information influencing a business decision comes by way of talking. The question is whether the decision-maker truly listens to the many types of spoken information.

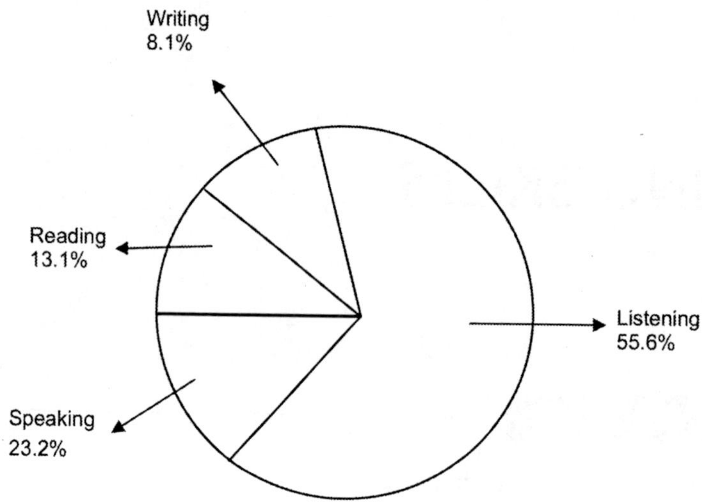

(Source: De Vinto, Human Communication, New York, 1994)

Figure 7.1: How communicative time is spent.

You cannot hope to be effective in the interview unless you listen well. Good decision making depends on the ability to listen to information. Skilled problem analysts must be able to listen if they hope to develop good solutions to potential problems. These and other skills depend on the ability to listen to and comprehend a message. The importance of the listening skill to messages has also been recognized by individual firms. Dr. Earl Planty in his role as executive counsellor Johnson and Johnson said, "By far the most effective method by which executives can tap ideas of subordinates is sympathetic listening in many day-to-day informal conducts within and outside the workplace. There is no system that will do the job in an earlier manner.... Nothing can equal an executive's willingness to listen."

Often we think we are communicating effectively, we may not be. This is equally true to listening, the process of learning and interpreting message. Listening is an integral part of the communication process. It is a skill just as writing, reading, and speaking are. It can be learnt and improved.

Listening is often a neglected skill. Think about it for a moment. How much of us truly listen? How many times has someone said to you, "You are not listening to me, are you?" One reason we have not developed our listening skills is the fast pace of contemporary culture. We do not seem to have time to listen, we are too busy in talking, and if we are not talking, we are formulating what we are going to say next.

7.2 WHAT IS LISTENING?

Listening is the act by which we make 'sense of sounds'. The most common form of listening involves spoken messages. However, the act of listening is not limited to language or even to people. We make sense out of other sounds as well. A doctor, for example, can learn about the state of a patient's health by listening to that person's breathing or heart-beat. Similarly, a skilled mechanic can identify a problem by listening to a running engine.

7.3 THE HEARING-LISTENING DISTINCTION

Listening involves much more than just hearing. Hearing is a passive activity and depends solely on the ears in a physical act. You may hear a speaker's words, but you do not necessarily understand their meaning. Hearing is simply what happens when a message vibrates over eardrums and causes a signal to move to the brain. Thus, hearing is simply perceiving sounds. When you perceive a sound, you are merely aware of it; you do not necessarily comprehend it.

On the other hand, listening is an active process which requires a purposeful and systematic response to messages. When you listen, the electrochemical reactions reach the brain, you interpret and meaning is given to the sounds. You listen not merely with the ears, but with the mind.

7.4 LISTENING PROCESS

Listening generally involves a five-step process: hearing, attending, understanding, remembering, and responding. These stages occur in sequence. This process is active rather than passive and involves using a number of behaviours and tools to be most effective.

The source has a message which is communicated to the listener. This can be affected by inferences, external or internal.

1. **External inference**

   This refers to noise or distractions external to the listener which may distract from the message. Examples of external inferences are a stuffy lecture hall, a strong wind, and other people speaking.

2. **Internal inference**

   This refers to mental or emotional distractions which may distract from the message. Examples of internal inferences are anxiety about an assignment, lack of knowledge of the subject matter.

Five Stages of Listening Process

Stage 1: Hearing

The first stage of the listening process occurs when sound waves are received. At this point, conscious perception of what is being heard does not take place.

Stage 2: Attention

In this second stage, the listener begins to focus on what is being said and how it is said. The brain selects only a few stimuli out of the mass of stimuli presented.

Stage 3: Understanding

In the third stage, the message content is analyzed and the non-verbal codes are interpreted. However, the meaning attached to the message differs from one listener to the next because of the unique frame of reference of each listener. Understanding is the essence active listening. It determines the response the listener will make.

Stage 4: Remembering

The fourth stage occurs when the message is stored for later recall.

Stage 5: Responding

The final stage occurs when the listener responds to the speaker. This response shows the listener's understanding of, and feeling about the message. The speaker sees whether the message was understood as intended, or whether it should be restarted or clarified.

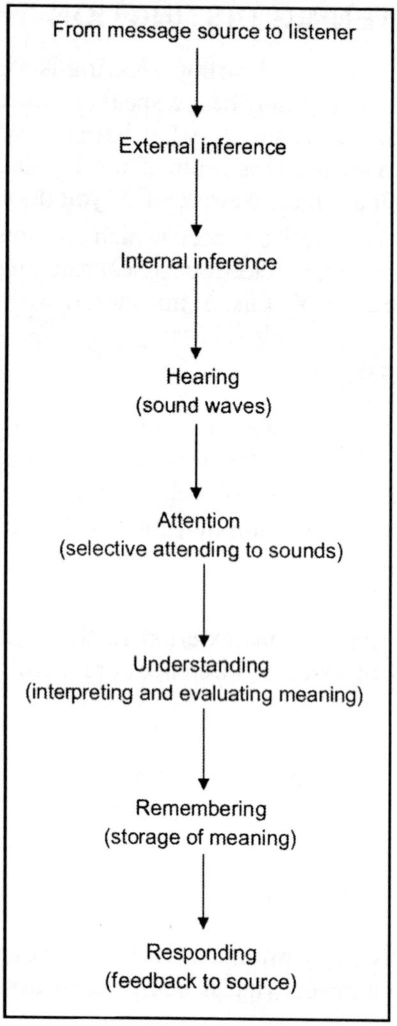

Fig. 7.2: Various stages of the listening process.

7.5 TYPES OF LISTENING

Efficient listening enhances your skills as a critical thinker and helps you to evaluate what you hear. However, just as a speaker has purpose in presenting a speech, audience has a purpose in listening to the speech. In other words, people listen at different levels depending on their degree of involvement in given situation. Besides, people use different types of listening when listening for different purposes.

Broadly speaking, the listening may be casual or active.

1. **Casual listening**
   - Casual listening is hearing and understanding a message but not trying to remember the message in the long term.

- Casual listening is sometimes called passive listening. Listening while watching a movie or making small talk at lunch are examples of casual listening.
- The casual listener expands little energy or effort. Although the listener may understand the message, remembering it for a long time is not important.
- Casual listening is relaxed. When you are talking with others, however, you must be careful not to listen so casually that others think you are not paying attention.

2. **Active listening**

   Active listening is hearing and trying to understand and remember a message. It has purpose. We can identify four types of active listening.

   (a) **Listening for enjoyment:** When you listen to music usually you are listening to relax. When you listen to your favourite radio programme, or to an entertaining speech, you listen for enjoyment, or pleasure. At such times, you may suspend your critical faculties, relax and enjoy the stimulation.

   (b) **Empathic or reflective listening:** In this type of listening, you provide emotional support for the speaker by showing affection, caring, and warmth. For example, you lend a sympathetic ear to a friend in distress. Listening and responding to friends during lunch sends the message that their thoughts and feelings are important to you. You listen to let people know that you are interested in what they have to say and that they are important.

   This type of listening is most often associated with interpersonal communication, but it occurs in the public speaking context as well. An audience listening to a leader's public apology for an inappropriate conduct may be considered as an empathic listening.

   (c) **Comprehensive or informative listening:** In this type of listening, people are primarily concerned with listening for information. Naturally people listen for different sorts of information. The student taking notes in a lecture or an employee receiving instructions about how to perform a new task is engaged in what is known as comprehensive or informative listening. The purpose is to understand and remember the information by following the logic of the message and concentrating on identifying and separating the main ideas from the material that relates to them. This type of listening, therefore, is also known as discriminative listening.

   (d) **Critical listening:** Critical listening is the type of listening people engage in when they have to evaluate a message in order to accept or reject it. In other words, when people are trying to persuade us to their point of view, it is engaged in critical listening. For example, listening to the campaign speech of a political leader, or to the sales talks to a car dealer or real estate agent.

7.6 LISTENING IN SPECIFIC SITUATIONS

In the business world, you will find two common listening situations – listening in a small group and listening in a conference setting.

7.6.1 Listening in a Small Group

When in a small group, all of your communication skills including your listening skills, are important. Practice active listening. Listen for both ideas and feelings. Use effective eye contact and body language that indicate to others that you are listening. Check your understanding by asking questions or restating ideas as appropriate.

7.6.2 Listening in a Conference Setting

As an employee, you will continue to learn new skills and information related to your job. You may attend meetings, seminars, or conferences designed to improve your skills and knowledge. In such a setting, you will need to listen effectively in order to learn. Following are the guidelines for taking part in a seminar or conference.

- Clearly understand your reasons for being at the conference. What do you need to learn or accomplish at the conference?
- Choose comfortable seating
- Choose seating where you can see the speaker and any visual aid that may be used
- Avoid judging the speaker's subject, ability to present, and appearance before hearing the message
- Take notes effectively
- Ask questions when permitted
- Review the content of your notes and add more details after the session

7.7 THE PROBLEMS OF POOR LISTENING SKILLS

Listening is the communication skill we use the most frequently, but have not been taught how to listen effectively. White-collar workers typically devote at least 40 per cent of their workday to listen. Yet immediately after hearing a ten minute oral presentation, the average person retains only 50 per cent of the information. Forty-eight hours later, only twenty-five per cent of what was heard can be recalled. Thus, listening is probably the least developed of the four verbal communication skills (writing, reading, speaking, and listening). There are many reasons responsible for poor listening skills, sometimes affected by the listener, sometimes by the speaker and sometimes by the environment.

7.7.1 Lack of Formal Listening Training

One of the major causes of poor listening is the lack of formal listening training we receive. Judith Pallack has described the problem this way, "We spend 80 per cent of our time communicating, but we only receive training in the speaking, reading and writing aspects. We never really receive training in listening, except at the hands of our teachers and parents." (Jones, 1999)

Patrice Johnson, Director of Spectra Incorporated in New Orleans, emphasized the importance of investing in listening training. She said, "I think listening is getting attention now because organizations do not have the luxury of redundancy. In the past, large organizations had plenty of people to do rework, unnecessary work and so forth. Failing to listen and the errors that it caused could be managed. (Salopek, 1999)

7.7.2 Speed of Thought Vs. Speed of Speech

Another factor that contributes to poor listening skill is the disparity between the speed at which we normally speak and the speed at which our brain can process data. Our thoughts are racing all the time. We can think faster than we can speak–about four times faster. Research reveals that an average person speaks at about 125 words per minute, whereas thinking speed is in the region of 500 words per minute. Thus, when listening to others, our minds begin to wander, and we lose our ability to concentrate on which is being said. If the speaker speaks very slowly, the listener may 'switch off' altogether.

7.7.3 Physical Distractions

At the physical level, our ability to listen can be affected by outside elements that may hamper our ability to hear, including noise, physical and technological dimensions.

1. **Noise:** Noise is any sound that disrupts or interferes with the delivery of a message. For example, if you are in a meeting with your manager and the phone rings and your mobile beeps at the same time to let you know that you have the message. It is very hard to listen carefully to what is being said. Noise can cause a listener to become frustrated or confused, or to give up on the message altogether.
2. **Physical diversions:** A physical diversion is any physical element that disrupts or interferes with the delivery of a message. Have you ever tried to listen in a room that is too hot or too dark?

7.7.4 Technological Diversions

A technological diversion is any element that disrupts or interferes with the delivery of a message. How many times have you initiated a conversation, only to have the phone or doorbell ring?

7.7.5 Informational Listening Diversions

Informational listening describes the stage when the message begins to be interpreted by the listener. At this stage in the listening process, we assign meaning to the words we hear and we listen for information. Many people conduct much of their business communication at this stage of the listening process, getting caught in a cycle of listening and responding, without moving onto the next stage, critical listening.

At this level, our ability to listen and gain information can be influenced by internal elements such as cultural, gender and language differences. Another factor that may interfere listening is our communication history with the person speaking.

7.7.6 Cultural Differences

Cultural differences affecting the situation can include the slang used by a younger or older generation, the language and tonal accents used by another nationality or race, the regional differences in language style, and the jargon used in a certain profession or industry. All too often, we focus on the cultural differences of the speaker and forget to the listener the message itself. In business, whose diverse cultures abound, this can become a serious communication problem.

7.7.7 Understanding the Non-verbal Cues

Most of the time listeners are unaware of non-verbal cues, although they dramatically affect how people listen. As many as 93 per cent of peoples' attitudes are formed by non-verbal cues. In most of the cases, the listener does not understand them. A person shows fingers to emphasize a point whereas the listener may comprehend that the speaker is pointing him out for something. Overuse of non-verbal cues also creates distortion and listener may be confused and unclear about the exact meaning.

7.7.8 Physiological Barriers

Hearing impairments or a noisy background can prevent a person from hearing well. If a person is sick, worried in shock, in pain or tired, he or she will not listen well. Some people may have genuine hearing problems or deficiencies that prevent them from listening properly. They may have difficulties in processing information, or memory related problems which make them poor listeners.

7.7.9 Uninteresting Information

Not all people find the same information interesting. A lecture on a subject, for example, would be deadly boring to many people, yet extremely interesting to just as many. If a person does not find the subject interesting, or if he or she thinks that he or she does not need the information or that it will be of no use, then the listener will not listen well.

7.7.10 Language Problem

People who cannot fluently understand the language that is being spoken to them will not be able to listen well. Words, phrases or whole sentences may be missed. Nuances of tones will not be picked up, and their associated meaning will be lost.

7.7.11 Pretending to Listen

Most of us pretend to listen even when we are not listening. This is damaging in the long run, because if the listener pretends to be listening very often, he or she will find it difficult to concentrate when he or she does not want to listen. Therefore, the listener cannot listen well.

7.7.12 Waiting Not Listening

Your opinions and experiences are very important to you. Most of us would prefer to talk then listen to somebody else talking. The result is that we wait for the other person to finish a sentence before cutting in with what we have to say. We concentrate on grabbing the space rather than on listening to what the speaker has said. If we spend time in conversation waiting like this, then we will not listen well. For example, many managers press ahead with their own agendas, sweeping away conversations with "yeah, I know what you are going to say, but here's what I think we should do..."

7.7.13 Attitudinal Barriers

Pre occupation with personal or work related problems can make it difficult to focus one's attention completely on what speaker is saying, even what is being said is of prime importance.

7.7.14 Over Assertiveness

Another common attitudinal barrier is egocentrism, or the belief that you are more knowledgeable than the speaker and that you have nothing new to have to learn from his ideas. People with this kind of close minded attitude may be poor listeners.

7.7.15 Gender Barriers

Communication research has shown that gender can also be a barrier to listening. Studies have revealed that men and women listen very differently and for different purposes. Women are more likely to listen for the emotions behind a speaker's words when men listen more for the facts and the content.

7.8 KEYS TO BETTER LISTENING

A research at University of Minnesota shows that individuals who receive training in listening improve their listening skills by 25% to 42% (Clear Communication Vol. 1, 1993). To learn to listen more effectively, whether you are involved in a one-to-one dialogue or are part of a mass audience, give the speaker your individual attention, stay open-minded, avoid interrupting, and involve yourself in the communication.

7.8.1 Pay attention

Give the speaker your individual attention. During a business presentation or a conference some members of the audience may make or take phone calls, doodle, play around with a pen or pencil, shuffle papers, or do other distracting things that distract the speaker. These activities give the speaker the impression that what he or she has to say is insignificant or uninteresting.

7.8.2 Resist Distractions

Adjust quickly to any kind of abnormal situation.

- Physical distractions can be easily eliminated. Simply shutting the door or asking someone to hold all calls will eliminate many interruptions during personal conferences. In a meeting try to tune out the distractions over which you have no control – noisy environment, too cold or hot temperature, dim light, or the uncomfortable chairs. Concentrate instead on the speaker and what he or she is saying.

- Mental distractions are more difficult to eliminate. But with practice and efforts, you can discipline your present psychological state. For example, forget about your fatigue or put wild thoughts out of your mind for sometime so that you can give the speaker your attention.
- It is also important for the listener to maintain eye contact with the speaker. Proper eye contact gives the message that you are interested in what the speaker has to say.
- You should focus on the content of the talk and not be overly concerned about how the talk is delivered. It is true of course, that non-verbal cues do provide important information. However, do not be put off by the fact that the speaker may have dressed inappropriately, spoken too fast or in an unfamiliar accent, or appeared nervous. Almost always, what is said is more important than how it is said. Likewise avoid dismissing a topic simply because it is uninteresting or its presentation is uninteresting. 'Boring' does not mean unimportant. Some information that is boring or difficult may in fact prove to be quite useful to you. So it requires your full attention.

7.8.3 Stay Open Minded

Listen objectively and empathetically. Be willing to accept new information and new points of view. Regardless of whom you are listening to or what the topic is, concentrate on the content of the message. How will you know unless we listen? An attitude of "I already know what they are going to say" can make you miss important information.

Keeping an open-mind results in a win-win situation. Always look at the situation as a 'win-win' proposition – the speaker win by convincing you of the merits of his or her positions, and you win by gathering new information that will help you perform your duties more effectively.

Try to understand why the speaker is arguing a particular point of view and evaluate the message objectively. This will help you gain the most of the information.

7.8.4 Don't Interrupt

Interrupting a speaker creates a barrier to effective communication. Because of time pressure, we sometimes get impatient. As soon as we have figured out what a person is going to say, we tend to interrupt to finish the sentence for the speaker. Such interruptions have many negative consequences. First, they are rude. Second, such interruptions interfere with the speaker's train of thought, causing back tracking.

The most serious negative consequence, however, is the non-verbal message. By looking at your watch, reading some book or newspaper, or looking away from the speaker should be avoided.

There is a difference between listening and simply waiting to speak. If you are constantly planning what you'll say next, you can hardly listen attentively to what the other person is saying. We should give enough time to the speaker. It helps create a quieter, calmer, more respectful atmosphere – that is more conducive to solving the problems at hand.

7.8.5 Involve Yourself

As we know hearing is passive and listening is active, involve yourself mentally in what the speaker is saying. You should avoid doing something – staring out of the window, or planning your afternoon activities – while the other person is speaking. Summarizing to yourself what the speaker is saying can process information much faster than the speaker can present it.

- Some listeners find it helpful to jot down points, translating their mental notes into written notes.
- Concentrate on the main ideas; if you get them, you will be much more likely to remember the supporting details later.
- Personalizing the information will help you to concentrate more easily and to weigh the evidence more objectively.
- Provide verbal and non-verbal feedback to what the sender is saying. In giving feedback, encourage the speaker by letting him or her know that you are actively involved in the exchange. Maintain eye contact, nod in agreement, lean forward, utter encouraging phrases such as 'I see', 'yes'. It tells the speaker that you are paying attention to the message.

7.9 LISTENING IS HARD WORK

We spend almost all our time in polishing our productive skills–talking and writing and sending the message. Yet listening is an even more important receptive communication skill. Do not neglect your own listening ability. Work on developing it to its fullest potential. You must make your brain struggle to understand what someone is saying. You must be objective and reflective in your communication behaviour. It is not easy to do these things. But once you have learned to do then you are well on your way to becoming a good communicator. As organizations be they private companies or public insituations-increasingly recognize the importance of listing they are also running communication causes where developing listening skill plays a large part.

REVIEW QUESTIONS

1. What role does listening skill play in effective communication in an organization?
2. What is listening? What does a person do when he or she listens?
3. Explain clearly the effective listening process. Describe listening in specific situations?
4. Distinguish between casual listening and active listening. What role does each play in effective communication in an organization?
5. What are the problems of poor listening skills? Suggest the various keys to improve listening skill in the communication?
6. Sit still for about five-six minutes with your eyes shut. Concentrate on the things you can hear, and identify as many different sounds as you can. At the end of the five-six minutes make a list, independently, of these sounds. Finally, discuss the results with your friend/partner. What conclusions can be drawn from listening?

8

ORAL PRESENTATIONS

Chapter Objectives

This chapter will enable you to understand:

- The role of business presentations
- Advantages of oral presentations
- Disadvantages of oral presentations
- Types of presentations
- Process to creating an effective oral presentation
- Use of body language
- Presentation environment
- Work-team presentations

The term 'presentation' covers a wide variety of instances. We mean opportunity you get to communicate your point of view to listening others. The opportunity to share your ideas at a meeting is a presentation. The opportunity to discuss in a one-to-one situation is also a presentation. Almost any kind of business transaction involves some degree of presentation skill. And almost everyone in business is required to give a presentation occasionally.

8.1 THE ROLE OF BUSINESS PRESENTATIONS

Presentation skills are very useful for business, sales, training, public speaking and self-development. Guiding a new colleague through the basic office procedures, reporting back to a departmental meeting, launching a new product, starting a training course, any kind of sales call (by telephone or face to face), presenting a new business plan, making a sales proposal, or giving the members of the board of a new product—in each situation you will be giving a presentation.

Thus, presentation can be defined as a visual or aural event intended to communicate, for the purpose of providing information, helping to understand, gaining agreement, and/or motivating to act.

Written reports and oral presentation both play important roles in helping an organization achieve its objectives. An oral presentation may be made either in combination with or in place of a written report. Nowadays, technology is changing the physical characteristics of oral presentations in business. For example, by making possible presenting via videotape, or interactive television rather than in person.

Advantages of oral presentations

1. **Immediate feedback:** The most important advantage of oral presentations is the immediate feedback that is possible from the audience. Questions can be answered and decisions can be made on the spot.
2. **Speaker control:** A second advantage concerns speaker control. The speaker can control the pace of the audience; question the audience to ensure attention and understanding and use non-verbal cues such as pauses, gestures, and changes in voice speed, and volume to add emphasis. In addition, visual aids used in an oral presentation are often more effective than those used in a written report.
3. **Less work for the audience:** A third advantage of oral presentations is simply less work for the audience. Listening is less strenuous and often more enjoyable than reading. The written report presents mostly verbal cues, whereas the oral presentation is filled with a variety of verbal and non-verbal cues to make comprehension easier and more interesting.

Disadvantages of oral presentations

1. **Impertinent:** Oral presentations are impertinent. They 'disappear' and within hours of delivery much of the information presented has been forgotten.
2. **No permanent record:** Listeners have only one opportunity to understand what they are hearing. In contrast, written report provides a permanent record that can be reread and referred to in the future. Video presentations, however, avoid this problem, but they are quite expensive.
3. **Very expensive:** Oral presentations are very expensive. A presentation is much more cost-effective to have 1,000 managers scattered around the country read a written report than to have them hear the same information in a mass meeting. Besides, the visual aids used in presentations are often more expensive than those used in written reports. For example, a coloured slide of a graph or chart costs many times more to produce than a black-and-white paper copy that has been printed directly from the computer.

   Considering the advantages and disadvantages of oral presentations, many presentations include both an oral and a written component.

8.2 TYPES OF PRESENTATIONS

There are three types of presentations, which are generally used.

8.2.1 Memorized Presentation

In this method the speaker writes and memorizes entire speech. Unless a presentation is short and significant, memorizing an entire speech is risky. But sometimes the speaker may forget some important point, and it spoils the entire effect of the presentation. In addition, memorized presentations often sound mechanical and do not let you adapt the material to the needs of the audience. That is why most speakers memorize key parts (first and last section of your presentation), a quotation, or a humorous story.

8.2.2 Reading the Paper

In this method the speaker writes out his entire speech and reads it out before the audience. Reading speeches are quite common in academic and scientific settings. This method is helpful in dealing with a highly complex and technical topic, or the subject is controversial. Advantage of this method is that accuracy is best maintained in it. Sometimes the reader sinks into dull monotones, miss punctuation marks, and fumble for words.

8.2.3 Speaking from Notes

By far the most common and generally the most effective method for business presentations is speaking from prepared notes. The notes contain key phrases rather than complete sentences, and you compose the exact wording as you speak. The notes help ensure that you will cover all the material and in a logical order. In preparing the notes, write on one side and do not staple the papers. Typed copy is better than handwritten copy and large type is better than small type. Type your notes in standard upper and lower case letters rather than in all capitals, which are more difficult to read because all the letters are of the same size.

8.3 OTHER BUSINESS PRESENTATIONS

In addition to the types of presentation described here, academics and professionals are often called upon to give ceremonial speeches or address audiences in other speaking situations. For example, welcome to farewell speeches, presentation or acceptance of honours, introductions. These presentations are part of professional life and as such deserve attention. In these types of presentations you act as a supporting player. Such situations include giving impromptu speech, making introductions and making or receiving special recognition.

8.3.1 Impromptu Speech

During the course of a meeting or in conjunction with other person's presentation, you may unexpectedly be asked to come to the podium to "say a few words about". In truth most such situations are not a complete surprise; you can often predict when you may be called on and should prepare accordingly. Mark Twain rightly says, "It takes three weeks to prepare a good impromptu speech."

8.3.2 Introductions

If you are the host of a presentation given by someone else, you are supposed to introduce the presenter and your action can set the stage for a successful performance. When introducing someone, remember that the speaker is the main event–not you. Briefly introduce the speaker, keeping the emphasis on the speaker and his or her qualifications. All of your remarks should be directed at welcoming the speaker. Avoid inserting your own opinion about the topic or speaking for too long, thereby cutting into the speaker's time. After the presentation, return to the podium and extend your appreciation to the person once again with some brief remarks about the importance and relevance of the speaker's comments. Also, lead the question and answer session if one is planned. Be prepared to ask the first question in case no one in the audience wants to go first.

8.3.3 Special Recognitions

When presenting an award or recognizing someone for special achievement, we give a short some special remarks. First provide some background about the award – its history and criteria for selection. Then discuss the awardee's accomplishments, emphasizing those most relevant to the award. When accepting an honour, show genuine appreciation and graciously thank those responsible for the award.

8.4 PROCESS TO CREATING AN EFFECTIVE ORAL PRESENTATION

There is a logical process to creating an effective oral presentation. In order to make a successful presentation one has to take the following steps:

1. **Planning:** Determining the purpose of the presentation, analyzing the audience, and determining the timing and method delivery.
2. **Organizing:** Collecting the data and arranging it in a logical order.
3. **Developing visual aids:** Selecting the appropriate type, number, and content of visual aids.
4. **Practicing:** Rehearsing by simulating the actual presentation conditions as closely as possible.
5. **Delivering:** Dressing appropriately, maintaining friendly eye contact, speaking in an effective manner, and answering questions confidently.

8.4.1 Planning the Presentation

Planning the presentation is the key to how successful it will be. It means that the person proposing to make a presentation must structure his presentation from beginning to end. He should keep in mind the following points:

1. Determining the purpose of the presentation
2. Analyzing the audience
3. Planning the timing of the presentation
4. Selecting a delivery method

8.4.1.1 Determining the Purpose of the Presentation

Keeping your purpose uppermost in mind helps you decide what information to include and what to omit, in what order to present this information, and which points to emphasize. Most business presentations have one of these four purposes:

- Reporting: Updating the audience or some project or event.
- Explaining: Detailing how to carry out a procedure or how to operate a new piece of equipment.
- Persuading: Convincing the listeners to purchase something or to accept an idea you are presenting.
- Motivating: Inspiring the audience to take some action.

Presentation format, media and purpose vary a lot according to occasion–the size of the audience, your need for immediate feedback, and the cost of the presentation, etc.

8.4.1.2 Analyzing the Audience

An audience is not just a gathering of individuals at one place. It has a collective personality of its own. Analyze your audience and target your presentation to their knowledge, understanding and psychological needs (values, attitudes, and beliefs). You must see

- The size of the audience that is likely to influence how formal or informal the presentation is going to be. The larger the audience, the more formal your presentation will be.

When you speak to a large group, you should speak more loudly and more slowly. Use more gestures and larger visuals. Usually allow questions only at the end of the talk. If you are speaking to a small group, you can be more flexible about questions and your tone and gestures will be more like those used in normal conversation.

- The age, sex, educational background, experience, nationality of audience, etc. have great relevance to the presentation. If your audience is unfamiliar with your topic, you will need to use clear, easy-to-understand language, with extensive visual aids and many examples. If the audience is more knowledgeable, you can proceed at a faster pace.
- It is also important to know whether one is going to make a presentation before on all male, all female, or a mixed audience.
- The audience's psychological needs will also affect your presentation. If you think your listeners will be hostile–due to some personal reason or to your message–you will need to give several examples instead of giving one or two examples.
- Audience analysis should continue during the presentation. Their body language immediately gives you the feedback as you speak and illustrate. Their facial expression, smiles, stares, lip movement, etc. give you ample idea of their reactions, and guide you through your speech.

The key is to put yourself in your audience's place so that you can anticipate their questions and reactions.

8.4.1.3 Planning the Timing of the Presentation

Consider two factors when scheduling presentations.

- Allow yourself enough time to prepare, including gathering data, writing and revising, producing visual aids, and practicing the presentation.
- Second, consider the needs of your audience. Avoid times when they need to be away or are so occupied with other matters that they will not be able to concentrate on your presentation.

8.4.1.4 Selecting a Delivery Method

During your planning the presentation, you have to decide upon the method of presentation– will you memorize your speech, read it or speak from notes? Consider the following questions:

- How long is your talk?
- How complex is the content?
- How formal is the presentation?
- With what method are you most comfortable?

8.4.2 Organizing the Presentations

For most presentations, the best way to begin is simply to brainstorm: write down every point you can think of that might be included in your presentation. Do not worry about the order or format – just jot down the points. Later separate your notes into four categories: opening, body, ending and questioning. Analyze and organize your material, collect additional information, if required.

8.4.2.1 The Opening

The purpose of the opening is to capture the interest of your audience. Your opening should introduce the topic, identify the purpose, and preview the presentation.

Remember that the first few minutes of your presentation are crucial. The audience will be observing you minutely – your dress, posture, facial features, and voice qualities, as well as what you are actually saying. In this way they will be making preliminary judgments accordingly.

The kind of opening that will be effective depends on your topic, how well you know the audience, and how well they know you. If most of the listeners do not know you, you will first have to gain their attention with a creative opening.

Effective openings may include a quotation, question, hypothetical situation, story, startling fact, or visual aid. Do not apologize or make excuses; for example, "I wish I had had more time to prepare my speech today…" or "I am not a good speaker in fact.", etc. Your opening should lead into the body of your presentation by previewing your remarks. For most business presentations, let the audience know beforehand what you expect of them.

8.4.2.2 Body

The body of your presentation conveys the real content. It includes:

- **Beginning**
  - (a) Introductory remarks
  - (b) Statement of the objective, giving reasons why you are making this presentation
  - (c) Draw the main points of the presentation.
- **Middle**
  - (a) Go through your points logically and sequence.
  - (b) Illustrate the points with examples.

(c) Put a time limit on each of the points. Certain points may need more time than others.
(d) Summarize as you go along.

- **Closing**
  (a) Give a summary of the whole.
  (b) Emphasize the main points made in the beginning or in the middle.
  (c) Give a conclusion.
  (d) End your presentation with something that the audience will remember. Even if it is something simple like a visual or a closing statement
- **Questions**
  (a) You should always be ready to answer any questions that are likely to arise.
  (b) Plan for questions and don't be taken by surprise.
  (c) Ask for them if none are forthcoming.
  (d) If you don't understand a question, ask for clarification.

Guidelines for organizing the body of presentation

1. Choose a logical sequence. Organize the body of your presentation logically, according to your topic and audience needs.
2. Establish your credibility. Convince the audience that you have done a thorough job of collecting and analyzing the data and that your points are reasonable.
3. Support your arguments, with credible evidence – statistics, actual experiences, examples and support from experts, etc.
4. Use objective language.
5. If your presentation has many facts and figures, prepare handouts to distribute for review.
6. Do not ignore negative information. To do so would surely open up a multitude of questions and subsequent doubts that would weaken your position. The effective tactic is to present all the information – pro and con – and to show through your analysis and discussion that your recommendations are still valid, in spite of the disadvantages and drawbacks.
7. Use humour in your presentation. Jokes, pun, satire, and especially real-life incidents are the examples of humour, all of which serve to form a bond between speaker and audience. Humour can be used anywhere in a presentation – in the opening to get attention, in the body to add interest, or in the closing to drive home a point. Humour should, of course, be avoided if the topic is very serious or has negative consequences for the audience.

8.4.3 Developing Visual Aids for Business Presentations

Today's audiences are accustomed to multimedia events. They often assume that any formal presentation must be accompanied by some visual element, whether it is chart, chalk board, flipchart, overhead transparency, slide, film, videotape, or actual model.

These visual aids should be used only when needed and should be simple, readable, and of high quality.

Visual aids help the audience understand the presentation and remember the information you are presenting, especially if it includes complex or statistical material. A University of Pennsylvania study found that presenters who used visual aids successfully persuaded 67% of their audience, whereas those who did not use such aids persuaded only 50% of their audience. In addition, meetings in which visual aids were used were 28% shorter than those that lacked such aids. Similarly, a University of Minnesota study found that the use of graphics increased a presenter's persuasiveness by 43%.

8.4.3.1 The Purpose of using Visual Aids

The presenters can use these devices according to the purpose of the message. The purpose of using visual aids can be

- To emphasize important points.
- To clarify complex ideas.
- To increase the audience's and speaker's interest in the subject.
- To provide notes, cues for the speaker, in case she or he goes blank.

8.4.3.2 Guiding Principles for the Use of Visual Aids

- Visual aids are used to emphasize the main points of the presentation.
- Whatever the visual aid used in the presentation, make sure that they are visible to the whole audience.
- Visual aids should add to the impact of your presentation. They must be fitted well into the presentation.
- Whatever you use, whether its OHP, flipchart or computer presentation, keep it simple and clear.
- Proper emphasis must be laid on the visual aid. The speaker must point to it with bodily action and with words.
- The speaker must look at the audience more than at the visual aid.
- Avoid turning your back on the audience when writing on the visual aids. If this isn't possible, be sure that you don't continue speaking when doing so.
- If the speaker is using a software package like Powerpoint, which is specifically designed to produce presentation material, bullet points are most effective.
- Keep the bullet point size large on slides. Use 18-24 point size, with up to 32 point for titles.
- Avoid italicized type. It is usually difficult to read when projected.
- Avoid all-capitalized words and phrases.
- Allow extra white space between lines of text.
- Keep graphs large and simple.
- Use colour to differentiate elements.
- Label graphics, graphs and maps clearly.
- A slide should carry only essential information.

8.4.4 Rehearsal of Presentation

Rehearsal is a necessary part of presentation.

- Practice is important so that the speaker can gain self-confidence.
- Repeated rehearsals help the speaker overcoming nervousness. He can make any changes if necessary and perfect his performance.
- Only a rehearsal can ensure coordination of efforts. It gives the speaker a clear idea of where, when and how to use visual aids to support his presentation.
- Rehearsal helps in keeping an eye on the time. Time management is important if you have a time limit.

8.4.5 Delivering the Presentation

- Be prepared: Don't forget pens even if you are using visuals, or anything else that you have prepared to use in your presentation. Keep your visuals in order to save time.
- Speak clearly. If you have a quiet voice, use a microphone. There's little point in being a brilliant speaker if no one can hear you.
- Vary the tone of your voice and the pace you speak at, though better slower than too fast.
- Be careful of the fillers/pauses like, 'ums', 'you know', etc.
- What people often remember are the mental pictures. If you have suitable anecdotes, do use them.
- Make eye contact with your audience, not the floor, the ceiling or the OHP.
- Use pauses. It gives you thinking time and the audience time to reflect.
- Be natural up there.
- There may be information/diagrams/charts on the visual that you don't want the audience to see until later. If so, cover that part with a piece of paper and remove when appropriate. This will stop the audience from reading ahead while you are talking about the current part.

8.4.6 Assessing the Audience

Always make sure that you are including the audience in your speech. Even if you're far away from the last row of the audience, the people there deserve to feel that you are trying to reach them.

There are several factors that you should consider in assessing an audience.

- Every audience has a set of unique demographics associated with it. Demographics are those general factual categories which can be used to describe any group people. Among those categories which might be included in a demographic analysis of the audience are average age, range of age, socio-economic level, intellectual level, and level of aesthetic and cultural understanding and sensitivity. Knowing these factors about your listener will help you to understand exactly who will be sitting in the room listening to your presentation.
- Make some guesses about the general attitudes of the audience. It will help you to characterize your audience as either 'willing to change', or 'resistant to change'.

Determining the general attitude of your audience will provide additional input to the presentation flow.

- If possible, collect some data to determine how much information the audience already has about the proposal. Audiences generally have some idea what you are going to talk about and some opinions, positive or negative, on the subject.
- After the initial assessment is accomplished, you must ask yourself two questions: (1) What does the audience expect me to say? (2) Is the purpose that I have developed consistent with the expectations of the audience?

8.5 USE OF BODY LANGUAGE

Body language accounts for over 90% of a conversation. Usually when we communicate with or see people, we only respond to what is being said, heard or generally seen. When we don't know someone, we use their body language to get the first impressions of them. Our body language gives others an impression of ourselves or shows our emotions.

8.5.1 Gesture

Make sure that you make proper gestures. Think about the following questions:

- Do you use your hands to describe or emphasize your points?
- Where are your hands when not gesturing?
- Are your gestures above the waist?
- Are your movements purposeful or random?
- Do your gestures give meaning to what you are saying?
- Are your gestures free flowing?

Audience see you before they hear you and the way you stand and move is important in establishing a professional image.

Tips for using better hand gesture

- Keep your hands by your side or neutrally in front of you, unless you can use them to make a point.
- Avoid putting your hands behind your back.
- Avoid putting them in your pocket
- Avoid putting them in front of you.
- Avoid using them to fidget.
- Keep most gestures at chest level.
- Think about what you are saying, and react with hand gestures to match and enhance your message.

8.5.2 Posture

Standing tall and upright as much as possible is the natural alignment of your head and body without the use of tension. Everyone has a different posture. This may be slumping your shoulders forward or hanging your head.

Your posture may show how you will approach a situation. For example, if you stand with your shoulders hanging, arms folded, and leaning to one side, it will look as if you aren't ready for or interested in the task in question. Should you stand with strong shoulders, head up, arms out by the side and closed fists, you will look as if you are ready for anything no matter how much stress is involved. Make sure that you have a proper posture. Think about the following questions

- Do your posture and stance command attention, without being stiff?
- Is your stance balanced? Are you pacing?

Tips for achieving better posture

Following are tips for achieving better posture:

- Before your presentation, sit or stand straight.
- Feet 12 to 18 inches apart and turned slightly outward.
- Weight evenly distributed over the balls of both feet.
- Body leaning slightly toward the audience.
- Hands at sides.
- Elbows loose.
- Move purposefully.
- Relax your hands at your sides unless you are gesturing. Look natural and spontaneous.
- Maintain erect posture, a balanced stance, and face your audience.

8.5.3 Facial Expression

Expression in your face captures the mood of your speech and keeps the audience involved. For example, a simple smile can make others feel more at ease where a frown can make people see that you are aggressive or unsure of something.

Think about the following questions

- What do you notice about your facial expression?
- Do you smile?
- Do your facial expressions convey enthusiasm? Envy? Excitement?

A smile is always appropriate and harmonizes your talk. It relaxes you and your audience.

Tips for using facial expressions to increase your persuasiveness

- Smile before you begin speaking.
- Act naturally.
- Think about what you are saying, and react with facial expressions to match or enhance the thought.
- Practice your speech in front of a mirror to evaluate your presentation style and body movements, and adjust accordingly.

8.5.4 Eye Contact

Of all the ways we communicate with people, eye contact is the most powerful. Maintain eye contact by knowing your speech well enough that you need only occasionally glance at your notes. Walk to the front of the group at a deliberate pace. Look around the room silently. Take a few seconds to arrange your presentation materials.

Great speakers make a point of engaging their audiences by moving around the stage and even sometimes around the audience, ensuring that they make eye contact with everyone. Find a few friendly faces in the audience that react to your message and concentrate on delivering your speech to them. Keep eye contact for four to five seconds at a time, and then more to someone else. If you do not have the courage to make eye contact with your audience, then the audience will quickly lose interest in your speech. Think about the following questions:

- Do your eyes move slowly through the audience?
- Do your eyes move rapidly?
- Do your eyes move to the floor, ceiling, or walls?
- Do you look eyes with one person in the audience before beginning to deliver the talk?
- Do you stay eye-to-eye with one person to finish a thought?

Focus on eye technique

Remember you want to be perceived as honest, sincere, confident, knowledgeable, and credible. What you do with your eyes plays an important role in how your audience perceives you, and how you look at people is more important from the fact that you look at them. Breathe. Focus on a pair of eyes in the audience and hold gaze for a few seconds before you speak. Always focus on eyes before you begin speaking. Complete a phrase or thought with your eyes staying on one person. Focus on another pair of eyes before beginning your next thought. This small pause serves as punctuation in your talk, and gives your audience time to register each idea. Each phrase or thought should take between three and five seconds. As you select people in different parts of the room, you will appear to be looking at more than one person at a time. This will give you control of the room and make the entire audience feel included. The 'focus on eye techniques have the added advantage of controlling nervousness, reducing the number of filler words, and providing the presenter with audience feel back.

8.5.5 Pace

When you get nervous, you often talk fast–very fast. You subconsciously think about the sooner you finish, the sooner you will be able to go back to the safety of your desk. To fight with this feeling of yours, consider the following questions:

- Is your pace rapid, slow, varied, uneven, or too even?
- Is it fluid or halting?
- Do you run out of breath or hear yourself sigh?

8.5.6 Fillers

The problem with using fillers when you speak is that they distract your listener–often to the point but she or he does not hear anything you say. Your message is entirely lost obscured by the dense fillers surrounding it.

8.6 OPTIMIZE YOUR PRESENTATION ENVIRONMENT

The atmosphere, layout, size, and general suitability of the room you use for your speech can directly affect your presentation. Although it is true that you will be unable to influence this in some situations, the presenter normally has the opportunity to change things in the environment. Factors that affect you and your audience are room size, light, temperature and ventilation, room layout, equipment, noise, access, and time of day.

1. **Room size:** The room should be enough to permit the audience to sit in comfort without being so large that they feel lost in the room. Awkward shapes can be distracting or tiring to the eyes.
2. **Light:** The amount of light should be enough to see and not excessive. If natural light is entering the room, it should be behind the audience so as not to be distracting or tiring to the eyes.
   - Make sure you know where the switches for the light are as well as the dimming capabilities in the room.
   - Brief whoever is operating the lights so he or she knows what lighting you will require at what stages of your presentation.
3. **Temperature and ventilation:** The hotter the room, the more likely the audience will fall asleep. Equally, the colder the room, the more distracted they are likely to feel by their discomfort. Therefore, a comfortable mid temperature should be the goal.
   - Ventilation is particularly important for health and presentation effectiveness. Remember clean indoor air laws in most states will prohibit smoking. When selecting a room, make sure that the ventilation system does not make excessive noise. Know where the controls are for the system.
4. **Room layout:** When selecting the appropriate layout for your presentation, consider whether your audience needs tables for note-taking, and whether they need to discuss things among themselves. The most common types of layouts are:
   - Cinema style: Rows of chairs, one behind the other, are most suitable for large audiences or for watching videos.
   - Classroom: Add tables between rows. This is suitable where information is being passed from the speaker to the audience and very little participation is required from them.
   - 'U' or 'V' shaped: Tables placed in the shape of a U or a V, and chairs behind them are particularly suitable when presentations may be followed by group discussion.
   - Boardroom style: Individuals are seated around a single table or several tables. This is useful when frequent interaction is required among audience members. However, visibility may be restricted with this type of layout.
5. **Equipment:** Determine, well in advance, your equipment and power requirements. You will need to make arrangements for such things as a microphone, television, VCR, overhead projector, screen, or extension cords.
6. **Noise:** Many locations have their own peculiar noises. Find out what they are in advance so you can avoid distracting yourself and the audience. Always know who is in the next room.

7. **Access:** People should normally enter the room from the back to avoid the disruption of late comers.
8. **Time of day:** Your audience is more alert in the morning. Whenever possible, plan to give your presentation early in the day. You will also avoid the 'running late' problems, usually created during the course of the day. Avoid late morning, early afternoon, and late in the day because the audience tend to be tired or distracted at these times.
9. **The space around you:** Those who stand always look more powerful to those people who are sitting down. This is because they are taking up more space. So if you feel comfortable standing, use it to look as though you have a higher status than those around you. When you move around, the more space you take up can make others seem influenced by your presence. If you are sitting, you can still give an image of power. If standing isn't appropriate, use more space by stretching your legs out or by having your arms at the side of the chair.

REVIEW QUESTIONS

1. Identify some of the users of presentations in the organization? Why should a manager be able to make an oral presentation?
2. What are the advantages and disadvantages of presentations as a means of communication? How can a presentation be made effective?
3. Why is audience analysis important? What function does it fulfil in helping to make a successful oral presentation?
4. Briefly describe the logical process for creating an effective oral presentation? What are the main presentation techniques or methods of delivery?
5. Write short notes on the following:
   (a) Memorized presentation
   (b) Impromptu speech
6. Discuss the significance of body language in presentation. How will you overcome nervousness if you are asked to make a presentation?
7. Write a note on presentation techniques. Why is it necessary to have an idea of the location/environment of the presentation?
8. What is the use of the audio-visual aids for enhancing presentation quality?
9. Describe what the following body movements suggest when someone exhibits them during a presentation. How do such movements influence your interpretation of spoken words?
   (a) Shifting one's body continuously while seated
   (b) Twirling and playing with one's hair
   (c) Rolling one's eyes
   (d) Extending a weak shakehand
   (e) Standing with arms folded
10. What are the important aspects to be considered while planning for a presentation? How can outlines help you writing and delivering of an oral presentation?

9

TEAM PRESENTATIONS

Chapter Objectives

This chapter will enable you to understand:

- Why Form Groups and Teams
- Four Phases of Team Development
- Conflict Resolution
- Positive and Negative Team Behaviour
- Characteristics of Successful Groups
- Virtual groups
- The ethical dimension of work-team communication

A team is a group of individuals who depend on one another to accomplish a common objective. Today's workplace is teaming with teams. You might find yourself a part of a work team, project team, customer support team, supplier team, design team, planning team, functional team, or cross-functional team. You might be assigned to a committee, task force, steering group, quality control circle, flat team, hierarchical team, advisory team, action team, or some other group. All of these teams are being formed to accomplish specific goals. On the other hand, teams can waste time, slow their decision-making, accomplish little work, and create an environment in which interpersonal conflict can rage. There is also the risk of 'social loafing', in which team members assume that other members will bear the burden. In other words, the risk of avoiding individual responsibility in a group setting is social loafing.

Groups may range from 2 to 25 members, although 4 to 5 is optimum for many projects. Smaller teams often do not have enough diversity of skills and intensity to function effectively as a team. If the group is too large, members may lack healthy team interaction. They may begin to form subgroups. Also, just a few people may dominate the discussions.

9.1 WHY FORM GROUPS/TEAMS?

Because much of the work in business today is done in teams, many presentations are planned and delivered by teams of presenters. Well-conducted team presentations give an organization an opportunity to showcase its brightest talent while capitalizing on each person's unique presentation skills. One member may be better at collecting and analyzing the information to be presented, other may be better at developing the visual aids and other may be better at delivering is the presentation.

Organizations are constantly looking for ways to do jobs better at less cost. They are forming teams for the following reasons:

1. **Better decisions:** Decisions are generally more accurate and effective because group and team members contribute different expertise and perspectives.
2. **Faster response:** When action is necessary to respond to competition or to solve a problem, small groups and teams can act rapidly.
3. **Increased productivity:** Because they are often closure to the action and to the customer, team members can see opportunities for improving efficiencies.
4. **Greater 'buy-in':** Decisions arrived at jointly are usually better received because members are committed to the solution and are more willing to support it.
5. **Less resistance to change:** People who have input into decisions are less hostile, aggressive, and resistant to change.
6. **Improved employee morale:** Personal satisfaction and job morale increase when teams are successful.
7. **Reduced risks:** Responsibility for a decision is defused, thus carrying less risk for any individual.

9.2 FOUR PHASES OF TEAM DEVELOPMENT

When groups are formed, they generally go through four phases, regardless of their purpose. These phases are forming, storming, norming, and performing.

1. **Forming:** During the first stage individuals get to know each other. As they search for similarities and attempt to bond, they begin to develop trust in each other. In addition, members discuss fundamental topics such as,
   - Why the team is necessary
   - How large the group should be
   - Whether membership is mandatory
   - What talents members can contribute
2. **Storming:** During the second phase, members define their roles and responsibilities, and decide how to reach other goals. Unfortunately, this stage often produces conflict, resulting in storming. But most often storm passes, and a cohesive group emerges. A good leader, however, steps in to set limits, control the chaos, and offer suggestions.
3. **Norming:** At this stage, tension subsides, roles are classified, and information begins to flow among members. The group periodically checks its agenda to remind itself

of its progress toward its goals. Important data are shared with the entire group and the group begins to move smoothly in one direction.

4. **Performing:** All those groups that survive first three phases, reach to the final stage. At this stage, establish routine and a shared language. They develop loyalty and a willingness to resolve all the problems. Fights subside and group members continue working together without grudges.

9.3 CONFLICT RESOLUTION

Conflict is a normal part of every workplace and every team. When managed properly, conflict can improve decision-making, clarify values, increase group cohesiveness, stimulate creativity, decrease tensions, and undermine dissatisfaction. Unresolved conflict, however, can destroy productivity and seriously reduce moral. Following an effective six-step procedure can help resolve conflicts through collaboration and corporation.

1. **Listen:** To be sure you understand the problem, listen carefully. If the other person does not seem to be listening to you, you need to set the example and be the first to listen.
2. **Understand the other's point of view:** Once you listen, it is much easier to understand the other's position. Show your understanding by asking questions and paraphrasing. This will also verify what you think the other person means.
3. **Show a concern for the relationships:** By focusing on the problem, not the person, you can build, maintain, and even improve the relationship. Show an understanding to the other person's situation and needs. Show an overall willingness to come to an agreement.
4. **Look for common ground:** Identify your interest and help the other person identify his or her interests. Learn what you have in common, and look for a solution to which both of you can agree.
5. **Invent new problem-solving options:** Spend time identifying the interests of both sides. Then brainstorm to invent new ways to solve the problem. Be open to new options.
6. **Reach an agreement based on what is fair:** Seek to determine a standard of fairness that is acceptable to both sides. Then weigh the possible solutions and choose the best option.
7. **The role of the team leader:** The effective team leader should lead the group in developing a cohesive strategy for the entire presentation. He should also prepare a tentative schedule.

9.4 POSITIVE AND NEGATIVE TEAM BEHAVIOUR

Positive team behaviour

- Effective team members are able to analyze tasks and define problems so that they can work toward solutions.
- They offer information and give ideas to stimulate discussion.
- They show interest in other's ideas by listening actively.

- They try to resolve differences.
- They review significant points and move the group toward its goal by synthesizing points of understanding.

Negative team behaviour

- They constantly put down the ideas and suggestions of others.
- They insult, criticize, and harass others.
- They waste the group's time with unnecessary recounting of their achievements, irrelevant topics, or inappropriate comments.
- They have nothing to say, either for or against ideas being considered.

9.5 CHARACTERISTICS OF SUCCESSFUL GROUPS/TEAMS

Effective group members share some or all of the following characteristics:

1. **Small, diverse groups:** Small, diverse groups often produce more creative solutions with broader applications than homogeneous groups do. Larger groups have trouble interacting constructively. More effective work groups generally have male and female members who differ in age, social background, training, and experience.
2. **A general purpose:** An effective group begins with a general purpose to specific goals.
3. **Agreement on procedures:** The ideal groups develop procedures to guide them. They set up intermediate goals with deadlines. They assign rules and tasks. Procedures are continually evaluated to ensure movement toward the attainment of the group's goals.
4. **Acknowledge conflict:** Conflict in a group is generally misunderstood. Many group leaders think a group experiencing conflict cannot run smoothly and distracts from a group's goals. Effective group members acknowledge conflict and discuss the root of the problem openly. Direct confrontation saves time and enhances team commitment in long run. In fact, the presence of conflict in a group indicates that members are actively discussing the issues. Conflict, then, is the essence of group interaction. Note, however, that the conflict involves debate about issues, not about personalities. Interpersonal conflict can, indeed, have serious negative consequences for work teams.
5. **Conformity:** Conformity is agreement with regard to ideas, rules, or principles. Members may be encouraged to disagree about the definition of a problem or possible solutions, but certain fundamental issues – such as how the group should operate – should be agreed to by everyone.
6. **Avoiding group think:** Conflict is normal in team-interactions, and successful teams are able to resolve it. But some teams avoid conflict and doing so may fall victim to 'group think'. This term was first used by theorist Irving Janis to describe faulty decision-making processes by team members who are overly eager to agree with one another. Groups suffering from group think fail to check alternatives, stifle opposing ideas and free flow of information, biased in collecting and evaluating information, and ignore the risks of the preferred choice.
7. **Use of good communication techniques:** The best teams exchange information and contribute ideas freely in an informal environment. Group members speak clearly and concisely. They encourage feedback, active listening, and positive body language. Tactful, constructive agreements are encouraged.

8. **Ability to collaborate rather than compete:** Effective group members are genuinely interested in achieving team goals instead of receiving individual recognition. They celebrate individual and team accomplishments.
9. **Consensus:** Consensus means finding a solution that is acceptable enough that all members can support it (though with reservations) and that no member actively opposes it.
10. **Acceptance of ethical responsibilities:** Members have a number of specific responsibilities to each other. As a whole, teams have a responsibility to represent the organization's view and respect its privileged information. They should not discuss with outsiders any sensitive issue without permission. In addition, teams have a broader obligation to avoid advocating actions that would endanger members of society at large.
11. **Shared leadership:** Effective groups often have no formal leader. Many teams operate under a democratic approach. This approach can boost morale, and create less resentment. However, in times of crisis, a stray team member may act as a leader.
12. **A sense of fairness in making decisions:** Effective groups resolve issues without forcing members into a win-lose situation.
13. **Giving constructive feedback:** The ability to give constructive feedback is a proven method for giving and receiving criticism that works equally well for giving and receiving praise. Feedback is vital, it is the only way to find out what needs to be improved and should be an overall part of the team's culture.

    Many people take good work for granted and give feedback only when there are problems. This habit is counterproductive. People are far more likely to pay attention to your complaints if they have also received your compliments.

9.6 VIRTUAL TEAMS

Many organizations are creating virtual teams. These are groups of people who work interdependently with a shared purpose across space, time, and organization boundaries using technology. Although they work in different time zones and rarely see each other, team members use e-mail and teleconferencing to exchange ideas, make decisions, and stay connected. Virtual teams may be local or global. Employees are allowed to work anytime and anywhere as long as they successfully complete their assignments on time.

How to form and participate in effective virtual teams

1. **Select team members carefully:** Choose team members who are self-starters, good communicators, and experts in areas needed by the team.
2. **Spend time together in the beginning:** If possible, meet face to face to work out procedures. Spending time together initially reaching consensus about goals, tasks, and procedures.
3. **Encourage unity:** Exchange team members to share information and to include each other in decision-making.
4. **Make use of technology:** Get the maximum benefit from technology, such as speaker phones, e-mail, teleconferencing, videoconferencing, blogs and wikis. Be sure that members are well-trained in their use.

5. **Build credibility and trust:** Encourage team members to pay close attention to the way others perceive them. Acting consistently, fulfilling promises, considering other's schedule, and responding promptly to mails and messages help build credibility and trust.
6. **Establish responsibilities:** Identify expectations and responsibilities for each other.
7. **Keep track of information:** Capture information and decisions in a shared database, such as wiki.
8. **Avoid misinterpreting message:** It is easy to misunderstand e-mail messages, be careful about responding quickly and negatively.

9.7 THE ETHICAL DIMENSION OF WORK-TEAM COMMUNICATION

When people form a group or a team to achieve a purpose, they agree to give up some of their individual sovereignty for the good of the group. They become interdependent and assume responsibilities to one another and to the group following are important ethical responsibilities for members to follow:

- Determine to do your best
- Decide to behave with the group's good in mind
- Make a commitment to fair play
- Expect to give and receive a fair hearing
- Be willing to take on a participant/analyst role
- As a leader, be ready to model appropriate team behaviour

REVIEW QUESTIONS

1. Name some of the potential uses of the group/team presentation in the organizations. Why are team presentations widely used?
2. Identify four phases of team development.
3. What is conflict resolution? How may unsolved conflict between group/team be resolved?
4. Comment on the positive and negative team behaviour affecting the team performance.
5. Write a short note on the ethical dimension of work-team communication. What will happen if there is no leader in the team? Is this potentially dangerous?
6. What are the characteristics of successful teams? Comment.
7. What functions do virtual teams fulfil in the organization? How one can form and participate in effective virtual teams?
8. How can organizations and employers benefit from successful teamwork?
9. Is conflict in a team good or bad? How can organizations help team members successfully reslove conflicts?

10

COMMUNICATION WITH PEOPLE FROM DIFFERENT CULTURES

Chapter Objectives

This chapter will enable you to understand:

- What is culture?
- Characteristics of culture
- Selected dimensions of culture
- Improving communication with multicultural audiences
- Making ethical decisions across borders

When we talk about diversity, we mean cultural difference not only within the country but also in the worldwide marketplace. International business would not be possible without international communication. Robert Rosen, in his book "Lessons on Business Leadership and National Cultures," (2000) writes, "Corporate survival and prosperity increasingly depend on our ability to interact with and manage people of different cultures, locally, regionally, nationally, and globally. Today, everyone is part of the global marketplace, even though many companies don't yet realize that fact." He continues, "To thrive all leader much adopt a global-centric approach to business. They must develop multicultural perspective and international knowledge base, and a global imagination – in other words, cultural literacy. A large part of cultural literacy depends upon communicating in a way that effectively gets the message across to all team members."

10.1 WHAT IS CULTURE?

Culture refers to the pattern of human activities and the symbols that give significance to these activities. Culture manifests itself in terms of the art, literature, costumes, customs, language, religion, and rituals of the society. Culture also includes the systems of ethical beliefs held by the people – their principles of life and their moral values – and their patterns of behaviour.

The word 'cultural' is derived from the Latin word 'cultura', which has its roots in the word 'colere', or 'to cultivate'. Hence, the way in which the minds of the masses are cultivated determines the culture of a particular region.

10.2 CHARACTERISTICS OF CULTURE

10.2.1 Culture is Learned

Human infants come into the world with basic drives such as hunger and thirst, but they do not possess instinctive patterns of behaviour which tell them exactly how to satisfy these drives. Likewise, infants are born without any cultural knowledge. However, they are genetically predisposed to rapidly learned language and other cultural traits. In fact, infants are amazing learning machines. Any normal baby can be placed into any family on earth and grow up to accept that family's culture as his or her own.

Culture is non-instinctive: Since culture is non-instinctive, we are not genetically programmed to learn a particular one. This is why every human generation has the potential to discover new things and invent better technologies. These new cultural skills and knowledge are added to what was learned in previous generations.

Culture is cumulative: Due to this cumulative effect, most high school students today are familiar with mathematical insights and solutions that ancient Greeks, such as Archimedes and Pythagoras, struggled their entire lives to discover.

10.2.2 Culture Change

All cultures change over time. Cultural knowledge does not perpetually accumulate. At the same time, new cultural traits are added, some old ones are lost because they are no longer useful in everyday life. The regular addition and subtraction of cultural traits result in cultural diversity.

10.2.3 People Usually are Not Aware of Their Culture

Most of us are basically unaware of our culture because we are so close to it and know it so well; it is as if our learned behaviour was biologically inherited. It is usually only when we come into contact with people from other cultures that we become aware that our patterns of behaviour are not universal.

Ethnocentrism: 'Ethnocentrism' – the belief that one's own cultural group is superior – is a normal human reaction. We instinctively feel threatened by what is obviously different. Many people view alien cultural traits as being not just different but inferior, even unnatural. For example, European cultures strongly condemn societies that practice the 'immoral and offensive' behaviour of polygamy. Meanwhile, the conservative Muslim societies of Afghanistan and Saudi Arabia consider European women immodest and immoral for going out in public without their bodies covered from head to toe. Ethnocentrism can prevent us from understanding, appreciating, even learning from other cultures.

10.2.4 We Do Not Know All There is to Know About Our Own Cultures

In all societies, there are people of specialized cultural knowledge that are gender-specific – known to men but not women or vice versa – or limited largely to particular social classes, occupation, religious groups, or special-purpose occasions.

In large-scale societies there are many professions with their own terminologies and specialized tools. Lawyer, medical doctors, soldiers, and other specialists use numeral technical terms in the professions. To make it even more obscure for outsiders, these professionals often use abbreviations to refer to their technical terms.

10.2.5 Culture Gives us a Range of Permissible Behaviour Patterns

Rules of behaviour are usually flexible to a degree. For example, culture tells us how we should dress based on gender, but allows us to dress in different ways in different situations in order to communicate varied messages and statuses.

10.3 SELECTED DIMENSIONS OF CULTURE

Informational cultures differ widely in their emphasis on context-sensitivity, individualism, long-term orientations, time orientation, power distance, formality, uncertainty avoidance, and materialism.

10.3.1 High- and Low-Context Cultures

Context is the most important cultural dimension. As a term developed by cultural anthropologist Edward T. Hall, 'context' refers to the stimuli, environment, or ambience surrounding an event. Communicators in low-context cultures, such as North America and Germany depend little on the context of a solution to convey their meaning; they assume that listeners know very little and must be told practically everything. In high-context cultures, such as Japan, China, Saudi Arabia the listener is assumed to be already 'contexted' and not in need of much background information.

Low-Context Culture	High-Context Culture
• Tends to prefer verbal interaction.	• Tends to prefer indirect verbal interaction.
• Tends to understand meaning in one level only.	• Tends to understand meanings only. Embedded at many sociocultural levels.
• Is generally less proficient in reading non-verbal cues.	• Is generally more proficient in reading non-verbal cues.
• Values individualism.	• Values group membership.
• Relies more on logic	• Relies more on context and setting.
• Employs linear logic – proceed from point A to point B to point C and finally arrive at a conclusion.	• Employs spiral logic – circling around a topic indirectly and looking at it from many divergent viewpoints.
• Says 'no' directly.	• Talks around a point, avoids saying 'no'.
• Communicates in highly structured messages, provides details, stresses literal meanings, gives authority to written information.	• Communicates in simple, unambiguous messages, readily understands visual messages.

10.3.2 Individualism and Collectivism Culture

An attitude of independence and freedom of control characterizes individualism. An individualist culture values individual effort and ability. A collectivist culture values the group over the individual. There is likely to be a strong emphasis on maintaining and achieving good group relationships. If there is a conflict between your individual feelings and the group needs, then you will be expected to meet the group requirements. The emphasis in an individualist culture is on the individual to achieve and do their best. If you come from a collectivist culture, then you may find it difficult to come to terms with the level of individual competitiveness and aggressiveness of more individualistic cultures.

In low-context cultures, particularly the United States is usually quoted as the typical example of an individualist culture and contrasted with more collectivist cultures. In America, individualism is highly valued. People believe that initiative and self-assertion result in personal achievement. They believe in individual action and personal responsibility, and desire a large degree of freedom in their personal lives. Members of high-context cultures believe in collectivist culture and emphasize membership in organizations, groups and teams. They encourage acceptance of group competition and confrontation instead of consensus. In group-oriented cultures, like many Asian societies, self-assertion and individual decision-making are discouraged. Business decisions are often made as a group. Similarly, in China, managers focus on the group rather than on the individual.

Many cultures, of course, are complex and cannot be characterized as totally individualistic or totally group-oriented.

10.3.3 Formality

People in some cultures place emphasis on tradition, ceremony, and social rules than do members of other cultures. Americans, for example, dress casually and quickly get on a first-name basis. Their lack of formality is often characterized by directness. In business dealings, Americans come to the point immediately. Indirectness, they feel, wastes time, a valuable commodity in American culture.

This informality and directness may be confusing in other countries. In Mexico, a typical business meeting begins with handshake, coffee, and an expansive conversation about weather, sports, and light topics. In Japan, signing documents and exchanging business cards are considered important rituals. In Europe, first names are never used without invitation. In Arab, South America, and Asian cultures, a feeling of friendship and kinship must be established before business can be transacted. In western cultures, people are more relaxed about social status and appearance of power. Deference is generally paid to individuals merely because of wealth, position, seniority, or age. In many Asian cultures, however, these characteristics are important and must be respected.

10.3.4 Power Distance

Power distance is about how people use and respond to power differences. For example, if you are a manager, do you expect your staff simply to obey every instruction that you issue? How would you react if one of your staff challenged or disagreed with one of these instructions? In a culture, when there is high power distance, powerful people will be expected to defend their ideas. Ideas will be accepted if they are convincing, regardless of who produces them.

10.3.5 Uncertainty Avoidance

Hof Stede (1994) defines uncertainty avoidance 'the extent to which the members of a culture feel threatened by uncertain or unknown situations'. In a society with strong or high uncertainty avoidance, you are likely to find many rules and regulations which ensure that people 'know exactly what to do' in as many situations as possible. Where the rules do not seem to apply or where others make requests which are 'outside' the rules then members of such a culture can become very uncomfortable.

10.3.6 Masculinity-Feminity

Men and women are expected to behave very differently in different cultures. However, this dimension is not just about sex roles. Cultures high on the masculinity index will typically value aggressive, ambitious, and competitive behaviour. A low-masculinity culture will have friendly and compassionate behaviour where conflict is resolved by compromise and negotiation.

10.3.7 Communication Style

People use their first language for a wide variety of functions, to express emotions, to give instructions, to exchange small talk at a social occasion, etc. each of these functions have different approach with different conventions.

People in high and low-context cultures communicate differently. To American and German words are very important, especially in contracts and negotiations. People in high-context cultures place more emphasis on the surrounding context than on the words describing a negotiation. A Greek may see a contract as a formal statement announcing the intention to build a business for the future. The Japanese may treat contracts as statements of intention, and assume changes will be made as project develops. In communication style, Americans value straightforwardness and are impatient with delays.

Cultures differ not only in their verbal language but also in their nonverbal language. Very few nonverbal messages have universal meaning.

O.K. sign (forming a circle with our forefinger and thumb)	
France	You are a zero
Japan	Please give me coins
Brazil	An obscene gesture
Mediterranean countries	An obscene gesture
Thumbs up	
Australia	Up yours
Germany	The number one

Japan	The number five
Saudi Arabia	I'm winning
Ghana	An insult
Malaysia	Thumb is used to point rather than the finger
Thumbs down	
Most countries	Something is wrong or bad
Open palm	
Greece	An insult dating to ancient times
West Africa	An insult

10.3.8 Time Orientation

Americans consider time a precious commodity to be observed. They correlate time by productivity, efficiency and money. Keeping people wait for business appointments wastes time and is, therefore, rude. Although Asians are punctual, they do not like to be rushed.

We intend to judge others by our own values. We expect others to react as we would, and they expect us to behave as they would. Misunderstandings naturally result. These misunderstandings can be reduced through knowledge of others and through development of increased intercultural sensitivity.

Differences in cultural backgrounds affect communication in the workplace

If an organization is employing workers from different cultural backgrounds, what does the organization assume about their perceptions? Does it assume that once people move into the workplace they will readily understand, believe, and accept the dominant norms and values?

There are many aspects of culture which affect business and which may not be understood and accepted by the entire workforce. These include:

- History
- Experience with institutions
- Attitude towards institutions
- Traditions and customs
- Experience with and attitude towards technology and the workplace
- Arts and religion
- Patterns of recreation and use of time

10.4 IMPROVING COMMUNICATION WITH MULTICULTURAL AUDIENCES

10.4.1 Oral Messages

- Learn foreign phrases. Even when English is used, foreign nationals appreciate it when you offer greetings and a few other phrases in their language.

- Use simple English. Speak in short sentences. Try to stick to the most common words. For example, old' rather than 'obsolete', 'rich, rather than 'luxurious', or 'sumptuous'.
- Eliminate puns, sports and military references, abbreviations, slang and jargons. Be alert to idiomatic expressions that cannot be translated, such as 'burn the midnight oil'.
- Speak slowly and enunciate clearly. Avoid fast speech. Do not raise your voice.
- Observe eye message. Be alert to glaze expressions or wandering eyes – these tell you that the listener is lost.
- Encourage accurate feedback. Ask probing questions and encourage listeners to paraphrase what you say. Do not assume that a 'yes' or 'no' or a smile indicates comprehension.
- Avoid waiting until you finish a long explanation to request feedback. Instead, make one point at a time, pausing after each to check for comprehension. Do not proceed to B until A has definitely been grasped.
- If a misunderstanding does occur, graciously accept blame for not making your meaning clear.
- Listen without interrupting. Restrain your desire to finish sentences or to fill out ideas for the speaker.
- Follow up in waiting. After conversations or oral negotiations, confirm the results and agreements with follow-up letters. For proposals and contracts, engage a translator to prepare copies in the local language.

10.4.2 Written Messages

- Adapt written materials to local formats. Learn how documents are formatted and addressed in the intended reader's country. Use locally common type faces and styles.
- Use short sentences and paragraphs. Sentences with fewer than 15 words and paragraphs with fewer than 7 lines are most readable.
- Avoid ambiguous expressions. Include relative pronouns (that, which, who) for clarity in introducing clauses. Stay away from contractions, like 'there's the problem.' Avoid idioms, slang, acronyms, and sporty expressions. Use action-specific verbs. ('Purchase a printer' rather than 'get a printer'.)
- Strive for clarity. Avoid words that have many meanings. If necessary, clarify words that may be confusing. Replace two-word verbs with clear single verbs ('return' instead of 'bring back', 'delay' instead of 'put off', 'maintain' instead of 'keep up'.)
- Use correct grammar. Be careful of misplaced modifiers, dangling participles, and sentence fragments. Use conventional punctuations.
- Be careful about numbers. In citing quantities and amounts, use figures instead of spelling them out; conversely, avoid using figures to express the month of the year. For international business, it is good idea to learn and use the metric system.
- Accommodate the reader in organization, tone, and style.

10.5 MAKING ETHICAL DECISIONS ACROSS BORDERS

Following are suggestions that acknowledge different values and provide practical solutions to the cultural challenges of global business interaction.

1. Broaden your views of other cultures. Become more sensitive to the values and customs of other cultures. Look especially at what they consider moral, traditional, practical, and effective.
2. Avoid reflex judgements. Do not automatically judge the business customs of others as immoral, corrupt or unworkable. Assume they are legitimate and workable until proven otherwise.
3. Conduct all business relations and negotiations as openly as possible.
4. Find alternatives. Instead of offering bribes, consider offering nonmonetary public service benefits, technical expertise, or additional customer service.
5. Do not be afraid to refuse business if opinions violate your basic values.
6. Do not try to rationalize shady decisions. If you try to justify yourself by thinking in terms of, "this is not illegal or 'immoral', or 'no one will find out', or, 'this is in the company's best interest', you are probably compromising with your own convictions.
7. Resist tactics that are legally safe but ethically questionable. Even in another culture, the following can guide you to the best decision.
    - Is the action you are considering legal?
    - How would you see the problem if you were on the opposite side?
    - What are some alternate solutions?
    - Can you discuss the problem with someone whose advice you trust?
    - How would you feel if your family, friends, employer, or coworkers learned of your actions?

REVIEW QUESTIONS

1. What is culture? Can culture be learned or it is instinctive? Explain the characteristics of culture.
2. Explain the various dimensions of culture. How can you improve communication with multicultural audiences?
3. Suggest some ways that help in providing practical solutions to the cultural challenges of global business interaction.
4. Explain the following:
    (a) Is it ethical to give gifts to get things done?
    (b) What would help a high-context new comer fit in a low-context culture?
    (c) Is it true that the people give more weight to negative information than to positive information?
5. How does non-verbal communication reflect cultural values?
6. It has been suggested in this chapter that culture refers to the pattern of human activity and the symbols that give significance to these activities? Explain.

7. Define the following:
   (a) Power distance
   (b) High and low context communication
   (c) Individualism and collectivism culture
8. What is ethnocentrism? How can it be overcome in communication?
9. How does high context culture differ from low context culture? In addition to contextual differences, what other categories of cultural differences exist?
10. What principles apply to ethical inter cultural communication and making ethical decisions across borders?
11. Why is it important to understand your own culture when attempting to communicate with people from other culture?
12. What are some ways to improve speaking and writing skills when communication with people of other culture?
13. What steps can you take to help someone from another culture adapt to your culture?
14. Make a list of the top five priorities in your life (for example, fame, wealth, family, spirituality, peace of mind, individuality, artistic expression). Compare your list with the priorities that are valued in the culture in which you are currently living? Do your personal priorities align with the cultural priorities of the other members? If not, how might this disparity affect your communication with the members of the other culture?

11
BUSINESS MEETINGS

Chapter Objectives

This chapter will enable you to understand:

- What is meeting
- Purpose of meetings
- Responsibilities of the chairperson
- Planning the meeting
- Conducting the meeting
- Following up the meeting
- Business etiquette

The ability to conduct and participate in meeting is a crucial managerial skill. Surveys done by researchers show that executives who run a meeting well are perceived to be better managers by both their superiors and their peers. ("Managing Meetings: A Crucial Role", 1989) To use meetings as an effective managerial tool, you need to know not only how to run them but also how to follow up afterwards.

11.1 WHAT IS A MEETING?

A meeting is an occasion when a group of people came 'together' to share ideas and experiences. Such meetings differ in their size, composition, organization, and purpose, but they all have certain things in common:

- Meetings exist for a purpose.
- They all involve people communication with one another.
- They all have someone in control.

11.2 PURPOSE OF MEETINGS

Meetings serve a wide variety of purposes in the organizations.

1. Information giving: They keep members informed of events related to carrying out their duties.
2. Meetings provide a forum for soliciting input.
3. They solve problems.
4. Meetings help in taking decisions.
5. They provide unity and cohesiveness among the members through social interactions.

It is fundamental to the success of any meeting that the purpose is clear and relevant. Unless the meeting serves a useful purpose, it not only wastes valuable time and effort, but also, it can cause a frustration, misunderstanding, and can demotivate people.

According to research by MCI World Com Conferencing, the average executive spends 25% to 70% of his or her day in meetings (an average of three hours per day), and considers about a third of them to be unproductive. (Rules for a better meeting, E.F. Wells, 1978)

11.3 RESPONSIBILITIES OF THE CHAIRPERSON

The leader of any meeting has a variety of responsibilities which include:

- Defining the purpose of the meeting
- Planning and preparation
- Attending regularity
- Conducting the meeting efficiently
- Controlling the discussions without doing all the talking
- Dealing effectively with problem situations and individuals
- Ensuring the meeting keeps to time
- Making sure the purpose of the meeting is achieved and members know what isexpected of them as a result.
- Initiating with the secretary to ensure that an efficient recording mechanism exists where required.

11.4 PLANNING THE MEETING

A well-planned meeting has a much greater chance of success than one that is called at five minutes' notice and has not been well thought out.

There are three areas where planning and thorough preparation can assist the leader of the meeting:

1. Identifying the purpose
2. Determining whether a meeting is really necessary
3. Preparing an agenda
4. Deciding who should attend
5. Planning the logistics

11.4.1 Defining the Purpose of the Meeting

The first step is to determine your purpose. There are two questions which need to be answered here:

- What is the purpose of holding this meeting
- Is the purpose going to be the best achieved by holding a meeting

Many meetings are ineffective because the purpose is not clear, not only to the person who has called it but also to others attending the meeting. For example, the main purpose of regular monthly meetings sometimes seems to be the self-perpetuation of the monthly meeting. The more specific you can be, the better results you will get.

11.4.2 Determining Whether a Meeting is Necessary

Determining whether a meeting is necessary is the best way to accomplish your goal. Sometimes meetings are not the most efficient than a face-to-face meeting to communicate routine information. Similarly, it does not make sense to use the weekly staff meeting of ten-twelve people to hold a long discussion involving only one or two of the members. A phone call or smaller meeting would accomplish that task more quickly and at less cost.

11.4.3 Preparing an Agenda

A group meeting agenda will serve as a guide to participants, making the meeting more efficient and productive. It helps focus the attention of both the leader and the participants.

11.4.3.1 Functions of Agenda

An effective meeting agenda, which states what activities will take place during the meeting, serves various important functions:

- It forces the meeting leader or group to think out what needs to be accomplished.
- Provided ahead of time (as it should be), the agenda lets people know what to expect and allows them to prepare as necessary, such as reviewing needed documents, bringing relevant records, deciding what questions need to be raised, and the like.
- It provides a blueprint or path for the meeting to follow.
- It reminds people of what there is left to cover if time gets to be an issue.

11.4.3.2 Elements of Agenda

Formal, recurring business meetings might follow an agenda like this one. However, it is not necessary that every agenda/meeting will contain all their elements.

- Call to order
- Roll call
- Reading and approval of minutes of previous meeting
- Reports of officers and standing committees
- Reports of special committees
- Old business

- New business
- Announcements
- Programme
- Adjournment

11.4.4 Deciding Who Should Attend Meeting

Everyone at the meetings should have a specific reason for being there. Before deciding who should attend the particular meeting, consider the following factors:

- If you decide who will attend a particular meeting, your primary concern is how the participants relate to your purpose. Who will make the decision? Who will implement the decision? Who can provide needed background information?

  Thus, in other words, you want to include all who can contribute to solving the problem.
- Keep the meeting to a manageable number of people.
- Consider also how the potential group members differ in status within the organization, in knowledge about the issue, in communication skills, and in personal relationships. The greater the differences, the more difficult it will be to involve everyone in a genuine discussion aimed at solving the problem.
- Do not underestimate the impact of potential group member's hidden agendas. If any member's personal goals for the meeting differ from the group goals, conflicts may arise, and the quality of the resulting decisions can be warned.
- Meeting separately with some of the important participants ahead of time might help to identify sources of potential conflicts or disagreements and provide hints for dealing with them.
- Membership in recurring meetings (such as committee meeting) is relatively fixed. Even for these meetings, the planner must decide whether outsiders should be invited to observe, participate, or simply be available as resource people.

11.4.5 Determining Logistics

To plan the logistics, consider the following factors:

- Date and time
- Location of the meeting
- Room and seating arrangements
- Types of audio-visual equipment
- Recording the meeting

11.5 CONDUCTING THE MEETING

Planning for a meeting goes a long way toward ensuring its success. Once in the meeting, to ensure maximum satisfaction for everyone, there are several things you should keep in mind:

11.5.1 Punctuality

An efficient leader begins and ends each meeting in time. Doing so will send a powerful non-verbal message to chronic late arrivers that business will be conducted and decisions made whether or not they are present.

If you wait for latecomers, you send the message to those who were punctual that they wasted their time by being prompt. As a result, they will probably arrive late for subsequent meetings. And the habitual late arrivers will then begin arriving even later.

11.5.2 Following the Agenda

One key to a focused meeting is to follow the agenda. At formal meetings you will be expected to discuss all topics on the given agenda and on items not on the agenda. However, in less formal meetings, the agendas are often flexible. But a leader must make certain that new topics are directly relevant.

11.5.3 Leading the Meeting

- Begin the meeting with a statement of your purpose and an overview of the agenda. As the meeting progresses, keep track of time.
- If certain people are dominating the conversation, make a point of asking others for views. Preventing people from talking from too much or deviating from the topic requires tact.
- If your purpose is to solve a problem, determine which problem-solving strategy is appropriate. You should consider ahead of time how you will structure the decision. The particular strategy you use (such as brainstorming, role play, or simulation) will depend on the nature and importance of the problem and the skills of the group.
- As leader, you will sometimes have to resolve conflicts among members.

Conflict may occur due to

- Unpopular decisions
- Bad news
- Lack of interest
- Discussion going offtrack
- Status differences

  Make sure that all members understand the facts involved and each person's position. However, some conflict may be good if arguments do not get personal and people are not driven into a 'this is my position' stance. Personal criticism may reflect tensions over another problem, and too little criticism may reflect fear or a sense that nothing real will come from the meeting. You need to examine each person's goals and search for alternatives that will satisfy the largest number of goals.
- At the end of the meeting, take some time to debrief. Summarize for everyone what the meeting has accomplished. What was decided? What are the next steps? Review the assignments and make sure that everyone understands his or her responsibilities. This will help you continue to improve your process of running effective meetings.

- In all cases it is essential that someone is appointed to take notes or minutes. A major cause of unsuccessful meetings is where the leader also tries to take notes. Neither role can be carried out effectively by the same person. Ideally, someone who is aware of the subject matter, but not directly involved, is in the best position to take notes.

11.5.4 Parliamentary Procedure

Every group needs to adopt rules that permit the orderly transactions of business in meetings. In the large groups it is important to establish rules of order, which is known as "parliamentary procedure". The basic principle of parliamentary procedure is that the minority shall be heard but the majority shall prevail.

Knowledge of basic parliamentary procedure is a strategic communication skill for managers. Anyone who runs a business meeting, whether at work or in connection with a professional, civic, or social organization, would do well to become familiar with the basic requirements of conducting meetings in a parliamentary manner.

11.5.5 Questions

Questions can be used to make sure there is maximum relevant participation. The following types are particularly useful.

1. **Opening questions:** These should:
    - be thought provoking and engage the attention of the whole group.
    - be specific and related to the experience of the whole group.
    - start with how, where, when, why, what, or who to avoid a 'yes' or 'no' reply.
    - point the meeting in the right decision.
2. **Overhead questions:** A question addressed to the group as a whole. For example, "what solutions can there be for this position?" This has the advantage of not embarrassing individual members who may be unprepared or unable to answer. Engaging the attention of all members, there is a good chance someone will reply. An overhead question is useful as an opening question.
3. **Direct questions:** A question addressed to a particular individual. This can be used for the following purposes:
    - to bring in a person with special knowledge, in dealing with the retiring, talkative or other problem individuals.
    - to help the meeting when flagging, by asking the resourceful member for an opinion.
    - to speed up the pace of the meeting.
4. **Re-directed questions:** To avoid the meeting's moving back and forth between individual members and the leader, questions raised by one member can be passed to another for comment. This can also be used as a link to coordinate a number of points and thus ensure continuity of ideas.
5. **Relay questions:** A question put to the leader is relayed to members for reply. This is useful when the leader does not wish to express any views, get involved in an argument, or influence the conclusion of the group.

6. **Reverse question:** The person posing the problem is asked to answer it himself. This may be useful if the person is known to have views which should be expressed, or to encourage that person to think again.

11.5.6 Participating Actively and Productively

Meetings are an opportunity for you to showcase your abilities and boost your career. To get the most out of the meetings you attend, try these techniques.

- **Arrive early:** You show respect and look well organized by arriving a little early.
- **Come prepared:** Bring the agenda and any distributed materials. Study the topics and be ready with questions, comments, and good ideas.
- **Bring a positive attitude:** Use positive body language; speak energetically.
- **Contribute respectfully:** Wait your turn to speak; raise your hand to be recognized.
- **Wait for others to finish:** Show respect and good manners by not interrupting.
- **Keep your voice calm and pleasant, yet energetic:** Avoid showing anger as this focuses attention on your behaviour rather than on your ideas.
- **Give credit to others:** Gain allies and enhance your credibility by recognizing others in front of peers and superiors.
- **Put the cell phone and laptop away:** Focus your attention on the meeting, not on answering e-mail or working on your computer.
- **Help summarize:** Assist the meeting leader by reviewing points you have noticed.
- **Express your views in the meetings:** Build trust by not holding postmeeting "sidebars" with criticism and judgements.
- **Follow up:** Send the signal that you are efficient and caring by completing the actions assigned to you.

11.6 FOLLOWING UP THE MEETING

Formal meetings require a formal summary known as 'minutes'. Routine meetings generally require only a short memorandum or e-mail as a follow-up to what was decided.

Minutes are an official record of the proceedings; they summarize what was discussed and what decisions were made. Generally, they should emphasize what was done at the meeting, not what was said by the members.

Thus, minutes present an intelligent summary of the points of view expressed on a particular issue, without names attached, followed by the decisions made. The minutes should be accurate, objective, and complete.

The first paragraph of minutes should identify the types of meeting whether it was regular or special. It includes the meeting date, time and place, the presiding officer, the name of those present or absent, and the fact – that the minutes of the previous meeting were read and approved.

The body of the minutes should contain a separate paragraph for each topic. According to parliamentary procedure, the name of the maker of a motion should be given in the minutes. The precise wordings of motion, exactly as voted on, should also appear in the minutes. It is also helpful to use meeting agenda as an outline for the minutes.

Remember that meetings are for future and outside readers as much as they are for the people present. Make sure whatever you write down must be clear to people coming into the process at a later time. The last paragraph of minute should state the time of adjournment and if appropriate, the time set for the next meeting. The minutes should be signed by the person preparing them. Before you submit the meeting minutes, proofread for typos and omissions. If someone other than the chair prepares the minutes, they should be read, and approved by the chair before being distributed.

11.7 BUSINESS ETIQUETTE

Etiquette implies conventional rules of polite, personal behaviour in society. Business etiquette is no exception and include much more. Your polite behaviour, courtesy and the appropriate mode of interaction contribute to etiquette. The rules of the etiquettes are not written. They are "an unwritten code of restricting professional person in what concerns interest of their colleagues of dignity of their profession." In other words, etiquette means polite and decent behaviour, upholding social codes and norms. It reflects your grooming and culture. It also brings out your sense of ethics and morals. Your behaviour and mode of communication need to be socially desirable. Only then will you be considered owing proper sense of etiquette. In the realm of business and enterprise, etiquette plays a pivotal role.

11.7.1 Be Careful With Your Appearance

1. Different positions, different companies and different parts of the country and world have different dress codes. For most businesses and most business occasions, you should choose well-tailored, clean conservative clothing for the workplace. Ask 'Am I successfully representing myself and my company'? You will have more credibility in a jacket than without, more credibility in long sleeves than in short, more credibility in conservative colours than in flashy. Combine business wardrobe items with casual allies.
2. Business etiquette is really concerned with any kind of interaction among a group of people or between persons telling a professional relationship. Each organization has its own rules about what is and is not considered fitting in terms of dress, ways of addressing superiors, importance of punctuality, and the like. Executives who follow correct business etiquette are more confident and appear more in charge. Good manners are good business; they communicate a strong positive message about you as a person.
3. Casual does not mean sloppy. Clothing should be clean, ironed or wrinkle free, and without holes.
4. Keep the focus on work quality. Avoid clothing that is too revealing or tight-fitting. Trendy or high-fashion clothing may communicate a pretentious attitude that is not suitable for most offices. T-shirts with messages other than company's logo should be avoided.
5. Leather shoes are generally preferable, but if athletic shoes are allowed, make sure they are clean, subtle in design, and scuff-free.

11.7.2 Making Introductions

1. The most essential thing about an introduction is to 'just do it', else people around you end up feeling invisible or uncomfortable.
2. Remember to have an eye contact and a smile, while shaking hands with the other person.
3. The person who is being presented or introduced is named last as a business etiquette.
4. Persons of lower rank are introduced to persons of greater authority, regardless of age and gender. For example,
   - "Mr. /Ms... (MD), I would like you to meet Mr. /Ms... (Junior Sales Executive)."
   - "Mr. /Ms... (MD), this is Mr. /Ms... (Junior Sales Executive)."
   - While introducing, look at and speak to the higher authority first, and then look at and speak to the lower authority. While introducing, a little information about those being introduced can be included
   - "Mr. /Ms... (Junior Sales Executive) has been with us for a year now."

   This little information gives them a point to get the conversation going. Once they start talking, you can discreetly withdraw as the situation demands it.
5. If the person you are introducing are equal in rank, mention the older one first, mention the guest first, or traditionally, mention the woman first.
6. Use a person's name in the conversation to help remember it.
7. At a business function, the host should greet the guests upon their arrival, and make them feel welcome. It is not necessary to introduce a newcomer to everyone. You can introduce him/her to the closest group, by saying his name first, and then naming the other. At a business function, if you are not introduced, you should introduce yourself.
8. If the person has forgotten your name, you should smile and offer to shake hands with the nearest person, and say, "I am...."
9. It is just as important how you make an introduction as how you respond to being introduced by others. The best way to respond to an informal introduction is by saying, "Hello", and can add a bit of information. In a formal introduction, it is always correct to say, "How do you do Mr./Ms...?"
10. In a formal introduction, do not use the person's first name unless he invites you to do so.
11. Everyone should stand up when being introduced. If for some reason, like being wedged behind the table, you cannot rise, at least lean forward, or rise slightly so as not to appear rude.
12. When someone visits you at the office, rise and come out from behind your desk to welcome the person, unless he is a co-worker, or someone who frequently visits you. When a senior officer visits his junior frequently, the junior should stop what he is doing and give full attention to his senior, even if he remains seated.
13. In a business world, a handshake is the only appropriate physical contact for both men and women. Otherwise fold your hands in a 'namesake', depending on the type of set-up at the office. Never offer your fingertips, that is, a weak handshake.
14. It is a serious business etiquette *faux pas* to mispronounce someone's name. If you miss it, or are in doubt, ask for it to be repeated in an apologetic manner.

15. Today, most business people have business cards. In business settings, you should present your card at the end of the encounter. Never present your card during a meal (wait until it is over), and never offer your card at any time during a social function.

11.7.3 Etiquette at Workplace

1. Proper etiquette at the workplace generates efficiency. Establish cordial and respectful relations with your staff.
2. Generally, you never ask your secretary to do some work that you yourself would shun.
3. When you speak on the telephone, speak clearly, but not too loudly. Avoid chewing, eating or drinking while speaking on the telephone.
4. If the other person is wasting your time with useless talk, politely excuse yourself stressing on your busy schedule, and that you will get in touch with him or her at a more leisurely hour.
5. Learn as much as you can about your job and how each fits into the organizational structure. Read the trade publication of your industry and profession.
6. However, your working hours working nine to five does not mean that you arrive at nine and leave at five. It means you work from nine to five. Socializing at the coffeepot or eating breakfast at your desk does not constitute working.
7. Never discuss or question salary or any other confidential or personal information with co-workers.
8. If you have to pay for the coffee, do so every time you take a cup. Do not force others to treat you to a cup of coffee. Never eat while talking to someone in person or on the telephone.
9. Many offices today have designated areas, and many prohibit smoking anywhere on the premises. If you smoke, follow the rules strictly. Smoking in public places is considered bad manners.
10. If you are using the copier or fax machine for a large job, and someone approaches with one or two sheets, let that person go ahead of you.

11.7.4 Business Card

1. Your business card is an important and personal part of your interaction within the corporate circle, you should know how and when to use it.
2. Your card should comprise your name, company designation, phone, fax, and e-mail address.
3. You can send your card with a document, photograph, magazine, etc. to someone who will find the information useful. You can send it with a gift or bouquet.
4. When you present your card to someone, see that the printed side faces up.
5. When someone gives you his card, look at him first and then the card to establish a connection.
6. Be selective about whom you present your card.
7. Always carry a few cards with you. You never know when you may need them.

11.7.5 Dining

1. The hotel or restaurant you select for a business meal reflects you and your organization. Your social skills and business acumen are evident by your ability to plan and organize, and your level of sophistication.
2. It is wise not to experiment. Choose some good restaurants where the food is of top quality.
3. Book a table that is in a quiet corner where business can be discussed without too many noisy disturbances. If a waiter/headwaiter seats you and your guest, your guest should precede you to the table. If you are seating yourselves, take the lead in locating an appropriate table.
4. Give your guest the preferred seat, facing the window with an attractive view or facing the dining room.
5. The guests wait until the host unfolds the napkin and places it in the lap before doing the same. Do not begin eating until the host takes the first bite of food.
6. To signal the waiter that you are ready to order, close your menu and lay it on the table. To get the server's attention say, "excuse me", when he or she is nearby or quietly signal for him or her to the table.
7. If you leave the table during the meal, leave your napkin on your chair. At the end of the meal, place the napkin, unfolded, on the table.
8. Do not put your elbows on the table all the time while eating, although you may do so between courses.
9. The person who issues the invitation is expected to pay the bill. Settle the bill quietly, without fiddling around with small bills or change.
10. Send a thank you note immediately after the meal. Be sure to write more than a token note, mentioning something special about the décor, the food, the service, the company of the people with whom you dined, or your satisfaction with the business discussed.

REVIEW QUESTIONS

1. What is a meeting? Justify the statement that meetings serve a wide variety of purposes in the organizations.
2. What things should be considered in conducting a successful meeting in an organization? Conduct a 15-20 minutes business meeting. Following the meeting, evaluate its effectiveness. Did you achieve your objective? Explain your answer.
3. Do you agree that the leader of any meeting has a variety of responsibilities. If yes, justify your point of view.
4. What are three areas where planning and thorugh prepartion can assist the leader of the meeting? Draft a detailed plan that you would prepare for the conduct of meeting.
5. Write a short note on the following up the meeting after a meeting how soon after should be the minutes be distrubuted?
6. Why etiquette is an important business skill? Is it necessary that everbody should learn what is considered appropriate behaviour in an organization?
7. As a team leader, what steps can you take to ensure that your meetings are successful and efficient?

UNIT–3
Written Communication Skills

12
THE PROCESS OF WRITING

Chapter Objectives

This chapter will enable you to understand:

- Business writing basics
- Writing process
  - Planning
  - Drafting
  - Revising
  - Formating
  - Proofreading
- Evaluating the writing
- The role of persuasion in communication

No two people speak or write exactly the same way. Your personal pattern, called your 'idiolect' is also unique. Nobody else knows or uses precisely the same words you do, or uses them in the same way. Every skilled writer develops a style that is unlike everyone else's. But one way or another, competent writers do have something in common. One of the most important is that they have learned to take their writing through a process–a series of step–that they know will get them from the idea stage through to the finished written product. The idea of writing step by step may at first sound as if it is a complex, difficult and time-consuming process. But, in fact, the step of planning gives you a sense of where you want to go and that, in turn, makes getting there faster and easier. The clearer you are about your goals, the more likely your writing will accomplish those goals. And if you review the document in the last stage of proofreading, your work will go more smoothly and efficiently.

12.1 BUSINESS WRITING BASICS

Business writing differs from other writing you may have done. In preparing business messages and oral presentations, you will find that your writing needs to be:

- **Purposeful:** You will be writing to solve problems and convey information. You will have a definite purpose to fulfil in each message.
- **Economical:** You will try to present ideas clearly but concisely. Length is not rewarded.
- **Reader-oriented:** You will concentrate on looking at a problem from the reader's perspective instead of seeing it from your own.

These distinctions actually ease the writer's task. In writing most business documents, you won't be searching your imagination for creative topic ideas. Furthermore, you won't be trying to dazzle readers with your exclusive knowledge, powerful vocabulary, or graceful phrasing. The goal in business writing is to express rather than impress. You will be striving to get your ideas across naturally, simply, and clearly. However, business writing requires hard work, especially for beginners. Following a process and practicing the draft can make nearly anyone a successful business writer.

12.2 THE FIVE STEPS IN THE WRITING PROCESS

Writing is a process that involves planning, drafting, revising, formatting, and proofreading. Each step of the process is important for good writing. All good writers do not use the same process, of course. They develop their own process that suits their own ways of tackling a problem. But there is a lot of commonality. One way or the other, competent writers typically perform these five stages when faced with a business situation that calls for a written response.

1. **Planning:** Determining what the purpose of the message is, who the reader will be, what information you need to give the reader to achieve your purpose, in what order to present the information.
2. **Drafting:** Composing a first draft of the message
3. **Revising:** Revising for content, style, and correctness.
4. **Formatting:** Arranging the document in an appropriate format.
5. **Proofreading:** Reviewing the document to check for content, typographical, and format errors.

12.2.1 Step-1: Planning

Planning, the first in writing, involves the following:

1. Making conscious decisions about the purpose
2. Audience
3. Content
4. Organization of the message

12.2.1.1 Purpose

The first decision relates to the purpose of the message. If you do not know why you are writing the message, then later you will have no way of knowing whether you have achieved your goal. In the end, what matters is not how well crafted your message was or how attractive it looked on the page; what matters is whether you achieved your communication objective. If you did, your communication was successful; if you did not, it was not.

The purpose should be straightforward and specific enough to serve as a benchmark for judging the success of the message. Most writers find it easier to start with a general purpose and then refine the general purpose into a specific one. The specific purpose should indicate the response desired from the reader. In addition, having a clear-cut purpose lets you focus on the content and organization, eliminating any distracting information and incorporating all relevant information. In fact, the purpose of the message determines content, organization, style, tone, and format.

12.2.1.2 Audience Analysis

To maximize the effectiveness of your message, you should perform an audience analysis; that is, you should identify the interests, needs, and personality of your receiver. Remember, each person perceives a message differently because of his or her unique mental filter. Thus, we need to determine the level of detail, the language to be used, and the overall tone by answering the pertinent questions about audience.

Asking the Right Questions to Profile Your Audience

Primary Audience	Secondary Audience
Who is the primary reader?	Who might see or read this message after the primary audience?
What is my personal and professional relationship with that person?	How do these people differ from the primary audience?
What position does the individual held in the organization?	How must I reshape my message to make it understandable and acceptable to others to whom it might be forwarded?
How will the audience likely react?	How much does the person know about the subject?
What do I know about that person's education, beliefs, culture, and attitude?	

Who is the primary audience?

It is much easier to personalize a message addressed to one individual than a message addressed to many individuals. For most correspondence, the audience is one person, which simplifies the writing task immensely. Sometimes, however, you will have more than one audience. In this case, you need to identify your primary audience (the person whose cooperation is crucial) and then your secondary audience (others who will also read and be affected by your message). If you can satisfy no one else, try to satisfy the needs of the primary decision-maker. If possible, also satisfy the needs of any secondary audience.

If, for example, you are preparing a proposal that must be approved by the General Manager but that will also require the cooperation of your colleagues in other departments, the General Manager is the primary audience and your colleagues are the secondary audience. Prepare your message mainly to the needs of the General Manager. Most often (but not always), the primary audience will be the highest-level person to whom you are addressing your communication.

What is your relationship with the audience?

Your relationship with the reader determines the tone and content of your message.

- Does your audience know you? If not, you will first have to establish your credibility by assuming a reasonable tone and giving enough evidence to support your claims.
- Are you writing to someone inside or outside the organization? If outside, your message will often be a little more formal and will contain more background information and less jargon than if you are writing to someone inside the organization. What is your status in the organization in relation to your audience? If you are writing to someone inside the organization, communications to your superiors are obviously vital to your success. A little more formal and less authoritarian in tone. Such messages use a direct organizational style and present the major idea in the first paragraph.
- When you communicate with subordinates, be polite but not patronizing. When praising or criticizing, be specific, and criticize the action—not the person.

How will the audience react?

If the reader's initial reaction to both you and your topic is likely to be positive, you can use a direct approach—beginning with the most important information and then supplying the needed details. If the reader's initial reaction is negative, you may like to use the first few lines of the message to get the reader's attention and convince him or her that what you have to say is important and that your reasoning is sound. Make sure your message is short and easy to read and that any requested action is easy to take. Use courteous, vivid, and conservative language.

If you anticipate that your reader will oppose your proposal, your best strategy is to supply extra evidence. Instead of one example, give two or three. Instead of quoting one external source, quote several. Begin with the areas of agreement, stress reader benefits, and try to anticipate and answer any objections the reader might have. Through logic, evidence, and tone, build your case for the reasonableness of your position.

What does the audience already know?

Determine how much information the reader needs. Understanding the audience's educational level and his knowledge about the topic is crucial to making decisions about content and writing style. You must decide how much background information is necessary. Consider whether the use of jargon is acceptable, and what readability level is appropriate. If you are writing to multiple audiences, gear your details according to the level of understanding of the primary audience who is the key decision-maker. However, as a general rule, it is better to provide too much rather than too little information.

What is unique about the audience?

The success or failure of the message depends on little things. If you are acquainted with your reader(s), you can actually visualize individual(s). Make the reader feel important by personalizing the content. Does the reader prefer to have important information straight—regardless of whether the news is good or bad? What level of formalities is expected? Would the reader be pleased or be angry by the use of his or her first name in the salutation? Has some good thing or bad thing happened recently at work or at home that may affect the reader's receptivity to your message?

Skilled communicators analyze their audience and then use this information to structure the content, organization, and tone of their messages.

12.2.1.3 Content

Once you have determined the purpose of your message and identified the needs and interests of your audience, the next step is to decide what information to include. Do not start writing until you have planned what you want to say. Many communication tasks require numerous decisions about what to include. How much background information is needed? What statistical data best support the conclusions? Is expert opinion needed? Would examples, anecdotes, or graphics aid comprehension? Will research be necessary?

Include enough information that you don't lose or confuse the reader. Avoid including irrelevant material that may obscure the important data. Do not start drafting immediately, deciding as you write what information to include. Instead, start with a basic outline of your message—whether it is in your head, in a well-developed typed outline, or in the form of notes on a piece of paper.

Brainstorming

One useful strategy is brainstorming—jotting down ideas, facts, possible leads, and anything else you think might be helpful in constructing your message. Aim for quantity, not quality. Do not evaluate your output until you have run out of ideas. Then begin to refine, delete, combine, and otherwise revise your ideas to form the basis for your message.

Mind mapping

Another possible strategy is mind mapping (also called clustering), a process that avoids the step-by-step limitations of lists. Instead, you write the purpose of your message in the middle of a page and circle it. Then, as you think of possible points to add, write them down and link them by a line either to the main purpose or to another point. As you think of other details, add them where you think they might fit. This visual outline offers flexibility and encourages free thinking.

12.2.1.4 Organization

The final step in the planning process is to establish the organization of the message—that is, to determine in what order to discuss each topic. After you have brainstormed or mapped out your ideas around a main idea, you need to organize them into an outline that you can use to draft your message into its most effective form.

Classification (grouping related ideas) is the first step in organizing your message. Once you've grouped related ideas, you then need to differentiate between the major and minor points so that you can line up minor ideas and evidence to support the major ideas.

The most effective sequence for the major ideas often depends on the reaction you expect from your audience. If you expect a positive response, you may want to use a direct approach, in which the conclusion or major idea is presented first, followed by the reasons. If you expect a negative response, you may decide to use an indirect approach, in which the reasons are presented first and the conclusion after.

12.2.2 Step-2: Drafting

Having now finished planning, you are finally ready to begin drafting, that is, composing a preliminary version of a message. Probably the most important thing to remember about drafting is to just let your ideas flow as quickly as possible onto paper or computer screen, without worrying style, correctness, or format. Do not combine drafting and revising. They involve two separate skills and two separate mindsets. As Marshall Cook (1987) has noted, "Writing is art. Rewriting is craft. Mix the two at your peril. If you let your inner editor (who, according to popular theory, lives in the left side of your brain) into the process too early, it's liable to overpower your artist, blocking your creative flow." Your first draft is just that—a draft. Don't expect perfection, and don't strive for it. Concentrate, instead, on recording all the points you identified in the planning stage. When you have finished and then begin to revise and prepare a final draft.

12.2.2.1 Writer's Block

This is the inability to focus on the writing process and to draft a message. The causes of writer's block are typically one or more of the following:

Procrastination: Putting off what we dislike doing.

Impatience: Growing tired of the naturally slow pace of the writing process.

Perfectionism: Believing that our draft must be perfect the first time.

These factors naturally interfere with creativity and concentration. In addition, they undermine the writer's self-image and make him or her even more reluctant to tackle the next writing task.

12.2.2.2 Strategies for Avoiding Writer's Block

1. **Choose the right environment:** The ability to concentrate on the task at hand is one of the most important components of effective writing.
2. **Schedule a reasonable block of time:** Schedule blocks of no more than two hours or so at one sitting.
3. **State your purpose in writing:** Having identified your specific purpose during the planning phase, write it at the top of your blank page. Keep it visible so that it will be uppermost in your consciousness as you compose.
4. **Engage in free writing:** Review your purpose and your audience. Then begin free writing; that is, write continuously for five to ten minutes, literally without stopping. It can be useful for helping writers "unblock" their ideas. While free writing, don't look back and don't stop writing. If you cannot think of anything to say, simply keep repeating the last word or keep writing some sentence such as "Now what?", or "I know".
5. **Avoid the perfectionism syndrome:** Remember that the product you're producing now is a draft—not a final document. Don't worry about style, coherence, spelling or punctuation errors, and the like.
6. **Think out loud:** Some people are more skilled at speaking their thoughts than at writing them. Picture yourself telling a colleague about what you're writing, and explain about the ideas you're trying to get across. Hearing your ideas will help sharpen and focus them.
7. **Write the easiest parts first:** You need not write the parts of a message in the order in which they will finally appear. Begin with the easiest parts. The opening paragraph

of a letter or memo is often the most difficult one to compose. If that is the case, skip it and begin in the middle. In a report, the procedures section may be easier to write than the recommendations. Getting something down on paper will give you a sense of accomplishment, and your writing may generate ideas for other sections.

Each of these strategies for avoiding writer's block into your writing routine those strategies that work best for you.

12.2.3 Step-3: Revising

Revising means improving the content and sentence structure of your message. Because few writers can produce a satisfactory copy on the first attempt, revision is an important step in the writing process. Although the communication process differs for individuals and situations, this phase should occupy a significant share of the total time you spend on a message. Rarely is the first version of the message satisfactory. The revision stage is your chance to make sure your message says what you mean. When you finish a first draft, plan for a cooling-off period. Put the document aside and return to it after a break, preferably after 24 hours or longer. Whether you revise immediately or after a break, examine your message critically. You should be especially concerned with ways to improve its clarity, conciseness, vigour, and readability.

Thus, revising is a process of modifying a document to increase its effectiveness. Having the raw material—your first draft—in front of you, you can now refine it into the most effective document possible, considering its importance and the time constraints under which you are working.

If possible, put your draft away for a period of time—the longer the better. Leaving time between creation and revising helps you distance yourself from your writing. If you revise immediately, the memory of what you "meant to say" rather than what you actually wrote may be strong that it keeps you from spotting weaknesses in logic and diction.

If you are a typical writer, you will have made numerous minor revisions even as you were composing; however, as noted earlier, you should save the major revisions until later. For important writing projects, you will probably want to solicit comments about your draft from colleagues as part of the revision process.

Although revising is considered as the third step of the writing process, in fact, it involves several steps. Most writers revise first for content, then for style, and finally for correctness.

12.2.3.1 Revising for Content

First reread your purpose statement and then the entire draft to get an overview of your message. Ask yourself such questions as these:

- Is the content appropriate for the purpose I've identified?
- Will the purpose of the message be clear to the reader?
- Have I been sensitive to the needs of the reader?
- Is all the information necessary?
- Is any needed information missing?
- Is the order of presentation of the points effective?

12.2.3.2 Revising for Style

Next, read each paragraph again (aloud, if possible). Reading aloud gives you a feel for the rhythm and flow of your writing. Long sentences that made sense as you wrote them may leave you out of breadth when you read them aloud.

12.2.3.3 Revising for Correctness

The final phase of revising is editing, the process of ensuring that writing conforms to standard English. Editing involves checking for correctness—that is, identifying problems with grammar, spelling, punctuation, and word usage. Writers who fail to check for grammar, mechanical, and usage errors risk losing credibility with their reader. Such errors may distract the reader, delay comprehension, cause misunderstandings, and reflect negatively on the writer's abilities.

12.2.4 Step-4: Formatting

No one format for any type of business document is universally accepted as standard; a fair amount of variation is common in industry. Letters are external documents that are sent to people outside the organization. Memos are internal documents that are sent to people inside the same organization as the writer. To some extent, technology is changing formatting standards. Today, most traditional memos have been replaced by email. Email messages and reports may be either internal or external. In addition, email messages all look like memorandums—whether they are sent to someone inside or outside the organization. They typically contain To:, From:, Date:, and Subject: lines just as memos do, and they do not contain an inside address as is typical in letters. The important point is to use the format that is appropriate for each specific message. A standard format not only saves time but also gives a consistent appearance to the organization's documents. Besides, readers expect to find certain information in certain positions in a document. If the information is not there, the reader is unnecessarily distracted. For all these reasons, you should become familiar with the standard conventions for formatting documents.

12.2.5 Step-5: Proofreading

Proofreading is the final quality-control check for your document. Don't proofread earlier because you may waste time checking items that are eventually changed or omitted. Proofreading is especially difficult because most of us read what we thought we wrote. That is why, it is important to look for specific areas. Remember that a reader may not know whether an incorrect word resulted from a simple typo or from the writer's ignorance of correct usage. And even one such error can have adverse effects. Take responsibility for ensuring the accuracy of your communication. Proofread for content, typographical, and format errors. Careful proofreaders check for problems in the following area:

12.2.5.1 Content Errors

Read through your document quickly, checking for content errors. Was any material omitted unintentionally? Check to be sure that your document makes sense.

12.2.5.2 Typographical Errors

Typographical errors may send a negative non-verbal message about the writer. Read through you document slowly, checking for typographical errors. Look out for repeated or omitted words. Double-check all proper names and all figures, using the original source if possible.

- **Spelling:** Now is the time to consult the dictionary. Is 'recommend' spelled with one or two Cs? Should there be 'from' or 'form'? Do you mean 'affect' or 'effect'? You may use your computer spellchecker, but do not rely on it totally.
- **Grammar:** Locate sentence subjects; do their verbs agree with them? Do pronouns agree with their antecedents? Are the sentences parallely constructed? Are the modifiers properly placed or dangled? You can use your computer's grammar checker. But before you decide that a grammar checker will solve all your writing problems, think again. Even world's highly developed software misses plenty of errors, and it also mismarks some correct expressions.
- **Punctuation:** Make sure that introductory clauses are followed by commas. In compound sentences put commas before coordinating conjunctions (and, or, but, nor). Double-check your use of semicolons and colons.
- **Names and numbers:** Compare all names and numbers with their sources because inaccuracies are not always visible. Especially verify the spelling of the names of individuals receiving the message. Most of us immediately dislike someone who misspells our name.

12.2.5.3 Format Errors

Visually inspect the document for appropriate format. Be sure that your document looks balanced on the page. Compare its parts and format with those of standard documents. Are all the parts included and in the correct position? What will be the receiver's first impression before reading the document? Does the document look attractive on the page? Do not consider the proofreading stage complete until you are able to read through the entire document without making any changes.

12.3 EVALUATING

As part of applying finishing touches, take a moment to evaluate your writing. How successful will this message be? Does it say what you want it to? Will it achieve your purpose? How will you know if it succeeds?

The best way to judge the success of your communication is through feedback. Thus, you should encourage the receiver to respond to your message. This feedback will tell you how to modify future efforts to improve your communication technique.

Your instructor will also be evaluating some of your writing. Although any criticism is painful, try not to be defensive. Look on these comments as valuable advice tailored to your specific writing weaknesses-and-strengths. Many businesses today spend thousands of dollars bringing in communication consultants to improve employee writing skills. Take advantage of this chance—one of the few you may have—to improve your skills. The best way to improve your skills, of course, is through instruction, practice and evaluation.

12.4 THE ROLE OF PERSUASION IN COMMUNICATING

The primary purposes for sending messages are typically to inform and to persuade. In fact, persuasion is a major purpose of any business communication. Whether your goal is to sell, to motivate, to convey bad news, or simply to inform, your ability to persuade ultimately determines the degree of success or failure that you will achieve.

The word 'persuade' in fact, stems from a Latin root that means 'agreeable'. Persuasion involves the persuader's awareness that he or she is trying to influence someone else. It also requires that the other person make a conscious or unconscious decision to change his or her mind about something. Communication scholars define persuasion in different ways:

- Persuasion is a communication process in which the communicator seeks to elicit a desired response from his receiver.

  –Anderson

- Persuasion is a conscious attempt by one individual to change the attitudes, beliefs, or behaviour of another individual or group of individuals through the transmission of some message.

  –Bettinghans & Cody

According to these definitions, following are the components of persuasion:

1. **A process of communication:** There is expression and interpretation of messages when persuasion occurs.
2. **Voluntarily:** The recipient is not forced into being persuaded. In the end he or she still has the right to choose, even though the choices are sometimes very limited.
3. **Forming, sustaining, or changing:** Persuasion does not only aim to change (as is the general perception). It is also used to sustain or to maintain, or even to intensify the attitudes or behaviour of recipients.
4. **What the communicator intends:** As in the case of communication, persuasion is intentional.

12.4.1 Persuasion Versus Coercion

Does persuasion differs from coercion? Persuasion deals with reason and verbal appeals, while coercion employs force, you suggest. Thus persuasion, of course, is not coercion. In some cases people may be forced to do something, but they cannot be forced to believe something. They must be persuaded in ways that are agreeable to them.

12.4.2 Aristotle's Art of Persuasion

Aristotle's (384-322 BC) 'Art of Persuasion' is today still generally considered to be the most important single work in the literature of persuasive oratory. (S. Steinberg, 2006) In his work 'Rhetoric' Aristotle identified three methods by which people can be persuaded:

Ethos: Ethos is an ethical appeal based on who you are and how your audience perceives you.

Pathos: Pathos appeals to an audience's emotions.

Logos: Logos is an appeal based on logic.

For most business communication situations, logic is the most effective form of persuasion—presenting facts, inferences, and opinion. Aristotle defined a fact as that which is indisputably true, an inference as that which is probably true, and an opinion as that which is possibly true. Competent communicators tend to rely on logical appeals and ensure that the facts, inferences, and expert opinion they use have relevance—both to their position and to their audience.

REVIEW QUESTIONS

1. Identify six different situations where writing might be used in an organization.
2. Describe five steps in the writing process? What is the role of audience analysis in the writing process?
3. This chapter has suggested that the goal in business writing is to impress rather than impress. How can a person become a successful business writer? Explain.
4. Write a note on the significance of proofreading a document to improve organizational writing.
5. Why do you think people in an organization choose to write things rather than say anything?
6. Following the five step process outlined in this chapter compose a one page letter to the administration discussing the quality of your cafeteria food in recent months. Brainstorm to generate ideas for the content of the letter.

13

PROBLEM SOLVING SKILLS

Chapter Objectives

This chapter will enable you to understand:

- Types of problem
- Alternative approaches to problem solving
- Creativity technique
- Mind mapping technique
- Brainstorming technique

Creative thinking, mind mapping, and brainstorming are the crucial problem-solving skills that you need in order to prosper in your management role or in your personal life. Problem solving is the process of analyzing and then seeking solutions to problems. The starting point is to analyze the problem to identify the nature of it.

13.1 TYPES OF PROBLEM

There are several different types of problem. Following are some of the main types:

1. **A deviation problem:** This is where desired results and outcomes are not being achieved. The problem solver, therefore, has to identify a way of getting back on track, that is, how to remove the deviation.
2. **An improvement problem:** This is where something is already working well but it may be possible to make it work better. The problem, therefore, is to find way of improving on current solutions.
3. **Creative problem:** This is where problem solving is used as a creative tool to generate new ideas for doing things, starting with a blank sheet of paper.

Thus, different types of problem solving require different types of thinking. For example, creative problem solving requires a far more flexible approach than solving deviation problem.

However, for most types of problem solving, first and foremost, you have to analyze the problem. In other words, find out what the nature of the problem is. This requires identifying data that is relevant to the problem, and the techniques that can be used to analyze and find solutions to it.

13.2 ALTERNATIVE APPROACHES TO PROBLEM SOLVING

Alternative approaches to problem solving can be employed such as creative thinking, mind mapping, and brainstorming.

Creativity is a skill which is needed in many areas of business life. Creativity is the key to inventions, improvements, solutions, breakthroughs, and brilliant suggestions. We sometimes refer creativity as thinking 'out of the box'. Thinking inside the box means coming up with standards 'tried and tested' solutions to problems that do not require a lot of imagination. In contrast, creative thinking involves developing novel solutions and ideas that nobody has thought of before.

Mindmapping as problem-solving technique offers exploration without traditional boundaries. It can be used to set out a graphic representation of a problem and its solutions. Mindmapping tells you how to use memory more effectively to improve recall. Exploring ideas without traditional boundaries provide freedom and creative energy. A mind map also shows relationships that help you organize and prioritize your information; you get a bigger picture much faster. Mind mapping can also be used before you make an important phone call or as a fine management technique.

Brainstorming involves generally a lot of ways of dealing with the problem. They can be as crazy as you like because at this stage they are not going to be followed through. Sometimes apparently crazy ideas can be structured into sensible solutions when they have the 'craziness' taken out. In a brainstorming situation participants simply suggest as many ideas as they can without justifying them or having them questioned. The idea is to generate as many solutions as possible.

13.3 CREATIVITY

With increasing competition and globalization, we have to negotiate with many more subtle and deeper issues in every profession. For example, how can we maintain our core identity while adapting to diverse cultures and rapid changes, and how can we create a work environment where people can grow to their fullest potential while still focusing on the organizational function and interests, and so on. Today, competence is becoming a commodity. State-of-the-art technology is a commodity. What is really going to matter is value creation. And value creation demands either copying from someone else or creativity.

Creativity in our day-to-day functioning and thinking offers solution to some of these problems. Realizing this, executives start looking around for a quick way of getting into the creativity business. The rewards will go to people who can create new products and industries, anticipate changes, focus resources where and when needed. The people who will survive best in this competitive environment are the motivated and creative people who can make a difference to the world around them.

13.3.1 Definitions of Creativity

According to Webster's dictionary, "Creativity is marked by the ability or power to create, to bring into existence, to invest with a new form, to produce through imaginative skill, to make or bring into existence something new.

H. H. Fox, the scientist defines creativity as, "Any thinking process in which original patterns are formed and expressed."

According to Rollo May, the writer and philosopher, "Creativity is the process of bringing something new into being."

Joseph Campbell, the great mythographer, sees creativity as a journey. According to him, "Creativity consists in going out to find the thing that society hasn't found yet."

13.3.2 Can Creativity be Learned?

Creative thinking is the process which we use when we come up with a new idea. It is the merging of ideas which have not been merged before. With changing perceptions we no longer believe that creativity is inborn, or only special, talented people are creative and you have to be born that way. Various researches reveal that we are naturally creative and as we grow up we learn to be uncreative. Creativity is a skill that can be developed and a process that can be managed. Generative research shows that everyone has creative abilities. The more training you have and the more diverse the training, the greater potential for creative output. The average adult thinks of 3-6 alternatives for any given situation. The average child thinks of 60.

Thus, creativity is a potential that every one of us possesses. The difference lies in whether we have been able to nurture, develop, and give it expression and direction. Some strongly believe that there cannot be creativity in their place of work. "If only I had a different work environment, then I could be creative." What we forget is that creativity comes from within, not from out.

Creativity is about the dynamic forces and impulses within us. Every situation has the potential to be creatively altered improved. You only need to clear you own blocks, think differently and see how best you can make the change happen. In 1904, Arnold Fornachou, an ice cream vendor, exhausted all his paper dishes while serving ice creams to customers at a fair. Luckily, he was then standing opposite a baker who was selling thin waffles. History has it that he bought a few, twisted them into cones, and scooped ice creams into them, and in this way an ice cream cone was born.

13.3.3 Situations and Creativity

Every person becomes creative at certain times. Even the most creative people are not equally creative at all times. Following are a few situations which are conducive for creativity and which make us think differently.

1. **Thinking up a new idea:** Creativity is not the realm of profound thinking only. There are many occasions when suddenly we look at a problem differently, and we find a new solution. Phrasing a thought, trying out a new recipe, or a child discovering how to fix a set of puzzles, or even writing a business report differently is also creativity. All these and many more are expressions of our creativity—the coming together of

intuition and logical thinking. Thus creativity is the ability to use different modes of thought to generate new and dynamic ideas and solutions.

2. **Spontaneous action:** Without using special techniques creative thinking does still occur, but usually in the spontaneous way, like a chance happening making you think about something in a different way and you then discovering a beneficial change. Other changes happen slowly through pure use of intelligence and logical progression. Sometimes in a moment of inspiration, we give a speech off the cuff, respond spontaneously and plead for justice in a public meeting. We think of a new game and spend a delightful day with children, spontaneously, sometimes we try a new route–a deviation in our daily way to office–we never thought existed, or try out a new combination of things, successfully. All these are outlets to our personal creativity. These are also moments when we are at our best, competent and confident.
3. **Creativity and building relationships:** Fostering a meaningful relationship too means creativity. The way we express ourselves in our relationships is a manifestation of creativity. Sometimes we change our approach to meaning deal with a person. We steer a relationship to a win-win situation and create a context that can be based on collaboration and cooperation. For example, we simply sit and relish the feeling that a co-worker is also a support and a reason to come back to work, or we get back to an old friend and strengthen an old relationship. All these and many more are expressions of our creativity. The way we establish and nurture our relationships are indicative of the quality of our underlying creativity.
4. **Changing your inner self:** Sometimes our attitude, perspective and feelings towards a person or situation change even though the situation remains the same. These are times when our inner self, our response to things outside undergoes a change. Allowing ourselves to be open to new changes or trying to organize our thinking differently are acts of creativity that make our lives richer and more fulfilling. If used purposefully, this can bring out our inner strength, and encourage openness rather than suppression of feelings.

   In fact, our inner experience is the most vital and fundamental arena of creativity. Opening ourselves to such experiences can enable us to shape events, organize activities, develop meaningful relationships, and make our own actions more meaningful and relevant.

13.3.4 Ways to be Creative

Creativity manifests itself in many ways. Different people experience it differently. Some of the ways in which creativity blossoms are:

1. **Creativity through visioning:** One way of finding creative solutions to problems is by visioning, through which you seek the ideal long-term solution to problems. During visioning you let yourself go, imagine what it would be like if dreams came true, or if problems were solved. It often helps in providing direction, inspiration, and momentum to creative projects.

   In career and business, visioning helps us form goals and give direction to our efforts. Questions like, "What would I like to be 10 years from hence", or "what would be the ideal wish of our customers" will help us form long-term objectives and focus our efforts. In 1961, J.F. Kennedy shared his vision with the nation. He had a dream that within the next ten years the US would send a man to the moon. By the time Neil Armstrong finally took his 'giant leap for mankind'. Kennedy's vision had become the vision of the nation.

2. **Creativity through modifying:** This method of exploring creativity seeks to explain and build on what you have already done. Here you modify and improve on what has already been initiated. Using this style involves looking at the previous situation, adapting solutions to fit a new purpose. The advantages of modifying are that it provides stability and exploits an idea to the fullest possible extent. The questions that can come up here are:
   - How can I build on the interests and experiences I have developed so far?
   - What measures can we take to further expand our sales and improve our functioning?

   In the 1850s, a 17-year old tailor Levi Strauss noticed that cloth trousers of miners wore off very quickly. He then started stitching overalls made of a stiff canvass that could stand wear and tear. Years later he substituted the canvass with a fabric called denim and dyed it blue to minimize the soil stains. Thus, came the blue jeans.
3. **Creativity through exploring:** This method of exploring your creativity involves questioning and challenging the core assumptions, making a radical breakthrough and coming up with new assumptions. This style of creativity works without any consideration of long-term goals, a specific incremental improvement, or even consideration of the practical realities. The typical questions one asks in this process are:
   - How can I breakaway from all the givens and establish an alternative?
   - How can I breakaway from convention and instil new wisdom in the profession?

   In 1948, George De Maistred, a Swiss mountaineer, was troubled by the prickly burns that tightly clung to his socks. As he sat tearing them off, an idea struck him. He studied the burr's clinging properties and invented 'Velcro', a fastener that made the zipper obsolete.

   It is important to remember that each of our styles of creativity is a mixture of all three. All of us function in all the three ways one time or the other.

13.3.5 Developing Creativity

How do we develop our creativity? Does it happen automatically, or is there a way whereby one can make it happen. If we analyze the nature of creativity we find in it a mixture of intuition and logical thinking. All discoveries have been made with logical thinking acting as the base for insight to flash and make the final connection or vice versa. It is one followed by the other or both together operating and forming a cognizable whole. Often creativity is also seen as an act of receiving-getting a thought or a flash. These experiences have a quantum effect. They show us something familiar in a strange, new light, or bring disparate elements of experience into an unexpected synthesis. We say:

- "The idea came to me."
- "I saw the light."
- "I see things differently now."

- "I could feel it in my bones."
- "I was struck by an insight."

And like quantum events, they are usually accompanied by a release of energy: an explosion of laughter or tears. It is seen as a phenomenon of ideas coming from our mind beyond our conscious awareness. This can happen at a time when the mind is relatively rested-alert but not involved in a stream of thought.

In 1972, Ray Tomlinson wrote the first electronic mail application by combining the code of an existing intra-computer messaging application with an inter-computer file transfer protocol. As Tomlinson describes: "It seemed like an interesting hack to tie these two together to use the file transfer protocol to send the email to the other machine. So that's what I did. I spent not a whole lot of time, maybe two or three weeks, putting that together and it worked... ."

The art of developing creative skills, thus, is to train the mind to produce these 'spaces', create opportunity for our intuition to act on our logic and form a whole. This sometimes comes to us in the form of metaphors or symbols. The mind should be in a state of 'active receptivity' to receive and interpret them. For example, Friedrich Kekule had been working for years to discover the molecular structure of benzene. One night, he says, he dozed off in front of the fireplace and saw a vision as if in a dream: "again atoms were juggling before my eyes...everything was moving in a snake-like and twisted manner. Suddenly, one snake got hold of its own tail and the whole structure was mockingly twisted in front of my eyes. As it struck by a lightning, I awoke." He had envisioned the closed ring structure of benzene.

13.3.6 Creating Intuitive Space

Intuition is ability to sense or know immediately without reasoning. Without doubt, we use our intuition all the time whenever we make a choice or a decision. Intuition uses the unconscious. It comes from a stratum of awareness just below the conscious level. We realize something without understanding how we come to know it. If we look into the history of inventions, we find that the most original ideas arise from the 'space' in between our thoughts. To improve one's creativity, thus, it is important to understand these 'spaces'. Eckhart Tolle writes in 'The Power of Now', "When an answer, a solution or a creative idea is needed, stop thinking for a moment by focusing attention on your inner energy field. Become aware of stillness. Then resume thinking, it will be fresh and creative... don't just think with your head, think with your whole body."

Einstein said that there is no logical path to the natural laws. Only intuition resting on sympathetic understanding of experience can reach them. For this, it is important to learn to enter into 'wandering'—a mindset that is attentive, alert, and curious and yet tranquil. Zen, the Japanese way of thinking calls it the 'Beginner's Mind', and in the Indian yogic system it is called the state of 'Conscious Unconsciousness'. New ideas spring from a mind that organizes these experiences, facts and relationships to determine a path not taken before.

This is the phenomenon, we can sometimes observe during someone performing at his or her best. What is significant is the grace and the confidence that comes in during this state of consciousness. The act is done as if it was natural, as if there was no other way it could be done. We find it during an athlete's peak performance, a speaker giving one of the best addresses, or a writer writing the most intense parts of his/her masterpiece- alert and active yet loose and cool.

We cannot summon up an intuition deliberately. We can, however, do something to prepare for it. It may come to use in disguise or in the form of symbols. We must be ready to interpret the form of our insight. Learn to read them. Practice is the only key to success her. Practise creating the empty spaces and even practise deciphering and trusting what comes to you as intuition.

13.3.7 Five Stages of Creativity

The five stages of creativity are preparation, effort, incubation, insight, and evaluation.

13.3.7.1 Preparation

Preparation includes being in the right mood or frame of mind to think deeply about the truth in hand. The problem must become part of you. Formulate the problem and think about it continually—sleep with it, eat with it, and play with it. Try and imagine looking at it from as many different viewpoints as possible. Let the problem brew in your mind. Redefine the problem using the words 'how to'. Read widely at this stage. To promote creativity you must diversify your interests and reading in order to generate diverse views. Collect the facts and materials required for the new solution, consult your staff, your colleague and your sincere friends also. Preparation in the form of education, training and research is an essential foundation to build creativity.

13.3.7.2 Effort

Develop and record all ideas and alternatives. Use the technique of brainstorming to formulate ideas. Besides, mind mapping will also be helpful to add and develop further ideas through reading, research observation, reflection, watching television, and consulting with others.

13.3.7.3 Incubation

Muse on the problem in your mind. The conscious mind usually looks for familiar channels which are known and thus not new or creative. Your subconscious mind will now be working on the problem. In fact, the subconscious mind, free from the constraints of the conscious mind is able to look at the issue from new angles or put information together into new combinations.

13.3.7.4 Insight

Insight is the 'Eureka' feeling. In other words, insight is a sudden flash of illumination and a release of tension when the problem has been solved. Frequently the insight turns out to be dissatisfactory and the thinker is back at the beginning of the creative process. In other cases the insight is generally satisfactory but needs some modification or the solution of minor problems to be a really good new idea.

13.3.7.5 Evaluation

The apparent solution is to test the idea to see if it satisfactorily solves the problem. It gives us a general picture of the steps frequently involved in the solution of problems by most talented and creative people. Another approach to the study of creative thinking is to see how it differs from the more routine kinds of thinking we do. However, discard ideas that are too costly, acceptable, inappropriate, or unethical.

13.3.8 Factors that Block Creativity

Look at the way a child plays. Carefully listen to the conversations they make. You will be amazed at the number of creative ideas that spring forth every second. Children are creative. But our adult life, our system of education and the thinking it promotes blocks our creativity. Many factors of our lives contribute to this. Some of them are:

1. **Fear:** Fear is one of the emotions that often force us to limit ourselves. Fear of being rejected, fear of uncertainty, fear of failure, and sometime even fear of success constricts us. It holds us back from moving ahead, finding new connections and exploring ourselves.
2. **Anger and guilt:** Guilt, depression and anger are emotion that blind us to the alternatives available to us. They prevent us from thinking of other possibilities, or exploring other possible probabilities. At the workplace they block us from fruitfully working together and bringing in positive vibrancy that can alter the way we function and look at work.
3. **Stress:** Stress that comes from our urge from growth and expansion can be positive, but the stress that results in tension and anxiety can be damaging and block the 'flow' in our thinking. Stress is not only a distraction, it also drains energy which could otherwise be used creatively. Pushing an individual to perform better may be positive at time. But a constant push to work at 110 per cent, continuous and 'urgent' projects that constantly stretch one to his/her limits can be dangerous. However, stress is often more psychological than real. If we enjoy the work we do, we rarely get stressed.
4. **Lack of imagination:** Our lack of imagination or unwillingness to go beyond the confines of our imagination also becomes a stumbling block. This can result in our inability to visualize certain types of growth or see ourselves as reaching certain heights.
5. **Routine:** Routines or set ways of performing tasks have their uses, but allowing them to become too entrenched in one's life causes one to limit the range of responses available and can lead to the development of the anathema of creativity.
6. **Beliefs:** Having a strong belief in something not only limits our response options, but causes us to limit the way in which we perceive and process information from the outside world. We may 'filter out' information which contradicts our belief, and end up in our own 'reality tunnel', in which we remain blissfully unaware of much that occurs in front of our very eyes.
7. **Ego attachment:** Having a strong ego identity with a particular belief exacerbates the situation and can lead us to aggressively defend it, to the detriment of ourselves, our creativity, and society. This is not to imply that one must have no beliefs, merely that one needs to be aware of one's beliefs and consequent limitations. This is the moment when we must sacrifice our attachment to our ideas, to let it go out into the world and fend for itself.
8. **Self-criticism:** Negative thinking and self-criticism are also limiting factors of an individual's creativity.

13.3.9 Creativity in Workplace

Creativity is a core competency for leaders and managers and one of the best ways to set an organization apart from the competition. In the recent years, the concept of organizational operation has undergone complete change. No longer are they seen as impersonal structures that have to be managed through systematic control. Creativity is fostered in organizational cultures that value independent thinking, risk taking, and learning.

Organizations are today looked upon as organisms where people are held together by shared purpose, and vision rather than audit and control. Such people are tolerant of failure and they value diversity. Open communication, a high degree of trust and respect between individuals are crucial.

In this altered work ethic, every person is also expected to contribute meaningfully, strengthen the bonding of teamwork and bring out the best of only in himself/herself but his/her co-workers as well. Fostering a creative climate that combines work with pleasure, that generates a sense of belongingness and strengthens a common vision for the organizations can do this. This can be achieved by building and strengthening innovative teams.

According to the French scientist Poincare, inventions consist in not making useless combinations but in making those which are useful. Creativity at workplace is the power to invent and design products and services that will ensure the success of your organization. It is characterized by the ability to perceive the world in new ways, to find hidden patterns, to make connections between seemingly unrelated phenomena, and to generate solutions. Generating fresh solutions to problems, and the ability to create new products, processes or services for a changing market are part of the intellectual capital that gives an organization its competitive edge. Specific areas in which skills in creativity and innovation generate solutions and improve performance include:

- Customer service
- Internal and external communications
- New products and services
- Branding
- Marketing
- Managing transition
- Team building
- Change management
- Organizational effectiveness
- Identity
- Work/life balance

13.3.10 Distinction between Creativity and Innovation

Creativity is typically used to refer to the act of producing new ideas, approaches, or actions, while innovation is the process of both generating and applying such creative ideas in some specific context.

In the context of an organization, therefore, the term 'innovation' is often used to refer to the entire process by which an organization generates creative new ideas and converts them into novel, useful, and viable commercial products, services, and business practices, while the term 'creativity' is reserved to apply specifically to the generation of novel ideas by individuals or groups, as a necessary step within the innovation process.

However, both, innovation and creativity go hand in hand. In order to be innovative, people have to be creative. Organizations that understand the relationship between creativity and innovation actively promote creativity in their employees. The root of innovation is creativity.

13.3.11 Creativity and Teamwork

Teams provide a golden opportunity to develop creativity. A good team environment can provide excellent pre-conditions for creativity thinking. Groups of people can produce more interesting ideas, and in greater numbers, than an individual.

Creativity, in turn, can bring enormous benefits to the team, by helping it to find new ideas and challenging assumptions, creativity can help to strengthen a team, renew its values and redefine its identity. Every team is composed of individuals. It depends on the diverse talent of its members. Authenticity in relationships helps bind a team better. Such groups have very few perceptual blocks. They are willing to make the best of one another's ideas. They create better synergy. Alignment of thinking lends single-mindedness and single-heartedness of purpose.

Once again, the benefits of teamwork and creativity are mutual. This approach seeks to develop teamwork by focusing on interpersonal dynamics. A healthy team will encourage individuals to think flexibly, express their thoughts freely suggest, question and challenge. A creative team will find itself in a cycle of positive, reinforcing behaviour, continually reinventing, re-energizing and realizing itself.

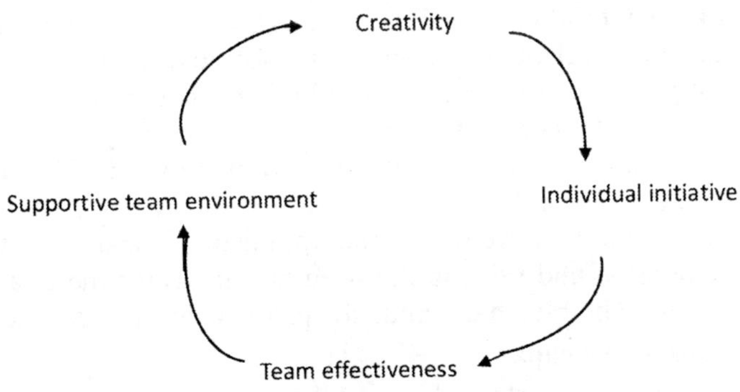

Figure 13.1

Once the team establishes a high-integrity relationship it becomes possible to explore one another's purpose and goals, blend them with the organizational vision and move towards it together. Following conditions will allow creativity to develop more easily in the team:

1. **Appraisal and rewards:** People are more likely to want to be creative if their work provides opportunities to develop their skills and knowledge. Besides, appraisal and rewards help motivate the teams and also see the good in one another.
2. **Empowerment:** Empowerment allows one to take risks, stretch oneself to face challenges and think of innovative ways during problem solving. Wherever possible, give

individuals complete task. Ownership of the whole piece of work, responsibility for it, and control over it will help to encourage a more creative approach to it, as well as promoting motivation, satisfaction and general mental well-being.

3. **Saying OK to failure:** Saying OK to failure gives confidence to experiment with new ideas. People should feel comfortable asking, and being asked for help. It does not nip creativity in the bud for the fear of thing going wrong.
4. **Reinforcing the vision:** Involve all the team in establishing the team's vision, objectives, tasks, and values. Individuals should have clear action responsibilities. It helps the group stay focused and goal oriented.
5. **The pressure trap:** Time pressure may be a trap. It provides scope for unstructured and unpressured time in the workplace. It is necessary to boost creativity. However, it has been found that low time pressure does not necessarily foster creativity. It works only when people would like to play around with ideas and have to experience with something new.

   There is no single universally approved way of boosting creativity. Every mind is unique, and therefore, it functions differently so the best that can be said is that observe and see. Find out what works best for you and your team and accordingly adopt your best way of working.

13.3.12 Creativity and Edward De Bono's Creative Techniques

Edward de Bono, who is one of the leading exponents of problem-solving techniques suggests that there are different types of thinking and that we can switch from one to another, particularly if we are aware of these different modes of thinking and we get into the habit of applying whichever is most appropriate to each problem.

In one of his books 'Six thinking Hats', he proposes different hats for different types of thinking. The white hat is neutral, objective, and non-emotional. White is effectively colourless. With this thinking hat you focus on the data. You look at the facts and figures and see what you can learn. The red hat by contrast is emotional hat, where you can present views on your intuition without explanation, or justification of your emotions. The black hat is gloomy and negative. You take time to look at the risks and why a proposed solution will fail. The yellow hat helps you to think positively. It is the optimistic viewpoint that helps you to see all the benefits of the decision and value in it. Green hat stands for the creation of new ideas, concepts and perceptions. The blue hat stands for process, control, or taking an overview.

De Bono's problem-solving techniques

1. Stop thinking about the problem for a while and come back to it later.
2. Think of other problems that are analogous to the one you're working on; either real or imaginary problems in real or imaginary domains. Solve those problems, and then translate the solution back to the original domain.
3. Write down the problem, and then translate it into various languages. Different languages divide things into concepts (words) in different ways, so this forces you to think about and re-cast the concepts that are involved.
4. Explain the problem to someone. For example, explaining a scientific problem to a layman, or to a scientist in a different field, forces one to think about the meanings of the concepts involved.

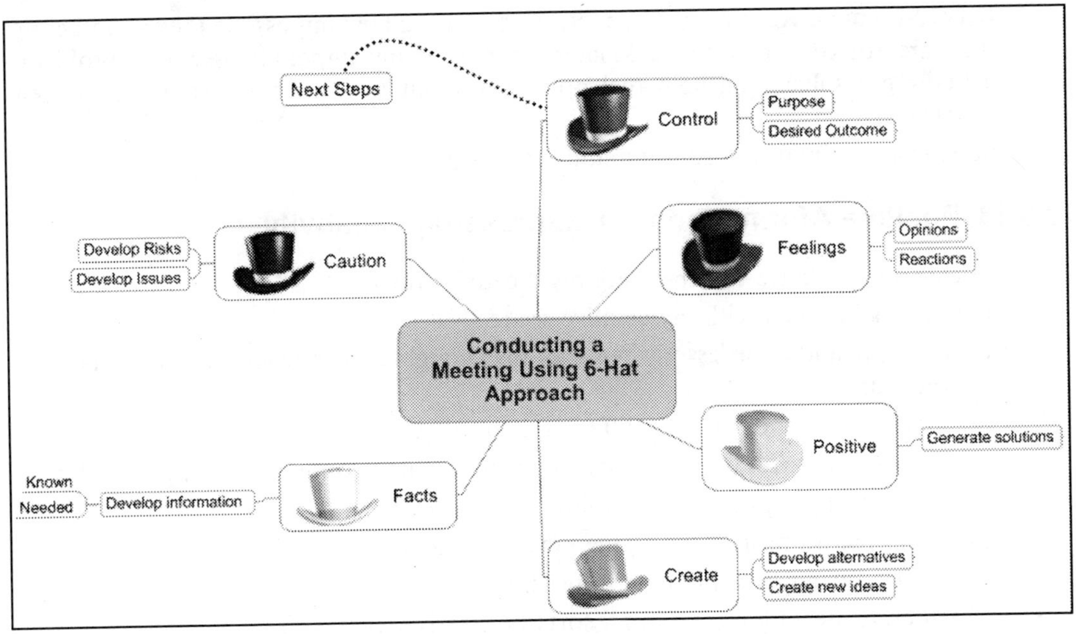

Figure 13.2

5. State the problem in much more vague, broad terms; or state it in much more specific, precise terms.
6. Physical methods: Get plenty of sleep. Consume brain-enhancing nutrients such as plenty of vitamin C. Get some exercise, and have a snack just before your thinking session so you have adequate blood sugar levels.
7. Think about the problem just before going to sleep. Tell yourself you are going to dream about a solution to the problem. Put a pen and paper next to the bed so you can write down your dreams.
8. Use your best time of day ... morning, perhaps ... for creative thinking.
9. Visual images: purposely think in visual images. Practice making images of the things related to the problem appear clearly and in detail in your mind. Manipulate the images.
10. Put pictures and objects around where you will see them, things that relate somehow to the problem.
11. Change track earlier than a blockage. For example, suppose you have been thinking over and over again, "A, therefore B, therefore C, therefore D, therefore E, and then where can I go from there?" There is a blockage at E: you have not been able to progress from there. Well, take a different crossroad of thought earlier on. Rather than searching for a route from E, search for a different route from, say C, and follow it. C, therefore X, therefore Y ...."
12. Imagine an alternate universe. Assume something that's false, that will make the problem easier to solve. Solve the problem in that universe, then see if the solution can be modified to work in this universe.
13. Broaden the perspective. Ask why the problem exists at all, and redefine the problem as the organization of the universe in such a way that problem exists.

14. Record-keeping. Keep a list of problems, recording how impossible they seem before they are solved. Looking back later on how many impossible-seeming problems actually got solved can help fuel optimism about the search for solutions to new problems.
15. Start from an imagined solution and work backwards.

13.3.13 Positive Affirmations for Expressing Creativity

- I release all resistance to expressing my creativity fully.
- I am always in touch with my creative source.
- I create easily and effortlessly when I let my thoughts come from the loving space of my own heart.
- I do something new or at least different–every day.
- There is ample time and opportunity for creative expression in whatever area I choose.
- My family totally supports me in fulfilling my dreams.
- All of my creative projects bring me great satisfaction.
- I know that I can create miracles in my life.
- I feel good expressing myself in all sorts of creative ways.
- I am my own unique self: special, creative, and wonderful.
- I direct my creative talents toward music, art, dance, writing–anything that gives my pleasure.
- The key to creativity is knowing that my thinking creates my experience. I use this key in every area of my life.
- I am a clear thinker, and I express myself with ease.
- I am learning to be more creative every day.
- My job allows me to express my talents and abilities, and I rejoice in this employment.
- I am discovering talents I did not know I had.
- My potential is unlimited.
- My innate creativity surprises and delights me.
- I am safe, and I am fulfilled in all that I do.
- My talents are in demand, and my unique gifts are appreciated by those around me.
- My heart is the centre of my power. I follow my heart.
- I am a joyous, creative expression of life.
- Ideas come to me easily and effortlessly.

13.4 MIND MAPPING

Mind mapping is a graphic technique for representing ideas and concepts on a particular topic. It is a visual thinking tool that helps structuring information, helping you to better analyze, comprehend, synthesize, recall and generate new ideas. Mind mapping is also used as an aid in study, organization, problem solving, decision-making, and writing.

In mind mapping information is structured in a way that resembles much more closely how your brain actually works. Here, in a mind map ideas move out from the centre to the fringes, branching out and associating with a network of other ideas. Every idea leads to a spray of associated ideas. Each of these again becomes the source of another spray of associations. This is a method primarily developed by Tony Buzan. He created the mind map concept in the early seventies. His inquiry began from basic questions like:

- How does one learn?
- What is the nature of thinking?
- What are the techniques of memorizing?
- What are the techniques of creative thinking?
- How can one read faster and more efficiently?

Based on his brilliant observation that our brains do not process information in a linear way, in mind mapping information is structured in a way that resembles much more closely how your brain actually works. Since it is an activity that is both analytical and artistic, it engages your brain in a much, much richer way, helping in all its cognitive functions.

13.4.1 How the Human Brain Works

Mind mapping originates from research into the human brain which shows that brain cells have a central body, its nucleus, with lots of branches and tentacles radiating from it. Thus the structure of human brain looks almost like an octopus. The branches and tentacles, called 'dendrites' carry information that is transmitted as electrical energy from one cell to another. At the end of the branches, we have synaptic buttons that contain the chemicals which are the message carriers in the human thinking process. It is made up of branches and tentacles called dendrites. Along the length of dendrites, we have synaptic buttons that contain the chemicals which are the message carriers in the human thinking process. Every synaptic button of a brain cell links with the buttons of other brain cells when electrical impulses travel through the liquid-filled space called the synaptic gap. This mechanism enables the cascading of bio chemical information across the brain, from one cell to the other. A small brain cell can receive impulses from thousands of connecting points every second, like a vast sophisticated telephone exchange and redirect it along the appropriate path.

Understood this way, successful thinking can be seen as an efficient system of networks. The pathways that are formed create a memory map; the greater the number of pathways, the more efficient thinking becomes. Every time you think a thought, the biochemical resistance along the way that carries the thought is reduced. The more you think a particular thought, therefore, the easier it is for the brain to think the thought. A pattern is thus created and the brain repeats the pattern. Learning put in the form of a familiar pattern, hence, is much more easily remembered and assimilated.

13.4.2 Brain Capacity

Psychologists now estimate that most people use less than one per cent of brain's potential. The brains potential is estimated by the number of connections it can make with 10–15 billion nerve cells, each one capable of making thousands of contacts. Recent researches estimate that our brain has about 30 billion numbers of nerves and the area of the brain is about 2,200 square centimetres. This gives us some idea of the cost capacity of the brain and its potential for learning if properly used.

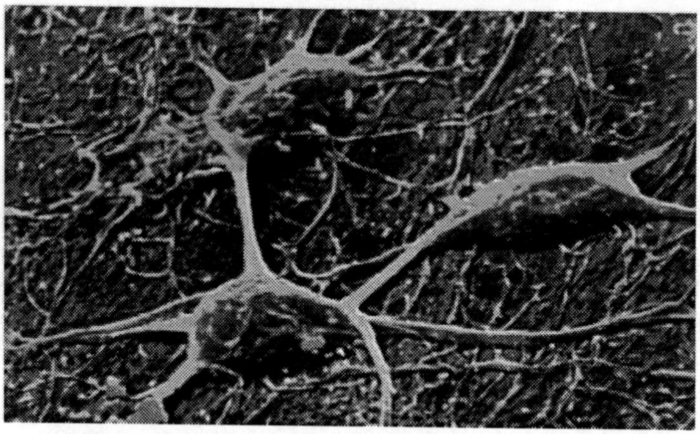

Figure 13.3: A scanning electron micrograph of three neurons in the human brain showing how associations are made.

13.4.3 Brain Hemispheres

Early left/right brain research was mainly conducted by Roger Sperry on split-brain humans in 1981. Briefly, 5-6 humans have their corpus callosums surgically cut to control severe epilepsy. Based on this and other research, many psychologists believe that the brain's hemisphere specialize in different areas. On left is the logic side, dealing with language, problem solving, convergent thinking, computer programming, and so on. The right is the artistic side, dealing with creativity, imagination, divergent thinking, face recognition, and so on. Although the brain is bifunctional and writing is considered a left-brain skill, it is now known the cooperation of both hemispheres. The most productive and creative intellectual functioning occurs when both are talking to each other. However, the research has found that the left hemisphere is automatically larger than the right hemisphere and is more active than the right in most adults.

13.4.4 The Brain Expands with Use

The brain is the only organ that expands through use. The more it is used, the more memory associations are formed, the more associations are formed, the easier it is to remember previously acquired information, and also to form new associations. Mind mapping use both sides of the brain. The words and logic of mind mapping call on left-brain skills whereas their radiant, non-linear format, with designs, pictures, symbols and colours call on right-brain skills. So by drawing mind mapping, you integrate both sides of your brain.

13.4.5 The Brain and Gestalt

As the brain creates and recreates patterns, it always tends to look for patterns and completion. If we see five pieces of wood lying close to one another, our brain will invariable perceive a pattern and make a complete picture of the disjoined wood pieces. Similarly, we perceive patterns in floating clouds and when someone leave a story incomplete, our mind completes it and produces a well-designed whole. This is otherwise called the brain's capacity to perceive in 'patterns'. This put very simply, is the mind's potential for gestalt.

13.4.6 Radiant Thinking

We have seen that our brain works through association. Often a smell, a taste or a sight acts as a triggering factor and starts a chain of associations and connections. Every stimulus entering the brain is like a central sphere that radiates millions of hooks that have other associations connects with them. The number of associations already made is stored in the data-processing system of the brain. But there is always scope for infinite more associations.

The brain thinking power can be thought of as a gigantic, branching, association-making machine, with line radiating from infinite number of data nodes. This, in short, is the concept of radiant thinking–the inherent process of the brain's functioning where thoughts move or radiate from one or many given centres and proceed from one association to the next.

Mind mapping is the external manifestation of this internal process. It radiates or branches out from a centre and each point in turn becomes a sub-centre of association. This can proceed infinitely, branching away from or towards a common centre.

Role of Images and Colours in Remembering

- A lot of learning material is prepared using the following devices:

1. Linear patterning	Matter put in straight lines, chronological hierarchical sequence
2. Symbols	Primarily letters, words, numbers
3. Analysis	Includes logical deduction, argumentative reasoning and point-by-point analysis

- What we find generally missing in all this is:

1. Variation of visual and aural patterns
2. Use of multiple colours
3. Use of images and other associations

When presenting material, people often make it monotonous with similar looking lists and lines. It rarely triggers the brain's creativity or aids association or memory.

Simple techniques sometimes make learning and remembering much easier and pleasurable. Colour variation aids memory and remembering much easier and highlights important points. Sometimes, different colour backgrounds are used to show the different aspects of the material being presented. Primarily, this helps the brain make and retain associations and note variations.

Experiments have shown that the brain's capacity to store images is infinite. Any material linked to images thus has more chance of being retained. Naturally, it reduces the brain's resistance to learning and creates a pattern for the brain to rely on. Difficult words are thus better learnt if they can be broken down and each part is associated with an image. It has also been seen that children categorized as having low IQ learn better with images. This can go on to prove that most of our learning methods as well as IQ tests rely on only one kind of learning, i.e. learning through words, numbers and logic. In all this the fact that finally emerges is that imagination, pictures, colours, rhythm, and images are as important learning tools as words and numbers are.

13.4.7 Mind Mapping and the Learning Process

Mind mapping is a tool that helps learning process closely imitates the way the brain works. It operates from various nodal points, branching out to multiple associations which, in turn, branch out again to more associations.

Mind mapping is an extremely powerful technique that can synthesize the various capacities of the brain and powerfully harmonize it to form a coherent whole. The spray of associations can radiate from various centres, and each goes on to become a centre of another spray of associations. The associations can be documented through images, words, varied colours, and even line of varying thickness.

There is another advantage the mind mapping technique has over the other. If you have forgotten a point or feel that there is more that can be added, just have blanks. Your brain's natural tendency to fill up gaps will eventually supply the missing point.

13.4.8 Mind Mapping and Genius

Buzan, the inventor of mind maps, claims that it enhances creativity. To support his claim he draws on the work of past geniuses, whose notebooks display the characteristics of mind maps such as non-linearity and images. For example, Leonardo da Vinci was as much scientist as artist, an engineer and architect, as well as sculptor and painter. Einstein, as well as being the most famous scientist, was also an accomplished violinist and painter. He thus had both scientific and artistic skills. The use of images and drawings by the great geniuses would seem to support the idea of the value of using the non-linear, spatial approach and visualization images, codes and symbols, in conjunction with words in mind mapping.

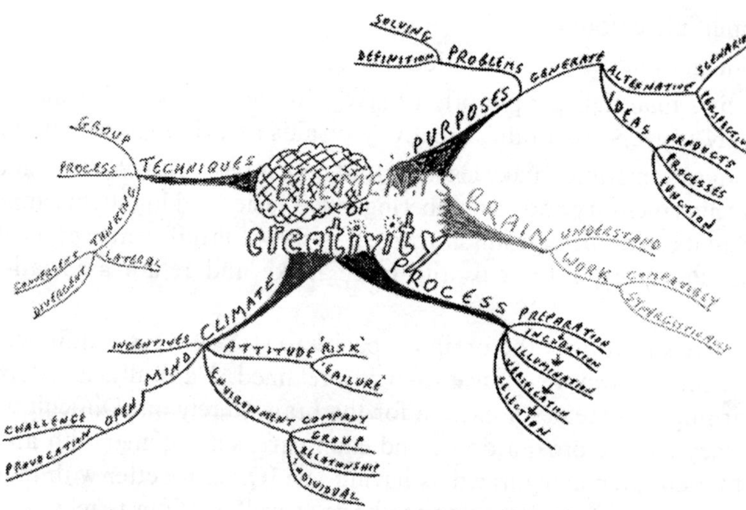

Figure 13.4: Mind map of the concept 'Creativity.'

13.4.9 Some Guiding Principles in Mind Mapping

- Begin from the centre. Put main idea in the centre.
- Use images wherever possible.

Figure 13.5: Mind map of the word 'Question.'

Figure 13.6: Mind map of the concept 'Happiness.'

- Keep the topics labels as short as possible, keeping them to a single word, or to only a picture.
- Use colours to separate one level of mental association from the other (break boundaries).
- Increase the line width to show main points and sub-points.
- Underline, highlight, encircle, or use any other means to highlight.
- Use arrow or dotted lines when you want to make connections across the branches.
- Use one keyword per line.
- Always ensure that the line length is equal to the word length. Write the keywords on lines.
- Use codes like ticks, crosses, circles to show the association between one word and another, however, distantly situated.
- Think fast. Draw quickly on unlined paper without pausing, judging or editing.

13.4.10 Mind Mapping–Don'ts

- Don't dismiss any idea even if it is irrelevant. Noting down somewhere will help the brain relax and proceed.
- Don't stop very often to think. If nothing occurs, keep making empty lines. Your brain's capacity for gestalt will fill it up later.
- Don't try very hard to organize when you are mapping, note down all the ideas first; organization can come later.

Advantages of mind mapping

- Mind maps work the way the brain works–which is not in nice neat lines.
- Memory is naturally associative, not linear. Any idea probably has thousands of links in your mind Mind maps allow associations and links to be recorded and reinforced.
- The mind remembers keywords and images, not sentences, allowing a lot more information to be put on a page.
- Because mind maps are more visual and depict associations between keywords, they are much easier to recall than linear notes.
- Starting from the centre of the page rather than top-left corner allows you to work out in all directions.
- The organization of a mind map reflects the way your own brain organizes ideas.
- Mind maps are easy to review. Regular review reinforces memory.
- We remember what stands out. Visual quality of mind maps allows you to make key points to stand out easily.

Uses of mind mapping

- **Notes:** Whenever information is being taken in, mind maps help organize it into a form that is easily assimilated by the brain and easily remembered. They can be used for noting anything—books, lectures, meetings, interviews, phone conversations.
- **Recall.** Whenever information is being retrieved from memory, mind maps allow ideas to be quickly noted as they occur, in an organized manner. There's no need to form

sentences and write them out in full. They serve as quick and efficient means of review and so keep recall at a high level.

- **Creativity.** Whenever you want to encourage creativity, mind maps liberate the mind from linear thinking, allowing new ideas to flow more rapidly.
- **Problem solving.** Mind maps help in confronting by a problem–professional or personal–see all the issues and how they relate to each other. They also help others quickly get an overview of how you see different aspects of the situation, and their relative importance.
- **Planning.** Mind maps help you get all the relevant information down in one place and organize it easily. They can be used for planning any piece of writing from a letter to a screenplay to a book or for planning a meeting, a day or a vacation.
- **Presentations.** Mind maps help you presenting information in a format that shows the overall structure of your subject.

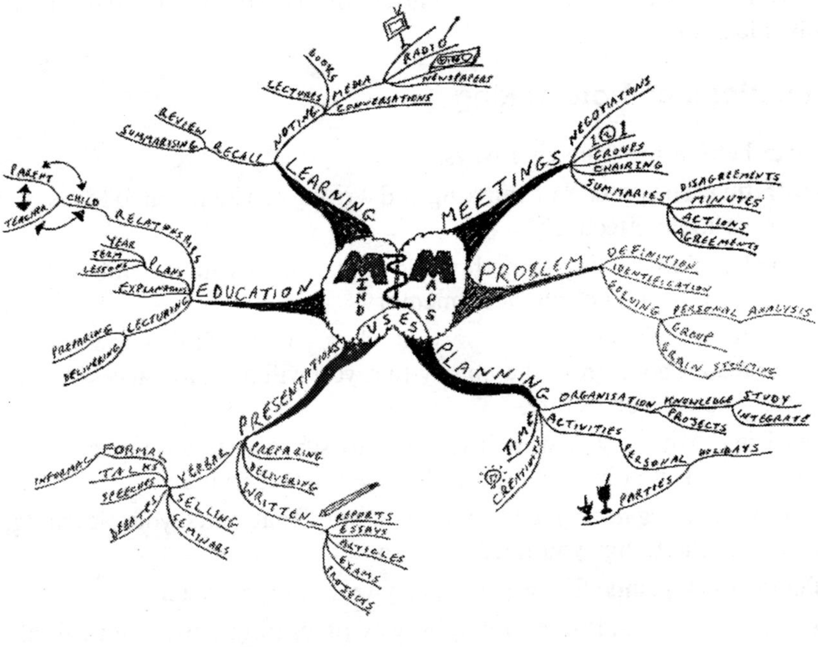

Figure 13.7: Uses of Mind Mapping.

13.4.11 Creativity and Mind Mapping

Mind mapping helps us pull information together in such a way that it exchanges making new connections. It concentrates our thoughts quickly into the insight stage of creativity. The structure of mind mapping helps to generate new ideas, integrate information and provide synthesis, links, combinations, relationships and associations between ideas. Surveys of critical thinking have emphasized the importance of encouraging initial right-brain visualization, an intuitive solution, which can then be evaluated logically by the left brain. Visual images appear to be a main communication medium of the right brain. Therefore, if the essence of a problem can be shown visually, as through mind mapping the creative capacities of the right brain can be more accessed in problem solving.

13.4.12 Note Taking and Mind Mapping

Note taking is the process of receiving other people's ideas from speeches or books and organizing them into a structure that reflects their thoughts. As a means of note taking mind mapping is a useful technique that improves the way you take notes. By using mind maps, you can quickly identify and understand the structure of a subject, and the way that pieces of information fit together, as well as recording the raw facts contained in normal notes. You can place each new idea in the right place, regardless of the order of presentations.

A good mind map shows the 'shape' of the subject, the relative importance of individual points, and the way in which facts relate to one another. Mind maps are more compact than conventional notes, often taking up one side of paper. This helps you to make associations easily. And if you find out more information after you have drawn the main mind map, then you can easily add it in.

13.4.13 Functions of Note Taking

Note taking can help in the following ways:

1. **Concentrating:** The process of thinking and writing can help you to focus your attention and so learn more effectively.
2. **Remembering:** Just writing something down can help you remember it, and you can also refer back to it to check your memory.
3. **Keeping a record:** This may be important when you are shown how to do something, when you read a book from the library that you will not have access to later, or when you listen to a talk or lecture.
4. **Summarizing:** You may wish to use notes to summarize a chapter in a book or to note down the key points of a procedure, you are learning
5. **Reordering or reorganizing material:** In a way that suits your learning, or which separates out the things you need to learn.
6. **Highlighting key points:** So you can easily refer to them later.
7. **Planning:** You may find notes a helpful way of putting down your initial ideas when you are planning an assignment, essay, report or presentation.

13.4.14 Mind Mapping for Essays

An essay is a kind of note making exercise where you have to first identify the essential topics of concern and then explore the related elements. Mind maps can help you in the early stages of your essay by summarizing your research and providing you with a picture of all aspects of the question. You can then move from your non-linear mind map to a more structured essay plan.

- Begin your mind mapping with a central image or an idea representing the essay.
- Decide the basic ordering of the ideas into divisions and subdivisions.
- Allow your mind to move freely, documenting all the ideas that come. Keep in mind the basic ordering principles and the levels to which the ideas belong. At this stage, you will need to be analytical, decide the hierarchy and the arrangement of ideas.
- Use different colours to show the different hierarchical structures. Use different thickness of lines for different levels. Use codes or symbols if you want certain points to be linked in the writing, draw arrows to show the flow. Move back and forth from one point to the other.
- If you face any problem in making associations or if you have a 'block', leave blank lines and continue working. Your brains natural capacity to form a whole will give you material and ideas to fill the gaps.
- Review the map for any other information and missing links.
- Begin the writing of the first draft of the essay. A well-ordered mind map would give you an ordered structure of the main and sub-points. Study the links, consider the points, and proceed with the main and sub-points.
- At the end, review the essay again, along analyzing the mind map. Give the finishing touches and ensure that you have sign-posted the different points well. Check your use of linkers and for general coherence.
- Reconsider your conclusion; review, modify, and expand it if necessary.

13.4.15 Mind Mapping for Summarizing Reading

There are five steps in creating mind maps which summarize your readings

1. **Skim:** Firstly, read the abstract, introduction , conclusion, key headings or chapter headings. When skimming through the text observe any diagrams, pictures or graphs. This gives you an overview of what you are about to read, puts it in context and may already give you some clues as to where the most relevant parts are located.
2. **Read:** Read the article in one sitting (or chunk it into sections/chapters if it is a whole book) and go over any parts you are not quite sure of.
3. **Mind map:** It is important to do the mind map from memory at this stage so don't consult the article or any other source of information.
4. **Study:** The mind map you have just done is very valuable as it will show both areas you have understood and also areas you are not sure of. Study your mind map to discover the gaps in your knowledge and refer back to the source material to fill in any of these gaps.
5. **Personalize:** Using different colours or symbols, add your own comments and questions to the mind map. Questions relating to relationships, implications, alternative approaches, usefulness, clarity, personal experience could all be considered at this stage. It is in this personalizing stage where your mind map really starts to help you with your learning. The trick now is to address all those questions you have raised and to keep returning to your mind map with the answers!

13.4.16 Mind Mapping for Lectures, Seminars, Workshops and Tutorials

1. **Adds structure:** All of these teaching strategies can be open-ended and free-flowing. Mind mapping can help you record information in a structure that suits your learning style and means something to you. The content may be coming at you thick and fast but a mind map allows you to put information where you want it and make the necessary connections.
2. **Helps review:** The open space of a mind map can allow you to revisit it in that first vital review after the session. It is in this first review that you can highlight key areas, gaps in your understanding and list questions that need to be addressed. Some students find it hard to consult a mind map during a lecture so they take standard notes in the lecture but construct a mind map afterwards in their first review of the lecture notes.
3. **Suits repeated reviews:** By continually returning to your mind maps of these sessions you can use the empty space to add new information and to expand on your understanding of the work covered in the session.
4. **Better recall:** By having all of the information covered in a session incorporated into a single mind map, many students find this an aid to them remembering what was covered.
5. **Prompts questions:** Your mind map should raise some questions about the information you have received. These questions will need to be followed up on so it is important to develop your own set of symbols which will prompt further action by you.
6. **Helps exam preparation:** Imagine how useful it would be if you had a set of mind maps for each of your lectures! These mind maps would show you the areas where you had difficulty and include the follow-up information you added in order to clear these problems up. You would also be able to construct a mind map of the entire subject prior to the exam and this would help you identify the key themes and likely exam questions.

13.4.17 Mind Mapping for Report Writing and Proposal Writing

A mind map lets you rapidly produce an almost infinite number of ideas, and at the same time organize them by placing each idea next to what it is related to. This makes a very powerful tool for report writing, where it is very important to get down all your ideas first. It is then a trivial matter to read the mind map and write a sentence or paragraph on each 'keyword'.

13.4.18 Mind Mapping for Self-Analysis

Most of us, in our daily lives, face the same problem—of taking a decision or finding a solution. Very often we stand at cross roads, confused over which career to chose, what decision to take, and so on. Using mind maps at such times can be of immense help. It can give you a better insight into yourself, your needs, desires, and aims. It can also show you how you can analyze yourself.

People from all walks of life, for example, Leonardo da Vinci, Isaac Newton, Albert Einstein, Thomas Edison, Beethoven, James Joyce, Vincent van Gogh, Mark Twain— all used mind mapping to express themselves in ways that reflect the full range of their mental skills.

13.5 BRAINSTORMING

Brainstorming, as we all know is a very crucial part of any organization. Brainstorming has been used in business in work simplification and cost reduction programmes and has achieved significant savings. Quality circle is a modern application of the idea. From advertising to IT, from computer setting to public relations, brainstorming has and always will be a fundamental process.

We can describe brainstorming as an activity that is done to make a mind map. It is also used as a technique in itself. Brainstorming is primarily an idea generating technique pioneered by Alex F. Osborn, an advertising executive, in the late 1930s. According to Osborn, brainstorming is "a conference technique by which a group attempts to find a solution for a specific problem by amassing all the ideas spontaneously by its members"

This technique could be applied individually but it should be better applied in group.

13.5.1 Individual Brainstorming

It generates a wider spectrum of ideas than the group's session, but with less efficiency, because often individuals try to give thought to problems that they won't be able to solve. On the other hand, individual could explore ideas in a better way, without being worried about wasting time or being criticized by someone else and, of course, without being dominated by the other members of the group.

13.5.2 Group Brainstorming

Brainstorming is generally done in a group. The normal view of brainstorming is where a group of people sit in a room and shout out ideas as they occur to them. They are told to lose their inhibitions and that no ideas will be judged so that people are free to shout out any ideas at all without feeling uncomfortable. People should build on the ideas called out by other participants. The purpose of this is to gain as many ideas as possible for later analysis. Out of the many ideas suggested there will be some of great value. Because of the free-thinking environment, the session will help promote radical new ideas which break free from normal ways of thinking.

Thus, a brainstorming session can be especially productive if the group is introduced to a few new problem-solving techniques. With a few good techniques, a good leader, and a mix of backgrounds and personalities any group can come up with dozens of new ideas. In addition to, brainstorming in a group may also provide benefits, such as boosting morale, enhancing work enjoyment, and improving teamwork.

13.5.3 Combining Individual and Group Brainstorming

Individual and group brainstorming could be combined together. For example, someone defines the problem individually and leaves the group free to find several superficial solution, if possible. Then, these solutions could be improved at individual level by specialists of each topic.

13.5.4 Rules of Brainstorming

There are five basic rules of brainstorming. These rules are intended to reduce social inhibitions among group members, stimulate idea generation, and increase overall creativity in a group.

1. **Focus on large quantities of ideas:** The more ideas we have the better. The assumption is that the greater the number of ideas generated, the greater the chance of producing a radical and effective solution.
2. **Welcome unusual idea:** To get a long list of ideas, all crazy ideas are welcome. This new way of thinking may provide better solutions.
3. **No criticism of ideas:** There should be no criticism or evaluation of one another's ideas. Participants should focus on extending or adding to ideas. In this way, participants will feel to generate unusual ideas.
4. **Every person and every idea has equal worth:** Every person has a valid viewpoint and a unique perspective on the situation and solution. Each idea presented belongs to the group, not to the person who said it. It is the group's responsibility and an indication of its ability to brainstorm if all participants feel able to contribute freely and confidently.

13.5.5 Running the Session Itself

1. During brainstorming, the group leader or the facilitator presents the problem, making it as specific, clear, and as tangible as possible. It is very important to ensure that the objective of the brainstorming session be clear all the members of the group. The people attending brainstorming sessions should come from different disciplines, with a wide spectrum of experience, so as to obtain more creative ideas from the session.

There are three methods of brainstorming:

1. **Freewheel brainstorming:** Here the group members give their ideas spontaneously and the facilitator or scribe simply records the ideas as they are suggested.
2. **Round-robin brainstorming:** In this style of brainstorming, the facilitator or scribe asks each member in turn for ideas. The members either may give an idea or pass their turn. The session continues until all members have 'passed' their turn during the round.
3. **The slip method:** This method differs markedly from the other two approaches. The facilitator asks members to write down their ideas on slips of paper or index card. The ideas are then collected, organized, and presented to the group.

Each approach has its advantages and disadvantages. Whatever is the approach, in the end of the session the output of the brainstorming session is reviewed and evaluated.

- **Post-Session Work and Idea Analysis**

  The facilitator first refers to each item on the list and make sure its meaning is clear. Then he tries to combine it with other items with the same meaning. Each cluster of items is brought together under a single title. Finally, there are a few large chunks of associated ideas and the group has to choose and decide their priorities among them.

This again is done in two ways: straight voting and dot voting. Straight voting is the method where the leader directly takes up each cluster of items and asks how many people have it at the top of their list. This way the cluster is found for which the maximum numbers of people have opted. Dot voting is where each member is given a certain number of small sticky dots to put up next to their choices on the organized list. This also ultimately shows the ideas for which the maximum numbers of people have voted.

13.5.6 How to make Brainstorming Effective?

To make brainstorming effective, we have taken care of the following factors:

- Use highly visual tools–meaningful colours and shapes–to organize and present ideas.
- Build and reinforce positive cooperative group behaviour.
- Generate interest, and stimulate interactivity.
- **Have a good leader.** A good leader will stop any criticisms, arguments, and even strong opinions, at least in the first part of the session. A brainstorming session needs to be spontaneous, open and uncritical. "Bad" or "silly" ideas can lead to helpful ones, so suggestions have to be left unjudged at first. Otherwise, you stifle the creative process. The leader's job, then, is to make everyone feel free to suggest any ideas.

Benefits of brainstorming

Brainstorming has numerous benefits to both you and your organization. You can profit from it by improving the products and services you provide and you can benefit your personal career by being the originator of good ideas and solutions to existing problems. Obviously, if the company's profits and market share increase because of you then you will get salary increases and will be promoted quicker than people who do not contribute in such a positive way.

If you are a manager of a group, then it is in your interest to promote better creativity and cooperation within your group and you will not only be praised for your successes by your own manager, but also your subordinates will like you all the better. A group which can operate in a more participatory way and which has the opportunity to put its ideas forward is a happier and more successful group. A better environment can be obtained just by holding regular brainstorming sessions because the freedom of thought in these sessions percolates to the normal working environment.

Limitations of a brainstorming session

Besides positive aspects there are also some limitations of the brainstorming technique that must be taken into consideration. As observed by Osborn, sometimes brainstorming sessions do not produce results as expected, fundamentally for two main reasons:

1. Faulty operation: Lack of adhesion with procedures based on experience
2. Overrated expectation: Sometimes people forget that miracles do not happen that often.

Brainstorming, however, is an important method of generating topics and ideas. It focuses on associative thought, jumping from one idea to another until you can come up with a good idea, a feasible solution, points for reports or other written work. It encourages creativity and free flow of ideas by stimulating the association form of thinking that can be very productive for producing topics for papers and reports, etc. Whether it is individual brainstorming or doing it in a group, it is an effective means of bringing out your creative flow.

13.5.7 Good Brainstorming: An Example

A company needs to cut delivery costs. The brainstorming participants start to suggest ideas and solutions. "Let's not deliver," one suggests, and when another criticizes this, he is reminded of the rules. "Negotiate lower shipping rates," is suggested, "Or just find a company with lower rates," another adds. Reducing package weight and charging customers more are suggested, and lead to other ideas. The leader keeps it simple, take notes, and eventually calls a halt to this free-for-all part of the session. Now it's time to further develop the ideas for whatever usefulness they may have. To keep the creativity flowing, the leader has participants defend or develop ideas that are not their own. This brings new insight to the ideas, and prevents the problem of people getting "stuck in a rut" with their own ideas. For example, he asks the man who criticized the idea of not delivering to work with that idea. "We have to deliver," he starts with, but then he thinks about it and says, "We could deliver in bulk to central distribution points instead of to the individual customers. The customers could pick up their orders there. I suppose that might save us money on shipping." Someone suggests that the customers may like the arrangement. They could return the product immediately if they were dissatisfied, with no need to pack and ship it. (It worked for Sears for years.) The leader assigns a couple people to look into it, and moves on to the other ideas. Good leadership keeps the whole process working. In the last example, a "bad" idea was used to come to a possible solution. That's good brainstorming.

REVIEW QUESTIONS

1. What do you mean by a problem? What types of problem can you face in an organization? Why is it said to be an opportunity for improvement?
2. Briefly explain alternative approaches to problem solving.
3. Define creativity. Explain briefly the factors that block creativity.
4. Describe why creativity is an integral part in many situations of business life. Describe how creativity manifests itself in many ways.
5. Can creativity be learned? How do you develop your creativity? Does it happen automatically, or is there a way whereby one can make it happen?
6. Describe five stages of creativity.
7. In what ways does creativity differ from innovation?

8. Do you agree with the statement that teams provide a golden opportunity to develop creativity? If yes, justify your viewpoint.
9. Discuss Edward De Bono's problem solving techniques for improving the creativity process.
10. Describe the guiding principles of mind mapping. What are the its various uses?
11. What are the benefits of brainstorming technique to an organization? Also describe some of its limitations.
12. What do you mean by brainstorming technique? Clarify whether it is better to be applied individually or in group? What are the factors that make brainstorming effective?
13. What do you mean by mind mapping? How does the human brain function? What operation does each hemisphere specialize in? What hemisphere is the 'seat of creativity'?
14. Explain the ten positive affirmations that improve creativity.
15. Why are creativity and innovation so important to the survival and success of a business?

14

BUSINESS CORRESPONDENCE

Chapter Objectives

This chapter will enable you to understand:

- Importance of an effective business letter
- Functions of a business letter
- Types of business letters
  - According to the function
  - On the basis of approach
  - Demi-official/form letters
- Essential characteristics of a business letter
- The layout of a business letter
- Planning the business letter
- Elements of a business letter
- Some practical examples of business letters

14.1 BUSINESS LETTER

The term 'correspondence' means 'communication in the form of letters'. The letters are written in order to send a message from a person to another. Letter writing is an art of conveying the required message. That means this particular skill can be developed through training.

Every businessman, whether big or small, has to maintain contacts with its suppliers, customers, prospects, government departments, and the like. When the letters are written on behalf of an organization to another organization and individuals to transact a business, such letters are called as business letters. Business correspondence includes all kinds of letters that may be written in conducting business transactions. As the name suggests, technical jobs deal as much in letter writing as in technical matters. A formal business letter follows a form and pattern that need to be learnt by anyone who aspires to be a smart letter writer. In this chapter, we shall take up only formal letters.

14.1.1 Importance of an Effective Business Letter

A good business letter is the backbone of a successful business house. Through correspondence, a businessman tries to open up and maintain business relations. He has to exchange information of varied types with different parties. Letters are the only channel, which facilitate a constant touch with the other business world. Men, who have never met, nor even likely to meet, can maintain close business relations with one another. A letter is the cheapest and the most common device for contacting parties. Easy and effective communication or information is possible through letters. It is only due to letter writing that a businessman can find markets easily all over the world. A written letter can carry assurance of transactions, confirmation of dealings and is a reliable record for further reference. To create the best relation, therefore, letters should be written in a clear and understanding way.

Of course, there exist other means of communication, like telephone, telex, telegraph, etc. Telephonic message is also widely used in business, but the message communicated through this media cannot be kept in memory for long. Besides, this media is quite expensive.

14.1.2 Functions of a Business Letter

1. **Record and references:** Written letter enjoys a distinct advantage over other means of communication. Written communication can be passed on to the concerned persons or departments as it is. They can be preserved for future references, as references are quite frequent in business communication.
2. **Making a lasting impression:** A letter makes a lasting impression on the reader's mind because it stays with him, goes with him and does its work effectively every time it is read.
3. **Widening the approach:** It is very difficult to send representatives to all places of its business connections by an organization. It is the letter that reaches any place at whatever distance. A letter finds easy access to one and all. Thus, a business letter helps widen the area of operation.
4. **An authoritative proof:** A letter, signed by a responsible person, is an authoritative proof of what is said in it. It can be treated as a legal document.
5. **Building goodwill:** A business letter aims at building goodwill in customer-company relationship, holding present customers to buy more and varied products.

Thus, business letters represent the firm just as much as the personality of the firm's salesman and the quality of its goods or services.

14.1.3 Purposes of a Business Letter

A major part of the success in business depends upon good correspondence. A businessman has to exchange information of varied types with different parties. A good and impressive letter promotes the business. An indecent and improperly worded letter may annoy the customer and ruin the business prospects. The purpose of every letter is to convert the reader into a customer. To be effective, it should catch the attention of the reader, excite his interest, and encourage him to buy the goods or services offered. Some of the purposes for which a business letter is written are as follows:

- Making and answering an enquiry.
- Placing an order for goods
- Acknowledging and executing orders
- Giving instructions
- Demanding and refusing credits
- Selling goods and services
- Making, accepting or responding to complaints
- Inviting quotations
- Placing order for products
- Making and collecting payments
- Seeking and giving information, etc.

14.1.4 Types of Business Letters

The business letters are written for various purposes in various contexts. Some important ramifications of the business letters are:

14.1.4.1 According to the Function

1. Enquiries and replies, quotations, orders and their execution, credit and status enquiries, complaints and adjustments, and collection letters, etc.
2. Circular letters and sales letters
3. Bank correspondence, insurance correspondence, import-export correspondence, agency correspondence
4. Job application letters, interview letters, references, testimonials, letters of appointment, confirmation, promotion, retrenchment, resignation
5. The correspondence of a company secretary, correspondence with State and Central government
6. Letters to the press

14.1.4.2 On the Basis of Approach

- Direct approach
- Indirect approach
- Persuasive approach

The kind of approach depends upon our assumptions about the reader's reaction to our letter.

Direct approach (Active voice)

It is generally seen that a reader immediately welcomes a 'good news' letter. In communicating good news, therefore, we can come directly to the point without wasting time in introductory remarks or lengthy explanations. This direct approach is suitable for:

- congratulating somebody
- making a request

- demanding information
- conveying good news
- enquiries, quotations, placing orders, etc.

Examples:

– "We are pleased to offer you the position of......"

– "With reference to your enquiry of...."

The indirect approach (Passive voice)

The indirect approach, on the other hand, has something in it that, we would not like to convey without some explanation, introduction or buffer statement. To convey something unpleasant we have to prepare the reader to receive the message as he is likely to resist or react negatively to it.

Such an approach is generally thought to be suitable for letter of:

- rejection of a request
- bad or unexpected news
- denial of a facility
- cancellation of an order etc.

Examples:

– "Thank you very much for your interest in buying our product. We really wish we had been able to dispatch it to you at once, but we are sorry to inform you that......"

Persuasive approach

Persuasive approach letters carry neither good news nor bad news but lie somewhere in between. This approach is generally found to be suitable for sales letters in which the writer persuades the reader to act, i.e., buy the product or avail himself of the service, we are offering him.

Examples:

– "Would you be interested in buying the...."

14.1.4.3 Official Letters, D.O.'S (Demi-Official Letters), Form Letters and Internal Letters

1. **Official letters:** Official letters are written to government or semi-government departments/ offices/bodies.
2. **Demi-official letters (D.O.'s):** Demi-official or D.O. letters are essentially official in purpose but are addressed to an official by name and not just sent to him by designation. D.O. letters may be written if
   - the matter requires personal attention of the addressee.
   - the matter is of confidential nature.
   - the matter is urgent and requires immediate disposal.
3. **Form letters:** Form letters are used for correspondence of routine nature. They are used in case of acknowledgements, reminders, interviews, notices, appointments, etc. They have a standard form with some blanks left in them. Form letters lack personal touch but they save the establishment a lot of time and labour.

4. **Internal letters:** Internal letters or memos are written to the people within an organization in the form of memorandum. These letters are used both in government offices and business houses for internal communication.

Every business letter is an ambassador of goodwill

Whatever be the purpose, every letter is an ambassador of goodwill. It gives the receiver a sensation of an actual meeting with the addressee, as it is customary to start writing a letter with salutation and to end the letter with a complimentary close, which is a sort of courteous leave taking.

A letter represents the work culture of an organization. In fact, in writing a letter one performs following functions:

- Achieves the specific purpose of one's organization.
- Creates a friendly relationship with other organization.

A major part of the success in business depends upon good correspondence. Through correspondence, a businessman tries to open up and maintain business relations. He has to exchange information of varied types with different parties. A good and impressive letter promotes the business by retaining the old customers and inviting the new ones. It will increase sales. An indecent and improperly worded letter may annoy the customer and ruin the business completely. A written letter can carry assurance of transactions, confirmation of dealings and is a reliable record for further references. In the world of competition an effective correspondence is a must.

Thus, a letter is that form of professional writing which vividly reflects the personality of an individual as well as organization.

A business letter acts as a messenger/salesman

A business letter is like a conversation—'a piece of conversation by post.' A businessman has to exchange information of varied types with different parties. The letter takes the place of a salesman and represents the whole company or organization. It serves as the medium for buying and selling goods, collecting debts, earning the goodwill of the customers and resolving all other important problems concerning business. Hence, letter writing is of vital importance in business.

The structure, layout and format of a business letter reflect the character of an organization. Like a salesman, the letter should create a good impression on the mind of the reader. A salesman representing his firm will create a poor impression if he is not properly dressed or if he does not know the etiquettes of approaching and presenting himself. Similarly, a business letter badly composed will make a poor impression on the customer. A letter bearing an unpleasant appearance fails to catch the reader's eye even if it contains an attractive preposition. A good letter must satisfy the following queries;

- What message is it expected to convey?
- What type of response is expected from the addressee?

In writing the letter, one should show one's willingness to serve or help the other person. So that after reading the letter, the reading must become curious and interested in the product. If the reader is interested, then half of the selling is done.

14.2 ESSENTIAL CHARACTERISTICS OF A BUSINESS LETTER

1. **Promptness:** As a rule, respond to the letter the day it is received. If you need time, acknowledge the letter and indicate how soon you will be sending a specific reply.
2. **Knowledge of the subject:** This indicates the knowledge of the past correspondence, if any, the requirement of the sender of the letter and the knowledge of the firm's policies.
3. **Appropriateness:** Vary the tone and language of your letter according to the need of the occasion as well as the psychology of the reader.
4. **Accuracy, completeness and clarity:** All facts, figures, statements, quotations etc. must be accurately mentioned. It is good to verify them before including them in your letter. If you are replying them to an enquiry, make sure that you have touched all the points. If it is a message, it should be absolutely clear and unambiguous so that it accomplishes the purpose for which it is being sent. The omission of a word, faulty punctuation, or faulty arrangement of words brings ambiguity. Make sure to avoid such pitfalls.
5. **Courtesy:** Courtesy implies that we seek favours politely and express our gratitude for the favours done to us.
6. **Tact:** Tact with courtesy is a quality, which is very important in handling complaints and adjustments, and letters seeking credit. Tactfulness helps in retaining the goodwill of someone even though his request has been turned down.
7. **Persuasion:** The letter should convince the reader as to the facts mentioned in it. Whatever is written in a letter must be capable of being believed by the reader. Each letter asks the reader to take action. If it wins the confidence of the reader, he will positively respond to the request.
8. **Conciseness:** The more concise your letter, the more effective it will be. Do not load your letters with irrelevant details and unnecessarily ifs and buts.
9. **Salesmanship:** Every letter going from your firm should carry a message. It must enhance your reputation.
10. **The 'You' attitude:** When we write letters to others, they are more effective and the readers response to our letters favourably only when we write from their point of view. To make your letters more effective, write your letters constantly keeping in mind the reader's point of view. Avoid 'I' and 'we' and include as many "you's" as possible.
11. **The positive and pleasant approach:** Avoid 'no' and 'sorry'. These are unwelcome words. Instead, emphasize pleasant and positive words. 'No' can be written as 'another time' and 'sorry' can be written as 'we'll try'.

14.3 THE LAYOUT OF A BUSINESS LETTER

The physical appearance of the letter is as important as its contents. The lay-out of a letter governs the impressions created in the mind of the reader. It is, therefore, necessary to remember the following points when a letter is written:

14.3.1 Stationary

1. **Paper:** A good letter typewritten on a paper of good quality gives a pleasant feeling to the reader. A good businessman, therefore, should use the best stationary.
2. **Size:** The size of the letter may be according to the suitability of each business. However, standard sheets measuring 11" x 8" are preferred these days.
3. **Colour:** Most business letters are written on white paper with black print. But there is now a growing tendency of using light coloured paper. Using coloured paper has the following advantages.
   - Colour coding makes papers noticeable and they are easy to trace at any point of time.
   - The colour becomes the symbol of the organization.
   - Colours have a psychological effect.
   - Colours also have a very strong association with moods and attitudes.

   Two points should be kept in mind while selecting colours. Firstly, light colours should be preferred. Secondly, only those colour tones should be selected which reproduce as clearly as white on copying machines.
4. **Envelopes:** Envelope should be made of matching material. The colour and quality of the cover must match with the inside letter. It should be a little longer than the width of the paper. An envelope must be impressive as it is seen by the receiver even before the letter is read.
5. **Letterhead:** The letterhead has a psychological significance, since it helps to form one's impression about the writer's firm. It should be ensured that the letterhead is aesthetically pleasing. The following information is neatly printed on the letterhead:
   - The full name of the firm
   - Address
   - Pin code
   - Telephone number
   - Fax number
   - E-mail and website address
   - Symbols and trademarks

14.3.2 Typing

Nowadays no businessman has handwritten correspondence. Typing not only saves time but also gives a pleasant appearance. The letter can be repeatedly edited till the writer is fully satisfied with his draft. Apart from this, making copies of the original to be sent to other people is quite easy. All the copies are as clear, bright and impressive as the original letter.

14.3.3 Margins, Blank Space at the Top and Bottom

As the frame of a picture, the letter should have decent margin on all sides. Generally, one-inch margin is left on the sides and one and half inches left on the top and the bottom in a standard size letter. The margins on all sides give attractiveness and beauty. **The general rule is: the typed part should look balanced with the blank part.**

14.3.4 Folding of the Typed Letter

When the letter is placed in a cover it must give a fine look. The folding of a letter must be based on the size of the envelope. It should be done with a minimum number of folds. The folds must be well pressed down. If window envelope is used, the letter must be folded in such a way that the address is fully and clearly visible.

14.4 PLANNING THE BUSINESS LETTER

A business letter should be properly planned and carefully drafted so that the purpose of writing it is adequately fulfilled. Even a two-line letter of enquiry is written with a specific purpose. If it is not drafted carefully, not only the purpose of writing will be defeated but also it may cause financial loss and embarrassment to the organization.

Apart from its primary purpose, a business letter always has the secondary purpose of building the goodwill of the organization which sends it. Carelessly written letters can never fulfil this purpose.

In planning the business letters, the following points should be considered:

14.4.1 Audience

A business letter should be reader oriented. Business letters do not deal with situations, they deal with people. Before writing a business letter, the writer must know the knowledge level of the audience who will receive the letter. Besides, in business letters reader's interest must be emphasized and not the sender's interest.

14.4.2 Tone

Tone is present in all communication activities. Tone in writing refers to the writer's attitude toward the reader and the subject of the message. The overall tone of a written message affects the reader just as one's tone of voice affects the listener in everyday exchanges. A business writer should consider the tone of his message, whether he is writing a memo, letter, report, or any type of business document. Ultimately, the tone of a message is a reflection of the writer and it does affect how the reader will perceive the message.

While planning a business letter, the writer should use clear tone and plain English. The use of personal pronouns, like "I", "you" and "we" are recommended in a more direct, plain and natural style. The tone of letter can be complementary, apologetic, sympathetic, persuasive, friendly but firm and polite, etc. It depends on the intimacy between the writer and the receiver.

14.4.3 Format (Punctuation and Style)

While planning a business letter, the writer should consider the format of the letter that he is going to use.

14.4.3.1 Punctuation

Punctuation means the marks of 'period' at the end of each line of the letterhead and the inside address. It helps to convey clearly the meaning of what is written. There are the three following punctuation styles:

1. **Open punctuation:** In this style, no punctuation marks (commas and full stops) are used in any part of the letter except in the body. It is the modern tendency that unnecessary commas and full stops should be omitted and in business letters open punctuation style should be used.
2. **Mixed punctuation:** In mixed punctuation, a coma is put after the date, the house number (if any), the salutation and the complementary close a full stop follows the last line of the inside address.
3. **Closed punctuation:** This style is conventional. In closed punctuation style, the main parts of the letter are punctuated. Of the three styles of punctuation, the mixed punctuation style is widely accepted by modern business entities. It is advisable to write the name of the city in the address in capital letters.

14.4.3.2 Styles of Presentation

The styles used by business organizations include the following:

1. **Indented style:** In this style of letter writing, the sender's name, designation, and (sender's) address are aligned right, no matter whether the letter is written on a plain paper or on a letter head. Just below the address line, leaving one space, is mentioned the date. The receiver's name, designation, and (inside) address are aligned left, once again leaving single space. Single space is a must between sender's name and address, date, receiver's name and address, attention line if any, salutation, subject line, and main body of the letter.

   The main point of this style is that the first line of each new paragraph in the main body of the letter is indented (space inward) 4 to 5 spaces so that the beginning of each paragraph is marked prominently. Throughout the letter **close punctuation** system is followed, i.e., comma, full stop, colon, etc. are used wherever necessary. Leave taking is again aligned right and the signature is put just below it. 'Enclosures' and 'copy to' (C.C.) are aligned left.

   Indented style consumes less space in addresses and leaves enough space for the main body. However, it is an obsolete style and hardly anybody follows this nowadays unless one has the constraint of space.
2. **Block style:** In this style, the sender's name, designation, (sender's) address, and the date line are on the right-hand side margin, rest of the matter is on the left and at the end the complimentary close, and the signature are aligned with the right margin. In it, generally the mixed punctuation style is used. Paragraphs are not indented in block style.
3. **Full-block style:** The full-block style is purely American style of letter writing. With open punctuation this kind of style is very popular these days. All parts of the letter begin at the left margin. A letter in this form saves more time because indentation is not required for any part. The only problem with this style is that it is too heavy on the left side and thus consumes more paper space.

4. **Hanging-Indented style:** This style is like the block style except the first line of each paragraph is aligned with the left margin. Subsequent lines in each paragraph begin a few spaces away from the margin. In it the mixed punctuation is used. Since this form involves many indentations, the typing consumes a lot more time. Therefore, this style is not popular in the world of business.

14.5 PARTS/ELEMENTS OF A BUSINESS LETTER

Most business letters, regardless of their purpose, have the following basic parts;

1. Heading or letterhead
2. Date
3. Reference
4. Inside address
5. Attention line
6. Salutation
7. Subject and reference
8. Body or substance of the letter
9. Complimentary close
10. Signature
11. Enclosure

14.5.1 Heading or Letterhead

Heading contains information relating to the name of the firm and its address. Most business organizations use printed letter head for correspondence. It is usual to provide the following information in the heading: the name of the organization, address, pin code, telephone/fax/telegraphical address/e-mail, website address, symbols and trademarks, etc.

The name of the firm and its address are usually given at the top centre or right side of the paper. If a firm prefers to put much of the information at the bottom of the letter head, we may call it letterfoot. But the firm's name should always be written at the top.

14.5.2 Date

Date serves the purpose of identification. It enables quick reference in future and helps in prompt action and orderly filing. The date consists of the month, the date of the month and the year.

Normally, it is written below the address (about 2 line space below the last line of letterhead) Write date in short, instead, name of the month in full.

Examples:

19 March, 20.. (or) March 19, 20.. (or) 19.3.20..

While writing the date, the abbreviations for months and the years should be avoided. The names of the month and the year are always written in full. No suffix as 'st', 'nd', 'rd', or 'th'(1st, 2nd, 3rd, or 8th) is added to the date.

14.5.3 Reference

The reference is printed below the date line. It is always written close to the left margin. The reference identifies either the department and its section from which the letter is being sent or the particular file in which the letter is to be found. The purpose of the reference is to enable replies to be linked with the previous correspondence and also to send replies to these letters to the proper official or department. Therefore, addresses are requested to quote this reference in their replies. Usual forms of giving the reference are:

- Reference No. ....
- Ref. No. ....
- In reply please quote..............

14.5.4 Inside Address

Inside address is typed on the top left-hand side, about 2 lines space below the date line. It contains the name and full address of the person or the organization, to whom the letter is written. These details should not be abbreviated. It is bad business manners to do so. Punctuation marks are generally not used in the address. The inside address must be similar to the address on the envelope.

Mode of address

- 'Mr.' and 'Shri' is used for men, both married and unmarried
- 'Miss' is used for an unmarried woman
- 'Mrs.' or 'Shrimati' is used for a married woman
- 'Ms.' can be used both for a married and an unmarried woman. (use 'Ms.' for women unless asked to use 'Mrs' or 'Miss')
- While addressing a firm, 'Messrs' (messieurs, meaning gentlemen) is used before the name as the plural for 'Mr'.
- 'Messrs.' is used in addressing firms with titles that contain personal names, as: Messrs. Williams Ltd. (or) M/s. Robert & Co.
- 'Mmes' (Mesdames) is used as the plural for 'Mrs.'
- Title of rank, such as 'Sir', 'Dr.', 'Prof.', 'Colonel', etc. are also used before the name. We can use either the title or 'Mr.'/ 'Ms.', but not the two of them together.

14.5.5 Attention Line

Attention line is used when the writer of a letter, addressed to an organization, wishes to direct it to a particular person or official (either by designation or name). It is written below the inside address but above the salutation and is underlined. For example,

Kind attention: Dr. R. K. Bansal, Director

Or

For the attention of Dr. R. K. Bansal, Director

Example:

SRM Institute of Management and Technology NCR Campus, Delhi - Meerut Road Modinagar - 201204 26.02.20.... Kind attention: Dr. M. K. Pandey, Director Dear Sir

14.5.6 Salutation

The salutation is the complimentary greeting with which the writer opens his letter. It is the written equivalent of the conversational 'Hello'. For ordinary business purposes, 'Dear Sir' (or 'Dear Madam') is commonly used for addressing a person. It is the term of politeness, respect or affection.

Salutation should be written below the inside address (or attention line, if any).

Salutations commonly used are:

Sir Madam	These are rather formal and are used in official correspondence. Government officials judges, ambassadors, editors of newspapers should be addressed as 'Sir' or 'Madam'. (not proper for use in business)
Dear Sir Dear Madam	These are very commonly used in business correspondence.
Dear Mr. Dubey Dear Dubey	These salutations are used when there is a close relation between the correspondents.

14.5.7 Subject and Reference

Purpose of writing subject is to enable the reader to know what the message is about. The subject tells us the main theme of the letter. It is written about one/two lines below the salutation, before starting the body of the letter. Salutation is written beginning from the place from where the first line of each paragraph starts, or it is placed in the middle of the line. Do not make the subject line very lengthy.

Reference, in the body of the letter, is the reference number of the letter in reply to which this letter is being written. Its reference no. and date may also be mentioned in a separate line below the subject. 'Reference' here may also be used to mention the Reference No.(s) of the previous letter (s) already sent by the writer to the same addressee.

These two, subject and reference, must be separate and must stand out clearly to attract the attention of the reader.

Examples:

Dear Sir

Sub: Overdraft facilities for ....

Ref: Your letter No. JK/B/10-20 dated 12 January, 20....

or

Dear Sir

Sub: Payment of Bill...........

Ref: Our letter No. SKB/95/99-20 dated 12 January, 20....

14.5.8 Body of the Letter

The main purpose of writing a letter is to convey a message. This is done through the body of the letter. It is better to divide body of the letter in two or more paragraphs.

Para-1 (Opening paragraph)

The Opening paragraph establishes relation of this letter to any previous correspondences taken place in the past. The letter should open with the expression of pleasure, gratitude, or acknowledgement. Therefore, it should reflect a positive approach and a friendly attitude and should arrest the interest of the reader. If the letter fails here, it will totally fail to achieve its purpose.

Para-2 (Main paragraph)

This paragraph contains the subject matter of the letter. It writes the main message the writer wants to convey. The writer should make himself absolutely clear about what he wants to say.

Para-3 (Closing paragraph)

In the closing paragraph, the writer may assure of his sincerity of purpose, expresses his confidence in the reader and also writes what exactly is needed. It is natural and logical; final and complete. It should stress the 'You' attitude and wherever possible, should use different forms of 'thank you'.

The entire body of the letter should reflect a positive approach and a friendly attitude and it must contain a definite sales appeal. Punctuations like commas, semi-colon and full stops should be marked in their proper places. Incorrect punctuation may alter the whole meaning of a sentence.

14.5.9 Complimentary Close

The complimentary close is merely a polite way of ending a letter. It is written in a separate line at the foot of the letter. Just as the salutation is the written equivalent of 'Good morning', so the complimentary close is the written equivalent of 'Good bye'. Salutation and complimentary close should correspond to each other. The use of 'yours sincerely' or 'yours faithfully' are conventional complimentary close. Generally, there is some confusion in the minds of students regarding suitability of the 'salutation' with the matching complimentary close. Here is a list of commonly used salutations and their appropriate complimentary close. Remember that there is nothing absolute about such usage, the only standard being present-day conventions and widely accepted norms.

Salutation	Complimentary close	Remarks
Sir/Madam Dear Sir/Madam/Sirs Ladies and gentlemen	Yours faithfully Yours truly (less formal)	If you don't know the name of the person you are writing to
Dear Mr. Atul Dear Prof. Garg Dear Ms. Parul	Yours sincerely	If you know the name of the person you are writing to
Dear Anil Dear Seema	Sincerely (yours) (Yours) cordially (Yours) sincerely Cordially (yours)	If you have friendly, or intimate relationship with the person you are writing to

Important points to be noted here are:

1. Only the first letter of the closure is capitalized.
2. at the end of the closure there may or may not be a comma depending on the style adopted.
3. Participle endings like, 'Thanking you', or 'Hoping to hear from you soon' are wrong, because they are incomplete sentences. Such endings should be either avoided or should contain suitable verbs.

14.5.10 Signature

The signature is the signed name of the writer. It is the writer's distinguishing mark. Generally, all important correspondence is signed by the head of the business firm. The name and designation of the signatory is typed in parenthesis below the closing line, providing enough space for the signature.

14.5.11 Enclosure

If anything, like cheque, draft or document, is to be attached to a letter, a mention should be made of these enclosures in the letter after the signature and at the left side margin. The short form of enclosure is Encl. or Enclos.

Further points

1. **Postscript (Latin: Post Scriptum or P.S.):** After completing a letter, if the writer wants to add further information, he can do so by writing a note at the bottom. This is called postscript. From the viewpoint of a good business letter, it should preferably be avoided as it indicates that the letter is not planned properly.
2. **Carbon copy notation (C.C.):** Sometimes copies of the letter are sent to different persons. At the left-hand side bottom of the letter, after writing C.C., the names and the addresses of these persons are written. The names of the persons should be arranged either in order of importance or alphabetically.
3. **Nota bene (N.B.):** It means take notice. When some special points are to be added in order to catch the attention of the reader, the writer can do so by writing N.B., below the letter at the left-hand side.

4. **Per pro signature (signature per procuration):** When the firm delegates the authority of signing letters to an officer by executing a legal instrument, called 'Power of Attorney' in his favour, the signature is called per pro (pp), signature. In all these cases, he will be binding the company legally.
5. **Identification mark or reference initials:** These marks are put in the left margin to identify the typist of the letter, one or two spaces below the signature. Usually, the initials of the officer who dictated the letter are placed first. After that the initials of the person are put who typed the letter. For example; JSK: NNB (JSK are the initials who has dictated the letter and NNB of the one who has typed it.)

14.6 SOME PRACTICAL EXAMPLES OF BUSINESS LETTERS

14.6.1 Letter of Enquiry

A letter of enquiry is an information-seeking letter. When a buyer wishes to get some information about the quantity, quality, price availability, of goods to be purchased, or about the terms of sale, etc., he writes a letter of enquiry to the seller. A good letter of enquiry and its reply can easily bring about an agreement between the customer and the businessman.

As a letter of enquiry is a direct approach letter, it should be

- Straightforward, compact, and courteous
- Positive and confident in tone
- Brief and to the point

Enquiries may be solicited, unsolicited, for some favour, or a routine enquiry.

1. **Solicited enquiry:** An enquiry made in response to the seller's advertisement and publicity.
2. **Unsolicited enquiry:** An enquiry made at the buyer's own initiative.
3. **Enquiry for some favour:** An enquiry about some other information or favour like some special price or relaxation of terms and conditions, etc.
4. **Routine enquiry:** An enquiry made by an old buyer in the usual course of business like some special price, relaxation of terms and conditions, etc.

Opening and closing sentences of a letter of enquiry

The opening line of a letter of enquiry sets the tone and the need for information. The closing line shows the writer's expectation of a quick response.

In order to make a letter of enquiry courteous, one should begin with such expressions as:

- We would be grateful if you kindly let us know about...........
- We would be grateful to get details of your price..............
- We are interested in filling of our stock of.......................manufactured by you. So could you kindly..
- We should appreciate details of..
- We request you to inform...
- With reference to your advertisement in 'The Times of India' of 10.02.2003, we are interested in knowing more details concerning the new model of.......................

In order to make a letter of enquiry courteous, one should close the letter with such expressions as:

- Anticipating an early response..................
- We would really appreciate an early response.
- Should your letter be favourable, we would be pleased to send our first order immediately.
- Since we plan to give you regular business, we are sure, you will quote your most favourable terms.
- We hope you will soon provide the information..............................

Guidelines for drafting a letter of enquiry

A letter of enquiry must clearly state the following points:

1. The purpose of the letter, whether the writer needs goods, service or information
2. Request for price-list, catalogue, etc.
3. Request for sample/demonstration.
4. Request for terms relating to discount, credit, delivery, packaging etc.
5. The details of the sender's business.
6. An idea of the quantity needed so that the supplier may quote the best possible price.
7. Language should be straightforward, compact, and courteous.
8. The writer should be positive and confident in tone.

While writing a letter of enquiry the writer should avoid the following points:

1. Lengthy and unnecessary statements.
2. Repetitions.
3. Apologies, like "We beg you to send..."

Reply to a letter of enquiry

All enquires must be replied promptly. It shows that the seller has a genuine respect for the buyer and his interest.

A reply to an enquiry must take care of the following points:

1. Refer to the date and/or number of the letter.
2. Thanks to the party for interest to the receiver.
3. All relevant information about goods, prices, discount, etc.
4. All the questions in the letter of enquiry should be answered in a courteous tone.
5. State the terms clearly and concisely.
6. State the time for which the offer is open if time is an important factor.
7. State whether the price list, catalogue, samples, etc., are enclosed or they are being sent separately.
8. Show your willingness to serve or help the customer in the form of additional information, etc. if needed.
9. Assurance of best service to the sender of enquiry.

Opening sentences of the letter of reply to an enquiry

- We thank you for the interest shown by you in our new model..............................
- Thank you very much for your letter no. .... dated..............

14.7 OFFERS AND QUOTATIONS

14.7.1 Offers

An offer is general and voluntary. It is like a sales letter sent to all prospective customers including existing customers. It can be made to large number of customers in general terms and in the form of a printed circular letter. An offer must be valid for a specific time.

Offers must be made attractive. They should be capable of arousing the recipient's interest in the goods. Besides, an offer must be valid for a specific time.

14.7.2 Quotations

A quotation is a specific offer for sale. It is made in response to an enquiry from a particular person or business house. It Includes details about the

- Prices of the specific goods desired,
- Terms of payment,
- Conditions of delivery, etc.

14.7.3 Difference Between Offers and Quotations

Replies to enquiries may be made in the form of offers and quotations. Both these terms are generally taken to mean the same but there is a slight difference between the two.

A quotation is a specific offer for sale. It is made in response to an enquiry from a particular person or business house. On the other hand, an offer is general and voluntary. It can be made to a large number of customers in general terms and in the form of a printed circular letter. An offer must be valid for a specific time.

A general offer to a customer is not bound by letters. It may be published in newspapers or presented through a TV as an advertisement but quotation is sent in response to an enquiry. However, a specific offer may be sent to a specific person only. Thus, a specific offer is very similar to a quotation.

Firm offer

Firm offer is an offer in which the seller undertakes to accept an order at the pre agreed price between the purchaser and the seller on the conditions stated only within a specified time.

Offer without engagement

It is an offer in which the seller is not bound by the price and conditions stated by him. He reserves the right to negotiate further before he finally accepts the order. While making offers, the seller must consider the following points:

- The quality of goods
- The unit of weight or measure
- Terms of payment, whether cash or credit
- The mode and place of delivery
- The mode of transportation (whether by post, courier, train, ship, etc.)
- The time of delivery

Offers must be made attractive. They should be capable of arousing the recipient's interest in the goods.

Example 1

Draft a letter to Hindustan Watch Company, 40, Munirka, Mumbai –1 asking for a copy of their latest catalogue. State that you propose to stock watches for sale. Ask for their best trade for supplying of watches and clocks.

A.B.C. Co. Ltd.
24, South Patel Nagar
New Delhi-8

Ref: 12345
15.4.20.....

The Hindustan Watch Company
40, Munirka
Mumbai-1

Dear Sir

Sub: Requisition for quotation and catalogue for watches and clocks

We take pleasure in introducing ourselves as one of the leading stockist of watches and clocks in Chandigarh. We deal with all the reputed watches and clocks manufactured in India. Our sales turnover last year was Lac Rs. 30.

In order to expand our business further, we would like to have an association with your company as a stockist and distributor of the clocks and watches manufactured by you for whole of South Delhi.

We, therefore, request you to please send your latest catalogue of clocks and watches along with the most competitive prices to us.

An early response will be appreciated.

Yours faithfully

(Sunil Kumar)

Proprietor

Example 2

Draft a suitable reply in response to the request for quotation and product catalogue of clocks and watches requested by Mr. Sunil Kumar.

The Hindustan Watch Company
Munirka
Mumbai-1

Ref: rrxy
29.4.20........

Mr. Sunil Kumar
A.B.C. Co. Ltd.
24, South Patel Nagar
New Delhi-8

Dear Sir

Thank you for your letter with Reference No. 12345, dated 15.4.20..... and the interest shown in our products. We have gone very carefully to the contents of your letter and appreciate your concern, desiring for becoming a stockist and distributor for the products manufactured by us.

We are enclosing herewith the latest product catalogue along with the quotation for your consideration. Kindly note that we offer a dealer margin of 15% over the maximum retail price (MRP). Apart from this, we also offer the bonus of 3% for meeting the sales target set mutually for each year.

Should you require any further clarification in this regard, please feel free to meet us or call our Sales Manager for any assistance.

Looking forward for a good business relationship with you,

Yours faithfully
(A B C)
Regional Sales Manager

Example 3

Ask a sports goods supplier to send their price list and catalogue.

BHARAT SPORTS
6, Mathura Road, Agra

12 September, 20....

Unique Sports & Co.
156, Gali No. 2
Sadar Bazaar
Meerut

Dear Sir

Kindly send us your latest price list for wholesale purchases. Since our annual requirements in sports goods of all kinds are large, we would like to place regular orders with you. Hence, please quote your most favourable prices and terms.

Yours faithfully

XYZ

Manager

Example 4

Reply to the above enquiry.

UNIQUE SPORTS & CO.
156, Gali No. 2, Sadar Bazaar, Meerut

22 September, 20....

Bharat Sports
6, Mathura Road
Agra

Dear Sir

We thank you for your enquiry of 12 September, 20.... We are glad to enclose the price list of our sports goods. You will be happy to know that our all sports items are approved by the ISI.

Our normal trade discount is 15%. In view of the large business promised, you will also get a special trade discount of 5% on all orders and an additional 5% on all orders exceeding Rs. 25, 000.

If you need further details or assistance in meeting your special requirements, you should feel free to write to us.

Yours faithfully

for Unique Sports & Co.

Sunil Kumar

Sales Manager

Encl: Price list

Example 5

On behalf of Jain & Jain Industries, 24, Industrial Area, Gurgaon, draft a letter to a retailer to handle a new water purifier, making a firm offer.

JAIN & JAIN INDUSTRIES
24, Industrial Area
Gurgaon

24 September, 20....

Messrs. Goyal & Co.
24, New Market
New Delhi

Dear Sir

We take pleasure in sending you today a sample of our newly manufactured 'Acquaria' water purifier.

Aquaria has been developed by our R&D wing after years of painstaking research. It is effective on all types of surfaces. You will agree that the effectiveness and comparatively low rates of Aquaria will make it a sure quick-seller. We have also undertaken a special publicity campaign both on leading newspapers and Zee channel to make its launching a special occasion. We can assure you that Aquaria is going to become a household name in the near future.

You will get Aquaria at a surprisingly low introductory price. A special discount of 15% will also be allowed on all orders placed with us during the month of October 20....Other terms and conditions are mentioned in the enclosed price list.

We now ask you to consider carefully this offer and look forward to your first order, which we are sure, will be the first of many orders.

Yours faithfully
Sanjay Garg
Sales Manager
Encl: Price list

14.8 ORDERS

For a buyer, making enquiries is the first stage. It enables him to get information necessary to place his order. On the part of the seller, his reply to the enquiry is the stage from where he expects and endeavours to obtain orders from prospective buyers. Thus, the quotations are the 'offeres' made by the seller and the orders by the buyers are the 'acceptance' of the offer. This acceptance, which is in the form of an order, is the 'thread', which establishes a legal relation between the seller and the buyer.

The order must be brief but clear, complete and accurate so that it may be correctly understood and promptly executed.

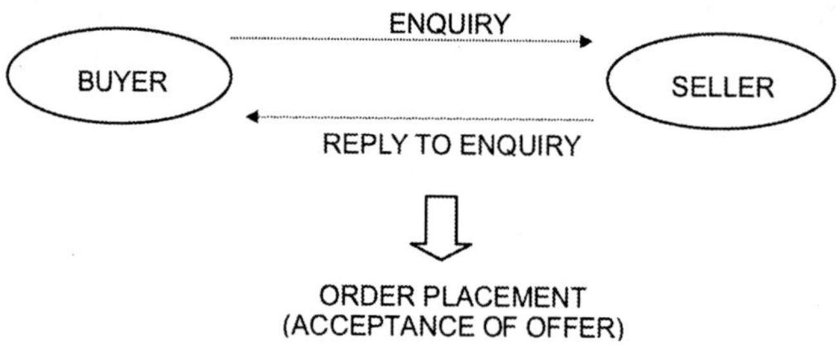

14.8.1 Guidelines for Drafting an Order

An order must contain the following points:

1. Thank the seller for his quotations, or add a note of appreciation in the case of a repeat order.
2. Give reference to the seller's letter no. date, etc.
3. Give the following specifications of the goods:
   - Exact trade name, catalogue number, size, colour, style, design, quality, etc.
   - Price and discount
   - Quantity desired for each item
   - Alternative goods, if acceptable
   - Forwarding directions (Goods to be sent by parcel post, goods or passenger train, truck or ship)
4. Give special instructions, if any, for
   - Packing, marking, insurance, etc.
   - The manner of payment
   - Withdrawal to account
   - Cash sent with order (C.W.O.)
   - Cash to be paid on delivery (C.OD.)
   - Invoice to be sent by post or through a bank
   - Bill to be drawn by the seller

5. The letter should be closed with what you wish to emphasize:
   - Quality
   - Prompt execution
   - Discount
   - Time factor (delivery time), etc.

14.8.2 Order Form (Purchase Order)

Generally, all firms use 'order form' to place orders, which contains all relevant information. These are standardized forms containing all the necessary instructions and blank space for the required details to be filled in at the time of sending out an order. As placing order is a kind of routine matter, these order forms are quite useful for repeat orders.

However, each order form, in all cases, is accompanied with a brief covering letter which includes all relevant instructions that is not given in the printed, pre-prepared order form. A sample order form is given below:

ORDER FORM

GARGA BROTHERS

16, Bank Street, Karol Bagh, New Delhi

Telephone:.................., Fax:................

Date:.......................

Ref. No. ....

To

____

____

____

Dear Sir

Kindly supply the following:

S.No.	Product No.	Product Name/ Description	Quantity	Cost each	Total

Kindly send invoice in duplicate.

Yours faithfully

....

14.9 CONFIRMATION LETTER

Confirmation letter means the letter of acceptance concerning supply of the ordered items. Every order is an opportunity for the seller to build a profitable relationship with the customer. So the acknowledgement of an order must express the seller's pleasure and gratitude, must appreciate the customer's interest in the goods, and must be a medium of mentioning the favourable aspects of the goods, terms, and services. The receipt of every order must be promptly acknowledged to the buyer.

As the acknowledgement of an order is a legal acceptance of all the points mentioned in the order, the order must be read carefully before accepting and acknowledging it.

Guidelines for drafting acknowledgement of an order

1. Thank the party for his order
2. Specify the goods you have dispatched or the time by which you will dispatch them.
3. State the total amount of the invoice and attach the invoice to the letter.
4. Refer to the need of prompt payment but do not stree this point.
5. Mention the mode of dispatch
6. Show your eagerness to the customer in all possible ways.
7. Mention that his order has been given personal attention.

14.10 DEFECTIVE ORDER

Sometimes an order may be incomplete or may not contain all the information necessary for its fulfilment or sometimes an item is not available. It becomes a problem for the seller how to deal with it.

Guidelines for drafting replies to defective or incomplete orders

1. We should thank the party for the order.
2. We should be tactful to point out that the order did not specify the requirements clearly.
3. We should be informative and suggestive.
4. We should see that the tone of our letter does not offend the customer.
5. We should help the customer in specifying his requirements clearly; giving necessary details, it is preferable to enclose catalogue, price list and other literature, if any, to guide the customer.
6. Indirectly we should make it clear that the information is sought in the interest of the customer.

14.11 DELAY IN EXECUTION

Hints for drafting letters intimating delay in the execution of orders

1. We should thank the party for his order.
2. We should explain clearly in a personal tone the reason for delay.

3. We should convince the customer that the circumstances are beyond our control.
4. We should state, if possible, the date when the order can be executed.
5. We should assure the party that his order would receive prompt attention on the date being mentioned.
6. We should end our letter with a reference to the inconvenience our customer might be put to and hope that he will not mind it.

14.12 REPLIES

Hints for drafting replies when the order is declined because of the unsuitability of prices desired or heavy orders on hand or at the new prices.

- If goods can be delivered after the lapse of a particular period, we should ask the customer whether he can wait till then.
- We should apprise the customer of our difficulties. However, we should offer our services for future orders from the customer.

14.13 CANCELLATION OF AN ORDER

Circumstances may arise sometimes that orders have to be cancelled. Some unforeseen situations create impossibility of execution, such as delay in the execution of order, variation in prices, insolvent party, etc. The letter cancelling the order must mention the reason of the cancellation. If the buyer is cancelling the order, the communication must reach the seller before execution of the order.

Example 6

Write a letter to any firm placing an order to purchase some goods.

ABC Limited
Gol Market
Dehradun
10.10.20....

M/S HCL Infotech Limited
28, Barakhamba Road
Connaught Place
New Delhi

Dear Sir

Sub: Purchase Order for 20 computers

Ref: Your quotation No. 123/XYZ/001, dated 20.09.20....

This refers to your above-mentioned quotation and subsequently the discussion we had with you on 05.08.20... on the subject matter.

We are pleased to place the purchase order for the supply of 20 numbers of computers to us as per the specifications, as mentioned in your quotation.

The cost of 20 nos. of computers has been mutually agreed to Rs. 10,00000 inclusive of all taxes.

You are requested to ensure the delivery of these computers to our office latest by 30.10.20....The terms and conditions and the warranty of the products will be governed as laid down in your quotation.

An early action will be highly appreciated.

Yours faithfully

(XYZ)

Manager- Purchase

Example 7

Write a letter to an organization confirming of order

Delhi Book Depot
46, Laxmi Nagar
New Delhi-911225
January 23, 20....

B.K. Trading Company
34 Avenue Street
Mumbai-982765

Dear Mr Amit

With reference to our telephone conversation today, I am writing to confirm your order for 100 reams of papers of superior 'B' quality, Ref. No. 856

The order will be dispatched within three days by passenger train and should arrive at your store in about 5 days. Please contact us again if we can help in any way.

Yours faithfully

Amit Arya
Sales Manager

Example 8

Write a letter declining to execute an order giving proper reason.

Raj & Company
Carvey Street
Chennai-600018

23.9.20....

Messrs. Kohli & Sons
Walia Street
Mumbai-400033

Dear Sir

Many thanks for your order No. 57 of 12 September, 20...., for 1,000 boxes containing an assortment of dry fruits. Your interest in the goods supplied by us is a source of great encouragement to us. However, we are sorry that we cannot accept your order at Rs. 2,600 per dozen boxes as desired by you.

Our letter of 17 August offers the lowest possible prices. We are left with a very thin margin of profit even at the prices quoted to you earlier at Rs. 3,200 per dozen boxes. This, therefore, does not allow us to reduce the prices any further.

We shall be glad to fill up your order, if you will confirm your order within 7 days, at Rs. 3,200 per dozen boxes.

Yours faithfully

XYZ
Sales Manager

14.14 COMPLAINTS AND ADJUSTMENTS

Irrespective of the best-managed business, mistakes and errors often occur. Therefore, the businessmen often receive letters of complaints about incomplete or defective order, delay in dispatch, wrong dispatch, defective packing that might lead to the damage of goods in transit, or mistakes by the accounts section in preparing the invoice, etc.

The following points should be considered while writing a letter of complaint:

1. When a complaint letter is sent, it is understood that it communicates the errors or mistakes made by the seller. It requests him to rectify those errors and mistakes at this end.
2. A letter of complaint must be persuasive in nature.
3. Clarity, courteousness, and an inoffensive style of writing are extremely important in a letter of complaint.
4. The complaint should be made politely but firmly without showing any kind of anger.
5. While writing about mistakes we should use passive voice.
6. As far as possible, the word 'COMPLAINT' should not be used. We should use the word 'REQUEST'.
7. A complaint must be genuine.
8. A complaint letter must be complete and clear.
9. A complaint letter must make concrete request for redress. (Compensation)
10. We should not show any threats.

The following points should be considered while writing a letter of reply for a complaint:

1. Thank the customer for pointing out something that needs improvement.
2. Express regret and sympathy for the customer's inconvenience.
3. Before making replies a proper investigation is must.
4. Reply must be sent promptly.
5. If the complaint is genuine, admit the fault at once and appreciate the customer.
6. Do not enter with a controversy with a customer.

Example 9

As a Purchase Manager of an organization you had ordered 5 generator sets of 5 kVA each. When the consignment arrives, you find 2 generator sets do not confirm to the specifications you had approved. Draft a claim letter asking for reasonable adjustment.

ABC Co. Ltd.
44, New Patel Nagar
Ahmedabad

10.8.20.......

The Regional Manager
ABC Yamaha Limited
A-2, South Extension
New Delhi

Dear Sir

Sub: Generator sets supplied by you, not confirming to the agreed specification

This refers to our order no. HPP/01-02/811 towards supply of 5 gensets of 5 kVA each.

We would like to inform you that we have received these gensets on 8.8.20……. and noted that 2 of the gensets received do not confirm to the specifications agreed by us mutually. You may kindly recall our discussion and the purchase order that all 5 gensets were required with an additional feature of self-start. However, out of the 5 gensets received, only three of them have this additional feature whereas the remaining two do not have this feature.

We would, therefore, request you to kindly depute your representative to our office for carrying out necessary modifications/replacement of these two sets.

We shall be grateful to you for your prompt action in this regard.

Yours faithfully

(XYZ)
Purchase Manager

Example 10

You had sent a parcel to your friend who lives in Mumbai. However, the parcel and its contents were found damaged at the time of receipt of the parcel. Write a letter to the Postmaster complaining about the damaged parcel and claiming the value of the same.

XYZ
23, New Friends Colony
New Delhi - 32

1.10.20....

The Head Postmaster
Cannaught Place
New Delhi-1

Dear Sir

Sub: Damaged Parcel

Ref: Parcel receipt no. 12568, dated 12.6.20....

Please be informed that I had sent a parcel on 12.6.20.... from Cannaught Place post office to the following address:

Naveen Chand Sharma
12/145, North West Junction, Worli
Mumbai-15

However, on receipt of the said parcel by Mr. Naveen Chand Sharma at Mumbai on 17.6.20...., it was noticed that the content of the parcel (Electronic calculator) was found damaged.

A complaint was lodged with Worli post office in the presence of the postman, who delivered the parcel. (Copy of the letter enclosed)

It is therefore requested that since the parcel was insured to the value of RS. 500/- (RS five hundred only), the said amount may kindly be refunded to me immediately.

I shall be grateful to you for your prompt action in this regard.

Yours faithfully

(XYZ)

Example 11

Assume that 12 room heaters out of 50 have been received by your firm in damaged condition from Jupiter Electrical Appliance Co. Ltd., 26 Park Street, Kolkatta. As a Manager of your firm write a complaint letter to the supplier, Mr. Ravi Mohan, seeking replacement or adjustment for the goods. Invent necessary details.

ABC Co. Limited
28, MG Road, Kolkata - 12

23.1.20.........

Jupiter Electrical Appliance Co. Ltd.
26, Park Street
Kolkata - 8

Dear Sir

Sub: Receipt of room heaters in damaged condition

Ref: Our Purchase Order no. xxxxxxx dated 12.12.20........

This refers to our Purchase Order as mentioned above for the supply of 50 numbers of room heaters.

We received the room heaters sent by your firm on 22.12.20......... as per the details as mentioned above. However, we would like to bring to your notice that on opening the cartoon boxes, we observed that out of 50 room heaters received, 15 room heaters were found in badly damaged condition.

These room heaters are beyond usage and we request you to look into this aspect and replace the damaged room heaters immediately.

Alternatively, you may like to adjust the equivalent amount of 15 room heaters against the supply of water cooler to us for which the Purchase Order will be released shortly by us.

Kindly confirm in either case and inform your line of action immediately.

Yours faithfully

(XYZ)
Commercial Manager

Example 12

As Sales Manager of Jupiter Co. Ltd., draft a letter offering replacement.

Jupiter Electrical Appliance Co. Ltd.
26, Park Street, Kolkata-8

Ref: RM/01-125

28.1.20.......

ABC Co. Ltd.
28, MG Road
Kolkata-12
Attention : Mr. XYZ – Commercial Manager

Dear Sir

Sub: Replacement of damaged room heaters

Ref : Your letter RKS/01/005 dated 23.1.20......

This refers to your letter about the receipt of damaged room heaters against our supply made to you last week.

We have advised our Service Department to immediately contact your office and take necessary steps towards replacement of these 15 damaged room heaters.

Apparently, it appears that the damage could have caused due to the negligence of the transporter as at the time of dispatch all room heaters were ensured in good condition by our Quality Assurance Section. However, we shall further analyze the cause of the damage and initiate necessary corrective actions at our end to prevent such damages.

We sincerely regret for the inconvenience caused to you. Assuring you of our best services.

Yours faithfully

(Ravi Mohan)
Regional Sales Manager

Example 13

As a Business Manager, you have ordered, for your firm, a supply of tractor tyres. The letter was sent to the supplier two weeks ago, but you have received no reply. Write a suitable and a polite letter to the supplier.

ABC Co. Ltd.
28, MG Road
Kolkata - 12

11.6.20...

Regional Manager-Sales
Ceat Tyres Limited
18, Venkateshvarya Road
Chennai-2

Dear Sir

Subject: Non-receipt of tyres against our purchase order

This refers to your quotation no. AB /Tyres/Ceat/022 dated 20.5.2006 for the supply of tyres of tractors.

We would like to inform you that we have sent you a draft of Rs. 250, 000 on 25.5.2005 towards supply of 50 tyres. As per the agreement, the tyres were to be received by us within a week's time.

Kindly note that we have neither received the tyres nor any communication from you in this regard.

We would request you to kindly acknowledge the receipt of our order and the demand draft and inform us the delivery schedule of tyres.

A quick response shall be highly appreciated.

Yours faithfully

(ABC)
Managing Director

Example 14

Draft a suitable reply to a customer who has complaint that quality of goods supplied to him was not up to the mark. Invent the necessary details yourself.

ABC Computers Ltd.
Chennai-28

15.4.20....

Personnel Manager
Infotech Limited
23, Kasturba Gandhi Marg
New Delhi

Dear Sir

This refers to your letter no. xxxxxxx, dated 10.4.20...., informing us about the quality of the switchboards supplied by us.

We would like to inform you that immediately after receiving your letter, we have checked all our stocks and have noticed that by mistake the switchboards of different specifications have been supplied to you. We sincerely apologize for our mistake. We are deputing our sales representative Mr. .... who will meet you tomorrow at 10 a.m. in your office and will organize the replacements.

We sincerely regret for the inconvenience caused to you. Assuring you of our best services.

Yours faithfully

(XYZ)
Personnel Manager

14.15 CREDIT ENQUIRIES

Credit is a means through which goods can be bought without cash payment. It is found to be useful both to the buyers and the sellers. It enables the buyers to conduct business with comparatively less capital and the sellers to attract longer sales. The sellers get the additional advantages of regular sales and guaranteed market for their goods.

Today, almost all of us use some form of credit to purchase the things they want or need. Most of us purchase on credit not only major items but almost everything else there is to buy. National and international credit cards have become a way of life. Through credit increases sales, It involves risks, particularly of bad debts and delayed payments. A sound credit policy, careful selection of credit customers and prompt collection are essential to successful function of credit system.

14.15.1 Requesting a Credit Account

The business customer who wants to open a credit account with another business can go about it in several ways:

1. Request credit orally or in writing before any transaction has taken place.
2. Request credit with the first order.
3. Place a first order, leaving the credit decision to the company.
4. Do businesses on a cash basis for a period of time, build a good credit rating with the company, and then obtain credit.

14.15.2 The Basis of Credit Decision

Those who have the power to decide whether to grant or refuse credit base their decisions on the four Cs – Character, Capital, Capacity, and Condition.

1. **Character**
    - Does the business applicant have character? That is, is the person reliable?
    - Is the person's business record steady and dependable? In dealings with others, does the person show a sense of responsibility?
    - Is the applicant honest and straightforward?
2. **Capital**
    - Does the business applicant have enough capital (funds)?
    - What is the relationship between the applicants assets and liabilities?
3. **Capacity**
    - Does the applicant have the capacity to successfully handle financials affairs?
    - Does the record show that the applicant has good business judgement and management ability?
    - How effectively has the applicant taken advantage of the opportunities available to him or her?

4. **Condition**
   - What is the condition of business in general?
   - Is business good, steady or poor?
   - Is business likely to improve, stabilize, or decline?

Each of the four Cs is vitally important, but the most important is character.

14.15.3 Specific Sources of Credit Information

Taking the four Cs into account, a credit officer or the trader can obtain specific information about an applicant from four main sources:

1. **The customer:** The person applying for credit supplies information, such as present salary, annual income, banking connections, ownership of property, current debts and credit accounts with other business firms. In addition, a business organization applying for credit provides commercial references and final statements.
2. **Other business firms:** Banks, savings and loan associations, and other business firms that do business with the applicant often share information about the financial record of the applicant.
3. **Credit bureaus and credit-rating agencies:** Credit bureaus, at the local and national level, are membership organizations that maintain computerized files describing the credit habits of individual as reported to them by members.
4. **Bank references:** Bank reference is the name of the credit applicant bankers who can supply all necessary information about him to be credit officer or the trader. While asking for references, the trader should be extremely polite so that he may not heart the feelings of the applicant.

14.15.4 Guidelines for Securing Credit Information from the Customers

1. Open courteously, thanking the person for the application.
2. Explain why you need the information.
3. Make a request for specific information – Bank references, financial statements, or personal interview etc.
4. Assure that the information will be kept confidential.
5. Tell the applicant that it will be in his own interest to send promptly the required information, complete in all details, for it will enable you immediately to open his account and dispatch the goods to him.

Example 15

You work in the credit department of 'M.H. Williams & Company', an authorized distributor of SONY equipment. Rajdeep Sahay, the owner of 'Raj Electronics', has asked to open a credit account with your company. As part of your investigation of this credit application, draft a letter requesting to the customer for credit information.

M.H. Williams & Company
24, Nehru Place
New Delhi-110019

28 July, 20....

Mr. Rajdeep Sahay
Raj Electronics
Laxmi Nagar
New Delhi

Dear Sir

Sub: Request for providing information for opening a new credit account

Thank you for your interest in becoming a new credit customer. We are pleased to have the opportunity of adding your name to our list of credit accounts. To open an account for you, we must first have from you routine references and information. Please complete the enclosed credit information request form and return it to us in the stamped, self-addressed envelope which we have provided. Should you have any questions, please contact us for clarification.

We hope the opening of this account will be the beginning of a long and happy association with you.

Yours faithfully

Geeta Mehta
Credit Officer

Granting and Refusing Credit

The credit information that you have acquired must be carefully evaluated and the references checked. On these bases, you will decide whether your company should grant or refuse the request for credit. Once your decision is made, you must inform the applicant in writing. The tone of your letter, granting or denying credit must be courteous and positive. The choice of words used in such written messages is the key to success or failure.

Granting Credit

1. Courteously state that the customer's request for credit has been approved.
2. Review the credit procedures
3. Stress the mutual value of a good credit relationship.

Example 16

A letter extending credit

M.H. Williams & Company
24, Nehru Place
New Delhi-110019

12 August, 20....

Mr. Rajdeep Sahay
Raj Electronics
Laxmi Nagar
New Delhi

Dear Sir

It is our pleasure to welcome you as one of our credit customers. A Rs. 1,000,000 credit limit has been established for your use. Your account statsment will be sent on the fifteenth of each month.

Credit is a privilege extended only to those whose excellent record of financial responsibility qualifies them for it. Your account with our company provides mutual benefits. It is a convenience for you to know that all your orders will be processed without delay. It is an advantage for us to know that you will be aware of 'M.H. Williams & Company when you need stereo equipment.

With these thoughts in mind, we look forward to the opportunity of doing business with you in the years ahead.

Yours faithfully

Geeta Mehta
Credit Officer

Nowadays, some companies prefer to send the customer a card instead of a letter. The card simply acknowledges that credit has been granted.

<table>
<tr><td colspan="2" align="center">M.H. Williams & Company
is indeed pleased to welcome
'Raj Electronics' as a Credit Customer
Your account is now available for your use and we hope
you will find it a convenience and a source of satisfaction.</td></tr>
<tr><td>MHW</td><td align="right">M.H. Williams & Company</td></tr>
</table>

A Printed Card Acknowledging Credit

Refusing Credit

1. Express appreciation for the customer's order and cooperation in providing credit information and references.
2. Mention the facts of the case straightforwardly, stating favourable factors before less favourable factors.
3. Suggest a cash purchase solution for the present, and encourage the customer to reapply in the future.
4. Close courteously.

Example 17

A letter refusing credit

M.H. Williams & Company
24, Nehru Place
New Delhi-110019

12 August, 20....

Mr. Rajdeep Sahay
Raj Electronics
Laxmi Nagar
New Delhi

Dear Sir

Your order of 28 July, 20.... for 10 sets of stereos and 10 numbers of digital cameras is ready to be dispatched. We appreciate the promptness with which you responded to our request for credit information and the references for the credit application which you submitted with this order.

From the references we have had, there can be no doubt that your integrity and business ability are very highly regarded. The problem we have encountered concerns the level of your current obligations. As you know, these obligations are exceptionally large at the moment.

In the meantime, we welcome your business on our most favourable cash terms, including our liberal cash discount. When the level of your current financial obligations improves, we urge you to resubmit your application for credit.

As soon as we hear from you concerning this suggested arrangement, your order will be on its way.

Yours faithfully

Geeta Mehta
Credit Officer

14.16 CIRCULAR LETTERS

On certain occasions a businessman has to communicate same message to a large number of his customers and suppliers. For this purpose, he uses circular letters—letters that circulate the same message. These circular letters are unsolicited letters written in an effective style and appropriate tone. The use of clarity, brevity, the 'you' attitude, catchy words and sentences are some ingredients of an effective circular letter.

14.16.1 Objectives of Writing Circular Letters

- Introducing a new product or service
- Expansion of an establishment
- Changing of address
- Seasonal Discount or announcing a prize scheme
- Increase in prices
- Change in the constitution of the firm

Example 18

Write a circular letter announcing change in premises.

WATSON INDIA LIMITED
Water Treatment Division
26, Kavi Nagar Industrial Area, Ghaziabad-201010

Dear friend

Owing to continued expansion of our activities, we have outgrown our existing office premises at the Watson Factory in Modi Nagar and have moved to larger office at the following address in Ghaziabad.

26, Kavi Nagar Industrial Area
Ghaziabad-201010

Today onwards we would be functioning from the new premises. Kindly ensure that all your correspondence is sent to the above address.

The move is part of our expansion and diversification policy, and integration programme with our Associate Company, Fine Chemical Industries Pvt. Ltd., Ghaziabad. We are committed to offering our clients the very best in water treatment ion exchange technology, backed with the best service possible.

Yours faithfully
for Watson India Limited

Example 19

Write a circular letter announcing a clearance sale.

HUMA VARIETY STORE
28, Kasturba Gandhi Marg, New Delhi - 110013

14 October, 20....

Dear Sir/s

DISCOUNT BY 50% OR MORE for almost all items!
HURRY UP! Offer Open Till 12th November!

On the eve of all festivals prices of many articles tend to go up but not at our shop. We have planned for you Grand Clearance Sale of our stocks before the arrival of Diwali-just the time you wish to buy cheap.

The present offer covers many of your favourite items. On purchases of Rs. 100, you will get a LUCKY DRAW COUPON. In the lucky draw arranged on 13th November, you get anything worth Rs. 200.

In addition, your purchases worth Rs. 500 entitle you to a FREE COUPON of Rs. 30. Your child will be very happy to exchange two such coupons for a beautiful soft toy in our kiddies' corner.

YOU GET RS. 200 WORTH OF GOODS OR EVEN MORE FOR JUST A HUNDRED.

We welcome you everyday till 12th November between 9 a.m. and 8 p.m., to enable you to chose any time convenient to you.

Yours faithfully
Sunil Dhar
Manager-Marketing

14.17 SALES LETTERS

The most important thing that a business letter does is to attract the reader towards the letter, to persuade him to read it and then to prepare him to buy the goods offered. Sales letter is the most important written form of business writing.

Its primary aim is publicity and to promote sale. Unlike general advertisements appearing in newspapers magazines, a sales letter is more particular in its appeal, for it is addressed to a selected class of customers, belonging to specific age groups, financial groups, professional groups, or having the same social status, or living at a particular place, etc. It is highly persuasive in its approach. Even if people are not interested in the product, the aim of the letter is to make them interested in it. The effectiveness of such letters depends on the writer's ability to use language suited to his purpose.

As a sales letter aims at capturing a customer it also holds out the promise to keep in touch with him and serve him in the best possible ways. Thus, it is a definite step towards turning service and maintaining relation.

14.17.1 Characteristics of Sales Letters

The prominent characteristics of a sales letter are as follows:

1. **Lengthy discourse:** Almost all sales letters are long letters in contrast with the other business letters. As the purpose of the letter is to persuade the reader, all this cannot be done in a short letter. Besides, it replaces the salesman it is generally lengthy, argumentative and conversational.
2. **Focus on a particular class:** No product can be of interest to all kinds of consumers, therefore, a sales letter is essentially meant for a particular class of consumers.
3. **Enclosures:** Very often a sales letter has enclosed with it
   - Literature about the product
   - Self-addressed reply envelope
   - Forms seeking information about the consumer.
4. **Arresting opening:** The beginning of a skilfully prepared sales letter includes words that attract the reader's attention in a positive way. It may be a catchy subject line, a slogan, or a straight question, etc. Here are a few examples:
   - Present a short story.
   - Share a mini testimonial.
   - Ask a question.
   - Make a comparison.
   - Report a fact of interest.
   - Use an "if" opening.
   - Make a claim. Refer to current events and developments
   - Offer a refund or rebate
   - Use a human interest approach.
5. **Highly conversational style:** A sales letter is generally written in a highly conversational style. It is supposed to replace the sales man in the sense that the writer enters into a heart-to-heart dialogue with the reader. It has a touch of intimacy and genuine interest in the reader's need. That is why, sales letters are often full of questions and answers, or suggested answers.
6. **You-attitude:** The writer of a sales letter has to put the reader in the centre of his concern and say all that he thinks the reader is interested in. for this purpose, he must write the letter with 'you-attitude' and make good use of the pronoun 'you'.
7. **Promise of continued contact:** As a sales letter aims at capturing a customer it also holds out the promise to keep in touch with him and serve him in the best possible ways. Thus, it is a definite step towards turning service and maintaining relation. For a businessman the most important person in his life is the customer and the customer is deemed as a friend to be cherished and taken care for.

8. **Highlighting important part of the message:** A sales letter highlights in bright colours or underlines all important parts of the message. It makes the letter at once appealing to the eye. Just as a sales man lays stress on significant facts and figures so does a sales letter emphasize them in print.

14.17.2 Preparation for Drafting a Sales Letter

As a sales letter draws attention to sales features that create in the reader a desire to own the product or at least to know more about it, you must first be able to answer the question listed below.

1. What is the product?
2. What is the market?
3. What response are you seeking through the letter as a step leading toward an eventual sale?
4. Which selling features will be most appealing, and which one of these deserves the greatest emphasis?
5. How can you best capture the interest of and appeal to your particular audience?
6. What message plan is likely to be most effective?

14.17.3 Guidelines for Drafting a Sales Letter

1. Begin your letter in a striking manner in order to arouse reader's curiosity and tempt him to read further.
2. Give a vivid description of the product, service, or proposition being offered.
3. Make an appeal to the reader by telling him how the article benefits him. Highlight the positive points: durability, low cost, satisfactory performance, etc.
4. Convince the reader by giving evidence: profits, testimonials, references to users' experiences, etc.
5. Persuade the reader to act at once, by offering different types of incentives, or by convincing words.
6. Tell the reader exactly what to do and how to do it so that the action becomes easy.

Example 20

Write a sales letter having an economy appeal.

AHLUVALIAS DEPARTMENTAL STORE
24, Gol Market, Bareilly

10 April, 2009

Dear Customer/s

Save Rs. 100 each time you buy a branded cotton shirt.

Buy AHLUVALIAS SUPERCOTTON SHIRT made specially by Caramel—a unit of Tata Textiles-for only Rs. 199. These shirts are stitched specially for you-the customer/s of Excellence Departmental Store, at an exclusive price, Rs. 199. Anywhere, in other showrooms, you would pay Rs. 200 for the same shirt. Even if you buy the material and have it stitched—it would cost still more.

AHLUVALIAS SUPERCOTTON is a quality shirt made of fine material and expert tailoring. Look for the exclusive SUPERCOTTON counter at Ahluvalias: Shirts Rs. 199, Duo shirts Rs. 250—in white and pastel colours.

AHLUVALIAS SUPERCOTTON shirts made from Caramel-Tata Textiles are offered at this exclusive price only for a limited period. ACT NOW AND SAVE RS. 100 AND MORE...

Yours faithfully

....

Example 21

Write a sales letter having special offer to old customers

MODERN BOOK STORE
4/B II Floor, Ali Ganj, Lucknow

22 August, 20....

Dear Sir/Madam

You will be interested to hear that we have decided to clear the present stocks of books at bargain prices. Only the old customers like you can enjoy the advantages, as the letters are being sent to the old customers only. The price list of the books, that shows the original price and the special discount offered to them, is enclosed for your ready reference.

The stocks of these books are already on sale and are limited for two more weeks. You can avail of this rare opportunity.

If you can spare a few minutes, please fill in the enclosed order form and post it today. The postage expenses will be free if your order is for more than Rs. 250.

You can take full advantage of this offer. Remember this offer is specially meant for our old customers only.

Yours faithfully

....

Encl: One bargained price list.

Example 22

As a manager of a firm, you intend to clear off your odd stocks lying in godown. Write a suitable but attractive letter to customer to purchase them at reduced prices.

Ahuja Garments
28, Kasturba Gandhi Marg
New Delhi - 110013

14.10.20....

Mr. XYZ
B-6, Lohia Nagar
Ghaziabad

Dear Sir

Sub: Clearance sales of woollen garments

This refers to your visit to our godown on 2.10.20...and the interest you have shown in purchasing the stock of woollen garments available with us.

We would like to mention that although the stock is lying in our godown for the last six months but it is still as good as fresh and latest in the fashion.

However, due to the fact that we want to change our business from woollen garments to automotive spare parts business, we intend to clear off our stocks.

You would be happy to note that in case you buy all the stock available with us, we shall offer you a discount of 40% on MRP.

This offer is valid up to end December, 20... and is a lifetime opportunity to the valued customers like you.

Should you require any further clarification, kindly feel free to contact us.

Thanking and assuring you of our best services.

Yours faithfully

....

Manager
for Ahuja Garments

14.18 BANK CORRESPONDENCE

These different types of services rendered by commercial banks have been so incorporated with general business activities that banks have become indispensable to organizations of all types and of different financial standing.

In performing these functions, a bank has to correspond with the customers, the Head office, and other banks. Most of this correspondence is of a routine nature and does not require any special skill for drafting. To facilitate correspondence and to save time and energy, banks generally prepare form letters in advance with some spaces left blank in them. On different occasions, relevant particulars are filled in blank spaces and the letters are sent to the concerned parties.

In situations, which are not a routine type, letters need a personal touch and a sales motto. Such letters have to follow the general principles of effective business correspondence in matter of style, tact, courtesy, brevity, completeness, and correctness, etc. In addition, banks are required to observe perfect secrecy about the financial standing and involvement of their customers.

Example 23

As a Personnel Manager of a firm draft a letter expressing a desire to open a current account of your firm in a bank. Invent the necessary details.

Agarwal & Sons
26, New Market
Ghaziabad-201010

20. 2.20……

Punjab National Bank
88, New Market
Ghaziabad-201010

Dear Sir

Sub: Opening of a Current Account

We would be grateful if a current account in the company's name is opened with the New Market Branch of your bank. We are enclosing the following documents along with the application form, duly filled in:

1. A copy of certificate of incorporation
2. Certificate of the registrar of the Companies granting permission to the Company to commence business.
3. Copy of the memorandum and articles of the Company.
4. Certified copy of the proposal of the Board of Directors to open a Current Account duly signed by the Chairman.
5. Letter of introduction by Mr. M. K. Jain, an account holder of your bank.

We are depositing Rs. 10,000 as initial deposit. Mr. R.K. Bansal, the Managing Director, is authorized to operate this account.

We are looking forward to a fruitful cooperation in our business transactions.

Yours faithfully

……………………

Personnel Manager

Encl: Eight

Example 24

As a customer request your bank to stop payment of a cheque.

Harish Chandra
426, Sector V
Vaishali
Ghaziabad

October 28, 20....

Branch Manager
Syndicate Bank
Vaishali Branch
Ghaziabad

Dear Sir

Sub: Cancellation of payment of a cheque

Ref: Ch. No. 212745 of 27 October 20...., for Rs. 5000

Please cancel payment of the cheque referred to the above mentioned details drawn by me in favour of 'Self', as it appears to have been lost.

Since it happens to be a bearer cheque, I request you to take immediate action to ensure that, if presented for payment, it is duly dishonoured.

Yours faithfully
Harish Chandra
Mobile: 9868379723

Example 25

Assume that you are the manager of a branch of a nationalized bank and that you have to cease the release of next instalment loan as the customer failed to furnish progress report of previous work done. Draft a letter based on the principles of trade ethos.

State Bank of India
Sector 23
Haridwar

10.2.20...

Mr. Anil Sud
44, Ganga Vihar
G T Road
Haridwar

Dear Sir

Sub: Stoppage of instalment against sanctioned loan

This refers to your letter for the release of the instalment of loan amount against the sanctioned loan of Rs. 70,00000 towards your project for manufacturing of electric fans.

As per the agreement, we are supposed to receive the progress report before release of instalment of loan to the customers. However, it has been noticed by us that the progress report for the month of January, 20... has not been received by us alongwith the request you have made for the release of instalment of loan.

We would like to inform you that as per the agreement, unless the progress report is made available to us, we shall not be in a position to honour your request for release of any loan installment against the sanctioned loan.

We, therefore, suggest you to kindly furnish the progress report to enable us to proceed with your request.

Yours faithfully

....

(Branch Manager)

Example 26

Write a letter to Telephone Department about the discrepancy in your telephone bill. Request them to adjust your telephone bill and send the revised bill. Invent necessary details.

XYZ
123, Shastri Nagar
New Delhi

23.01.20.........

The Assistant Engineer (Telephones)
Shastri Nagar Exchange
New Delhi

Dear Sir

Sub: Discrepancy in my Telephone Bill

Ref: Telephone no. 2775894, Bill no. 234567, dated 15.01.20......

This refers to the telephone bill received for the period November-December, 20......... against my telephone connection as mentioned above.

I would like to inform you that in the said telephone bill, the amount of Rs. 3500/- has been charged towards five international calls made to USA. It may kindly be noted that we do not have STD facility in our telephone connection.

It appears that some mistake has happened at your end at the time of billing resulting to this discrepancy in my telephone bill.

I, therefore, request that:

-You may kindly get your records verified for these international calls made from my telephone

-Based on the investigation, my bills be corrected and the revised bill sent to me immediately for further actions

I shall be thankful for your immediate response.

Yours faithfully
(XYZ)

14.19 LETTERS TO THE EDITOR

Almost all newspapers and magazines have a special column as 'letters to the Editor'. Through this column readers can express their views on various matters such as;

- any news that has been published by the paper
- any event in the field of politics, education, administration, labour, management, or other social activities
- any defect in the working of public institution like, a library, a sports organization, a hospital, a charitable institution, etc.

It is through this column that one can draw attention of the public and win its sympathy for a particular issue that requires attention, or action of the government, or some institutional authorities. Sometimes this column provides a platform for a 'debate' or 'discussion' on a certain issue which gets invaluable opinions from qualified and experienced persons. Thus, it is highly beneficial to many interested readers in general and to the person/s responsible for creating the issue, in particular.

Example 27

Write a letter to the Director–Ministry of Environment & Forests to initiate necessary actions towards the noise pollution caused due to loudspeakers in the daytime by the shopkeepers.

Amit Khanna
44 Govind Apartments
Ghaziabad

16.12.20.......

Ministry of Environment & Forests
Paryavaran Bhawan
CGO Complex
Lodi Road
New Delhi

Dear Sir

Sub: Noise pollution caused due to loudspeakers

I, the resident of Govind Apartments, New Delhi, am concerned with the noise pollution caused due to the loudspeakers, which are invariably played every day by the shopkeepers (mainly music shops). This affects me and the other students living in this locality. We are unable to concentrate our studies due to the noise pollution caused by them.

We understand that there is a provision in the law, issued by MOEF, that the noise level should not be more than 75 dB(A) (Decibel) in the daytime. However, this law is not adhered by the shopkeepers and there is no enforcement of law by the concerned Pollution Control Board, namely, Uttar Pradesh Pollution Control Board, Lucknow.

We request that the Pollution Control Board should enforce such laws, which have been laid down for the benefit of society at large.

This will assist the students like us to concentrate more towards our studies.

Hoping to have a favourable response from you

Yours faithfully
(Amit Khanna)

Example 28

Write a letter to the president, Municipal Committee of your town, pointing out the inadequacy of the street lights in your locality

Rajendra Prasad
44, Adarsh Colony
Surat

11.02.20.....

The President
Municipal Committee
Surat

Dear Sir

Sub: Inadequacy of street light in our locality

I am a resident of Adarsh Colony and would like to draw your kind attention that in the locality of Adarsh Colony, most of the streets of this area present a picture of complete darkness after the sunset and it is sometimes difficult to pass through them without bumping against a cyclist or fellow pedestrian.

The main road passing through the central part of the locality is lighted only at a few points. The side streets running from this road are almost entirely unlighted. It is not difficult to imagine how troublesome it is for the residents of this locality to move from one house to another or from one street to an adjoining one in the lightless nights these days.

Adarsh Nagar is a beautiful locality where all other amenities such as good roads, drainage system and the water supply systems etc have been provided. However, the pathetic maintenance conditions of the street light projects the image of this area as a deserted place.

I would, therefore, request you to please depute your supervisor/engineer for reviewing the present conditions for the lighting arrangement of the streetlights and initiate a long-term corrective and preventive action for maintenance of these facilities so that a common man is not deprived of these basic facilities any more.

I shall be thankful for your immediate action in this regard.

Yours faithfully
(Rajendra Prasad)

Example 29

Write a letter to concerned authority, complaining the irregularity of electric supply in your locality.

XYZ
23, Gandhi Nagar
Varanasi

20.9.20........

The Executive Engineer
Uttar Pradesh Electricity Board
Vidyut Bhawan
Varanasi

Dear Sir

Sub: Irregularity in Electric Supply in Gandhi Nagar, Varanasi

We, the residents of Gandhi Nagar, would like to bring to your kind notice the hardship we have been going through due to the irregularity in supply of electricity by your department. Apart from a regular power cut in the morning from 4:30 a.m. to 7 a.m., the power goes off intermittently on many occasions during day and evening times.

We are the students of B.Tech and MBA and have to get up and study in the early hours of the morning. However, due to frequent power cuts, this has not been possible and thus is affecting our performance in the class.

We would like to draw your kind attention that this power cut situation be kindly reviewed for changing the power cut timings from early hours to daytime so that the power is available in the morning and evening hours.

We shall be thankful for your immediate action in this regard.

Yours faithfully
(XYZ), (ABC), (OPQ)

14.20 PUBLIC RELATIONS LETTERS

Public relations letters, or goodwill letters, are friendly letters sent by organizations to their customers or prospects. Their main function is to convey a friendly, usually unexpected, message that builds goodwill and brightens the image of the organization among the general public. Letters of invitation, thanks, congratulations, and sympathy are the examples of public relations letters. Since these letters come to the recipient rather unexpectedly, they come as a pleasant surprise and are always welcome.

A public relation letter should be

- a 'you-attitude' letter
- honest and sincere
- short and direct in its approach
- free from any sales motive

Example 30

On behalf of the Secretary, Indian Tyres Manufacturers Association, Kamla Nagar, New Delhi, draft a formal invitation to Mr. R K Dubey, Managing Director, Herculus Tyres Pvt. Ltd., Dehradun, for lunch on 20th January at Hotel Holiday Inn, New Delhi.

INDIAN TYRES MANUFACTURERS ASSOCIATION
44, Kamla Nagar, New Delhi

12.1.20.......

Mr. R K Dubey
Managing Director
Herculus Tyres Pvt. Ltd.,
Dehradun

Dear Sir

You will be pleased to know that our association-Indian Tyres Manufacturers Association, Dehradun has now been registered and we have formally received all the necessary approvals from the competent authorities.

In order to discuss further and chalk out the strategy for representation to the Government for reduction of excise duty on tyres, it is desired that we meet at a common place along with other association members.

In this connection, we have fixed a meeting at 11 a.m. followed by lunch at Holiday Inn, New Delhi on 20 January 20.......

Kindly make it convenient to attend and confirm.

Yours faithfully
C L Narang
Secretary

Example 31

Assuming that you are R K Dubey, Managing Director, Herculus Tyres Pvt. Ltd., Dehradun, draft a letter in reply to the above-mentioned invitation.

R K Dubey
Managing Director
Herculus Tyres Pvt. Ltd.
Dehradun

18.1.20............

C L Narang
Secretary
44, Kamla Nagar
New Delhi

Dear Mr. Narang

I am in receipt of your letter dated 12.1.20.......and noted the contents therein. The news of registration of our association is really encouraging.

As suggested, I shall be attending the meeting at Holiday Inn as per the plan for further discussion on the sensitive issues.

Yours faithfully

R. K. Dubey

Example 32

As a bank manager write a letter of congratulation to a newly elected Chairman of Traders' Association.

S. K. Bansal
Branch Manager
Punjab National Bank
Nehru Nagar Branch
Saharanpur

12.2.20.....

P. K. Arora
Chairman
Nehru Nagar Traders' Association
Saharanpur

Dear Mr. Arora

Please accept our hearty congratulations on your election as Chairman of Nehru Nagar Traders' Association, Saharanpur.

I am sure that under your leadership the Association will work as a cohesive unit committed to the welfare of the members as well as the society.

Yours sincerely
S.K. Bansal

REVIEW QUESTIONS

1. Briefly describe the importance of effective business letters in an organization.
2. Write a short note on the various functions of a business letter.
3. What are the essential characteristics of a business letter? Why is 'you-attitude' regarded so important in business correspondence?
4. Compare the two most commonly used styles of business letter writing used by organization and write in brief their differences. Which of the two would you like to use and why?
5. This chapter has suggested that 'the physical appearance of the letter is as important as its contents'. Write a detailed note on the appearance of business letter.
6. Draw a format of a business letter. Wirte a brief note on the elements of a business letter.
7. Write a note on the necessity of planning letter, showing how an unplanned letter can be disadvantageous to an organization.
8. What is the motivating objective of writing a sales letter?

9. What are the broader guidelines for drafting a letter of claim? Bharat Dairy Products at Vaishali, Ghaziabad supplied 100 tins of condensed milk to Messers Raj Khanna and Brothers at Noida. 25 tins out of it were found to be in damaged condition. Draft a letter of complaint on behalf of buyers.
10. Write a letter to a bookseller ordering books worth Rs. 1000/-. Invent the necessary details.
11. Write a letter to the principal of your college requesting him to issue a character certificate.
12. Write a letter to a dealer ordering a TV set for your house.
13. Write a letter to a hotel manager at a hill station inquiring about accommodation in the hotel for your forthcoming visit.
14. Write a letter to a complaining against the delay and lack of proper attention from the bank staff experienced by you.
15. Draft a suitable reply to a customer who has complaint that quality of good supplied to him was not up to the mark. Invent the necessary details yourself.
16. You have noticed that a local bus service has become inefficient in recent weeks. Buses are infrequent and sometimes a number of them are going to the same place at the same time. Write a letter complaining to the General Manager, State Roadways Transport Services, Ghaziabad about the inadequate services and to initiate necessary corrective action.
17. You had sent a parcel to your friend who lives in Mumbai. However, the parcel and its contents were found damaged at the time of receipt of the parcel. Write a letter to the Postmaster complaining about the damaged parcel and claming the value of the same.
18. Home Appliances Co. Ltd. has produced a new mixer grinder, and you as a sales manager have asked to promote its sales. Draft a letter to be sent to ladies' clubs and hotels in NCR region.

15
BUSINESS REPORTS

Chapter Objectives

This chapter will enable you to understand:

- Meaning and definition of report
- General characteristics of business reports
- Significance of a business report
- Types of report
- Structure of a business report
- Planning and preparing report
- Style of report writing
- Team written reports
- Some practical examples of report writing

Report writing is an essential skill for professionals in almost every field: engineers, accountants, teachers, graphic designers, business executives, information scientists, and the list goes on. In business the information is needed for reviewing and evaluating progress, planning for future course of action and taking decisions.

15.1 MEANING AND DEFINITION OF REPORT

The word 'report' is derived from the Latin word 'reportare' that means to carry back. (re = back + portare = to carry). In a broad sense, we define a business report as an orderly and objective presentation of information that helps in decision-making and problem solving. According to this definition,

- The report must be orderly so that the reader can locate the needed information quickly.
- It must be objective because the reader will use the report to make decisions that affect the health and welfare of the organizations.
- It must present information–facts, data.
- The report must aid decision-making and problem solving.

15.2 GENERAL CHARACTERISTICS OF BUSINESS REPORTS

A report should be easy to read, and professional in its presentation. Here is a brief review of some of the chief characteristics of the business report:

1. **Clarity:** Clarity depends on proper arrangement of facts. The purpose of a technical report is to transmit conclusions and their supporting evidence. To do this, your report must convey your exact meaning to the reader. You must proceed systematically. Make your purpose clear, define your sources, state your findings and finally make necessary recommendations. The text must be clear and unambiguous, mathematical symbols must be fully defined, and the figures and tables must be easily understood.
2. **Conciseness:** Most of your intended readers are busy. Therefore, your reports should be concisely written. But conciseness should not be achieved at the cost of clarity. Nor should it be at the cost of completeness. You should include everything significant and yet be brief. Give enough information to enable them to understand clearly what you are describing and why you are describing it. Include enough background information to make the context clear. Do not assume that they will remember details of a previous report—or have even read it. Include all details needed to understand the current report. In short, make your reports brief but comprehensible.
3. **Information sources:** Your report should make use of information sources. These may include not only books and articles that can be found in libraries but also technical brochures, interviews or correspondence with experts, as well as first-hand inspections.
4. **Documentation:** When you use borrowed information in your business report, be sure to cite your sources. The style of citing your source is also called "documenting" your sources.
5. **Reader orientation:** As report is a piece of communication, it is always written with a reader in mind. While drafting a report, it is necessary to keep in mind a real or realistic group of readers who exist in a real or realistic situation.
6. **Special format:** The technical or business report uses a rather involved format including covers, binding, title page, table of contents, list of figures, transmittal letter, and appendices. These have to be prepared according to a set standard, which will be presented later in the section 'Structure of a Report'.
7. **Objectivity:** Business reports should be objective and show restraint. Be honest with your readers. They expect you to evaluate the data honestly. If recommendations are made at the end of a report, they must be impartial and objective. Do not try to hide deficiencies in your research. They should come as a logical conclusion to investigation and analysis. Your readers will be persuaded by facts, but they may become irritated if you attempt to impress them with your cleverness or to claim credit for accomplishments.
8. **Simple and unambiguous language:** A good report is a kind of scientific document of practical utility. Therefore, it should be written in a simple language.
9. **Grammatical accuracy:** The grammatical accuracy of language is of correct fundamental importance. It is one of the basic requisites of a good report; because faulty construction of sentences makes the meaning obscure and ambiguous.
10. **Visual aids:** Report writing communicates visually with graphs, tables, and drawings. Reports that explain experiments or projects almost always include tables or graphs.

You should use highlighting techniques (bullets, numbers, headings lists, diagrams, etc.) in order to communicate effectively and to make the report easy for quick reading.

15.3 SIGNIFICANCE OF BUSINESS REPORTS

1. **Making important business decisions:** Report serves the purpose of taking important business decisions. A number of business decisions are made on the basis of information and recommendation provided by reports.
2. **Analysis of present situation:** It is a useful tool to be competitive in the market. Through the analysis of present situation, it is easier to initiate necessary corrective actions to improve the present situation.
3. **Planning and evaluating the business activities:** The analysis of present situation with regards to the target helps an executive perform his functions and assists in planning the activities, resources, and action plan to be initiated to reach to the defined goals.
4. **Monitoring and controlling the business activities:** In order to have an effective monitoring and controlling of a business activity where thousands of employees are working, it is not possible to keep oneself informed of what others are doing without the aid of a report. Therefore, writing the reports from associates is an important aspect in managing and controlling the activities effectively.

15.4 TYPES OF REPORT

There is no such document as a standard report–in length, complexity, formality, or format. Reports are used for various purposes and to perform various actions. You can classify business reports in various ways according to their form, their purpose and their subject matter.

Report may be **oral** or **written**. It may be **short** or a **long** one.

The following tree diagram summarizes the various types of reports that have been mentioned in this section:

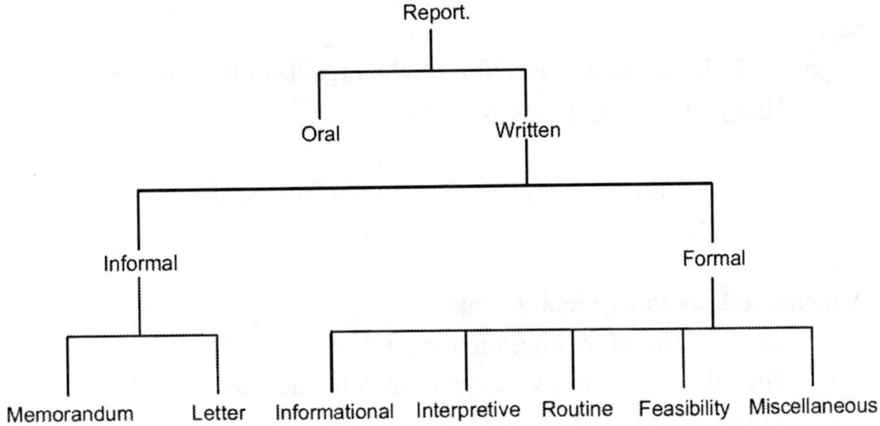

An **oral report** is a piece of face-to-face communication about something seen or observed. A business oral report includes the most routine and informal situations in the daily conduct of business to highly formal presentations.

Though an oral report saves the reporter's time, it is more time-consuming for the receiver, as he has to listen to every word of the report. Most of contents, if not important, are easily forgotten and an oral report cannot be retrieved.

A **written report** is relatively more accurate and permanent. In certain cases the reader may just skim through the report or read the abstract or conclusion or recommendations only. A written report is more formal than an oral report. It can be referred again and again. On the basis of legal formalities to be complied with, we can have **informal** and **formal** report.

15.4.1 Informal Report

An informal report is usually in the form of a person-to-person communication.

In day-to-day working in the industry, the written reports made are comparatively informal unless specifically asked for. Very short reports (one page or two page reports) generally do not follow the usual format of report writing very strictly. These are in the forms of:

1. Memorandum
2. Letter report

1. Memorandum: Memorandum form report or memo report is the simplest form of a report. It is a short official note generally used by the employees of an organization for communicating among themselves. That is why, it is called 'Inter-office Memorandum' too.

Thus, memorandum is a written statement, inside the organization, that is prepared especially for a person or committee on order to give them information about a particular matter.

Memo format: (Steps in writing memo)

A memo includes nothing except the message in its simplest form. Usually, each organization has printed memo form. There are four main parts in a memo:

- **1st part**
  - □ 1st part includes name and location of the organization. For example;

    Hindus Levers Limited: Mumbai
- **2nd part**
  - □ 2nd part includes the date, to, from, subject, reference, if any.
  - □ There is no salutation, and the writer's signature is put without the complimentary close.
  - □ A memo follows this general format:

    Date: Date of writing the memo

    To: Readers name & designation/All concerned

    From: Sender's name and designation

    Subject: The subject matter of memo

- **3rd part**
  - ☐ What is the purpose of writing the memo?
  - ☐ The action statement
  - ☐ The conclusion
  - ☐ Necessary information is provided in a sequential manner, dealing with the subject matter.
  - ☐ If two or more points are dealt with in a memo, it is usual to put them in separate paragraphs and to number the paragraphs.
- **4th part**
  - ☐ 4th part includes the signature of person writing the memo.

2. **Letter report:** The letter report uses letter format with letterhead, date, inside address, salutation, subject, matter, complimentary close, signature area and reference section. It is usually single-spaced and may go outside and inside the organization.

15.4.2 Similarities and Differences between Memorandums and Letters

Similarities

- Like a letter, a memo must be clear, concise, courteous, etc. Even in negative messages, courtesy should be observed as far as possible.
- The subject in a letter as well as in a memo must be clearly written and underlined.

Differences

- Memorandum are written to people within an organization. While, the letters are written to people within an organization as well as to people outside the organization.
- A memo is different from a letter, both in format and in its effect on the addressee. It does not have a salutation and complimentary close. (But the subject is clearly written and underlined.)

Press release

A memo written to make newsworthy information available to the public is called press release. It is written for the outside world and is not meant for internal circulation. The information may be in regard to launching of new products, significant change, merger with another organization, etc. Its style is direct, concise and clear.

In press release the emphasis is given on focusing the information that would be of immediate benefit or interest to society.

A press release is different from an advertisement. A press release is strictly factual while an advertisement is written to attract and persuade the prospective consumer.

15.4.3 Formal Report

A formal report is one that is prepared in a prescribed form and is presented according to an established procedure to a prescribed authority. A formal report can be statutory or non-statutory.

A report prepared and presented according to the form and procedure laid down by law, is called a statutory report. Report submitted at the statutory meeting of shareholders, Director's report to the Annual General Meeting, Auditor's report are statutory reports.

A formal report, which is not required under any law, but which is prepared to help the management in framing policies or taking other important decisions, is called a non-statutory report.

According to their purpose and contents, a formal report can be divided into the following:

1. Informational
2. Interpretive
3. Routine/progress
4. Feasibility
5. Miscellaneous

1. Informational report

- As the name indicates, an informational report deals with information about a survey, analysis or an investigation, etc.
- It contains only the data collected or the facts observed in an organized form as required by the management.
- An informational report presents the situation as it is should be.
- It does not contain any conclusions or recommendations.
- It is useful because it presents relevant data put together in a form in which it is required by the management to take decisions.

2. Interpretive report

An interpretive report, like an informational report, contains facts but it also includes an evaluation or interpretation or analysis of data and the reporter's conclusion. It includes

- The analysis of the data collected.
- Conclusion or the inference of that data.
- Recommendations for action.
- Also known as recommendatory report.

3. Routine/Progress report

A routine or progress report is usually written in a prescribed form at regular intervals.

- **Periodic report**
  - ☐ A periodic report is prepared and presented at regular, prescribed intervals in the usual routine of business.
  - ☐ It may be submitted annually, half-yearly, quarterly, monthly, fortnightly, weekly, or even daily.
  - ☐ Such report contains a mere statement of facts without an opinion or recommendation. Many business firms use printed forms and standardized headings for the text section of such reports.
  - ☐ It helps the management to keep a given situation under control and gives it direction so that short-term and long-term objectives could be achieved.
- **Project report**
  - ☐ When long-term project or work is undertaken, the administration keeps itself informed through progress reports. The project may be the construction of a bridge or a building, the installation of equipment in a factory, or the investigation of some problem.

- ☐ A project report informs the management about ongoing projects or activities.
- ☐ It is a systematic presentation and discussion of the date collected.
- ☐ It may be external or internal.
- ☐ Necessary for monitoring and controlling of a project/process.
- ☐ Concerned persons and the management are kept informed periodically and this information assists them to take stock of the situation and act accordingly.
- ☐ It includes chronology of events taken place since the last report submitted
- ☐ Generally speaking, a progress report may contain the following information:
    - › Name of the work or project
    - › Total work to be completed
    - › Date
    - › Work completed to date
    - › Work to be completed
    - › Possible date for completion
    - › Remarks, if any
    - › Signature and designation of the reporting officer.

However, the format of such report may differ from organization to organization.

- **Laboratory report**
    - ☐ Laboratory report is considered to be an essential part of scientific investigation and experimentation.
    - ☐ It is an account of experiments done in the laboratory.
    - ☐ In lab report various steps–choosing the right equipment, arranging various instruments appropriately, and arriving at valid conclusion–are put together in a logical order.
    - ☐ Generally, these reports contain the following elements:
        - › Heading
        - › Experiment No.
        - › Date
        - › Statement of objects
        - › Apparatus used
        - › Method
        - › Procedure followed
        - › Observations
        - › Conclusions
        - › Signature
- **Performance appraisal report**
    - ☐ At a regular interval, performance appraisal of the employees is done by the personel department.
    - ☐ Assess and evaluate the employees as per their performance.
    - ☐ Sent to the management for evaluation

4. Feasibility report

- A feasibility report is related to future.
- This kind of report is prepared when an organization intends to start a new venture or to open a new branch.
- Cutting costs, introducing new equipment, market expansion, production of a new product, moving into new areas, and collaboration with another firm are a few of the areas where this report makes decision-making easy and smooth.
- A feasibility report explores possibilities for effectively improving a given situation. It helps the management to determine whether a proposed scheme is practicable and profitable or not.

All the reports have their own importance. Informational and evaluation reports are commentaries on the past, the present and the future. Progress reports are concerned with the present. Feasibility reports are related to future.

Evaluation comments on existing projects, Progress with existing projects and Feasibility deals with new projects.

5. Miscellaneous reports

- **Inspection report:** The report which incorporates the result of the inspection of a product or a piece of equipment to ascertain whether it is functioning properly or requires any repair or replacement is termed Inspection report. .

  It is made on a typed format supplied to the reporter. The reporter has to simply measure the test data and fill in the blanks.
- **Inventory report:** It is customary for every organization to take periodic stock of equipment, furniture, stationary, etc. at regular intervals. The person who checks the stock, files in a prescribed form.
- **Audit report:** This kind of report is prepared on financial records or accounts of a firm.
- **Technical report:** This kind of report is prepared on a discussion of a technical problem. We present data on a specialized subject, with or without comments.
- **Blank format report:** This report is prepared on a typed format supplied to the reporter. The reporter has to just fill in the blanks in the form. This kind of report is generally used by companies and organizations to get information or feedback of their employees. The positive point in this kind of report is that there is much scope for objectivity since the writer does not have to write anything from his side but to fill in the blanks.
- **Situational report:** Situational report is a one-time only report made in unique problems and opportunity. It deals with non-recurrent problems. A report on the desirability of opening a new branch or on the unrest among staff in a particular department is called a situational report.
- **Newspaper report:** Objective of the newspaper report is to bring the happenings in various aspects to the knowledge of the concerned persons/society for making them aware of the facts. Generally, newspaper reports are on the matters of public interest, any happening in society, function, procession, accident, gathering, etc. A good newspaper report should contain an impressive and catchy title. It should begin with introductory

paragraph with place and date of the event. The news related to the event should be put in logical order. Conclusion of the report should be written in a separate paragraph.

15.5 STRUCTURE OF A REPORT

A business report has a typical pattern and format of its own. However, there are no hard and fast rules about the structure. The basic structure gets changed as per the purpose, scope and the contents of a report. Following is the order in which various elements of a report are organized:

Front matter*

1. Cover page
2. Frontispiece
3. Title Page
4. Copyright Notice
5. Forwarding Letter
6. Preface
7. Acknowledgement
8. Table of Contents
9. List of Illustrations
10. Abstract and Summary

Main body*

1. Introduction
2. Methodology
3. Discussion or Description
4. Conclusion
5. Recommendations

Back matter*

1. Appendices
2. References
3. Bibliography
4. Glossary
5. Index

In practice, only long formal reports are likely to contain all the above-mentioned elements. In short reports, the title page, the introduction and the discussion or description are mandatory. In very short reports even a separate title page is not required. We write the title on the top of the first page and start with the introduction.

The structure discussed here is also applicable to other formal writings such as articles, research papers, books, monographs, etc.

* None of these parts are mentioned in the report. They form only the organizational structure of the report.

15.5.1 Front Matter

1. **Cover page:** The cover page of a report is usually made of a hard sheet. It protects the manuscript from damage and gives the report a neat appearance.

   The cover page has:
   - The name of the organization
   - Title of the report
   - Report number, if assigned
   - Full detail of the person(s) who prepared the report
   - Full detail of the person(s) for whom the report was prepared
   - The date of the presentation/submission of the report

   Example of Cover Page:

   > Report No. 68
   >
   > <u>**BHARAT SANCHAR NIGAM LIMITED, BHOPAL**</u>
   >
   > **A Report**
   >
   > On
   >
   > **The Installation of E/A Sets at Various Stations in Bhopal**
   >
   > By
   >
   > T.R. Sharma
   >
   > Asst. Engineer (Elect.)
   >
   > BSNL, Elet. Dvn. Bhopal
   >
   > To
   >
   > Sri. V.K. Mongia
   >
   > Executive Engineer (Elect.)
   >
   > BSNL, Elet. Dvn. Bhopal
   >
   > 28, November 20....

2. **Frontispiece:** A frontispiece is usually a decorated page which generally appears in bound reports. The photographs, maps, diagrams, and artistic drawings, etc. are given on this page. However, it is not a necessary item in a report. Normally this is ignored in the internal reports. However, when the reports are to be submitted to outside world, it may be useful and brings the attention of the reader.
3. **Title page:** Usually, the title page is the first right-hand page of the report. It is the most essential part of the front matter. In addition to all the information given on the cover page, the title page of a report shows
   - Title of the report
   - Sub-title
   - Name of the author

- Designation or position of the author
- Name of the person for whom the report is written
- Submission date
- Approval by the concerned authorities
- Distribution list

Example of Title Page:

Report No. 68

BHARAT SANCHAR NIGAM LIMITED

BHOPAL

A Report

On

The Installation of E/A Sets at Various Stations in Bhopal

By

T.R. Sharma

Engineer (Elect.)

BSNL, Elet. Dvn. Bhopal

To

Sri. V.K. Mongia

Managing Director

BSNL, Elet. Dvn. Bhopal

Approved by
Sri Vinay Kumar
Sr. Engineer (Elect.)
BSNL, Elet. Dvn. Bhopal

28 November, 20....

4. **Copyright notice:** Copyright notice is given on the inside of the title page as:

   @ All rights are reserved with the author.

   This notice forms part of those confidential and voluminous reports which are protected by copyright so that no part of the report is used by anybody in any form without prior permission of the author. Sometimes the following note is added (same you find a copyright notice inside a book):

   "All rights are reserved. No part of this report may be reproduced in any form or by any means without the permission in writing from the publisher/author."

   This is an optional arrangement and does not find place in short or routine reports.

5. **Forwarding letter:** The forwarding letter is a simple letter issued to the author by the forwarding authority. Routine/day-to-day reports rarely have any forwarding letter.

6. **Preface:** The preface tells about the salient features of report. Basically, the preface introduces the reader with the contents of the report (not the subject matter like scope/content, etc.). It is written by the author himself.

The preface is different to forwarding letter. Preface is written by the author himself, while forwarding letter is written by an authority or expert in the field commending the work done.

7. **Acknowledgements:** Acknowledgements is that page where we express our sincere gratitude (acknowledge the help received) to all those people and the organizations who have been helpful to us, in any way, directly or indirectly, in the process of writing report.
8. **Table of contents:** If report is long enough, more than ten pages, table of contents is made to give the reader
   - overall view of the report.
   - helps in locating the particular topic easily.

   This table lists the contents of the report serially arranged according to their page numbers. The page numbers are carefully checked against the text. The contents are compiled from the headings and sub-headings of the report. The important point to be considered here is that sub-titles are generally indented.

   The table of contents is not recommended if the report is of 4-5 pages only.
9. **List of illustrations:** A separate list is given immediately after the table of contents if there are a large number of (a dozen or more) tables and figures. Its layout is the same as that of the table of contents.
10. **Abstract and summary**
    - **Abstract:** An abstract is the presentation of the essence of the report. In other words, Abstract is presented only as a brief write up on the whole report.

      The abstract usually contains three paragraphs. The first paragraph talks about the main aim of the report or discusses in brief the objective in writing the report. The second paragraph discusses in brief the methodology adopted to achieve the objective. The third paragraph merely spells out the conclusion but does not elaborate the same.
    - **Summary:** Presentation of the main points of the report is 'summary'. A summary is often presented chapter-wise, i.e., what is there in each of the chapters. This familiarizes the reader with the contents of the report and facilitates in taking a decision whether to pursue the entire text or shelve it.

      A summary can be written in either paragraph format or in a point format. In a summary, the emphasis should be given on stating the idea in its accurate form without any copying from the original material.
    - **Difference between abstract and summary:** Many of the characteristic features of writing an abstract are similar to that of a summary. However, there is a minor difference:
      1. Summary presents the report in a nutshell, without any illustrations and explanations and abstract tells the reader what the report is about in concentrated form.
      2. By its nature an abstract is shorter than a summary. It is generally agreed that the length of the abstract should be about two to five per cent of the original whereas that of the summary between five to ten per cent.

3. Summary is often presented chapter-wise while in an abstract only the concepts are presented. Their development is not discussed. A reader, who is interested in knowing only the extent of coverage, will be satisfied with the abstract. But if he also wants to know the method of analysis, the significant findings, the important conclusions and the major recommendations, he will need a summary.

- **Executive summary:** A summary written in a point format is called executive summary. This type of executive summary is normally written for those top officials, who probably, have little time to go through a summary. In such instances, we normally lift the points as they exist in the original. The basic purpose in observing this type of formulation is that as few changes as possible should be brought about in the summarizing process. The reader would definitely be closer to the text of the report if the points presented in point format are in their original form.
- **Summary and synopsis:** The terms, summary and synopsis, can be used interchangeably. However, normally the gist of any academic work is called as synopsis. It has more connection with academic. A summary, on the other hand, can be used on almost all occasions, academic and professional both.

15.5.2 Main Body

The main body of the report is generally divided into chapters or units. If required, the units are subdivided into subunits and then into sub-subunits. The main units in a detailed report are the following:

1. **Introduction:** Introduction to report provides a better starting point to a reader who is not familiar to the subject matter of the report. It should be well drafted to catch the attention of reader.

   Introduction describes the following points:

   - **Technical/historical background:** This section provides the background for the report and spells out the basic purpose for which the report was written. The required history of the situation helps the reader in analyzing or understanding the case more effectively.
   - **Objective/purpose of writing the report:** Immediately after giving the background history, the purpose of writing the report is given which helps in giving the entire report a proper direction.
   - **Scope and limitations of study:** A report cannot be all inclusive. There must be certain limitations or shortcomings in a typical report. This section spells out the area to be covered and not covered by the report. It familiarises the reader with the complexity and the size of the report.
   - **Difference between contents of introduction and preface:** Preface in a report is a personal statement of the author and is written in personal style. Introduction is a part of the main report and is written in formal, impersonal style.

     Preface prepares the reader by introducing the theme of the report. The preface may also contain acknowledgements. Introduction in a report is an extension of the preface.

2. **Methodology:** Methodology describes the process of writing the report, the sources and method of collecting data, the analytical methods/tools used, the methods to arrive at the conclusion and various other important aspects related to the report.
3. **Discussion/description:** This section is different in different cases and depends upon the type of project/subject matter the writer is dealing with. It discusses the main business of the report. In some cases, it may be discussion and in other it can be data collection, data analysis, situational analysis/problem analysis or countermeasures, etc.

   The main function of this part is to present data in an organized form, discuss their significance, analysis and the result.
4. **Conclusion:** As the title suggests, the conclusion sums up the main points of the report which are drawn by the author through study and analysis.

   In normal business report writing, this section concludes the observations, findings, analysis, etc., in the form of remarks. In data-based reports, it tells the inferences and the judgement formed, which could be derived from the collected data and its analysis.
5. **Recommendations/suggestions:** These are suggestions for future action. Based on the conclusions, the line of future course actions is recommended. Recommendations should be formulated after considering all aspects of the question examined in the report. It assists the management to take quick decisions.

   Recommendations should be given in the descending order of their importance.

15.5.3 Back Matter

Back matter appears at the end of the main report. Generally the elements in back matter are given in separate page numbers, but it is not mandatory. Following are its elements:

1. **Appendices:** An appendix contains material which is too detailed, technical, or complex to include in the body of the report. The material that has been used in the process of writing the report but which is not necessarily to be documented in the main body finds place in the appendix.

   All appendices should be referred to in the text and their significance and meaning pointed out. If their number is more than one, they should be designated as Appendix A, Appendix B, and so on. If the reader wants to go to the details, he can refer appendices or can simply skip. Questionnaires, letters from the respondents, statistical data, various charts, diagrams, maps, sample documents, and other materials which must be included for records are documented in the appendices.
2. **References:** Any term, point or quotation (published or unpublished) referred in the main body of the report but not explained there for fear of break of flow in the text is explained further in the reference section. This is done by citing such works in the text and listing them in alphabetical order at the end of the report. If their number is small, they may be mentioned in the footnotes at the bottom of the page on which they are cited.

   The attention of the reader is drawn to the footnotes either by putting a printer's mark (*) or by putting a number in superscript at suitable places in the text.

The style of documentation followed in the reference section is MLA style (Modern Language Association: an international organization that determines internationally recognized style of documentation for reports, thesis, dissertation, books, etc.) as shown below:

Alan Moorhrad, "The expanding Universe," in 'Science' published from NASA, USA. Vol. 275. No. 4. 1998. Pp. 1025-36

3. **Bibliography:** A bibliography is a serially numbered list of published and unpublished works, which are consulted before or during the preparation of the report. Bibliography is documented in hanging-indented style and the name and the surname of the author are reversed in writing. For example, if the author's name is N.P. Singh, it will be written as Singh N.P. If the book's authors are more than one, the next names are written as usual. Example:

   Mohan Krishna and N.P. Singh. 1995. Speaking English Effectively. New Delhi: Macmillan India Limited

   The difference between bibliography and reference:

   (a) The bibliography may contain works which the author may have consulted for the purpose of report but may not have used them in his report while references contain books or journals which the author has actually used in his report.

   (b) The bibliography may contain works recommended for further study, whereas the reference does not perform any such function.

   (c) The entries in the bibliography are in alphabetical order, whereas the reference may sometimes be recorded in the sequence in which they have been cited in the text.

   (d) The author often prepares the bibliography before writing the report to remember the work he intends to consult. The list of references, on the other hand, is prepared while the report is being written.

   (e) There is a difference in the style of documentation of the two. No page numbers are mentioned in the bibliographical list, whereas page numbers are mentioned in the reference section.

4. **Glossary:** Glossary is a list of technical words used in the report and their explanation. In glossary, we provide meanings of the difficult/uncommon words or terms.
5. **Index:** Index serves as a quick guide to the material in the report. It is the list of important terms/names arranged alphabetically with page numbers. There is a need of giving index only in bulky reports where the Table of Contents cannot do this job. It is provided for the convenience for the reader. It enables reader to find out easily any topic/content of the report.

15.6 PLANNING AND PREPARING REPORT

An effective report is the result of careful preparation and execution of the plan. The following are important preparatory steps to writing a report:

1. Defining the purpose and scope
2. Determining the audience

3. Collecting data
4. Organizing material
5. Making an outline

1. **Defining the purpose and scope:** Reports are produced in response to specific demands or instructions which are generally called 'Terms of reference'. Terms of reference tell you what you are required to do and guide you in your job before you actually begin to collect data. It is also advisable to spend some time in working out the exact scope of your report.
2. **Determining audience:** A report is always written with an audience in mind. The terms of reference generally make it clear who will read your report. In some cases, it may be just your immediate boss who needs information on some aspects of work with which you are connected. At other times it may be a number of readers to whom your report will be circulated.

   Remember that a report is a piece of communication and can be considered successful only if it produces in the reader the desired response. One way of testing is to place yourself in the position of the reader and then examine the effect it produces.
3. **Collecting data:** The next step of writing a report is to gather the relevant data. There are various methods of methods of collecting information and the sources from which you can collect the relevant material. We may place them into the following catagories: (a) Methods of collecting data, (b) Sources of data.

   (a) Methods of collecting data

   - **Personal observation:** Some reports will be based on your personal observation. For example, you may be required to write a report on an experiment you conducted in the laboratory or an event to which you were an eyewitness.
   - **Telephone/personal interview:** Telephonic interviews as well as personal interviews are the other methods of collecting data. If the information you seek is of a routine nature and only brief answers are required from a small number of people, you may contact them on telephone. But often you may not get as effective a feedback on the telephone as in the case of personal interviews. It will help you to draw your own conclusions better.
   - **Questionnaires:** When a wide geographical coverage is required and a large number of people have to be contacted, the most efficient and convenient method is to collect data through questionnaires. In preparing the questionnaire, the following hints will be of help:
     - ☐ Questionnaire should be brief, and convenient to handle.
     - ☐ Each question should be clearly framed and should seek to obtain the information related to the topic of your report.
     - ☐ It should be precise.
     - ☐ Questions which may embarrass the respondent should be avoided.
     - ☐ Ensure that your questions are easy to answer.
     - ☐ Questions should be arranged in a logical order.
     - ☐ Questions should be neatly printed.

(b) Sources of data

- **Internal records:** Relevant data for the reports you have to write can be assembled from internal records. Most activities of an organization are recorded in written documents–letters, memoranda, reports, orders, office notices, circulars, agreements on files, etc. figures for annual statements of income and expenditure, sales, purchases, production, distribution, etc. are collected from account books.
- **Library:** In library written material is collected and kept for use by its members. One of the main aims of a library is to ensure that the best possible use is made of its collections, to bring the right reader to each book, and the right book to each reader.
- **Internet:** Internet has emerged as a mighty global mechanism of information dissemination. It has facilitated the processing of information, reproduction of documents, and communication with persons/organization anywhere in the world.

4. **Organizing material:** The best way to organize material is to prepare the outline of a report before you actually start writing it. Thus, an outline will indicate the pattern of your report and provide you with a starting point for writing. It will also show which topics are more important, which are of equal status, and which are subordinate.
5. **Making an outline:** The last step is to prepare an outline according to the principles of sequencing and categorization. An outline is a framework which would help organize and plan the presentation of the material you have gathered. As a mechanical structure, an outline is an arrangement of words, phrases, or sentences which indicate the nature and sequence of topics and sub-topics to be discussed in your report. A proper outline can prove useful not only in writing the main body of the report but also in preparing its abstract, and summary.

   These steps, if taken properly, would lead to the writing of an effective report.

15.7 STYLE OF REPORT WRITING

Style is that feature, which distinguishes one person's writing from another's. Thus, style is the way of writing or as Chesterfield says, " the dress of thought." All writing has style; it may be poor, good, excellent, personal, and impersonal. Several writers have made an attempt to define 'style'. According to Jonathan Swift, "Style is proper words in proper places." Emerson says, "A man's style is his mind's voice." In this respect, style is like the character attributed to man, be it good or bad.

The following are the basic features of style in a report:

1. Scientific attitude
2. Reader oriented
3. Readability
4. Choice of words and phrases
5. Construction and length of sentences
6. Construction and length of paragraphs

15.7.1 Scientific Attitude

Scientific writing relates to logical thinking and result-oriented views. It is reflected in our handling of matter: collection of data, various sources of knowledge, analysis of data using different tools of analysis and then the presentation technique of the entire material. Since the main purpose of a report is the presentation of facts, it should be able to command the attention of the reader and to clearly convey to him the message.

To achieve this, it is necessary to develop a scientific attitude in writing. Therefore, the language of the report should be terse, direct and informative. The report writer should be objective in his approach to problems, impartial in the analysis of data, and truthful in the presentation of facts. Literary figures of speech and emotive words have no place in report writing.

A report writer, as far as possible, must approach his subject with a scientist's objectivity detachment, and passion for truth. In reports there should be honesty about facts and their presentation in a language the reader can understand. Since every report is written to meet a unique situation, one pattern cannot suit all situations. If the writer has personally collected the data and written the report he may use the first person and active voice. If the work is done as a member of a group or on behalf of a group, the use of 'we' is advisable. To sum up, the reporter should be objective in writing. Objectivity demands that one should not involve one's personal opinions and attitude in a report.

15.7.2 Reader Oriented

Relationship between the report writer and the reader is one of the factors that determine the style of a report and ensures readability. The style of a repot meant for circulation among subordinates will be quite different from a report on the same subject to be circulated to the top management or among other organizations.

15.7.3 Readability

Readability factor determines the language used in a report. A report is always written for a specific readership. If the reader is an expert in the field, we can use all the technical terms and jargons in the report. But if the presentation is for laymen, the writer is supposed to make it as simple as possible, avoiding all the obscure jargons and technical terms. Sometimes the report writer knows the intellectual ability of the reader and sometimes he does not know the reader. In all situations, the report writer should try to make his language reader oriented.

In writing a report, simplicity should be applied not only at the level of vocabulary but at the level of sentences and paragraphs too.

- **Readability formula:** Robert Gunning in his book 'The Technique of clear writing' has suggested a formula, which serves as a guide to test whether the report is likely to be understood by the reader or is difficult and needs revision. It is one of the easy and simple methods to check the readability of a report.

  Robert Gunning uses the word 'fog' to refer to the level of difficulty of a piece of writing. From the reader's point of view, the higher the fog index of writing means the more difficult to understand.

To calculate the fog index of a passage, following steps should be considered:

- To get the average sentence length, the total number of words should be divided by the number of sentences.
- The difficult words, which have three or more syllables, should be counted. While doing so (a) Capitalized words, unless they begin the sentence, (b) Combinations of short easy words (e.g., gentleman), (c) Verb forming of three syllables, including-es or-ed, will not be counted.
- Work out the percentage of difficult words.

  $$\frac{\text{No. of difficult words}}{\text{Total no. of words}} \times 100$$

- Add the average sentence length and the number of difficult words as worked out and multiply the total by 0.4 to get the fog index.

If the passage is long, to calculate the fog index random samples can be taken. According to Gunning, a fog index of ten or less indicates easy reading level.

15.7.4 Choice of Words and Phrases

We should carefully choose the words in preparing a report. In fact, style does not consist in displaying one's vocabulary but in how successfully the writer can communicate his meaning to the reader. Therefore, a careful collection of words is very important.

Sometimes the meanings of words overlap. No two words in a language convey exactly the same meaning. What the dictionary lists are not synonyms but only near- synonyms. The report writer should use such words as would evoke in the mind of reader the same thought, which is in his mind. Sometimes a wrong choice of words may lead to embarrassment, confusion and misunderstanding. Therefore, a careful selection of words is equally important.

Following are the characteristics, which shall be kept in mind in selecting the right words suitable for report writing:

1. **Precision:** In a report one has to be specific in order to be precise. A precise statement will commit the report writer to a specific thing or idea.
   - ☐ One should use a specific word instead of a general term.
   - ☐ One should use a concrete word instead of an abstract word. Abstract words have general meaning while concrete words are the specific words.

For example:

Abstract	*Concrete*
a significant loss	a 53% loss
good attendance record	98% attendance record
the majority	62%
in the near future	by noon Thursday
a labour-saving Robot	does the work of seven workers
light in weight	feather light
a particular newspaper	The Hindustan Times
by road transport	by a truck

- Adjectives and adverbs are weak words. They should be used sparingly in report writing.
- Verbs are action words and attract attention. It is better to use the verbs instead of phrases having ' -tion words' formed from verbs. For example,

Phrases	*Verb*
Take into consideration	Consider
Offer to make a selection	Select
Suggestion	Suggest
Make an application	Apply

- We should prefer the active voice to the passive voice. Active voice is stronger, it emphasizes the action and saves words. However, sometimes passive voice is preferable.
  - When the doer of the action is not important.
  - Passive voice helps avoid accusing the reader.
  - When the performer is not known.
  - When the writer prefers not to name the performer.

2. **Conciseness (to the point):** Every word that is used in report writing should contribute something to the meaning you wish to convey. Special attention should be given to modifiers, elaborate prepositions, and conjunctions, and phrases to introduce a new idea. But abbreviations such as 'O.K.' 'Phone' 'ad', 'exam', 'lab', 'auto', or shortened forms like 'isn't', 'aren't', 'don't', etc., have no place in report writing.

For example

(a) Let us make an approximation of how much money it would cost.

Improved: Let us estimate its cost.

(b) There is a considerable amount of time needed for collecting data, which will be adequate for writing this report.

Improved: For preparing this report, data collection will take considerable much time.

(c) One distinctive feature of which this piece of equipment has and which makes it particularly desirable is that its running cost is very low.

Improved: Low running cost is the distinctive feature of this equipment.

(d) The committee is involved in the task of revising service conditions.

Improved: The committee is involved in revising service conditions.

(e) Various devices that have been experimented on have given very encouraging results.

Improved: Experiments on Different devices have given very hopeful/ good results.

3. **Plainness:** Plain words are usually short and familiar. The writer can catch the reader's attention more easily by using such words. In fact, style does not consist in displaying one's vocabulary but in how successfully the writer can communicate his meaning to the reader. Instead of using the long and unfamiliar words it is better to select the simple words. Following are the few examples of unfamiliar and long words, which we often come across.

Long and unfamiliar words	*Plain words*
activate	start
accomplish	do
aggregate	total
commence	begin
compensation	pay
discern	see
discontinue	stop
endeavour	try
optimum	best
verbose	wordy
initiate	start
ramification	branches/subdivisions

4. **Clichés, and jargons should be avoided in reports:** Cliché can be defined as a phrase that has been used so often that it no longer has much meaning and is not interesting. A cliché very often comes to mind unbidden and finds its way in to writing almost unnoticed. Some of the common clichés are; 'acid test', 'burning question', 'unturned', 'melting point', ' heart and soul', etc.

   Jargon is a lineage full of technical or special words. Every profession has its jargon and is used by the specialists. The use of jargon creates a gap between the professional man and common man and makes writing difficult to understand.

   Foreign words sometimes are used to impress the reader. But the reader of the report would be more interested in what is said rather than how it is said. For example, there is no point in using 'infra dig' when the same meaning can be conveyed by using the word 'below dignity'. By avoiding such words and phrases the report can be kept within easy reach of the reader. There are certain foreign words, which are commonly used in the reports because most people understand them. For example,

Short form	*Full form*	*Meaning*
etc.	etcetera	and so on
ibid	abides	in the same
a.m.	ante meridian	before noon
p.m.	post meridian	after noon

Those are generally set in italics in printed report.

15.7.5 Construction and Length of Sentences

Sentences can be classified on the basis of structure, form, and function. According to structure there are three types of sentences: simple, compound, and complex. A simple sentence consists of one independent clause; a compound sentence has two or more independent clauses joined by coordinate conjunction like and, but, or, etc.; and a complex sentence contains one independent clause, with one or two dependent clauses. These dependent clauses are linked with the independent clause by subordinate conjunctions like 'while', 'because', 'since', 'although', etc. or by relative pronouns like 'who', 'which', etc.

On the basis of form, the sentences are classified into statements, commands, requests, questions, and exclamations.

On the basis of function, the sentences are classified into illocutionary, emotive, expository, descriptive, and narrative. Illocutionary sentences are used for socialization. The emotive sentences express strong feelings or sentiments. The expository sentences explain a process, plan, theory, etc. The descriptive sentences give a picture of something in words or say what qualities an object has. The narrative sentences give an account of events, show their sequence, and establish a relationship among them. Therefore, every sentence in report should perform the function the writer intends it to perform. In a report most sentences are likely to be simple or compound in structure, statements in form, and expository, descriptive, or narrative in terms of function.

There is no rule about the length of a sentence and there cannot be. A survey has been made to find out whether the length of a sentence causes difficulty in understanding and if so, when. According to the survey, the maximum length of a sentence ranging from 15 words to 25 words has been recommended on the basis of these studies. It is difficult to suggest how long the sentences of report should be. But it is certain that communication becomes difficult if too many subordinate ideas are crammed in to one sentence. If the sentence has several, let us say more than three, conjunctions the report writer should try to see whether greater clarity can be achieved by splitting it into two or more smaller sentences. If it is not possible, the predicate should be kept close to the subject and the modifiers, near the words they modify.

- The words, which do not perform a function, should be removed.
- To avoid monotony, the report writer should vary the construction and length of the sentences. Variety would give freshness to style and make the report interesting and easy to read.
- While constructing a sentence, a subject should be chosen about which the reporter is going to say something. Normally sentences have both the subject and the predicate. Sentences such as 'what' 'if' 'so', 'oh', etc. have no place in a report.
- The part of a sentence should be arranged carefully in order to provide the proper emphasis.

15.7.6 Construction and Length of Paragraphs

A paragraph is a group of sentences related to one core idea and arranged in a logical order. The core idea is expressed in a sentence, generally called as topic sentence or theme sentence. All other sentences in the paragraph clarify the idea, compare and contrast it with other similar ideas, give supporting facts, details and proof, illustrate, or provide additional information. Thus, a paragraph must have unity of theme, coherence of sentences and emphasis of main points.

In the report, the topic sentences may occur in the beginning, in the end and occasionally in the middle of the paragraph. If the topic sentence is placed in the beginning, it provides a good basis for writing the summary. If the topic sentence occurs in the middle, the preceding sentences introduce the main idea. If the topic sentence occurs in the end, it summarizes the contents of the paragraph. However, in a report, it is a good practice to place the topic sentence in the beginning, it will help you keep your focus on the point you wish to discuss in the paragraph.

The most important factor that should govern the length of paragraph is whether the development of the core idea is adequate.

It is necessary to have one or more breaks on every page. Solid running matter tires the reader. However, a writer has a number of choices to decide what constitutes one unit of thought or idea.

15.8 REPORTS ARE OFTEN A COLLABORATIVE EFFORT

Short, informal reports are usually a one-person effort. Many formal reports in organizations, however, are multiperson efforts. it is not likely, for example, that management would ask a single person to study the feasibility of entering the generic-product market. Instead, a combination of talents would be needed-marketing, manufacturing, human resources, and the like. Such joint efforts require well-defined organizational skills, time management, close coordination, and a genuine spirit of cooperation.

Advantages of team written reports

- They draw on the diverse experiences and talents of many members.
- They increase each manager's awareness of other viewpoints.
- They typically result in higher-quality output than might be the case if single person worked alone on a complex assignment.
- They produce a final product in less time than would be possible otherwise.
- They help develop important networking contacts.
- They provide valuable experience in working with small group.

15.9 SOME PRACTICAL EXAMPLES OF REPORT WRITING

Let us take some practical examples of report writing here:

Example 1

Your company has decided to held a three-day conference to discuss outstanding industrial problems. Representatives from foreign firms and expert speakers will be invited to it. The Board has asked you to arrange the programme including the discussion, accommodation and entertainment of those attending it. Draft a status report (in memorandum format) summarizing what you have arranged so far.

NORTH INDIA SILICON LIMITED, NEW DELHI

TO : THE BOARD OF DIRECTORS
FROM : XYZ
DATE : 05.03.20....
SUBJECT : ARRANGEMENTS MADE TOWARDS THE CONFERENCE

A three days conference is to be held from 12.04.20...-14.04.20... for discussing the outstanding industrial problems. As desired, the details of the various arrangements made towards the conference, accommodation and the entertainment of the guests are as under:

1. **Arrangements for conference/discussion:** We have made arrangements for 22 participants and 6 panel discussions spread over three days. The entire programme is as follows:

Venue : Hotel Taj Mahal, New Delhi

Timings : 9:00 a.m.-5:30 p.m.

During the presentation, all relevant presentation facilities like, computer, LCD projector, overhead projector, mikes (standing and table) will also be made available for facilitating the presentation.

The hotel shall organize the following facilities:

- U-shaped sitting arrangement for the participants.
- The delegates will be sitting in the front and their name plates will be provided for easy identification by the participants
- Tea will be served two times along with the snacks at 9 a.m. and 3 p.m.
- The lunch will be served at 1:30 p.m. The menu for the lunch can be as per our choice. (Continental/Chinese/Indian)

2. **Arrangements for accommodation:** The total number of delegates expected from India and abroad is 24. Out of which, 16 are from India and 8 from abroad. We have made elaborate arrangements to receive our foreign visitors from the airport. Two cars are provided for the purpose and two volunteers are on duty to welcome the guests. Indian guests shall be received at the railway station and airport by two volunteers.

   The hotel accommodation has been booked for the expert speakers and the foreign delegates in the same hotel. The Indian delegates are put up at the company guesthouse, provided with single room facility.

3. **Arrangements for entertainment:** We have arranged for the entertainment programmes as follows:

Date	*Time*	*Programme*
12th April	6-8 p.m.	Cultural programme by company artists
13th April	6-9 p.m.	City sight-seeing programme
14th April	6-8 p.m.	Handicrafts exhibition

4. **Expenditure:** The expenditure for the above-mentioned activities is as under:

S. No.	*Particulars*	*Expenditure (Rs.)*
1.	Conference for three days including 2 teas and the lunch	40,000/-
2.	Accommodation for the delegates @ Rs. 6000/- per person	1,28,000/-
3.	Entertainment of guests	60,000/-
	Total estimated expenditure	2,28,000/-

This is submitted for your information and necessary advice for further actions.

(signature)

(XYZ)

Example 2

ABC Limited, New Delhi is in the business of marketing Refrigerators. An internal committee has been appointed by the Board of Directors to suggest a suitable place for the location of new branch. As incharge of the committee, draft a feasibility report to be submitted to the Board of Directors.

ABC LIMITED, NEW DELHI

A REPORT

ON

SUITABLE LOCATION FOR A NEW BRANCH

By

XYZ
Area Manager
ABC Ltd., New Delhi

To
Board of Directors
ABC Ltd., New Delhi

September 08, 20....

Abstract

This report explores the scope for the location of the new branch. The committee, constituted to suggest a suitable place for the location of new branch, has studied the various aspects pertaining to the product, demand and the possible locations for its new branch. On behalf of all committee members I take this opportunity to present this report to the Board, regarding suggestions for the most suitable place for the location of a new branch of our company. The findings are as under:

Present situation

Presently, the company has five branch offices at Mumbai, Chennai, Bangalore, Hyderabad and New Delhi. It has been noticed that there is a good demand of refrigerators in the eastern region of Uttar Pradesh. The head office at New Delhi is unable to fulfil the customers' needs and the demand for our refrigerators is gradually decreasing. The competition on the other hand is very strong in terms of Publicity and Promotional activities.

Situational analysis

In spite of a very good potentiality of our product especially in the eastern region of UP, the main constraints the branch office at New Delhi is facing are:

- Inadequate timely after sales services, especially in the rural areas.
- Weak dealers

- Distance, which the area manpower has to travel, is very long. Though representative travels from Delhi to Lucknow at least 2 times per week but this area needs to be concentrated in depth.
- There is no office of our company in this area whereas the other competitive companies have their sales offices with a 6 members' team. This is one of the reasons that the competitors are selling almost 3 times as compared to us.

Recommendations

It is, therefore, suggested that the company should have the new branch in the eastern region and the possible city for opening the branch office is Lucknow.

It is recommended that the office be initially opened at Lucknow as we have been losing our business heavily. At a later date, we may review to have another branch office at Gorakhpur, which can concentrate its peripheral/nearby towns.

(signature)

XYZ

Example 3

As a marketing executive you have been sent to investigate Lucknow District market for your company's products. Write your report on the conditions and prospects. Also include your recommendation for the best method of working in the district.

Compaq Systems India Limited, Banglore

A REPORT

ON

MARKETING POTENTIAL OF COMPAQ COMPUTERS

By

S.K. Nigam
Marketing Executive
Compaq Systems India Ltd.
Bangalore-23

To

The Chairperson
Board of Directors
Compaq Systems India Ltd.
Bangalore-23

March 10, 20.....

1. **Introduction:** A visit to Lucknow District of U.P. was made from 20.02.20…-25.02.20…. with a view to find the marketing potential of Compaq computers. The following three were taken into consideration for the survey:

(a) The existing number of computer users in the area
(b) Choice of the users for the computer set
(c) Buying potentials of the computer users

The data collected through the survey was put to analysis and startling facts came into light as a result. The discussion and the conclusion parts in the following pages reveal the facts of market potential of the new brand of computer launched in the market-Compaq.

2. **Discussion**

   (a) **Widening field:** Computers have found wide scope of use in UP, especially, in the prosperous Lucknow district selected for this survey. It is found that established business concerns, industries, research centres, educational institutions, individual users, libraries, travel agencies, and well-to-do business houses use computers extensively and the demand for PCs is ever increasing. Where computers have been in use for years and now the PC version in use is found to be outdated. It is preferred to be replaced by a P IV model. Educational institutions have either updated their computer labs or replaced the DOS with Windows NT Workstations. The approximate number of computer users in the area is estimated to be 10 lac, excluding the newly opening engineering colleges and private computer training centres in the area. This number is ever increasing at the annual rate of 10% increase.

   (b) **The best preferred:** The survey revealed that most users go for quality and do not care for the investment. Initially, people used Wipro brand computers and individual users preferred assembled sets. But slowly established and good quality products like Compaq are leaving impact on people and making their way into the market. People in this area believe in quality and good after sale service. There is no doubt Compaq will soon get a good share of market because of competitive prices and high quality as well as better services.

   (c) **Investment no bar:** As revealed by the analysis, computer users in this area do not hesitate to invest good amount of money on a reliable product. The area is rich and people are affluent as well as well educated. Now they are aware of the umpteen functions performed by computer, they put faith in it. Compaq is a slightly costly venture initially if compared with the other cheaper brands available and the assembled ones. But its quality and our service have attracted people resulting in no bar in this initial investment.

3. **Conclusion:** It may be safely concluded that Compaq has a bright future in this area. Compaq computers with free multimedia kits and printers have immediately caught people's imagination. At the same time the market is free from competitors and Compaq is the only brand of its functions and performance. No other brand available in the market can boast of such a fast processing speed, superior multimedia facility and good quality ink-jet printers. So, buyers will naturally flock to Compaq.

4. **Suggestions:** Though Compaq brand in itself is publicly yet the market potential of Compaq will boost up if supported by publicity campaigns. We can arrange demonstration classes in educational institutions, engineering colleges, and in industries and I hope we'll obtain good results. Big advertising campaigns will certainly help. Compaq should start its own training centres too.

Example 4

Draft a recommendatory report to expert committee of Board of Directors appointing to inquire into the cause of fire in the basement, resulting in a considerable loss to the company.

ABC LIMITED, NEW DELHI

10.09.20....

A report on cause of fire in the godown

As per the advice of the expert committee of Board of Directors, an investigation was carried out to ascertain the cause of fire and propose corrective actions for prevention of such accidents in the future. The detailed report is as under:

Situational analysis

The fire broke out on the night of 8.09.20... in the basement. At that time there was no body inside the basement and it was locked from the outside. The discussions were held with the concerned security guard and the officers of the company. The observations followed by the recommendations are furnished below.

Observations

- The fire broke out at around 11:30 in the night.
- The security guard was the first person, who saw the smoke and flames coming out of the godown.
- On seeing the flames, the security guard raised an alarm to seek the assistance of the persons nearby and simultaneously gave a call to the fire brigade also.
- The security guard could not inform the branch manager and other responsible officers of the branch, as he did not have their telephone numbers.
- The fire brigade reached within 30 minutes to the site and took control of the situation. But by that time it was too late to act and the fire destroyed a large stock of material stored inside.
- The exact cause of the fire could not be established. However, it is believed that the fire must have been caused due to the short-circuiting of the electrical wires as the basement was closed from the outside and there was no body inside it at the time of fire.

Analysis

The analysis of the observations/discussion points out that

- The security guard was not provided the telephone numbers of the key persons of the organization so that he could have informed them for assistance.
- There was no written down procedure available in the basement and other locations to deal with the fire emergencies.
- The guard was not trained on firefighting methods and the usage of firefighting extinguishers.
- The firefighting equipment was not kept nearby basement to take care of such accidents. As a result the fire broke out in a big way by the time firebrigade reached to the site.

Suggestions/recommendations

It is suggested that:

- The telephone numbers and the names of the key contact persons, telephone numbers of fire brigade and police, etc. should be displayed on the key locations prone to fire.
- A written down emergency procedure is made and explained to the security guards and the concerned persons of the emergency team to control such eventualities.

- Adequate number of firefighting equipment is kept at the designated places and persons are trained for their usage.
- Since the actual cause of fire could not be established and there is a possibility of an electrical short-circuiting, there should be a periodical maintenance of the distribution boxes and electrical wiring.

This investigation report is submitted for the kind perusal of the Board of Directors.

XYZ

(Personnel Manager)

Example 5

Write an acknowledgement letter (letter of submission) for any business report. Invent necessary details yourself.

Acknowledgements

The report, which has been submitted, is the result of the teamwork of all the members on this project. I sincerely thank all my colleagues and all other people who have been associated with this project, directly or indirectly.

My sincere gratitude to the director of the institute Dr. R.S. Tiwari who has provided me with all the infrastructural facilities to carry out my research work and all the help I needed towards completion of the project. My special thanks are due to Dr. C. P. Nigam who has helped me conceptualize this project.

XYZ

Example 6

Prepare a report to be sent to press, on the inaugural function of any handicraft exhibition held in your town.

Inaugural function of the handicrafts

Meerut, 9 January. Meerut city is slowly acquiring the status of the cultural centre of western U.P. Apart from Nauchandi fair, an annual event at Meerut, the city is abuzz with frequent fairs, exhibitions and cultural programmes. For example, Saharanpur was reported to be the place for the best woodwork in western UP but the exhibition of woodcarvings and furniture held at Gandhi Park, Meerut has proved that Meerut is not legging behind Saharanpur in this craft.

The three-day exhibition (January 8, 9, and 10) was declared open by the chief guest of the occasion, Mr. D.K. Goel, DM Meerut city at 9 in the morning. In his inaugural address, Mr. Goel stressed upon the need and significance of such exhibitions in the life of local people, artisans and the visitors alike. He emphasized upon the need to hold such exhibitions frequently. He took a round of the exhibition compound and showed much interest in the articles displayed. He was much impressed by the furniture that has a local touch in its design and decoration.

There are at least 1200 pandals in the exhibition, some of them displaying only woodcarvings and some only furniture. One is impressed by not only the designs, patterns and decorative work displayed but also by the fact that some artisans have used local raw material like, bamboo, cane, scrap wood, and lightweight metal. On the first day of the exhibition, the compound was full. One wishes the place should have been a little more spacious to accommodate such a large crowd of visitors.

Example 7

As a Production Engineer of public sector organization, write a memorandum report to the General Manager suggesting ways and means to enhance rate of production there.

ABC Limited: New Delhi

TO : THE GENERAL MANAGER
FROM : XYZ
DATE : 21.02.20
SUBJECT : REPORT ON INCREASE OF RATE Of PRODUCTION

As desired by you, I am furnishing the details on the increase of production volumes in our company. The objective of this report is to:

- Assess the present situation with regards to the installed capacity in various departments.
- Suggest ways and means to increase the production volumes.

Present situation

Presently, we have the capacity of 100,000 nos. per annum for the manufacturing of diesel engines in our company. It has been observed that the shop wise manufacturing capacity is, however, different and is as follows:

S. No.	*Production Department*	*Capacity for Manufactureing Disesel Engines (Units/year)*
1.	Press	125,000
2.	Weld	100,000
3.	Paint	125,000
4.	Assembly	120,000
5.	Machining	120,000

It is desired that the production capacity be enhanced to a level of 120,000 nos./annum.

Situational analysis

The data on the present available capacity shows that except Weld section all other sections have an adequate capacity to raise the production volumes to a minimum of 120,000 nos./annum. However, the following constraints are available in these sections for enhancing the capacity:

Weld shop

The main problem is of low capacity of TIG (Tungsten Inert Gas) welding machine. Rest of the machines are having enough capacity to make 120,000 units/annum.

Suggestions

The following options are available to enhance the capacity of these shops to a level of 120,000 nos./annum:

Option 1: We purchase one TIG welding machine for weld shop. The total investment works out to Rs. 4.5 lac.

Option 2: We send the components to the vendor who will supply the components to us after welding.

Option 3: Presently, the plant runs on a two-shift basis. Since the proposed volume increase per annum is only 20,000 nos., we may have a policy decision to run these shops in three shifts on need basis.

Merits and demerits of the options

Option	*Merits*	*Demerits*
1	An asset to company. Quality to be monitored at vendor place	Inverstment required
2	No liability	Dependency on the vendor.
3	All facility available with the co. No further investment	Working in III shift Supervision and general admn., Transportation, Canteen facility, etc. required

Recommendation

Considering the available options and their merits and demerits, it is recommended to exercise option 2, i.e., we off load some of the components requiring welding operations to a vendor.

This proposal is for you kind perusal please.

XYZ

(Production Engineer)

Example 8

Draft a report on the feasibility of merging the purchase and store departments of your company.

REPORT ON FEASIBLITY OF MERGING PURCHASE & STARE DPT.
ABC LIMITED, NEW DELHI

REPORT

ON

FEASIBILITY OF MERGING PURCHSE AND STORE DEPARTMENTS

By
XYZ
Manager-Personnel
ABC Ltd., New Delhi

To
Managing Director
ABC Ltd., New Delhi

02.03.20....

Summary

The company's store and purchase departments are presently located at different locations and cause the operational problems. Also it requires more staff and managers to manage purchase and store departments separately.

A study has been conducted to see the feasibility of merging these two departments, which will finally assist in effecting management and control of the day-to-day operations and reduction of manpower. The observations are as under:

Observations

1. The manpower in purchase & store dept.

Purchase Dept.	Manager	1
	Officers	3
	Staff	3
Store Dept.	Manager	1
	Officer	1
	Staff	4

2. The material is first ordered and sent to stores. These are located at a distance of 50 km. Considerable time and efforts are lost in knowing the stock situation and the status of receipt of ordered material by stores.
3. This results in improper utilization of manpower and loss of time.
4. Store dept. has a big unutilized building. This can be easily used by purchase department.
5. An estimated investment of Rs. 15 lac is required to make proper office for purchase dept.

Analysis

1. By combining these two departments, the estimated manpower is:

Manager	1
Officers	3
Staff	5

2. The reduction of manpower is mainly due to better monitoring and control as these two departments are in close proximity to each other.

Recommendation

It is recommended that these two departments be merged which will result in the substantial saving of manpower and also will improve the overall efficiency of the organization.

XYZ

(Managar – Personnel)

Example 9

The head of your organization is worried about the time employees are spending during the tea break. Draft a memo to be signed by him and circulated to all employees asking them to be at their workplace during duty hours.

ABC LIMITED: NEW DELHI

Date : 10.03.20....
To : All Concerned
From : XYZ (Personnel Manager)
Subject : Absence from workplace during duty hours

It has come to the notice of the management that some of the employees of Accounts and other departments visit very frequently to the canteen and spend time in discussion/ other activities with other colleague. This results to unnecessary crowding of employees in the canteen during working hours.

It may please be noted that we have two scheduled timings of tea, each of 10 minutes as per the following time schedule.

Morning tea : 10:00 a.m.-10:10 a.m.
Evening tea : 3:00 p.m.-3:10 p.m.

All concerned persons are requested to observe the above tea timings and assist in maintaining the discipline in the organization.

(XYZ)

Example 10

In Weld Shop of ABC Limited, it has been noted that on many occasions the operators remain on unauthorized absence especially one day prior or after any declared holiday. The Section Incharge has informed the operators and advised verbally but in vain. The matter has now been referred to the Personnel Manager. You consider yourself the Personnel Manager and write a note/memo advising the operators to refrain themselves from such type of activities else the disciplinary action will be initiated as per the standing

ABC Limited: Dehradun

To : All concerned operators of Weld Shop
From : XYZ (Personnel Manager)
Date : 18.09.20.....
Subject : Unauthorized absence

It has come to the notice of the management that the following operators have been absenting from the duties quite frequently. Unauthorized absence not only reflects the careless approach but results in the loss of production also. On many occasions, this matter has been personally discussed with the concerned operator by the Section Incharge – Mr. P K Bhalla but no improvement has so far been reported. Therefore, it has become imperative that such practices should be stopped immediately.

The details of the operators who have indulged themselves in such type of unauthorized absence are listed below:

S. No.	Operator	Unauthorized Absence				
		Jan	Feb	March	Apr	Total
1.	Mr R S Rawat	2	-	4	-	6
2.	Mr P K Saklani	2	1	-	-	3
3.	Mr Gurmeet Singh	1	7	2	-	10

We bring to the notice of all the above-mentioned persons and the like minded in the organization that these activities should be stopped immediately in the best interest of the self and the organization. The company's policy for getting the prior approval from the Section Incharge for any absence should be strictly adhered to.

It is, therefore, in the best interest of the operators to comply to the rules and regulation otherwise the following actions may be initiated:

- No payment of salary for the unauthorized absence.
- Disciplinary action as per the standing rule of the company.

XYZ

REVIEW QUESTIONS

1. What are the general characteristics of a business report? Elaborate.
2. How can you classify business report in various ways? Explain various types of reports with the help of tree diagram.
3. What is an informal report? Describe the basic structure of a memorandum?
4. What aspects of a report are dealt with in the 'front matter' and 'back matter' of a business report?
5. You have recently attended a conference. Write a site visit report for your co-workers.
6. Comment on the following:
   (a) Scientific attitude in report writing
   (b) readability of report
   (c) Title page of a report
   (d) Executive summary
7. Why is the 'you-attitude' especially important with long, complex reports?
8. What is the function of a report introduction? Explain.
9. What information might you include in the back matter of a report? Discuss.
10. What types of material does an appendix contain? Why do some writer's cite references in the report?
11. Write a note on the style of business report. Does the style of report differ from that of a literary article?
12. What is the desirable structure of a business report? Also elucidate precautions to be taken while preparing and writing a business report.
13. Write a report in which you use a table or graph to explain any one of the following problems and its solution to your manager:
    (a) A sales decline in a store at a mall
    (b) Difficulties with a measuring device in a lab
    (c) Problems in the shipping department of a furniture companay

    Use at least one visual aid.
14. Assume that you have just returned from a conference on sales promotion to which you were deputed by your college. Write a memo to your managing director, reproting to him the important matters discussed at the conference and indicating the significance of the conclusions arrived at.
15. Your manager has asked you to determine whether or not the office staff would welcome the introduction of canteen facilities. Most of the staff have indicated that they would, but only if the facilities were of a high standard. Some of the staff would prefer luncheon vouchers. Make your recommendation in a report to your manager.
16. You are working in a company which is dealing in foreign exchange functions and its impacts on business. Your Managing Director has asked for your advice in the matter and has requested for a brief report on the subject.

16
BUSINESS PROPOSALS

Chapter Objectives

This chapter will enable you to understand:

- Meaning of proposal
- Difference between report and proposal
- Types of proposals
  - External proposal
  - Internal proposal
- Format of journal proposals
- Some practical examples of proposal writing

16.1 BUSINESS PROPOSAL

The proposal is one of the most important forms of business writing. The word 'proposal' has been derived from the word "propose" which means 'to offer' or to 'put forward for consideration'. A business proposal is a persuasive communication that may be defined as a written offer to solve a business problem or to undertake a project of a practical or theoretical nature.

You might have to write a proposal for your own business or try to persuade your employer to make a few costly changes. Or, may be, you would like to suggest a few changes in the marketing policy of your company. To do all this, you will have to write good proposals. And, if you work for a government agency, non-profit organization, or a large corporation, the proposal can be a valuable tool for initiating projects that benefit the organization or the employee-proposer (and usually both). Proposals may contain other elements—technical background, recommendations, results of surveys, information about feasibility, and so on. But what makes a proposal actually a proposal is that it asks the audience to approve, fund, or grant permission to do the proposed project. It convinces the reader(s) that:

- the proposal is good (scientifically and economically)
- the writer(s) is qualified to accomplish the task.

In writing a good proposal, there are three things you need to identify:

The problem: It is important to state the problem convincingly. Talk about the needs and why the proposal is important.

Solution: The solution to the problem is another important feature in a proposal. The readers will be interested in knowing what you want to propose exactly and how it is related to the problem presented.

Costs: The next important thing in a proposal is the cost factor. What will be the cost of the changes and is the cost worth the changes.

16.1.1 Comparison Between Report and Proposal

A report as well as a proposal imparts information and they both form an essential part of the business correspondence. But there is a basic difference between the two.

1. A proposal is written before the event where as the report is written after the event has taken place.
2. The proposal aims at getting the approval and acceptance of what one wants to do, whereas the report usually deals with what has already been done.

Imagine that you have a terrific idea for installing some new technology where you work and you write up a document explaining how it works and why it's so great, showing the benefits, and then end by urging management to go for it. Is that a proposal? No, at least not in this context. It's more like a feasibility report, which studies the merits of a project and then recommends for or against it. Now, all it would take to make this document a proposal would be to add elements that ask management for approval for you to go ahead with the project.

16.2 TYPES OF PROPOSALS

Consider the situations in which proposals occur. A company may send out a public announcement requesting proposals for a specific project. This public announcement—called a request for proposals (RFP)—could be issued through newspapers, trade journals, Chamber of Commerce channels, or individual letters. Firms or individuals interested in the project would then write proposals in which they summarize their qualifications, project schedules and costs, and discuss their approach to the project. The recipient of all these proposals would then evaluate them, select the best candidate, and then work up a contract.

But proposals come about much less formally. Imagine that you are interested in doing a project at work (for example, investigating the merits of bringing in some new technology to increase productivity). Imagine that you visited with your supervisor and tried to convince her of this. She might respond by saying, "Write me a proposal and I'll present it to upper management." As you can see from these examples, proposals can be divided into several categories:

16.2.1 Internal, External

If you write a proposal to someone within your organization (a business, a government agency, etc.), it is an internal proposal. The internal proposal persuades the higher authorities or the management of the same organization to accept an idea–usually to change something (for example, new pieces of lab equipment), or to fund something, or both. With internal proposals, you may not have to include certain sections (such as qualifications), or you may not have to include as much information in them.

An external proposal is one written from one separate, independent organization or individual to another such entity. Ranging from lengthy (100 pages or more) to short (3 to 5 pages), these documents secure contracts for firms. The typical example is the independent consultant proposing to do a project for another firm.

Government agencies and large and small corporations issue a Request for Proposal (RFP), which explains the project and lists its specifications precisely. For example, a government agency, such as the Ministry of Defence, often sends RFPs to several large firms to solicit proposals for a specific type of item, for example, a truck. The RFP contains extremely detailed and comprehensive specifications, stating the important characteristics of that truck (height, weight, colour, speed, carrying capacity, and so on) and specifying the content, format and, deadline for the proposals.

Companies that receive the RFP write proposals to show how they will develop the project. They must be prepared to prove that their product will meet requirements of all specifications. A team assembles a document demonstrating that the company has the technical know-how, managerial expertise, and budget to develop the project.

After receiving all the proposals, the firm that requested them turns them over to a team of evaluators. The evaluators rate the proposals, judging the technical, management, and cost sections in order to select the best overall proposal.

External proposals are also commonly written by state, and local governments, public agencies, education and industry.

16.2.2 Solicited, Unsolicited

If a proposal is solicited, the recipient of the proposal in some way requested the proposal. Typically, a company will send out requests for proposals (RFPs) through the mail or publish them in some news source. But proposals can be solicited on a very local level: for example, you could be explaining to your boss what a great thing it would be to install a new technology in the office; your boss might get interested and ask you to write up a proposal that offered to do a formal study of the idea. Unsolicited proposals are those in which the recipient has not requested proposals. With unsolicited proposals, you sometimes must convince the recipient that a problem or need exists before you can begin the main part of the proposal.

16.3 PLANNING THE EXTERNAL PROPOSAL

To write an external proposal, you must consider your audience, research the situation, use visual aids, and follow the usual format for this type of document.

16.3.1 Consider the Audience

The audience of an external proposal consists of potential customers. These customers know that they have a need, and they have a general idea of how to fill that need. Usually, they will have expressed their problem to you in a written statement (RFP) or in an interview. Generally, a committee will decide whether to accept your proposal. You must assess their technical awareness and write in such a way that they all understand your proposal. To write to them effectively, you should follow these guidelines:

- Address each need they have expressed.
- Explain in clear terms how your proposal fills their needs.
- Express the relevance of technical data.

16.3.2 Research the Situation

To write the proposal effectively, you must clearly understand your customer's needs as well as your own product or service. Your goal is to show how your product fill the customers' needs. You must research their needs by interviewing them or by reading their printed material. Make sure you understand exactly what they want.

16.3.3 Use Visual Aids

Many types of visual aids may be appropriate to your proposal. Tables might summarize costs and technical features. Maps or layouts might show where you will install the workstation and the electrical lines in the company premises. Remember that your goal is to convince the decision- makers that your way is the best.

16.4 MAIN PARTS OF A PROPOSAL

Four main parts, however, are found in a proposal:

1. Front Matter
2. Technical Section
3. Management Section
4. Financial Section

16.4.1 Front Matter

Front matter includes Cover Page, Title Page, Table of Contents and an executive summary.

1. **Cover page:** The cover page includes
    - The title of the proposal
    - The name of the organization
    - The name and designation of the author
    - Name of the person for whom the proposal is written
    - The date of submission

2. **Title page:** Usually, the title page is the first right-hand page of the proposal. It may have the following information:
   - The title of the proposal
   - The name of the organization
   - The name and designation of the author
   - Name of the person for whom the proposal is written
   - Project number
   - Approval by the concerned authorities
   - The date of submission
3. **Table of contents:** A table of contents is a list of the major headings in a proposal in their order of appearance and with their corresponding page numbers.
   - Recommended only if proposal is of or more than 10 pages long.
   - If proposal is long enough, table of contents is made to give the reader:
     - ☐ Overall view of the report.
     - ☐ Helps in locating the particular topic easily.
   - The contents are compiled generally from the headings/sub-headings of the proposal.
   - The page numbers are written on each page.
4. **Executive summary:** The executive summary is the entire proposal in a nutshell. A well-written, comprehensive and concise summary persuades the reader to appreciate the writer's idea. In short external proposal, this section should be reduced in proportion to the body. It should succinctly present the contents of the technical, managerial, and financial sections.

16.4.2 Technical Section

This is perhaps the most important section of the proposal. Technical section begins by stating the problem to be solved. Clarity of presentation is the essential requirement of technical section of the proposal. The proposers must clearly demonstrate that they understand what the customer expects. In this section, the proposal should describe:

- the nature of the problem and its background.
- its approach to solving the problem and present a preliminary design for the product if one is needed.
- alternative methods for solving the problem.
- any major technical problems visualized by the writer of the proposal and the solutions offered thereof.

16.4.3 Management Section

The management section describes the personnel who will work directly on the project. In the case of company the recipient would obviously be interested in assessing whether the writer has the ability and talent as well as basic resources to execute the project. This section clearly explains:

- educational qualification and professional achievements of the people responsible for the project. It's like a mini-resume contained in the proposal.
- the firm's success with similar projects and its willingness to service the product.
- a description of the existing facilities and technical assistance.
- a schedule for the project.
- deadline for each phase.
- the additional facilities required for the proposal work.

This section specifies how the work will be divided, who will be responsible for each division and how much time would be taken to complete it. It may tabulate the time schedule for the activities matching it with person responsible for each job or task.

16.4.4 Financial Section

The financial section provides a breakdown of the costs for every item in the proposal, whether internal or external. In external proposals the amount and type of cost data required are given in the Request for Proposal (RFP). The estimates should be realistic, accurate and complete.

Most technical proposals, however, contain the cost analysis of the following items:

- Materials
- Equipment
- Salaries of technical personnel
- Salaries and wages of other personnel
- Travel
- Contingencies (Allocation of reserved funds for any unforeseen activity)
- Publications
- Outside consultant services

16.4.5 Conclusion

It is an optional element; it may be given when the situation demands. But if it is given, it states the significance of the project and highlights once again the benefits that would accrue from it.

16.5 EVALUATION/FEASIBILITY OF A PROPOSAL

The three significant aspects of the proposal, namely, the technical content, the management plan and the cost estimate are put to detailed scrutiny by experts in this area. The evaluators rate the proposals, judging the technical, management, and cost sections in order to select the best overall proposal. This evaluation is generally known as feasibility of a proposal.

A proposal may be rejected if it does not stand the test of evaluation. There are, however, other reasons for the rejection of a proposal. For example,

- Adequate funds are not available for the execution of the proposal.
- The proposed project has low priority.
- The improvement proposed is not significant or is too meagre (thin) to justify the overall effort and cost.
- Another competitive proposal is found superior to it.

16.6 INTERNAL PROPOSAL

When someone within the organization makes a proposal and passes it on to the higher authorities or the management of the same organization, it is known as internal proposal. The internal proposal persuades someone to accept an idea-usually to change something (for example, new pieces of lab equipment), or to fund something, or both.

16.6.1 Planning the Internal Proposal

The goal of an internal proposal is to convince the person or group in authority to allow the writer to implement his or her idea. To achieve this goal, the writer must consider the audience, use visual aids, organize the proposal well, and design an appropriate format.

1. **Consider the audience:** Writer should consider the audience of a proposal in at least three ways: in terms of their involvement, their knowledge, and their authority.
   - **How involve is the audience?**

     In most cases, readers of a proposal either have assigned the proposal and are aware of the problem or have not assigned the proposal and are unaware of the problem. In the assigned proposal and the reader is aware of the problem, the writer does not have to establish that a problem exists, but does have to show that how the proposal will solve the problem. If the audience does not assign the proposal and is unaware of the problem, the writer must first convince the audience that a problem exists and only then can he/she go on to offer a convincing solution.
   - **How knowledgeable is the audience?**

     The audience may or may not know the concepts and facts involved in either the problem or the solution. You must learn to estimate your audience's level of knowledge. If the audience is less knowledgeable, take care to define terms, give background, and use common example or analogies.
   - **How much authority does the audience have?**

     The audience may or may not be able to order implementation of your proposed solution. A manager might assign the writer to investigate problems with the material flow of a particular product line, but the manager will probably have to take the proposal to a higher authority before it is approved.
2. **Use visual aids:** Use of Visual aids—tables, graphs, gnatt charts and diagrams—can enhance a proposal. Visuals can support any part of the proposal—description of the problem, the solution, the implementation, or the benefits.

3. **Organize the proposal:** Organize the proposal around four questions:
   - What is the problem?
   - What is the solution?
   - Can the solution be implemented?
   - Should the solution be implemented?
   - **What is the problem?**

     Describing the problem is a key part of a proposal. The writer must establish three things about the problem:

     ☐ the data

     ☐ the significance

     ☐ the cause

     The data are the actual facts that a person can perceive. The significance is the way the facts cause a falling off from a standard you hope to maintain. To explain the significance of the problem, you show that the current situation negatively affects productivity or puts you in an undesirable position. The cause is the problem itself. If you can eliminate the cause, you will eliminate the negative effects.
   - **What is the solution?**

     To present an effective solution, explain how it will eliminate the cause. If the problem is causing undesirable condition, then the solution must show how that condition can be eliminated. If the Instrumentation Lab of Electronics department is running with obsolete equipment, then the writer must show how the modernization of lab can improve its functioning and efficiency. You should analyze the solution in terms of its impact on technical, management/maintenance, and financial aspects of the situation.
   - **Can the solution be implemented?**

     The writer must show that all the systems involved in the proposal can be put into effect. To make it clear, you would explain:

     ☐ the cost

     ☐ The effect on personnel

     ☐ The schedule for implementing the changes
   - **Should the solution be implemented?**

     To convince someone that you should be allowed to implement your solution, the writer should demonstrate the benefits of the proposed solution, stressing how it will eliminate the negative aspects of the situation.

16.7 DESIGNING A PROPOSAL

To design a proposal, select an appropriate format, either formal or informal. A formal proposal has a title page, table of contents, and summary. In informal proposal you can use the memorandum format or some kind of preprinted form.

16.8 FORMAT OF FORMAL PROPOSALS

Format of a formal proposal has the following features:

Topic	*Point of persuasion*
1. **Introductio** What do you propose to do	• Give some background information to help readers understand what you have in your mind.
2. **Problem** *Why is it important*	• State the problem convincingly • You will have to persuade you readers that the problem is significant to them. • The manner in which you describe the problem is very important for the success of the proposal. • Present the problem from your reader (s) point of view.
3. **Objectives** *Make your objectives clear*	• The features necessary to make a successful solution • Talk about how the action will solve the problem.
4. **Solution** The detailed overa plan of overall plan of what you intended to do	• Link up your solution to the objective • It is the best way of achieving the objectives.
5. **Plan of action** The resources with which you have to do the work, the schedule you have fixed for it, your plan to execute it.	• Tell your audience that you have the resources, the equipment and the expertise necessary to carry out the proposal. • Present a viable and suitable schedule. • State what else you would need for the work and how they can be procured. • Give your audience a very clear picture of how much time the work will take.
6. **Cost estimation** How reasonable is the cost.	• Give a clear picture of the cost to be incurred. • To convince your reader give a calculation of how much can be saved as a result of the project.

16.9 REVISION CHECKLIST FOR PROPOSALS

As you reread and revise your proposal, watch out for problems such as the following:

- Make sure you use the right format. Remember, the memo format is for internal proposals only; the formal format of proposal is for proposals written from one external organization to another. (Whether you use a cover memo or cover letter is your choice.)

- Write a good introduction—in it, state that this is a proposal, and provide an overview of the contents of the proposal.
- Make sure to identify exactly what you are proposing to do.
- Think from the point of view of the readers. Keep their goals and perspectives in mind when you are trying to persuade.
- Break out the costs section into specifics. Be realistic about the cost but show that it is necessary.
- For internal proposals, don't omit the section on costs and qualifications. For example, how much time will you need, will there be printing, binding costs? Include your qualifications, if your proposal will go to somebody in the organization who doesn't know you.
- Some of your proposal readers may know the technical side of your project—but others may not. Bring difficult technical concepts down to a level that non-technical can understand.

16.10 SOME PRACTICAL EXAMPLES OF PROPOSAL WRITING

16.10.1 Cover Letter with Separate Proposal

In this format, you write a brief cover letter and attach the proposal after it. The cover letter briefly announces that a proposal follows and outlines the contents of it. In fact, the contents of the cover letter are pretty much the same as the introduction. This is because the letter may get detached from the proposal or the reader may not even bother to look at the letter and just dive right into the proposal itself.

Example 1

As the Branch Manager of the Punjab National Bank, Sarvodaya Nagar, Mumbai you wish to expand the services and facilities of your branch on popular demand. These include provision of fifty lockers, one teller counter and one additional office room. Invent the necessary details and prepare a proposal to be sent to the Divisional Manager of your Bank.

Punjab National Bank
Sarvodaya Nagar
Mumbai
26.3.20....

Divisional Manager
Punjab National Bank
Thane, Mumbai

Dear Sir

Sub: Proposal for incorporating additional facilities in our Branch at Sarvodaya Nagar, Mumbai

Kindly note that we have been operating our branch at Sarvodya Nagar, Mumbai for the last 5 years and have a customer base over 10,000 nos. Of late, customers have been requesting to provide with the additional facilities like lockers and teller system facilities for which a proposal has been prepared by us and is enclosed for your kind perusal and necessary approval.

We request you to kindly give your feedback for further planning of activities at our end.

Yours faithfully

XYZ

Branch Manager

Punjab National Bank
Sarvodaya Nagar, Mumbai
A Proposal
for
Incorporating Additional Facilities in our Branch
By
XYZ
Branch Manager
Punjab National Bank
Sarvodaya Nagar, Mumbai
To
Divisional Manager
Punjab National Bank
Thane, Mumbai
08/03/20....

Summary

Punjab National Bank has been functioning in Sarvodaya Nagar, Mumbai for the last 5 years. The bank has a customer base of over 10,000 nos. However, over a period of time with the increase in the transaction per day, it has been noticed that the usual time taken for the clearance of cheque/withdrawal is 25 minutes as against the bank norms of 15 minutes. Also, the customers have been requesting for improved facilities with regards to the safe deposits (lockers). This is a common facility being provided by other banks in the same vicinity. We propose to provide better services and facilities to the customers by having

- Teller counter
- Fifty lockers
- A separate office room to deal with the esteemed customers as the existing space available is inadequate.

It is, therefore, proposed that the above-mentioned services and facilities be extended for improving the bank image, which in turn will add to more customer base in future.

The total expenditure to be incurred is approximately 1,55,000 rupees and this will be implemented in a time frame of six months.

A detailed proposal is made for your perusal.

Objective

To provide improved services and facilities to the bank customers.

Present situation

- The bank handles on an average 1000 customers every day but it has one extension counter. It takes approximately 25 minutes for clearance of a cheque / withdrawal, which is much higher than the bank's norms of 15 minutes. This leads to lot of inconvenience to the customers.
- Further, the bank does not extend any facility to the customers for safe deposits by providing lockers. This has resulted to shifting of customer base to other banks in the vicinity that provide such locker facilities.
- The bank does not have a separate office room due to inadequate space availability and the discussions with the customers are held in the main hall. This causes inconvenience to the customers.

Proposal

It is desired that the services and the facilities to the customers be improved by:

- Facilitating a teller counter for speedy clearance of cheques/withdrawal and comply with the bank's norms of 15 minutes.
- Extending locker facilities for safe deposits.
- Providing separate office room for official work and discussion with the esteemed customers.

Implementation approach

- The teller counter will be built of a wooden partition and will be managed by the existing staff by rescheduling their job responsibilities.
- The lockers will be bought from Godrej, which is the best in safe deposits. Initially, we plan to have 50 nos. of such lockers and subsequently add more lockers based on the demand.
- A separate office room of 3 metre X 3 metre to be constructed, which will have a capacity to accommodate 6 persons at a time.

Cost estimation for implementation of proposal

Following expenditure is estimated implement the proposal:

S. No.	Description	Expenditure (Rs.)
1.	Construction of teller counter	20,000
2.	Lockers (50 nos.)	100,000
3.	Construction of office room	35,000
	Total	155,000

Inplementation schedule

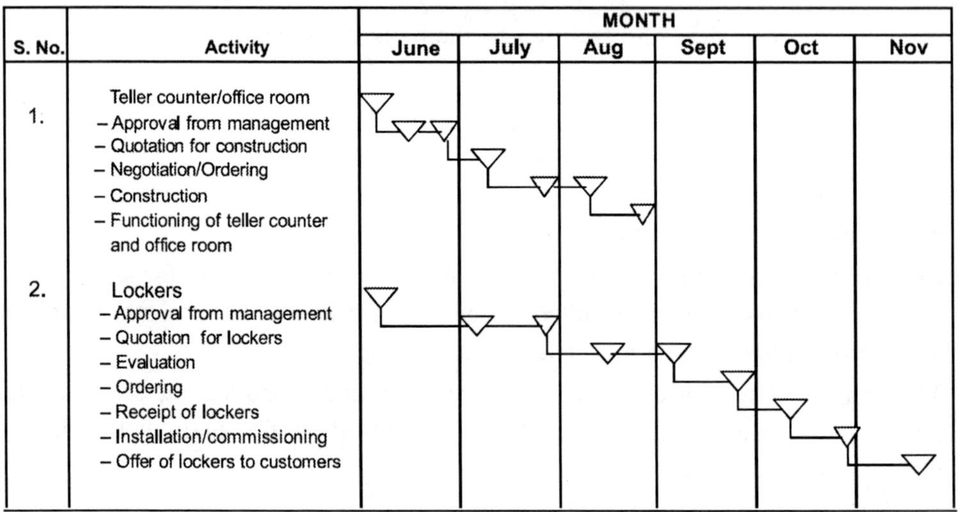

Benefits

By way of implementation of above-mentioned proposal, it is expected that the bank will be able to meet the expectations of the customers and increase the customer base and overall improvement in the image of the bank.

It is, therefore, requested that an amount of Rs. 1,55,000 be sanctioned to implement the above-mentioned proposals in the interest of the customers at large.

Example 2

As a fresh graduate in engineering you have decided to establish a manufacturing unit in your town. You wish to avail of the subsidized loan facility under the self-employment scheme. Draft a proposal for the manufacture of an item of your choice, seeking loan from the State Industrial Development Finance Corporation, Lucknow, Uttar Pradesh.

XYZ
24, Friends Colony
Sector 68
Noida
10.8.20....

Branch Manager
State Industrial Development Finance Corporation
Lucknow
Uttar Pradesh

Dear Sir

Sub: Requisition for obtaining loan towards establishing a manufacturing unit for electric fans.

I am an unemployed engineer from ABC Engineering College, Greater Noida and intend to have my own small-scale industry for manufacturing of electric fans.

As per the policy of the government to promote self-employment through small-scale industries, I understand that your branch has been offering subsidized loans on a long-term basis.

I am keen to have a loan of Rs. 6 lac for installing a small-scale unit of electric fans. The detailed proposal has been made and is annexed for your kind perusal.

I request that the loan of Rs. 6 lac may kindly be granted for the above-mentioned purpose.

(XYZ)

A PROPOSAL
FOR
MANUFACTURING UNIT FOR ELECTRIC FANS
By
XYZ
24, Friends Colony
Sector 68, Noida
To
Branch Manager
The State Industrial Development
Finance Corporation
Lucknow, Uttar Pradesh

10.8.20....

Summary

There is a good demand of electric fans in India. Government has been promoting small scale units through unemployed youth engineers by way of granting subsidized loans on a long-term basis.

A project for assembly of electric fans in Noida has been prepared with a capital expenditure of Rs. 11 lac. Out of 11 lac, the promoter shall incur 5 lac from self-finance, whereas the balance of 6 lac is intended to be borrowed from the bank on soft terms (6% per annum). The return of investment at the break-even point of 30,000 fans per year is estimated to be 2.5 years, which is quite good and thus makes the project feasible.

A detailed proposal is made and is as follows:

Objective

To seek the loan from State Industrial Development Finance Corporation, Uttar Pradesh towards establishing a manufacturing unit for manufacturing of electric fans in Noida.

Present Situation–Demand of Electric Fans

The electric fans are required in every house. There is a growing demand at a rate of over 10% per annum with the increase of housing and commercial sector. It is expected that this industry will further grow in the years to come.

The government has also been promoting the educated unemployed engineers to come to the mainstream of development of the nation and has been granting easy long-term loans to promote small-scale units operated by such unemployed engineers.

The following graph demonstrates the growth of electric fans in small-scale industry and in the organized sectors.

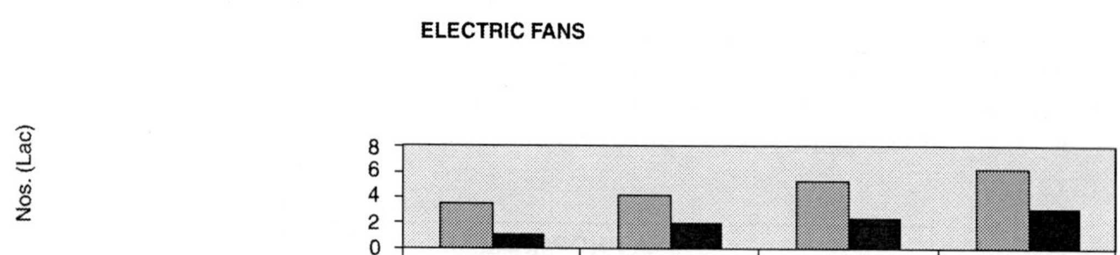

	98-99	99-00	00-01	01-02
Organized sector	3.5	4.1	5.2	6.2
Unorganized sector	1.0	1.9	2.3	3.1

Year

Proposal

A feasibility study has been conducted to promote such a small-scale industry to manufacture electric fans. The proposal consists of the following assumptions:

- The installed capacity of the unit is 30000 fans per year.
- The main parts of the electric fans shall be procured from the following vendors.

Components	Vendor
Electric motor	Rajhans Industries, Meerut
Covers	Prem Auto, Noida
Blades	Jai Prakash Industries, Noida

- The company intends to perform only assembly at its premises. The electric fans shall be subjected to quality control tests before being sold through the distributors.
- The company plans to tie up with such distributors initially in four districts of Uttar Pradesh, which will be increased subsequently to other districts and other states.

Investment required for establishing assembly unit

S. No.	Description	Expenditure
1.	Building cost	500,000
2.	Conveyor	100,000
3.	Working equipment	50,000
4.	Officer capital	50,000
5.	Working capital	300,000
6.	Other miscellaneous items	100,000
	Total	1,100,000

Cash management (Cash Flow)

Out of the total cost requirement of the project, the funds are proposed to be managed in the following way:

Self-financing - Rs. 500000

Loan from bank - Rs. 600000

Return of investment (ROI)

It is expected that the sales of the electric fans will be met right from the day one and no problem is envisaged in meeting the sales target of 30000 fans per year. With these assumptions and considering the overall net profit of 15%, which is the lowest considered as per the industry practice, it is expected that the return of investment will be in 2.5 years.

Implementation schedule

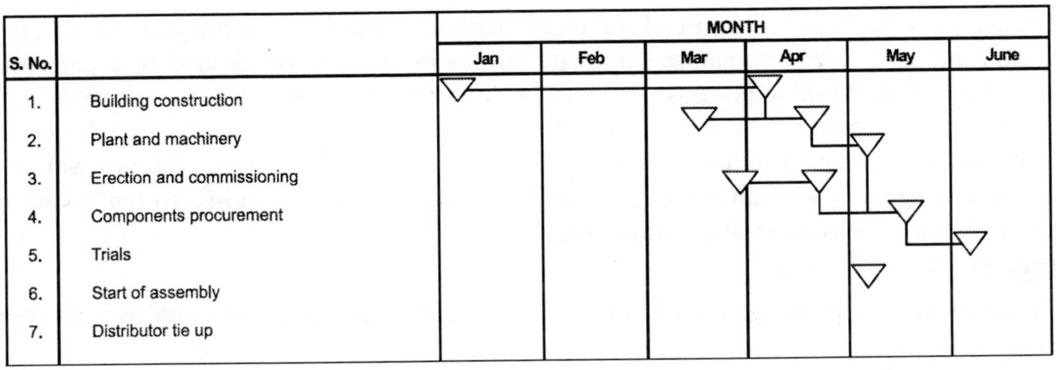

Cover memo with separate proposal

In this format, you write a brief "cover" memo and attach the proposal after it. The cover memo briefly announces that a proposal follows and outlines the contents of it. In fact, the contents of the cover memo are pretty much the same as the introduction. This is because the memo may get detached from the proposal or the reader may not even bother to look at the memo and just dive right into the proposal itself.

Example 3

A large public limited company has been spending about Rs. 7 lac per annum on getting its various documents such as routine forms, brochures, reports, proposals, manuals, etc. printed by outside agencies. For greater economy and efficiency it has been decided to have its own printing unit to cater to all its printing needs. As Personnel Manager write a proposal for the creation of this Unit for consideration of the Board of Directors.

ABC LIMITED: DEHRADUN

Date: 10.3.20...

To: The Board of Directors

From: Personnel Manager

Subject: Proposal for in-house printing of documents

The company has been procuring various printed documents from outside printers for over last 3 years. The total expenditure incurred/year on an average is Rs. 7. lac.

It is desired to explore the possibility of having in house printing facility for printing of documents in use. This is aimed to improve overall economy and the efficiency of the organization.

A proposal in this regard has been prepared and is annexed along with for the kind consideration of the Board of Directors. We propose to initiate necessary work in this regard once the Board of Directors accepts the proposal.

XYZ

Proposal for In-house Printing of Documents

Executive summary

The company has been using printed stationary material worth Rs. 7 lac per year. The printed documents/stationery are organized through various printers. It was desired to explore the possibility of establishing in-house printing facilities for improvement in the economy and the efficiency. Accordingly, it was studied that by investing Rs. 4.5 lac, we can establish our own printing facilities. The return of investment has been worked out to 2.5 years, which is very encouraging by all standards. A detailed proposal is hereby proposed to the Board of Directors for their consideration and approval.

Objective

To economize the printing cost of various documents in use by establishing own printing unit.

Present Situation

The company has been using various documents for day-to-day purpose. The documents are printed by various printing units and incur a total annual expenditure of about Rs.7 lac, which is a significant amount.

A feasibility study was carried out to explore the possibility of economizing the printing cost by way of having our own printing unit. The quotation from various printing press manufacturers were organized and based on the evaluation, it was decided by the evaluation team members that the offer received from M/s Jaya Printing Press is most price competitive.

Investment required for establishing in-house printing unit

S .No.	Description	Expenditure
1.	Building cost	100,000
2.	Printing press	300,000
3.	Installation and commissioning	25,000
4.	Contigency amount	20,000
	Total	445,000

Return of investment (ROI)

The yearly expenditure incurred on printing stationery is around Rs. 7 lac. The cost of infrastructure and the printing press is estimated to Rs. 445,000. The return of investment as calculated by Finance Department is worked out to 2.5 years.

(ABC)

Proposal

Since ROI is only 2.5 years, it is, therefore, proposed that the in-house facility for printing of various documents be generated by having our own printing unit. This will add to the overall improvement in economizing the operations.

Implementation approach

The following approach is suggested for establishing printing facility.

- The printing unit can be housed beside the administration block.
- Build a separate room for printing unit.
- Place an order on M/s Jaya Printing Press
- Start our own printing for various documents in use.

Implementation schedule

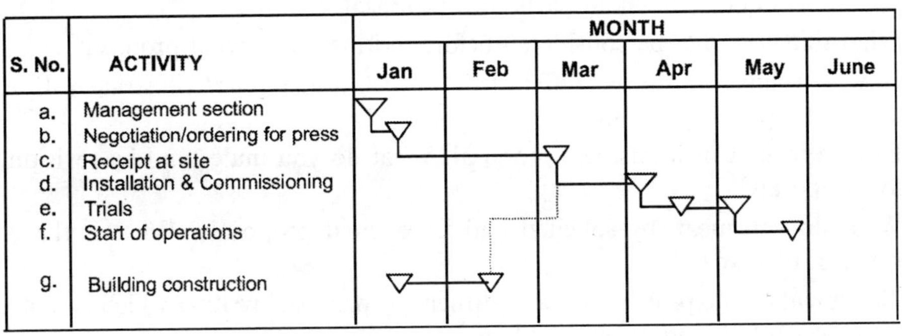

Benefits

It is estimated that by having the in-house printing of documents, the company shall be benefited by Rs. 1.1 lac/year. Also there would be flexibility in printing schedules and the inventory carrying cost can be further brought down, which is not included in the saving proposed.

Memo proposal (Internal proposal): In this format, you put the entire proposal within a standard office memorandum.

Example 4

The instrumentation lab of your institute is running with obsolete equipment. A company interested in this job has struck an agreement to modernize it. Write a proposal in 100 words along with its salient features as per job requirement.

ABC Institute of Technology, Panipat

Date: 10.3.20....

To: Prof. Y. Kumar, Director

From: Sunil Kumar, Lecturer, Dept. of Electronics

Subject: Proposal for modernization of Instrumentation Lab

The Instrumentation Lab of our institute has been running for the last 3 years with the obsolete instruments. We have hired the services of M/S ABC consultant for modernization of this lab.

M/S ABC consultant has agreed to buy our existing instruments at the cost prevailing in the market and to equip the lab with the latest instruments as per the list submitted by us. The total additional expenditure works out to Rs. 3.5lac and the activity of modernization shall be completed in a period of three months from the date of placement of firm order.

With this modernization activity, our students will get better insight of the subject for their overall understanding.

(XYZ)

REVIEW QUESTIONS

1. Define proposal. Explain in detail the factors, which should be considered while writing an external proposal.
2. Describe in detail the main parts of a proposal.
3. What things should be considered before writing an internal proposal?
4. How a technical proposal differs from a technical report? Illustrate with examples different types of proposal.
5. Draw a format of a business proposal. What do you undestand by revision cheklist for proposals?
6. What do you mean by solicited and unsolicited proposals? What is the difference between the two?
7. 'Statement of the problem is a constituent of proposal writing which is written in the front page of the proposal.' Explain.

8. You are Mr. Shishir Kumar, Manager, ABC, Electrical Devices, Delhi. Submit a proposal to your Managing Director for the supply of new air conditioners to replace the old and insufficient ones in the office.
9. Design a proposal for levying of financial support in order to establish a sister concern of the company Cooper & Brewery Pvt. Ltd.
10. Write a proposal to the Director, State Corporation for Industrial Development, Lucknow for the modernization of the commercial section.
11. You are Mr. Shishir Kumar, Manager, ABC, Electrical Devices, Delhi. Write a proposal for the manufacturing of transformers. Invent the necessary details.
12. As a manager of State Corporation for Industrial Development, Lucknow, write a proposal to your Director, for the modernization of the reception and commercial section of the office.

17

MODERN COMMUNICATION DEVICES

Chapter Objectives

This chapter will enable you to understand:

- Role of technology in communication
- Accessing electronic information
- The internet
- E-mail
- Fax
- Telephone/cell phone
- Teleconferencing and videoconferencing

How people communicate, seek information, and obtain intelligence is changing rapidly. It is obvious that our society grows more complex so do our communicating. This can be attributed partially to exponential growth of new knowledge in almost every area of professional knowledge. Not too long ago, a pen, typewriter, and telephone were the primary equipment for business communicators. Then came word processors, fax machines, and e-mail. Today, we can choose from a host of tools that includes cell phones, web pages, videoconferencing, and instant messages, each one ever increasing its features and benefits.

17.1 ROLE OF TECHNOLOGY IN COMMUNICATION

We are becoming electronically interdependent. Relationships being formed across international boundaries were not possible a few years ago. Because technology changes so rapidly, adaptation to staying current, and being open to learning new technologies is a must. It is important to note that these tools and techniques will not, simply by their use, result in effective communication. Essential ingredient for effective communication must be present when using the technology. The idea of media choice is not what you say but how and where you say it. Although you use the telephone to talk to someone, you need good communication skills. The telephone serves only to enhance the process. Hence, technology, as an enhancing mechanism is good only when we apply it effectively.

17.2 ACCESSING ELECTRONIC INFORMATION

The computer is the widely used instrument today. An electronic database is a computer-searchable collection of information on a general subject area, such as business, education, or psychology.

1. Electronic databases are fast. You can collect more data electronically in an hour than would be possible in an entire day of conventional library research. They are available either on CD-ROM or online via computer network or telephone hookup.
2. Electronic databases are typically more current than printed databases; most are updated weekly or monthly.
3. Electronically databases are extremely flexible. You can use different search terms, combine them, and modify your search at every step.

Computer assisted information retrieved has now become so widely available, economical, and easy to use that it has emerged as a powerful tool for helping managers solve problems and make decisions.

17.3 THE INTERNET

The Internet is a vast information system that connects millions of computers worldwide, allowing them to exchange all types of information and to conduct many types of business transactions, such as online banking and shopping.

On the Internet you can send and receive email, transfer files between computers, search for information, and participate in discussion groups.

17.3.1 Internet Resources

- **Mailing list:** A mailing list is a discussion group in which messages are sent directly to members via email. On the Internet, these mailing lists are called 'list serves'. Mailing-list messages are sent directly to you as email. To become a member, you must first subscribe to the list, by sending an email message to the list server. From then on, any messages posted to the list are automatically sent to your email address.
- **News group:** The news group is a discussion group in which messages (called articles) are posted at the news group site. Anyone can connect to the site via an Internet 'Usenet' connection as frequently as desired to read any newly posted articles.

  The difference between the mailing list and news group is that news group members have to 'visit' the news group site to see any new messages, whereas new messages are automatically sent as email to mailing-list members.
- **World Wide Web:** The newest and fastest segment of the Internet is the World Wide Web, known as www or simply the web. Web documents, called 'pages' can contain text, graphics, sound and video, all written hypertext. Hypertext links in the document enable the reader to explore as much or as little of a document as desired.

  Users access this type of information by using a software program known as a 'web browser', the most popular of which are 'Microsoft Internet explorer' and 'Netscape Navigator'.

17.4 EVALUATING THE QUALITY OF ELECTRONIC INFORMATION

Nobody owns the Internet; that is there is one governing authority that can make rules and impose order. Thus, anyone with access to the Internet can post pretty much anything that he or she wants online. There is no law, regulation, or Internet policy that states that the information posted on the Internet has to be true, objective, intelligent, or politically correct. However, information posted by government and educational institutions (those sites that end in ".gov" or ".edu") is most often comprehensive, accurate, and up-to-date. Most pages sponsored by commercial organizations (those sites that end in ".com") are also of high quality. Personal home pages and those sponsored by advocacy organizations should be evaluated especially carefully for accuracy, fairness, and coverage. The same is true for Usernet newsgroups and mailing lists.

Avoid accepting something as fact just because you saw it on the Net. You are responsible for the quality of information you include in your correspondence, reports, and presentations.

17.4.1 Guidelines for Evaluating the Quality of Internet Resources

1. **Authority**
   - Is it clear who sponsors the page and what the opener's purpose in maintaining the page is?
   - Is it clear who wrote the material and what the author's qualifications for writing on this topic are?
   - Is there a phone number or postal address to contact for more information?
   - Is the material is protected by copyright and the name of the copyright holder given?
2. **Accuracy**
   - Are the sources for any factual information clearly listed so they can be verified in another source?
   - Has the sponsor provided a link to outside sources?
   - Is the information free of grammatical, spellings, and other typographical errors?
   - Are statistical data in graphs and charts clearly labelled and easy to read?
   - Does anyone monitor the accuracy of the information being published?
3. **Objectivity**
   - Is the sponsor's motivation for providing information clear?
   - Is the information content clearly separated from an advertising?
   - Has the sponsor presented his views in a clear manner, with well-supported arguments?
4. **Correctness**
   - Are there dates on the page to indicate when the page was written, first placed on the web, and last revised?
   - Are there any indications that the material is kept current?
   - If the material contains graphs or charts, is it stated when the data was gathered?
   - Is there evidence that the page has been completed and is not still in the process of being developed?

17.5 SHARING ELECTRONIC INFORMATION

Technology helps us not only access information but also share it with others.

17.5.1 E-mail

In e-mail (electronic mail) messages are composed, transmitted, and usually read on computer screens. E-mail software allows users to send notes to other users in a fast and organized manner. E-mail messages are coordinated or sent to specific individuals without fear of losing information in the distribution system. Messages can be tagged to indicate to the sender that the receiver read the note. Time is saved in coordinating and conveying a message via e-mail and this improves communication. Word processing, spreadsheet, and database management packagers make information transmitted easier to perform. New programs have increased the efficiency in how we organize, analyze, and present information. Using communication software allows the sending of large documents via telephone lines fast and efficiently. Transmittal of information is significantly faster than mail delivered by postal service. Online catalogue and bulletin boards allow us to order goods and services and learn new ways to use the computer for communication.

E-mail has, in fact, become so popular that it can be time-consuming to read and answer. Another problem relates to the fact that e-mail is typically written – composed, and sent while keyboarding. Writers sometimes tend to ignore effective writing principles.

Effective e-mail practices (Netiquette)

- Use short lines and short paragraphs.
- Do not type your entire message in all capitals. Use capital letters only for emphasis. It is text-based form of shouting at your reader and is considered rude.
- Pay attention to spelling, grammar, and proofreading.
- Re-read and proofread your message before sending it.
- Choose your recipients carefully. Do not send a message to an entire mailing list.
- Use a brief, but descriptive subject line. It should be specific, concise, and catchy.
- Greet your recipient. Start your message with a friendly salutation, such as 'dear—'.
- Insert previous messages appropriately.
- Use a direct style of writing.
- Think twice and then write. Do not be indiscreet in e-mail. Although e-mail feels informal, it is not private, as a conversation might be. Always assume the message you send will never be destroyed.
- Provide an appropriate closing. Include your name, e-mail address, contact no., and any other identifying information at the end of your message.
- All the principles of good writing still apply with e-mail. Remember 'you –attitude' and 'positive approach'.

17.5.2 Fax

According to Maury Kauffiman, author of 'Computer-Based Fax Processing', fax machines are the one true global communications standard. They are fast, inexpensive, easy to use and available worldwide.

Another technology called 'broadcast fax' allows organizations to automatically send documents to a large number of people quickly using fax technology and programmed telephone lists. Basically broadcast fax is form of electronic direct mail. In turn, using fax on demand (FOD) technology, clients or customers can call a company, key in their fax number, and have specific documents automatically faxed to them.

Guidelines for faxing a document

- Always use a cover sheet when you send a fax. Include a name, company address, phone number, and fax number for both you and the recipient, the date, the total number of pages, and a brief note regarding the reason you are sending the fax. Cover sheet should be neatly typed so that it will have a professional appearance.
- Ensure that the document to be faxed is legible. The paper to be faxed is free of smudges, wrinkles, and the font is readable.
- Avoid sending lengthy documents, unnecessary, or complex 'graphics'. It will cost both companies time and machine.
- Be courteous. If someone is waiting behind you to fax only one page and you have many pages, let that person go ahead of you.
- Be ethical. If someone inadvertently leaves an original document behind, return it to him or her – unread.

17.5.3 Telephone/Cell Phone

Telephone, a central part of modern communication, is a useful tool at home and work. We cannot perform effectively without having the instrument. It is rare to find a home or a desk at the office without one. The popularity of the cellular phone, which allows us to converse with others while driving to and from works or while working in the backyard, is increasing. New generations of cell phones allow limited television reception, in addition to camera, email, and instant messaging capabilities.

1. Telephone voice quality

It is necessary that your telephone voice convey your message accurately and favourably.

Thus, to train your voice to convey a pleasing quality over the telephone, you should practice according to the following suggestions.

- Demonstrate a warmth; a pleasantness in your voice. Greet the caller with a smile.
- Cultivate a natural tone.
- Show that you are alert and interested.
- Speak neither too softly nor too loudly. Use a moderate, normal volume.
- Vary the pitch occasionally. Raise and lower the sound of your voice when appropriate.

2. Telephone speech pattern

A pleasant voice is only effective if it is accompanied by good speech patterns. Remember that your caller cannot see you as in face-to-face conversation. Try to develop the following effective speech patterns.

- Pronounce your words properly. Remember to always speak clearly and carefully.
- Enunciate your words distinctly. Your language must be distinct you are to communicate effectively.

- Pace your rate of speech. Speaking too slowly can be just as bad as speaking too rapidly.
- Use an appropriate vocabulary. Slang words and expressions should not be used in your telephone speech vocabulary.

3. Telephone manners

As you know manners are codes of behaviour for certain situations. Appropriate manners are just as important when dealing with telephone callers as when dealing with office visitors.

- Sit or stand tall and avoid chewing gum or eating.
- Treat every call as an important call.
- Answer promptly.
- Identify yourself immediately.
- Show interest and courtesy.
- Use common sense.
- End positively and appropriately.
- Keep a pad and pen near the phone for note taking.

4. Using a cell phone

- Avoid making or answering calls when driving.
- Speak clearly and get to the point quickly.
- Turn off your cell phone while in a social environment and during meetings.
- If you get disconnected, redial the party if you initiated the call. Wait for the other party to redial if you received the call.
- Be aware that others may be listening to your calls, either intentionally or unintentionally.
- Cell phones are not secure and should not be used to discuss confidential information.

17.5.4 Teleconferencing and Videoconferencing

A teleconferencing is a meeting of three or more people, who communicate via telephone. The primary advantage of teleconferencing is that they save time and money. As in all telephone communications, however, the participants 'see' each other only through their voices. There are no body language or non-verbal signals to help complete the picture.

Videoconferencing has grown tremendously in recent years. A videoconference is an interactive meeting between two or more people using video linkups at two or more sites. The audio or video signals that transmit the live voices and images may be transmitted through telephone lines, direct cable connections, microwave or satellite.

In addition, personal one-to-one videoconferencing is becoming popular as people take advantage of the advent of inexpensive personal video cameras attached to personal computers.

Thus, conferences and meetings are conducted by integrating use of telephone, television and satellite technologies. Benefits can be measured by time and money saved. Conferences and meetings are held without attendees leaving their office environment. This translates into travel savings, and subsequently, into productivity savings.

Guidelines for conducting a teleconference or videoconference

- Plan ahead. Prepare a detailed agenda and follow it.
- Involve all participants frequently during call.
- Speak normally.
- Be prepared. Provide participants with copies of the agendas, handouts or other visual aids, etc. ahead of time.
- In a teleconferencing, encourage participants to position themselves near the phone when talking.
- In a videoconference, when you want to speak, introduce yourself; then wait until the camera is focused on you before beginning to speak.
- Prepare any graphics with video in mind and ensure that your visual aids are simple. With readable font size.
- Avoid sudden movements. Maintain a quiet posture.

Thus, advances in technology are altering ways people relate and communicate. We may be less inhibited when communicating through technology, and tend to be less self aware.

REVIEW QUESTIONS

1. What role does the technology play in business communication? How can the organization use modern communication devices more effectively?
2. Briefly discuss the changes brought about in the field of communication by the newly introduced electronic devices.
3. Discuss the advantages of the following:
   (a) E-mail
   (b) Internet
   (c) Fax
   (d) Videoconferencing
4. Describe three technology trends and how they affect business communication?
5. Explain the Internet resources and discuss guidelines for evaluating their quality.
6. What things should be considered during telephonic communication? Describe how to use cell phones/telephones effectively and safely.
7. 'Technology helps us not only access information but also share it with others.' Justify and explain the statement with reference to e-mail messages.
8. What do you mean by the netiquette? Describe the legal and ethical issues brought about by use of e-mail and the Internet.
9. What is the use of Fax machine as one of the technology tools that affects business communication? What are the legal and ethical issues that arise with its use?
10. How can teleconferencing and videoconferencing increase business productivity of an organization? Give guidelines for conducting a teleconference or videoconference.

UNIT–4
Employment Communication

18

RESUME AND JOB APPLICATION LETTER

Chapter Objectives

This chapter will enable you to understand:

- The career search
  - Personal characteristics, skills and abilities
  - Sources of available jobs
  - Growth career areas
- Preparing your resume
- Two different resume types
  - Chronological format
  - Functional format
- What a resume should look like
- Resume vs. CV
- Electronic resume
- Job application letter/covering letter

An occupation is a task or series of tasks that is performed to provide a good or service. People are hired to fill occupations, and they are paid for the work they perform. A career is a goal for work that is fulfilled through an occupation or series of occupation. Career planning is the process of studying careers, assessing you in terms of career. This process begins by carrying out a personal assessment, your interests, values, talents, and abilities provide the basis for a career choice as you develop new interests and abilities. Thus, the study of careers is a continuous process. New career opportunities occur all the time. You do not just decide to study career for one day or one week. Skill requirements and job responsibilities change rapidly due to technology, corporate restructuring, a global economy, and the socio-political climate. As a result, people change jobs frequently; and many people change careers several times during their lives.

18.1 THE CAREER SEARCH

Finding a job that satisfies your personality and professionally helps you maintain both mental and physical health. Conduct your career search seriously. Make sure you stand out from the crowd of applicants.

1. Analyze your personal characteristics skills and abilities
2. Determine and evaluate your job-related skills and abilities
3. Research employment opportunities

18.1.1 Personal Characteristics, Skills, and Abilities

You must do some soul-searching to decide exactly how you wish to spend the working hours of your life. How can you make sure you select a job you will enjoy and that fits your life situation?

Analyze your personal characteristics, needs, and interests, think about your talents and abilities. Do you perceive yourself as a leader, or are you more comfortable supporting someone else? Which is more important – salary or job satisfaction? Do you want to work with many people or a few people?

- **Interests:** Many sources are available in print and online to determine the activities that give you satisfaction. Your interests provide a basis for your employment goals and possible paths.
- **Values:** Your values are things that are important to you. You can learn about your values with exercises and activities. These exercises show how you rank items such as prestige, money, power, achievement, independence, security, belongings or serving others. Each of these may influence you, directly or indirectly, when you select your life's work.
- **Talents and abilities:** Each of you has certain talents and abilities. A talent is a natural, inborn aptitude to do certain things. People often say "someone has a natural talent". Ability is the quality of being to perform a mental of physical task. Your talents and abilities, along with your career goals and interests are important in career planning. You can learn about your abilities in a number of ways. Think about the causes you have taken and the grades you have received in school? What kinds of courses have you taken? In which ones have you done your best? Answers to questions such as these will identify your talents and abilities. Abilities can be developed. If you are weak in a certain area, you may want to take courses that will improve that area. Work to strong your weak areas before you go into full-time work.

Such introspection will help you make sound career decisions.

18.1.2 Sources of Available Jobs

Some experts indicate that 80 per cent of the open positions are not found in newspapers, on job boards, etc. That means that as many as 80 per cent of available jobs are found through other sources. Your job search strategy should include investigating many different sources. Net working, employers, career related experiences, publications, employment agencies, and the internet are excellent sources for career and job information.

- **Networking:** Network is people connecting, and when you connect with people, you begin to assemble your network. Networking is often considered the most valuable source for jobs.

  Once your network is in place, you will continue to make new contacts and communicate with established members. People in your network will provide advice, information, and support in helping you achieve your career goals and aspirations.

  Networking accounts for up to 70% of the new opportunities uncovered. Many people assume that they should call all the people they know personally and professionally and ask if they know of any companies that are hiring. A successful networker starts by listing as many names as possible on a street of paper. Those names can include family members, relatives, friends, co-workers, and managers (past and present), other industry contacts, and anyone else you know.

  The next step is to formulate a networking presentation. Keep in mind that it need not address potential opening. In networking the aim is to call your contacts to ask for career or industry advice. Do not show yourself as a desperate job hunter but as a researcher.

- **People connection:** Many job seekers begin their search for occupational information by interviewing one or more currently employed in the career or industry that interests them. Such sources can provide the current and detailed information you seek, and they are likely to be more objective than a recruiter. Locate such sources by asking friends, relatives, and acquaintances, or consulting with your college placement cell or your professors.

- **The media:** You can plan your course and future activities to help you grow towards your chosen career.

  Newspaper help wanted ads can be useful in career planning. Ads in newspapers give you an idea of what jobs are in demand, what training and skills are needed. The career and business sections of newspapers publish articles on a range of career planning topics.

  Although the major purpose of such contacts is data gathering, these sessions also advertise your availability for and interest in a position.

- **Memberships:** Memberships are a valuable source of employment information and opportunities. Membership in a career-related association shows commitment to the profession and a desire for professional growth. Many professional associations operate online job boards for members.

- **Online sources for industry and company information:** Websites are available to help you with career planning. Besides, go online and visit the homepage of a prospective employer. Don't consider such website sources of objective information because companies use them to market themselves, but they can reveal how a firm likes to see itself and provide key details about the company. Look especially for current company news, its mission statement, most recent annual report, and advertised career opportunities.

- **Career fairs:** Career fairs are often held at colleges or community centres. These events allow a chance to contact several prospective employers in a short time. You will be asked a few questions to determine if you qualify for a longer interview.

  Get ready for job fairs by being prepared to quickly communicate your potential contribution to an organization. Knowing something about the company will help set you apart from other applicants.
- **Government-employment offices:** Local and state government offices are another source for information about available jobs. These offices help people find jobs and provide career information, and work with employers to find qualified workers. Offices can provide up-to-date information about the job market in your area. They can help you look for part-time, summer, or full-time work.

  No one source is necessarily better than others. You need to let as many people as possible know that you are looking for a job. Your relatives, friends, neighbours, and others are all potential sources of job leads.

18.1.3 Growth Career Areas

The life work you choose could be affected by the career available in a field. Future employment opportunities are influenced by geography and business trend.

- **Geographic influence:** You may have to decide whether you want to work in the geographic area in which you now live or whether you are willing to move to where the jobs you really want is located. There may be reasons why you would prefer to live and work near your home. People who successfully pursue the careers of their choice often have mobility. Mobility is the willingness and ability of a person to move to where jobs are located. The lack of mobility can lead to locational unemployment. This occurs when jobs are available in one place but go unfilled because those who are qualified to fill those jobs live elsewhere and are not willing to relocate.
- **Economic and industry trends:** Career areas with the most potential are influenced by economic trends and current business activities. Consumer demand, changing demographic trends and new technology are factors that often affect career opportunities. Think about your personal interests and abilities in addition to economic and business trends.

18.2 PREPARING YOUR RESUME

A resume is a brief record of one's personal history and qualifications that is typically prepared by an applicant for a job. The emphasis in the resume should be on the future rather than on the past. You must show how your education and work experience have prepared you for your future jobs—specifically, the job for which you are applying.

Right from the beginning, be realistic about the purpose of your resume. As a purpose of a resume is to get you a job interview (not to get you a job), the resume and accompanying application letter (cover letter) are crucial in advancing you beyond the mass of initial applicants and into the much smaller group of potential candidates invited to an interview.

18.2.1 Resume Length

Today, employers do not have the time or the patience for verbose documents. Most recruiters prefer a one page resume for entry-level positions. In fact, recruiters typically spend no more than 35 seconds looking at each resume during their initial screening to pare down the hundreds of applications for a position into a manageable number to study in more detail. Thus, how much information can the recruiter be expected to read in less than a minute? It won't matter how well qualified you are if no one ever reviews those qualifications.

Although one-page resume is the norm, a two-page resume may be warranted if you have had extensive job experience or have changed careers and truly need the space to properly position yourself. Your resume must be attractive and easy to read. If, after careful editing, you still need more than one page to present yourself, it is acceptable to use a second page. A crowded resume with small type and narrow margin would be the worst of your choices.

Do not make your resume too short. A resume that does not fill one page may tell the prospective employer that you have little to offer.

18.2.2 Resume Format

Choose a simple, easy-to-read typeface, and avoid the temptation to use a lot of 'special effects' just because they are available on your computer. One or two typefaces in one or two different sizes should be enough. Use a simple format, with lots of white space, short paragraphs, and a logical organization. Through the use of type size and style, indentation bullets, and the like, make clear which parts are subordinate to main features. Your resume and application letter must be 100% free from error—in context, spelling, grammar, and format. 99% accuracy is simply not good enough when seeking a job.

18.2.3 Elements of a Resume

An effective resume is composed of information that employers are most interested in knowing about a prospective job applicant. The following is a list of elements that are found in most resumes—some essential, some optional

- Heading
- Job objective
- Education and training
- Work experience
- Professional memberships
- Publications
- Personal information
- References

Let us take a look at each of these important elements individually so that you can judge their appropriateness for your resume.

There is not a standard resume; each is an individual the person it represents. The standard and optional parts of the resume are discussed here in the order in which they typically appear on the resume of a fresher graduate.

Heading

Although the heading may seem to be the simplest section of your resume, be careful not to take it lightly. It is the first section your prospective employer will see, and it contains the information she or he will need to contact you. Your name and complete address, including phone number and e-mail address are crucial, which helps recruiter to locate you easily to schedule an interview.

Your name should be the very first item on the resume, arranged attractively at the top. Give your complete name, avoiding nicknames and do not use a personal title such as Mr. or Ms. It is not necessary to include the heading "Resume" at the top. You can make name to be the main heading.

If you will soon be changing your address (as from a college address to a home address), including both, along with the relevant dates for each. The heading must contain your phone number where you can be reached easily.

Your e-mail address not only provides another means of contact but also sends a non-verbal message that you are computer savvy.

Job objective

The job objective is a short summary of your area of expertise and career interest. Mention a particular position that suits your educational qualifications and experience.

Normally the objective is one or two sentences long. Its contents will vary depending on your field, goals, and personality. Your objectives can be specific or general, but it should always be to the point.

The vague, high-flown objectives do not help the recruiter find a suitable position for you. They waste valuable post on your resume. Your objective must be personalized—both you and for the position you are seeking.

Vague Objectives	*Effective Objectives*
• Challenging position in a progressive organization.	• Position in personal sales in a medium-sized manufacturing company.
• A position that offers both a challenge and opportunity for growth.	• A paid, one-semester internship in marketing.
• To seek a management position in the tourism industry.	• To obtain a junior level management position in a tourism company which gainfully uses my summer training and internship experience.
• A sales position in a reputed and growing publishing organization which uses my education.	• Textbooks sales requiring an academic background in marketing.
• A challenging career in the field of event management which offers growth and advancement opportunities.	• A position as an event manager for cultural and social programmes that incorporates my fluency over both English and Hindi.

In some cases, this element is not necessary but usually it is good idea to include your objective. It gives your prospective employer an idea of where you are coming from and where you want to go. Many career experts suggest not including a career objective on the resume if you are uncertain of the exact title of the job you seek. Often a career objective is too vague or too general. In such a case, this goal is better addressed in the cover letter when you connect your abilities to the organization's needs.

Education and training

Your education background is often a deciding factor in an employer's decision to interview you. If you are looking for your first job, your education will be your greatest asset, since your work experience will most likely to be minimal. Be sure to include any degrees or certificates you received, your major area of concentration, any honours, and any relevant activities. Again, be sure to list your most recent degree first and then work in reverse chronological order.

List the title of your degree, the name of your college and its location if needed, the name of your university and year of graduation, overall percentage, job-related courses.

Work experience

Work experience is a definite plus your current and former positions will provide the central focus of the resume. By thoroughly examining your work experience, you can get to the heart of your accomplishments and present them in a way that demonstrates and highlights your qualifications.

Remember that the purpose of describing your work history is to show the prospective employer what you have learned that will benefit the organization. No matter what your previous work, you have developed certain traits or had certain experiences that can be transferred to the new position. On the basis of your research into the duties of the job you are seeking, highlight those transferable skills.

As you create this section of your resume, remember the need for accuracy. Include all the necessary information about each of your jobs, including your job title, dates of employment, name of your employing company or companies, job responsibilities, special projects you handled, and accomplishments. Also include in this section all of the honours you earned, and any relevant activities you participated in, organized, or chaired. If your work experience is directly related to your job objectives, consider putting it ahead of the education section, where it will receive more emphasis.

The most common way to list your work experience is in reverse chronological order. Start with your most recent job and work your way backward. This way, your prospective employer seeks your current position before considering your past employment. If you were promoted or given greater responsibilities or commendations, be sure to mention the fact.

In relating your work experience, use either a chronological or a functional organizational pattern. In actual practice, the two patterns area actually exclusive; you can use a combination. Regardless of which type of organizational pattern you choose, provide complete information about your work history.

Show in your resume that you have developed as many of the following characteristics as possible:

- Ability to work well with others
- Communication skills
- Competence and good judgement
- Innovation
- Computer proficiency

- Reliability and trustworthiness
- Enthusiasm
- Honest and moral character
- Increasing responsibility

When preparing your resume, be completely honest about your qualifications. Keep in mind that employees check resume information. Providing false information can cause you to lose your job.

Remember the resumes are usually skimmed quickly. Some companies even use scanners to check for keywords. You need not to write complete sentences. Instead, start your descriptions with action verbs, to demonstrate what you have achieved. Use present tense for current duties and paste tense for previous job duties or accomplishments.

Action Verbs for Resumes and Cover Letters

Achieved	Directed	Organized
Accomplished	Edited	Planned
Administered	Established	Presided
Assisted	Facilitated	Produced
Coordinated	Initiated	Researched
	Implemented	
Created	Managed	Supervised
Designated	Monitored	Trained
Developed	Negotiated	Updated
	Operated	Wrote

Avoid weak words such as

Attempted	Error
Endeavoured	No
Hoped	Not
Tried	Sorry
Fear	Doubt

Work experience need not be restricted to paid positions. If you have little or no actual work experience, show how your involvement with professional, social, or civic organizations has helped you develop skills that are transferrable to the workplace. Volunteer work, for example, can help develop valuable skills in the management, working with groups, handling money, speaking, accepting responsibility, and the like.

Never write 'no experience'

As a fresh graduate, you may have little opportunity to acquire professional work experience. But every graduate student gains some experience by organizing functions, running clubs, associations, societies, or managing events, undertaking visits to industries, and so on. Young applicants, in the early stage of their career can include voluntary work done for clubs, associations or charitable organization, vacation jobs or any other informal experience. All such exposures form a fresh graduate's "experience". You must demonstrate that the experience has added to your ability to be useful to the prospective employer.

Other relevant information

If you have special skills that might give you an edge over the competition, list them on your resume. Common examples include fluency in a foreign language, extensive travel abroad, or knowledge of a particular computer application. Special skills can encompass a wide range of talents, and this section can be used creatively.

- **Professional and board affiliations:** Memberships and active participation in professional and trade associations demonstrate to a prospective employer that you
    1. are a contributing member of your profession.
    2. want to advance your own knowledge and improve your skills.
    3. are committed to the future of your vocation. Pertinent affiliation should appear in your resume.

  If you sit on boards of directors, this indicates that you are well respected in your community and give your time to other organizations, be they for profit or non-profit entities. These distinguishing credits should be included in your resume.
- **Awards, honours, and recognitions:** No doubt these are critical to your resume because they represent your achievements in a powerful and convincing manner. It is one thing to boast about your accomplishments. You can illustrate your honours and recognitions
    (a) Under professional section or work experience
    (b) As a separate section
- **Technical expertise/computer skills:** Incorporating a section describing your specific technical and computer skills may be an effective way to introduce your skills to the reader quickly. In a high-tech, ever-changing business environment, employers are looking for people with specific skills and, even more important people who have the ability to learn, adapt, and embrace new technologies. In this section consider using short bullets so that the information is easily accessible.
- **Teaching assignments:** If you have conducted, facilitated, or taught classes, seminars, workshops, or classes, include this on your resume whether you were paid for it or not. Teaching, training, and educating are in demand skills. They exhibit confidence, leadership, and the ability to communicate.
- **Licence, accreditation, and certification:** You may choose to include a section exclusively for licence, accreditation, and certifications. Consider using bullets as an effective way to communicate your significant qualifications quickly and effectively.
- **Languages:** We live and work in a global economy where fluency in multiple languages is an asset that is in great demand. Be sure to list your language skills at the beginning of the resume if you think these skills are critical to being considered for the position. Otherwise, note them clearly toward the end.

Personal information

Personal data consist of information such as date of birth, marital status, social security number, height, weight, sex, health, number of dependents, citizenship, travel and relocation preferences, and employment availability.

Employers by law, cannot discriminate by age, race, religion, creed, sex, or colour. For this reason, this is generally not recommended. Unless you have a specific reason to include it, it is probably a good idea to limit or eliminate most personal information. Do not include a photograph with your application papers.

Other optional information includes hobbies and special interests. If you think that your hobby and talent has some bearing on the position you are seeking, include it. Provide one line of information to show the reader your diversity of interests. This gives the prospective employer a good profile of who you are outside the work.

Here is a good test for determining whether to include personal information on a resume. Ask yourself, "Will this information dramatically improve my chances for getting an interview?" If the answer is 'yes', include it. If the answer is 'no' or 'I don't know', omit it.

References

A reference is a person who has agreed to provide information to a prospective employer regarding a job applicant's fitness for a job.

As a general rule, references are not usually given on the resume itself, but a prospective employer needs to know that you have references who may be contacted if necessary. All you need to include is a single sentence at the end of the resume: "References are available" or "Available on request." Have a reference list ready—your interviewer may ask to see it! Contact each person on the list ahead of time to see whether it is all right for you to use him or her as a reference. This way, the person has a chance to think about what to say before the call occurs. This helps ensure that you will obtain the best reference possible.

Letter requesting references or recommendations

Recommendation letters are written by the people to a prospective employer who knows the candidate well.

Example : A request letter to any authority requesting for a reference.

ABC Computers
Mumbai
23.4.20....

Mr. R. K. Sharma
11, Maharani Bagh
New Delhi

Dear Sir

This refers to the contract for annual maintenance of your computers and the peripherals, which is being carried by us for the last three years successfully.

We have many more clients who are interested for awarding similar annual maintenance contracts to us and have requested to demonstrate the satisfaction letters from our present clients to entrust our credentials before awarding the contracts.

We shall be highly grateful to you for issuing a satisfaction/reference letter for the work being carried by us at your office.

We shall be thankful for your immediate response.

Yours faithfully
for ABC Computers
Ravi Kulkarni
The Personnel Manager

Example: A letter of recommendation for any former employee working with your organization.

ABC Computers
Sector-36
Chandigarh
15.4.20....

Personnel Manager
Infotech Limited
23, Kasturba Gandhi Marg
New Delhi

Dear Sir

This is with reference to your letter no. SKW/2301/09 dated 11.4.20... inquiring about Mr.............. who is an ex-employee of our organization and has applied for the post of Asst. Manager-Marketing in your organization.

We would be pleased to inform you that Mr.................. has served our organization with sincerity and dedication and resigned due to his own domestic problems. In fact, our organization has lost a good person who could have otherwise made a career with us.

We have no reservation in recommending Mr.................... for your organization and wish him a good success in his career.

Yours faithfully
(XYZ)
Personnel Manager

18.3 TWO DIFFERENT RESUME TYPES

It is important you choose a design and approach that is concise and effective and highlights the skills your perspective employer is looking for in an applicant. For example, place education before work experience if you are fresh out of college or include a summary of skills instead of a job objective if you want to highlight your skills over your previous jobs. In order to determine how to best position your skills and accomplishments, ask yourself these questions

- What in my background best proves I can do the job.
- Should I put my emphasis on my skills, or where I have worked, or on the courses that I have taken in school?
- What are my major selling points?

There are two major types of resumes, chronological and functional.

18.3.1 Chronological Format

The chronological format is preferred by many employment professionals and hiring authorities because it demonstrates continuous and upward career growth. It does this by emphasizing employment history. A chronological format lists the positions held in a progressive sequence, beginning with the most recent and working back. The one feature that distinguishes the chronological format from the others is that under each job listing you communicate your

1. Responsibilities
2. Skills needed to do the job
3. Specific achievements

The focus is on time, job continuity, growth, and advancement, and accomplishments.

Advantages

- You are planning to stay in the same field/work area.
- You want to show off your promotions.
- The name of your employer is highly prestigious.
- It is easy to see whom you have worked for and what you did in each particular job.

Disadvantages

- Not necessarily a great format if you are planning to change career direction.
- You have frequently changed employers; this will highlight each are listed.
- Your work history has been inconsistent in recent years through unemployment, time taken off, job hopping, and so on.
- You do not have many achievements or your achievements are not consistent with what you are targeting.

18.3.2 Functional Format

A functional format emphasizes skills, abilities, credentials, qualifications, or accomplishments at the beginning of the document but does not correlate those characteristics with any specific employer. Titles, dates of employment, and employment track record are deemphasized in order to highlight qualifications. The focus is squarely on what you did, not on when where you did it.

A functional resume is useful when you want to change career fields and need to identify skills that may be used in a new situation, you have limited work experience, but still have skills, that can be identified and grouped, you want to enter or reenter paid employment and have acquired skills through unpaid or paid experience, or you have had many different work experiences that are not directly related to the job you are seeking.

Some hiring managers consider that this format is used by problem career designers—job hoppers, older workers, career changers, people with employment gaps or academic skill-level deficiencies, and those with limited experience. Some employment professionals feel that if you cannot list your employment history in a chronological fashion, there must be a reason and that reason deserves close scrutiny.

Advantages

- You may emphasize abilities and achievements that have not been used in your most recent work.
- You are changing your career direction.
- You have had a large number of jobs and would prefer to describe the experience you have gained in total.
- Your work history has been patchy in recent years through unemployment, redundancy, self-employment, ill health, and so on.

Disadvantages

- You want to highlight promotions and career growth. You could include this sort of information on the second page of a functional resume, but it would not be as prominent as it is on a chronological resume.
- Your job has only a limited number of functions.

- Because of its unusual layout, many hiring managers do not like this format and may generalize that it is used by people with employment gaps or problems.

18.4 WHAT A RESUME SHOULD LOOK LIKE?

There is no single appropriate layout that applies to every resume. However, there are a few basic rules to follow in putting your resume on paper:

- Leave a comfortable margin on the side, top, and bottom of the page (usually one to one and a half inches).
- Use appropriate spacing between the sections (two to three lines spaces are usually adequate).
- Be consistent in the type of heading you use for different sections of your resume. For example, if you capitalize the heading EMPLOYMENT HISTORY, don't use initial capital and underling for a section of equal importance, such as 'Education'.
- Do not use more than one font in your resume. Stay consistent by choosing the font that is fairly standard and easy to read, and don't change it for different sections.
- Highlight the points you want the reader to notice.
- Short phrases are easier to read than long sentences and long paragraphs.
- Use dashes (—), or dots (…), or asterisks (***), different kinds of type, and underlining to guide the eye, but be sure not to make it too crowded.
- Choose quality bond paper for your resume. White, ivory, or gray looks best.
- Finally, your resume and application letter must be 100% free from error—in context, spelling, grammar, punctuation, and format. Have at least three other people proofread your resume to make sure all spelling, grammar, punctuation, and information are correct.

18.5 RESUME VS CURRICULUM VITAE (CV)?

A CV has different meanings in different places. In the United Kingdom, for example, the 'CV' is an interchangeable term for 'resume'. In America, it is a type of resume, a subset of the genre.

As a good rule, a Curriculum Vitae (CV) is a longer detailed synopsis of your professional history, which generally runs three or more pages in length. It includes a summary of your educational and academic backgrounds, as well as teaching and research experience, publications, awards, honours, affiliations, and other details.

A CV is used primarily for admissions applications to graduate or professional institutes, independent consulting in a variety of settings, proposals for fellowships or grants, or applications for positions in academia. You should only send a CV when one is specifically requested by an employer of institution.

Like a resume, your CV should include your name, contact information, education, skills, and experience. In addition to the basics, a CV includes research and teaching experience, publications, grants and fellowships, professional associations and licenses, awards and other information relevant to the position for which you are applying.

Difference between a CV and a Resume

Category	Curriculum Vitae	Resume
What is it?	A full list of your professional and educational history.	A summary of your experience and skills that are most pertinent to the advertised position.
How long is it?	Usually many pages; length is not important.	Usually one page only. Multiple pages only for senior level positions.
When do you use it?	Used for academic positions and research positions in government and industry.	Used for every other type of job outside of academia and research science.
Do you include your publications?	A full list of publications is essential.	Even a partial list of publications is rarely included.
How important is style and layout?	Style doesn't matter that much; content is what matters most.	Style and content are important. Bad style is real liability.
Should you modify it to match each specific job to which you are applying?	CVs do not need much alteration to fit each specific job opening.	Resumes should be adapted to fit each specific job to which you are applying.
Are references listed?	Typically references are listed at the end of the CV.	References are not listed on the resume. If required, you may submit a separate list of relevant references for each position (usually only when these are requested).

18.6 ELECTRONIC RESUME

An electronic resume is a resume that is stored in a computer database designed to help manage and initially screen job applicants. These resume come from variety of sources:

- Applicants may simply mail or fax a paper copy of their standard resume.
- They may send the resume as an email message.
- They may post their resume on the internet, using a bulletin board system, a newsgroup, or a personal homepage on the World Wide Web.

18.6.1 Benefits of Electronic Resume

Electronic resume provide many benefits—both to the recruiter and to the job seeker.

- The job seeker's resume is potentially available to a large number of employees.
- The job seeker may be considered for positions of which he or she was not even aware.
- The initial screening is done by a bias-free computer.
- Employers are relieved of the drudgery of having to manually screen and acknowledge resume.
- A focused search can be conducted quickly.
- Information is always available until the individual resume is removed from the system.

When jobs need to be filled, the computer is fed a list of keywords and phrases. It then looks through the database and prints out a list of candidates with the most keywords matches. A person picks it up from there, manually studying each selected resume to determine when to invite for an interview.

18.6.2 Special Tips for Electronic Resume

The following guidelines will ensure that your resume is in a format that can be scanned accurately and transmitted accurately as an email message.

- Think 'nouns' instead of 'verbs'. Use concrete words rather than descriptions.
- Use a variety of different words to describe your skills, and do not overuse important words.
- Use standard fonts in which none of the letters touch.
- Keep in mind that underlining, italics, and fancy scripts may not scan well.
- Use boldface and capitalization to set off elements. Again, make sure letters do not touch. Leave at least a quarter inch between lines of type.
- Keep information and elements at the left margin. Centering, column, and even indenting may change when the resume is scanned.
- Do not use lines, boxes, or graphics.
- Place the most important information at the top of the first page. If you use two pages, put "page 1 of 2" at the bottom of the first page and put your name and "page 2 of 2" at the bottom of the second page.
- List each telephone number on its own line in the header.
- Make sure you always save the document as a text file—not as a word processing document.
- To ensure accurate reading by computer software, make the format as plain as possible.
- Remember you cannot change margins in a text file.
- Use white 8 ½-by-11-inch paper, printed on one side only.
- Do not fold or staple the paper as this might interfere with scanning.
- If responding via mail, use the job title or noted reference number as the subject of your message. Always send the resume in the body of the email message. Do not assume that you can attach a word-processed document to an email message, it may or may not be readable.

18.7 WRITING JOB APPLICATION LETTERS

An application letter communicates to the prospective employer your interest in and qualifications for a position within the organization. The letter is also called a cover letter, because it introduces (or 'covers') the major points in your resume, which you should include with the application letter.

A solicited application letter is written in response to an advertised vacancy, whereas an unsolicited application letter (also called a prospecting letter) is written to an organization that has not advertised a vacancy.

Because the application letter is the first thing the employer will read about you, it is of crucial importance. Make sure the letter is formatted appropriately, looks attractive, and is free from typographical, spelling, and grammatical errors. Do not forget to sign the letter and enclose a copy of your resume.

Most job applicants use the same resume when applying for numerous positions and then use their application letter to personalize their qualification for the specific job for which they are applying.

Your cover letter is a sales letter as you are selling your qualifications to the prospective employer. You should use the same persuasive techniques you learned earlier; provide specific evidence, stress reader benefits, avoid exaggeration, and show confidence in the quality of your product.

An application letter should be no longer than one page.

18.7.1 Address and Salutation

Your letter should be addressed to an individual rather to an organization or department. Ideally, your letter should be addressed to the person who will actually interview you and who will likely be your supervisor if you get the job. Gather enough information about the prospective employer. If necessary, call the organization to make sure you have the right name—including the correct spelling and position title. In your salutation, use a courtesy title (such as Mr. or Ms.) along with the person's last name.

However, some job agency ads are blind ads; they do not identify the hiring company by name and provide only a box number address, often in case of the newspaper or magazine that contains the ad. In such a situation, you have no choice but to address your letter to the newspaper and to use a specific generic salutation such as "Dear Human Resource Manager." Insert a subject line to indentify immediately the purpose of this important message.

18.7.2 Opening

The opening paragraph of a solicited application letter is fairly straightforward. Because the organization has advertised an opening, it needs quality application. Use a direct organization–state the reason of your letter, identify the particular position for which you are applying, and indicate how you learned about the opening.

For unsolicited application letter, you must first get the reader's attention. You can gain that attention most easily by talking about the company rather than about yourself. One effective strategy is to show that you know something about the organization—its recent projects, awards, changes in personnel, and the like—and then show how you can contribute to the corporate effort.

Your opening should be short, interesting, and reader-oriented. Do not address the reader by a first name.

18.7.3 Body

Treat your letter as a persuasive sales letter. In a paragraph or two, highlight your strongest qualifications and show how they can benefit the employer. Do not repeat all the information from the resume. Provide specific, credible evidence to support your statements, using wording different from that used in the resume. Tell an anecdote about yourself. For example, "Recently I...." Your discussion should reflect modest confidence rather than a hard-sell approach. Avoid starting too many sentences with 'I'. Maintain an air of formality throughout your letter.

18.7.4 Closing

Close your application letter by asking for a personal interview. Indicate flexibility regarding scheduling and location. Provide your phone number and email address, either in the last paragraph or immediately below your name and address in the closing lines. In addition, invite further inquiries, and state how you can be contacted. Some ways of concluding job application are as follows:

> I hope that my qualification will merit your consideration.
>
> I would appreciate an opportunity of attending an interview.

Use a standard complementary closing. Leave enough space to sign the letter, and then type your name, address, phone number, and email address. Sign your name neatly in blue or black ink. Make sure the finished document presents a professional, attractive, and conservative appearance and that is 100% error-free.

18.7.5 Guidelines for Drafting a Covering Letter

The applicant, therefore, must take care of the following points while drafting a covering letter for his resume:

- Use of a standard quality paper.
- The letter must be typed unless specifically asked for a handwritten application.
- The name and address of the employer must be carefully written.
- The source of the information regarding the vacancy must be mentioned.
- The applicant must express desire to be considered for the position.
- He must express enthusiasm and optimism towards receiving a favourable reply from the employer to discuss more details in an interview.
- He must use an active and positive tone.
- He must mention that the resume and other papers, if any, are enclosed.
- If the employer has given only a box number, the covering letter must be addressed to "The Advertiser, Box No......
- The style of the covering letter should be formal.

Example

Following is an example of an application letter.

XYZ
B-63 Adarsh Colony
Chandigarh
23.4.20....

The Personnel Manager
ABC Limited
Rajouri Garden
New Delhi–100011

Dear Sir

Sub: Requisition for the post of Production Manager

Ref: Your advertisement in The Hindustan Times, dated 10.10.20......

This refers to your advertisement as mentioned above for the post of Production Manager at your Bhiwani plant.

I am a first class B.Tech in Computer Science from Institute of Engineering Technology, Chandigarh and have been presently serving M/S Satyam Computers, New Delhi in the capacity of Asst. Manager – Production.

Please find enclosed my detailed resume for your kind perusal. I believe my training has given me the skills to make a valuable contribution.

Sincerely

(XYZ)

REVIEW QUESTIONS

1. Describe factors for personal assessment for career planning
2. What are the main sources of information about available jobs?
3. What are your short-term and long-term career goals? What factors affect the career areas in demand in the future?
4. As part of writing assessment, organize and prepare your resume in the two ways described in this chapter.
5. Why should job hunters keep two versions of their resume? How do you decide whether to use a chronological or a functinal resume?
6. List ten technical terms used in your career that you could include in your resume.
7. Write a sample cover letter to accompany your resume for a position in your field?
8. Because of the growing use of Internet for job hunting, what are the changes happening to traditional resume?
9. Describe the purpose of and procedure for searching the new career opportunities which satisfy your personality and job related skills.
10. Make a list of elements (essential and optional both) usually found in most resumes of a fresher graduate.
11. What are the standard basic rules to put your resume on paper?
12. What benefits does the electronic resume provide to the recruiter and to the job seeker?
13. Give some guidelines for making the electronic resume more effective?

19
INTERVIEW SKILLS

Chapter Objectives

This chapter will enable you to understand:

- Definition of a job interview
- Interview myths
- Structured and unstructured interviews
- The special nature of interviews
- Types of interviews
- Factors relevant to all interviews
- The interviewer's preparation
- The interviewee's preparation
- Parts of the interview
- The panel interview
- Useful interview questions
- Conducting yourself during the interview
- Communicating after the interview

An interview is a special type of interpersonal communication. Interviews may be conducted by one interviewer or by a panel of several interviewers. The interviewer controls the interviewee by asking a set of prepared questions. The interviewee is expected to answer these questions. At its best the interview should be a controlled conversation, rather than a random flow of information.

19.1 DEFINITION OF INTERVIEW

General definition

An interview is a planned conversation between two parties, during which questions are asked and answered. This conversation is designed to exchange information and attitudes about a specific subject.

Definition of a job interview

A job interview is a planned conversation about a specific job. During this conversation the interviewer(s) ask questions, which the interviewee answers. These questions are designed to exchange facts and opinions. They are also designed to help both parties form an impression of the other.

These definitions are relevant to all one-to-one interview and a panel interviews. They stress:

- a conversation, rather than an interrogation.
- a planned, rather than a random flow of information.
- properly designed questions.
- the need to exchange facts and opinions.
- the need to form impressions on both sides.

19.2 INTERVIEW MYTHS

All of us know that the purpose of interview is for an interviewer to hire someone who will perform well in a particular job, but beyond that few people fully grasp how interviews really work and makes one candidate stand out more than another. This lack of understanding represents a major obstacle to maximizing preference when sitting before an interviewer and trying to give his or her best answers. There are several misconceptions or myths, about what really happens during the course of an interview.

1. The best person for the job gets it

Sometimes this is true, especially in a situation where everyone knows everyone else, such as when a company is recruiting internally. The reality is that it is often the person who performs best at the interview gets the job. The important lesson here is, if you happen to know that you are the best person for the job, avoid taking the interview for granted. Take the time to prepare properly. Just because you have got a lot of experience does not mean you know how to convey this message at a interview.

2. Interviews are like school exams –The more you say, the better you'll do

Yes, interviews are a bit like exams insofar as that you are asked a number of questions to which you need to respond intelligently. But interviews are more about interacting and rapport building. Long and overly detailed answers can drive interviewers to distraction, despite their technical accuracy. Articulate smart answers. Knowing when to stop talking is a skill all successful interviewees have. Unlike any exams, there are often no right or wrong answers in interviews. We are all different and come to interview from different backgrounds and business situations. What is important at an interview is to justify your actions and talk about your achievements in a confident manner.

3. Interviewers know what they are doing

Some interviewers are very good at what they do, especially full-time professionals. However, many managers flounder because interviewing is not something they do on a regular basis. Remind yourself that interviews are just as much about rapport-building as they are about answering questions. So nod your head, smile, make all the right noises—talkative interviewers love people who agree with them.

4. 'I don't know'

Interviews are about making a possible impression by answering questions intelligently. If you do not know the answer to something it is better to admit to it rather than pretend to know and start talking.

5. Good looking people get the job

This is not to say that appearance and a bright personality are not important factors at an interview. It is very important that you dress appropriately and try your best to demonstrate all your friendly qualities. Good looks are certainly overrated in interviews, but an appropriate appearance and a friendly personality are not.

6. If you answer the questions better than the others, you'll get the job

Interviews are much more than just giving the answers. They are also about convincing the interviewer that you will be a nice person to work with.

7. You should try to give the perfect answer

The reality is that in most cases there is no such thing as the perfect answer. It makes a lot of sense to settle for a good answer that gets to the point rather than meander all over the elusive perfect answer.

8. You must ask questions to demonstrate your interest and intelligence

Only ask questions if you have a genuine query. Interviewers never mind answering questions about such matters, but they do mind answering questions they perceive to be irrelevant.

9. Relax and just be yourself

Most interviews are highly formalized events in which otherwise innocuous behaviours are deemed unacceptable.

10. Interviewers are looking for flaws

If you believe that the interviewer is assiduously searching for your flaws, it will more than likely undermine your attempts to establish that all important rapport and trust. It may also prevent you from opening up and giving really good answers.

Understanding the myths surrounding interviews give you a great start for success.

19.3 STRUCTURED AND UNSTRUCTURED INTERVIEWS

Interviews may be structured or unstructured. Structured interviews are carefully prepared in advance with questions written out. Such interviews are designed for very specific purposes.

Unstructured interviews are more flexible. The interviewer may depart from her or his specific plan, the interviewee is allowed scope to answer questions in detail even if these details are not fully relevant to the plan. The interviewer will, however, try to keep to a general plan.

19.4 THE SPECIAL NATURE OF INTERVIEWS

Interviews differ from ordinary conversations for a number of reasons:

- They demand specialist knowledge if they are to be successful.
- They take place in a controlled setting.
- They are two-sided and are conducted in a predictable way.
- The roles of interviewer and interviewee are prescribed.
- They are conducted with specific purposes in mind.
- They rely on effective verbal and non-verbal communication for their success.
- They rely on active listening.
- They are based on formal questions and answers.

19.5 TYPES OF INTERVIEW

The most common types of interview that are used in organizations are informational, employment, counselling, appraisal, sales, public relations, and customer interviews. Some of these types of interviews occur only between a superior and a subordinate. Others occur between peers within the organization. Still others occur between a member of an organization and someone outside the organization.

19.5.1 Informational Interview

The informational interview is a technique for gathering data. It might be defined as an exchange between two people for the purpose of enabling one or both persons to gain information from each other. The informational interview is often used by peers, between superiors and subordinates, and between members and non-members of an organization.

In each of these situations, a member of an organization is seeking information. This type of interview is used in a wide variety of organizations and professionals. In the typical large organization, people obtain information from a variety of sources. Sometimes the bulletin board or the memorandum is used to send information to members. However, members of organizations prefer to receive information by written and oral channels. The interview is an important oral channel.

Often the interviewer and the interviewee will both be attempting to transmit information to one another. For example, imagine an interview between a superior who wants to find out how a subordinate is doing in his job and a subordinate who wants to find out what his boss thinks of his performance. Each has a preconceived purpose in mind. Informational interview may occur in various contexts. It may take place in a highly formal atmosphere, as when a boss and subordinate sit down at a table to discuss a matter of mutual concern. Two members of a department may stop on their way to lunch to exchange information. A reporter may stop a political figure in the hallway while both are going into a fund-raising banquet. Two managers may exchange information over a friendly drink in the local tavern. Informational interviewing takes many forms and can accomplish many purposes. It is an important method of communication in the organization.

19.5.2 Employment Interview

The employment interview is conducted to determine if an individual is well suited for employment in a given organization. It is a special kind of informational interview. The goal of each participant in the employment interview is to gather information. The company interviewer wants to learn from the applicant whether he or she is suitable for employment in the organization. The applicant wants to learn about the organization in general, and specifically about the position for which he or she is applying. Occasionally applicants attempt to sell themselves for the position in addition to gathering data.

The employment interview is actually three separate interviews. It usually falls into three chronological phases, and a different interview is conducted in each phase. These phases are illustrated in the following figure.

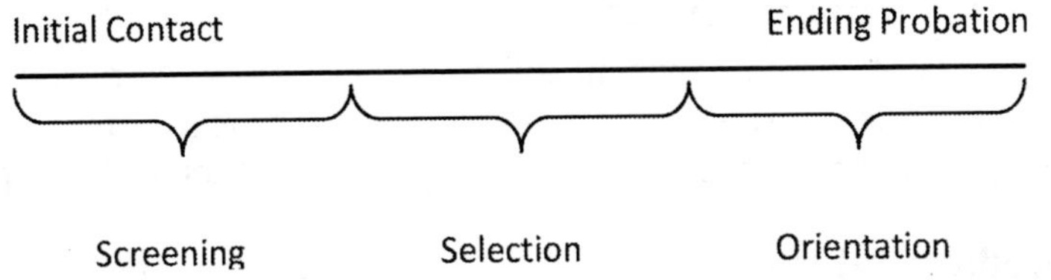

19.5.2.1 Phases of the Employment Interview

1. **Screening phase:** The screening phase occurs between the time when the initial contact is made between the potential employer and employees and the time when the serious candidates are finally chosen. Initial contact between an organization and a potential employee usually takes place by mail or telephone. An applicant may send a resume in response to a newspaper advertisement or make a telephone call after learning of a possible opening. After the contact has been made, the organization will have a contact person conduct a short interview with interested candidates. Sometimes the organization will decide to call in a few candidates for further interviews based on the resumes.

   Screening interviews are often short. Often in these screening interviews, the focus is on the "hard qualifications" – technical expertise, education, experience, and so forth. These interviews may be conducted by a member of the employment relations or personnel department. After all the candidates have been screened, the employer chooses the three or four best ones. The process then moves to the selection phase.

2. **Selection phase:** The goal in the selection phase is to reduce the number of applicants from three or four to one or two. During the selection phase a typical organization is likely to use various techniques such as group discussion and aptitude test in addition to the face-to-face interview to help it make decisions. The primary task of the organization, during this phase, is to get adequate information about the applicant in order to judge his or her potential as a member of the organization. The applicant, during this phase, would normally attempt to persuade the organization that he or she would be a valuable employee by calling attention to his or her background, experience, and talents and by demonstrating potential use to the organization.

3. **Oriental phase:** The oriental phase begins when the applicant has been selected for a position. In many organizations there is a trial period of a few weeks or months after the employee has come on the job during which he or she must perform satisfactorily. This is called a probationary period. During the probationary period, the applicant will probably be given a variety of jobs to determine where he or she will fit the best.

   The interviewing during the oriental phase really has two functions. The first is educational. The applicant will probably be taught various aspects of one or several jobs. The second has to do with placement. During the orientation phase, the applicant will probably be interviewed several times by the personnel department or by his or her orientation supervisor to determine the type of permanent position for which he or she is best suited. Data collected from the applicant's various training positions will be used to determine the best permanent job.

   All three phases of the employment interview have the same purpose: to attempt to generate a complete exchange of information between the applicant and the organization, to enable the organization to decide whether to hire applicant.

19.5.3 Counselling Interviews

People who work in organizations are often called upon to conduct counselling interviews. In a counselling interview, one participant attempts to aid and advise the other. The counselling interview may be initiated by either participant or by a third party. It is used in a wide variety of circumstances. A supervisor calls in a subordinate to determine why the subordinate's work has grown erratic. An employee who has outgrown his or her present job makes an appointment to talk with an employee representative in the personnel department.

Most managers eventually find themselves obliged to conduct a counselling interview. Often, the counselling situation will involve job-related matters (low productivity, inability to get along with others). Occasionally, the manager will have to counsel the subordinate about a personal problem (an upcoming divorce, alcoholism). Good counselling interviews recognize those areas in which they are qualified to counsel and will refer the counsellee to someone else when they are not qualified.

19.5.4 Appraisal Interview

Members of organizations are periodically evaluated by means of interviews. These evaluation interviews are known as appraisals. Employees of industrial organizations are normally called into their supervisor's office about once a year to be told how the organization perceives their work over that period of time. Sometimes appraisals are conducted by means of unique formats and forms. Other times, the employee just chats across the table with a supervisor.

For the appraisal interview to be successful, two things must occur. First, the goal of the interview must be job improvement. Second, a problem-solving climate must exist.

The communication that takes place in the appraisal should emphasize problem solving, not punishment or reprimand.

19.5.5 Sales, Public Relations, and Customer Interview Credibility

Organizations often use the interview in their "external" communications activities. A salesperson talks about a new product with a potential customer; a credit manager discusses an account with a buyer; a public relations representative outlines the construction plans for a new plant to the local newspaper editor. In each of these interviews, a member is communicating the organization's message to a non-member.

19.6 FACTORS RELEVANT TO ALL INTERVIEWS

1. **Level of preparation:** Interviewing needs special skills and careful preparation. Interviewers need to be well prepared to make the interview a successful transaction. They need to understand other people's motivation. In addition, they need to understand:
   - How to plan an interview
   - How to prepare effective questions.

   Interviewees need to understand exactly what job they are applying for. They should also study the company and anticipate the questions that are likely to be asked.
2. **Perception:** Both parties will arrive at the interview with different perceptions. They should strive to understand these perceptions by using careful questions and answers.
3. **Types of questions:** A good interview should be conducted by means of carefully prepared open questions in specific areas. These questions enable the interviewee to talk freely. Closed questions, demanding exact answers, should be used only to fill in details.
4. **Motivation of both parties:** Both parties need to be motivated to give their best. Lack of motivation from one side will soon become obvious and could destroy the interview.
5. **Listening skills:** Both parties need to practise active listening. They should listen both for the facts and the attitudes and motivations behind those facts. The interviewer should hear the interviewee out and not jump to conclusions. The interviewee should listen carefully to questions. She or he should strive to answer exactly what was asked.
6. **Thinking patterns:** These may be different for each party. Each should, therefore, strive to understand the thinking patterns of the other. A good understanding will lead to a better transaction.
7. **Language ability:** Ability to use language clearly and accurately is extremely important. If the interviewer is uncertain about his or her language ability, then she or he should write out each question. The interviewee should practise answering questions beforehand so that she or he has an exact word stock to draw from. Both parties should keep in mind that meanings are in people. They should, therefore, ensure that they give the same meaning to words.
8. **Sensitivity to non-verbal communication:** Each party should strive to be sensitive to the other's non-verbal communication. They should show that they are listening actively and should regulate their turn-taking. Interviewers should analyze their non-verbal biases and stereotypes. This analysis should help them to judge people more fairly.

9. **Ability to receive feedback:** This is especially imported for interviewers. They should be sensitive to responses from the interviewer so that they can adjust their answers.
10. **Person bias and attitudes:** Both sides should be aware of their own biases and attitudes. This general awareness will help them to be more sensitive both to the types of questions asked and to the replies.
11. **Memory:** Both the parties should strive to remember exactly what the other has said. Accurate remembering will help the interviewer to guide the interviewee(s). She or he will also be able to return to key points for clarification. The interviewee will be able to remember difficult questions. She or he will also be able to refer to earlier points to strengthen present answers.

19.7 THE INTERVIEWER'S PREPARATION

The interviewers should go through the following procedure:

1. Prepare a job description.
2. Read the applications and summarize key points about each applicant.
3. Define the objectives of the interviews and prepare a plan.
4. Prepare a range of general and specific questions suitable for each candidate.
5. Make sure that the interview room has been well prepared.
6. Prepare a checklist of desired characteristics. This will help quick note-taking during the interview. These kicked-off points can then be used for detailed note-taking after the interview.
7. Prepare a scoresheet so that each candidate can be rated out of ten on a set of characteristics. This will help the interviewer make quick comparisons.

Candidate Scoring Grid

Points \ Candidate	1	2	3	4	5	6
Appearance						
Honesty						
Ability to Communicate						
Knowledge of the Job						
Suitability for the Job						

19.7.1 Types of Questions

19.7.1.1 Open and Closed Questions

The interviewer should plan a range of questions for each stage of the interview. Open questions require general information. They enable interviewees to expand on a topic, express opinions, to give the reasoning behind opinions. Open questions usually start with, Who? Why? What? When? Where? How? Closed questions, on the other hand, demand specific answers, even 'yes' or 'no'. They restrict the interviewee's choices.

Examples of open questions

The following are examples of open questions:

- How would you......?
- What are your thoughts on.........?
- In what ways do you think that you could increase sales?
- How would you evaluate the success of our new job policy?
- What is your opinion about foreign trade policy of the government?

Advantages of open questions

The major advantages of open questions are as follows:

- They help to show the interviewee's ways of thinking and priorities.
- They give an interviewee freedom to construct an answer.
- The candidate feels relaxed when he is asked to respond without any restriction.
- They show how much an interviewee knows.
- They show how articulate the interviewee is.
- They help to build up a good relationship because the questions do not imply a judgement.
- They can be less threatening if the interviewer becomes tense.

Disadvantage of open questions

The major disadvantages of open questions are as follows:

- They take time and energy to ask and answer.
- They need expert preparation.
- They make it more difficult to control the interview.
- Recording the answers during the interview is more difficult.
- Answers may be interpreted differently if there is a panel.

Examples of closed questions

The following are examples of closed questions:

- Have you ever tried to satisfy your employer?
- Are you capable enough to carry out this responsibility?
- When did this problem start?

Advantages of closed questions

Closed questions have the following advantages:

- They save time.
- They allow the interviewer to control the flow of information.
- The enable the interviewer to obtain exact information.
- They enable the interviewer to fill in gaps in the interviewer's replies.
- They help a shy interviewee to start talking.
- They enable interviewer to ask a number of questions in a short time.

Disadvantages of closed questions

The main disadvantages of closed questions are as follow:

- They limit the replies.
- They can turn an interview into an interrogation.
- The interviewee could become defensive if too many closed questions are asked.
- They can restrict the interviewee's choices of answer and need to explain.

Preparing a range of questions

Interviewers should prepare a range of open and closed questions under the following headings:

- Home background
- Work history
- Education and training
- Career plan
- Reasons for applying for job
- Leadership
- Initiative
- Flexibility
- Independence
- Ability to get on with others
- Motivation
- Communication skills

19.8 THE INTERVIEWEE'S PREPARATION

It is estimated that 90 per cent of all jobs failures result from personality clashes or conflicts—not incompetence. (Shelley Liles, 1989) Just as any good sales representative would never attempt to walk into a potential customer's office without having a thorough knowledge of the product, neither should the interviewee. So he or she should do his/her homework–both on himself/herself and on the potential customer.

19.8.1 Gain as Much Knowledge as Possible About the Company

The interviewee has to prepare himself for the interview in order to make good impact on the interviewers. He has to find out everything he can about the organization and has to decide whether he really wants to become a part of it. He can collect information about the organization from the business periodicals, chamber of commerce, business bureau, local newspapers, and personal contacts. This information may give him an idea of the company's public image.

He has to get the basic information about the company's recent developments, its affiliated organizations, its main products or services, etc. It can enable the interviewee to give intelligent answers to the questions like, "Is he or she interested in working for that organization?", "Why does he think that he would be successful in that organization?"

The candidate's acquired knowledge about the company and his sincere interest in it can create a good and favourable impression on the interviewer.

19.8.2 Analyze His or Her Strengths and Weaknesses

The interviewee should be confident about himself or herself. He or she needs to evaluate his or her strength, weaknesses, opportunities, and threats, that is, he should carry out his own SWOT analysis. This will help him or her to know where he/she stands.

19.8.3 Draw Up a List of Questions That She or He Would Like to Ask

The interviewee can anticipate the questions which are likely to be asked in the interview. The interviewee can participate effectively in an interview if he or she improves his or her ability of anticipating typical questions and practices answering them. He or she must prepare, practice, and rehearse his answers and non-verbal responses.

Besides, the interviewee must thoroughly study his or her resume to be ready to answer any questions related to it.

19.8.4 Have Presentable Appearance

Everybody appreciates a pleasant personality. In an interview the concerned person's appearance is a part of the message. The most effective strategy for making a good impression is to pay careful attention to your dress, grooming and posture. Since an interview is a formal occasion, prefer a well-tailored, clean, conservative outfit for the interview. Pay attention to personal hygiene and grooming including mustaches and beards should be neatly trimmed and combed. Hands and fingernails should be clean. Perfume and cologne should be used with moderation and should not overpower the interviewer. Avoid excessive or distracting jewelley, and elaborate hairstyles. Do not smoke, chew gum, or eat during the interview. This can detract substantially from your presentation and overall image.

19.8.5 Show Interest by Making Effective Use of Body Language

Keeping eye contact with the interviewers at once, shows that interviewee is genuinely interested in the event is keen to participate in it. Be alert to your body language throughout the interview. He or she should also sit in a correct, confident posture. Be careful not to slouch down in the chair. This may be interpreted negatively by the interviewer (i.e., you are disinterested in what is being said, you are lazy or sloppy, you are not concerned with your personal appearance, etc). Conversely, do not sit rigidly or on the edge of the chair. If too rigid, you may project the image of someone who is overly formal, unfriendly, or distant. Likewise, sitting on the edge of the chair may take you appear nervous, anxious, high strung, or overly aggressive. Maintain good posture and a relaxed, but attentive demeanour throughout the interview.

Be straight, balanced, and not stiff in the chair offered. The hands should be neatly logged in the lap or be comfortably placed on the arms on the chair.

Gesticulate appropriately to make a key point. However, be careful not to over-gesticulate, since this can draw the interviewer's attention away from what you are saying and can detract substantially from your overall presentation. Avoid unnecessary fidgeting with your hands or finger, such as tapping your fingers, playing with pencils and paper clips, stroking your beard of hair, pulling your ear, resting your shoulders on the table, rubbing your nose, and so on. All of these suggest nervousness and will distract interviewers, thereby causing them to pay less attention to what you are saying.

19.8.6 Be Honest in Answering the Questions

Since the primary aim of an interview is to exchange information, it should be done effectively. If the interviewee is not clear about a suitable answer to a question, there is no harm in admitting it. Do not try to pretend to know what you do not know. One must never try to bluff.

19.8.7 Be Polite

The interviewee should be pleasant, friendly, warm, and polite throughout the interview. Remember to smile from time to time and try to establish and maintain good personal rapport with the interviewer throughout the discussion.

In addition to, be polite, courteous, and friendly to the interviewer's support staff (i.e., secretary, administrative assistant, assistant). These individuals will frequently relay their impressions of an employment candidate to their supervisor.

19.8.8 Avoid Talking Too Much or Making Boastful Statements

Be factual and honest, but be brief. Try to present this information in as positive a light as possible, but do not over-explain or apologize. The interviewer is intelligent enough to find out the interviewee's intelligence and suitability for the job.

19.8.9 Avoid Negative Statements or Criticism

Never volunteer negative information to the interviewer. Avoid criticism of the previous employer or anybody else. However, should such information come to light as a result of the interviewer's questioning, do not dodge the issue.

19.9 PARTS OF THE INTERVIEW

Every interview has an introduction a body, and a close. Interviewers should prepare different approaches and questions for each part.

In the opening, good interviewers will try to put the candidate at ease. Some interviews will open with easy questions about your education or interests. Others open by telling you about the job or the organization. If this happens the candidate should list a carefully so he or she can answer later questions related to the job or contribute to the organization that is being described.

The body of the interview (10 to 15 minutes) enables the interviewer to move into the interview properly. She or he will now start obtaining facts, opinions and attitudes from the candidate. Detailed questions about the job will be asked. The candidate will be encouraged by open and closed questions to give details of specific answers.

The closed of interview (two to five minutes) enables the interviewer to sum up. She or he will also tell the candidate.

- What will be done with the responses.
- What will happen next.

The candidate is encouraged to ask questions at this stage. The interview is then concluded on a friendly note.

19.10 THE PANEL INTERVIEW

A panel is normally controlled by a chairperson, who allocates duties. There may even be a secretary who records the proceedings. A panel has the following advantages:

- Each person can be responsible for a specific set of questions.
- The other members can concentrate on the candidates' answers and take notes.
- Each member can use his or her special knowledge to help the panel to choose the best candidate.

There are, however, some major disadvantages of a panel:

- Panel needs a great deal of time to prepare.
- Members may not be well prepared and questioning may be poor as a result.
- Members may not agree on candidates. They then make compromises and do not necessarily choose the best candidate.

If panel ask to work well, they need to get together well in advance. They can then discuss the best ways of tacking the interview. Duties can be allocated in advance so the questions can be prepared.

19.11 USEFUL INTERVIEW QUESTIONS

Here are some job interview questions that are often asked during an employment interview. Questions such as these provide the interviewer with important clues about the candidate's qualifications, personality, poise, and communication skills. The interviewer is interested not only in the content of your responses but also in how you react to the questions themselves and how you communicate your thoughts and ideas. Before going for your interview, practice your response to each of these questions. Answer each question honestly, but in a way that highlights your qualities.

- Tell me about yourself?
- How would you describe yourself?
- Why are you interested in this job?
- Why should we offer you the job?
- What are your strengths for the job?
- What are your goals and ambitions?

- What has been your most valuable work experience?
- What are your hobbies?
- What is your proudest achievement?
- What would you like to be doing in five years time?
- What are your plans for further education and training?
- How ambitious are you?
- What are some of the things you find less satisfying?
- Why do you think you would be capable supervising/managing people?
- Have you innovated in your previous/present job? In what way?
- What do you know about this job?
- Why do you think you are suitable for this job?
- What was it about _____ that interest you? (for example–technology, personal)
- Why did you leave that job?
- What are reasons for leaving the previous job?
- What do you know about our organization?
- How do you react to pressure? Give examples.
- What do you think distinguishes a good manager from a bad one?
- What have been the milestones in your career?
- What would you do if _____? (Some problem related to the job)
- Why did you move from _____ to _____?
- What experience do you have which is most relevant to the job on offer?
- In what ways have you been able to stamp you own personality on the jobs you had?
- Give me three reasons why you are especially qualified for this job.
- What weaknesses have previous employers identified over the years?
- What part of this job would probably give you the most trouble?
- What are your expectations about the salary?

19.12 CONDUCTING YOURSELF DURING THE INTERVIEW

- Observe the organizational environment very carefully and treat everyone you meet, including the receptionist and the interviewer's assistant or secretary, with courtesy.
- Maintain an air of formality. When shown into the interview room, greet the interviewer with a firm handshake, direct eye contact, and a smile.
- If you are not asked to be seated immediately, wait until the interviewer is seated and then take your seat. Sit with your feet planted firmly on the floor, lean forward a bit in your seat, and maintain comfortable eye contact with the interviewer.
- Avoid taking notes, except perhaps for a specific name, date, or telephone number.
- Recognize that certain parts of the office are off-limits—especially the interviewer's desk and any area behind the desk. Do not rest your hands, purse, or notes on the desk and never wander around the office.

- Show interest in everything the interviewer is saying. Do not concentrate so hard on formulating your response that you miss the last part of any question.
- Answer each question in a positive, confident, forthright manner. Remember that more than yes-or-no answers are expected.
- Control nervousness during the interview the same way you control it when making an oral presentation. Therefore, practice until you are confident you can face whatever the interviewer throws your way. Participate in mock interviews conducted by your college. Practice answering lists of common questions.
- Through the interview your attitude should be one of the confidence and courtesy. Assume a role that is appropriate for you. Remember, you are applying–not begging—for a job. If the match works, both you and the employer will benefit.
- Do not try to take charge of the interview. Follow the interviewer's lead, letting him or her determine which questions to ask, when to move to a new area of discussion, and when to end the interview.
- Answer each question put to you as honestly as you can. Keep your mind on the desired job and how you can show that you are qualified for that job.
- If asked about your salary expectations, try to avoid giving a salary figure, indicating that you would expect to be paid in line with other employees at your level of expertise and experience. If press, however, be prepared to reveal your salary expectations, preferably using a broad range. If salary is not discussed, be patient. Few people have ever been offered a job in industry without first being told what they would be paid.
- You might participate in a group interview, in which several people interview you at once. In such a case, address your responses to everyone, not just to the person who asked the question or to the most senior person present.
- It is also likely that you will be interviewed more than once. Be on the alert for clues you can pick up from your early interviews that might be of use to you in later interviews.
- When the interview ends, if you are not been told, you have a right to ask the interviewer when you might expect to hear from him or her.
- You will likely be evaluated on education and experience, mental qualities, manner and personal traits, and appearance.

19.13 COMMUNICATING AFTER THE INTERVIEW

- Immediately after the interview, conduct a self-appraisal of your performance. Try to recall each question that was asked and evaluate your response. If you are not satisfied with one of your responses, take the time to formulate a more effective answer. Chances are that you will be asked a similar question in the future.
- Reevaluate your resume. Were any questions asked during the interview that indicated some confusion about your qualifications? Does some section need to be revised or some information added or deleted?

- Determine too whether you can improve your application letter on the basis of your interview experience.
- You should also send the interviewer(s) a short thank-you note or email message as a gesture of courtesy and to reaffirm your interest in the job. Remember, however, that your thank-you note may or may not have any effect on the hiring decision. Most decisions to offer the candidate a job or to invite him or her back for another round of interviewing are made the day of the interview, often during the interview itself. Thus, your thank-you note may arrive after the decision, good or bad, has been made.
- The real purpose of a thank-you note is to express a genuine appreciation for some courtesy extended to you; you do not write to earn points. Also avoid trying to resell yourself. You have already made your case through your resume, cover letter and interview.

Letter of Acknowledgement

This letter is used to follow up an interview, thanking the interviewer.

XYZ
42, Nai Sadak
Lucknow

7.3.20...

Personnel Officer
M/S Paroons Tools Limited
A-4, Industrial area
Kanpur

Dear Sir

Sub: Acceptance of appointment letter

This refers to my interview with your organization, held on 11.2.20..., for the post of Sales Manager and subsequently appointment letter which has been received by me yesterday, i.e., on 6.3.20....

I am very much thankful to you for the appointment letter and give my consent to accept the offer and join your company.

I would like to draw your kind attention that although you have asked me to report for joining in the next 15 days time but my present employer has requested me to stay with the company for another two months due to the important assignment which I have been handling independently. I too feel that considering the present situation and my long association with the company, it would be better to stay with the company for at least one month so that another person can be trained on the jobs, presently handled by me independently.

I shall be grateful for your confirmation for extending my joining period by another fifteen days.

Kindly confirm

Yours faithfully

(XYZ)

Letter of resignation

When the person wants to leave his current position under the best circumstances possible, he writes a letter of resignation.

XYZ
Employee No. 00125
Sr. Engineer-Assembly Shop

15.2.20..

The Production Manager
Atlas Cycles Limited
Sonipat

Dear Sir

Sub: Resignation from the post of Sr. Engineer – Assembly Shop

I bring to your kind attention that due to some personal reasons, I am not in a position to serve your organization anymore. Therefore, I resign from the post of Sr. Engineer Assembly shop with immediate effect.

I am very much thankful to you and the management of the organization for their time-to- time guidance and the cooperation during my short tenure of two years with the organization.

I request that my resignation be kindly accepted and relieved by 14.3.20.. as per the terms and conditions of my appointment letter.

Yours faithfully
(XYZ)

Letter Informing Non-Selection

A letter of rejection to a candidate is an indirect approach letter.

Example: A letter of rejection to a candidate who appeared for an interview as a programmer

SOFTNET SOLUTIONS
Sector-62, Noida

24.3.20....

Mr. XYZ
26, Gandhi Nagar
Roorkee
Dear Sir

This refers to the interview you had with us on 12.03.20.... for the post of programmer in our IT department.

Kindly note that although our interview committee found your performance satisfactory but we require a person who has an experience not only in programming but also in the upgradation of hardware.

We thank you once again for the interest shown in our organization.

Yours faithfully
(XYZ)
Personnel Manager
SOFTNET SOLUTIONS

REVIEW QUESTIONS

1. Define interview? What are the different types of interview?
2. What are the objectives of job interview? Identify at least five specific uses of the interview in the typical organization.
3. Describe various phases of a typical interview.
4. Describe several misconceptions or myths that create a major obstacle during the course of an interview.
5. List some of the factors that are relevant to all inteviews.
6. How should interviewers prepare themselves for the interviews?
7. How an interviewee should prepare himself for the interviews?
8. How should a candidate behave during the interview?
9. How should the interviewers and interviewees prepare themselves for the interview?
10. What is the significance of appraisal interview? Suggest some ways and means of making an appraisal interview successful.
11. Write a note on the most common type of interviews that are used in organizations. Describe various phases of employment interview.
12. What type of questions often form basis for an interview strategy? Mention at least ten questions?
13. How do successful interviewees communicate? How do you use your interview strategy during an interview?

UNIT–5
Grammar, Mechanics, and Usage

20

LANGUAGE: BASIC TOOL FOR BUSINESS COMMUNICATION

Chapter Objectives

This chapter will enable you to understand:

- Language as the basic tool of communication
- Definition of language
- The background of language
- Different forms of English
    - Historical differences
    - Geographical differences
    - Educational differences
    - Situational differences
- Language characteristics
- Appropriate and effective English
- Correct business English

Whatever language you speak – Hindi, English, Chinese, Japanese – helps to define you personally and identify the community you belong to. But the fact that we can talk to all, the fact that we have a language, is inextricably bound up with our humanity. To be human is to use language, and to talk is to be a person.

20.1 LANGUAGE AS THE BASIC TOOL OF COMMUNICATION

The ability to communicate is basic to our daily lives. Language is our basic tool for communication at home, at college, at work, and in countless other situations. Thus, we use this tool in many different ways for many different purposes. Through speaking and writing, we are able to give and receive information. We use language to express ourselves and to learn about others. In fact from a person's language, we can learn not only what the person is saying but also many extra things about that person.

1. Your language tells others about your education, intelligence, priorities, family, and neighborhood background.
2. Your vocabulary, sentence structure, ideas, use of logic, and sensitivity of expression provide clues about you and your abilities.
3. Your voice characteristics disclose your sex and approximate age.
4. Your pronunciations and phrasing patterns indicate the part of the country where you grew up.
5. Your tone of voice and manner of speaking tend to reveal your mood and feelings.

To an observant person, such as a job interviewer, these factors suggest a good deal about your maturity, personality, and outlook on life.

It is obvious, then, that both what you say and how you say it will affect those you meet. As a result, your use of English will directly affect the success you have in dealing with other people. Whatever you can do to improve your skill in using English will contribute to your ability to make a favourable impression upon others. This ability in turn increases your chances of success in all your undertakings.

20.2 DEFINITION OF LANGUAGE

"A language is a system of conventional vocal signs by means of which human beings communicate." – The Origins and Development of the English Language"

— John Algeo and Thomas Pyles.

According to Lewis Thomas, "Language is, like nest-building or hive-making, the universal and biologically specific activity of human beings. We engage in it communally, compulsively, and automatically. We cannot be human without it; if we were to be separated from it our mind would die, as surely as bees lost from the eyes" (Lives of Cell, .89).

The language that is innate in us is not English or indeed any specific language. It is indeed the ability to learn and to use a human language. This ability is language in the abstract, as distinct from any individual language system.

20.3 THE BACKGROUND OF LANGUAGE: A BRIEF VIEW

In 1755, Kant explained that language was the result of gradual evolution and natural causes that influenced development of humans. The very existence of language is something of a miracle, extending back in various spoken forms more than a million years. The history and development of language depicts that language as a tool of communication varies from period to period, place to place, social/occupational group to social/occupational group, and situation to situation.

How the English language changed from being the speech of a few small tribes to becoming the major language of the earth – and in the process changed radically has had a remarkable history. In contrast to spoken language, written language is a comparatively recent invention, dating back only about 8,000 years. From early pictorial forms, alphabetic writing developed, with each written symbol generally corresponding to one of the sounds in spoken language. Written language, then, comes from spoken language, and each written word and sentence is a rough graphic representation of the corresponding spoken word and sentence. In written language, punctuation marks have come to stand for pauses and other features of speech.

20.4 DIFFERENT FORMS OF ENGLISH

English is one of more than 2,500 languages spoken by human beings throughout the world. However, it is one of the most important because of its widespread use and influence. There are many different dialects (varieties) of the English language spoken in the world today. These various forms of English have resulted for four main types of differences or influences which affect all languages: historical, geographical, educational, and situational.

20.4.1 Historical Differences

English existed for centuries in different spoken dialects. During this early period, there was no written form of English. However, in 597 A.D., Christian Missionaries from Rome brought the Roman Alphabet to England. These missionaries adapted that alphabet for writing English. Since that time, written English has been in use. For about the next 850 years, all written English had to be transcribed by hand. All records and other written communications were in manuscript form. The invention of movable type about 1452 A.D. changed all that. This invention made it possible to print and distribute identical copies of a written work in large numbers. Printing greatly increased the use and importance of written languages for purposes of sharing information and knowledge.

English, we speak and write today is much different in pronunciation, spelling, vocabulary, forms and constructions from the English of King Alfred 1100 years ago.

The differences are so great that if you try to read the English of his time, you would think you were looking at a foreign language. English speaking people in the thirteenth century will probably feel the same way about the English we use today.

The reason for these differences is that every language is continuously undergoes changes. New words are added to the vocabulary and others become outdated. Some words change in sound and appearance. For example, the high irregular plurals of nouns like man – men, mouse – mice, goose – geese, and ox – oxen. The result is that over centuries, these accumulate to such an extent that the language reaches a new stage of development.

20.4.2 Geographical Differences

When you speak English, you unconsciously imitate the pronunciation and expressions used by your family and friends. Thus, you adopt the patterns of pronunciation, phrasing, and timing characteristic of these around you. As long as you remain in the region where you grew up, your pronunciation and other speech characteristics blend in with those of the other people in your locality. However, if you move to another part of the country, your new friends might take a special interest in the way you talk. Due to historical changes, dialects of English vary from region to region and country to country. The English spoken in North India differs from that spoken in southern part of India. Likewise, the English spoken in the United States differs from that spoken in the Great Britain.

20.4.3 Educational Differences

The English used by those who have had a good deal of formal education often contrasts with that used by those who have not had similar opportunities. For example, those who have had the advantage of more education are likely to have read widely. For this reason they probably have a good deal of information and a long vocabulary at their command. These people have had chances to develop their capacity to express themselves on a range of subjects in both speech and writing.

On the other hand, those without much formal education often develop the habit of using pronunciation, forms, and expressions that would not be appropriate in business dealings. For example,

- Smith *don't* have the schedule yet.
- *Ain't* Mr. Walker going to attend both meetings?
- Ms Ruth had already w*rote* the new guidelines.

20.4.4 Situational Differences

Consciously or unconsciously, you adapt your English to fit various situations. You speak and write differently in different circumstances. For example, you have many different roles at this point in your life. You have a certain role as a family member, and this role involves certain expectations about the language used around your home. You have another role as an employee, and this role involves certain expectations about the language used in the organization and in written documents. You probably have additional roles in our social activities. Each of these roles carries with it certain expectations about the formality and informality of your language. The language you might use in a family discussion with your family members, for example, would very likely be entirely out of place in a business discussion with your employer. Likewise, the language you would use when writing a letter to a friend would differ from the language you would use when writing a letter for a job.

20.5 LANGUAGE: CHARACTERISTICS

The human mental ability to use language and process information, including our articulatory mechanisms, results for the unique biological evolution of humans. Hockett in 1960 outlines the following features which prove that humans have unique linguistic and communication capabilities.

1. Duality of patterning

A language is not just a collection of words; such as we find in a dictionary. It is also the rules or patterns that relate our words to one another.

Every language has two levels to its systems – a characteristic that is called 'duplicity of patterning'. One of these levels consists of meaningful units. For example, the words and word parts such as Adam, liked, apple, and – s in the sentence "Adam likes apples."

The other level consists of units that have no meaning in themselves, although they serve as components of the meaningful units. For example, the sounds represented by the letters a,d and m in the word 'Adam'. The distinction between a meaningful word 'Adam' and its meaningless parts (a, d, and m) is important. We have 44 sounds in English, but we have hundreds of thousands of words. Duality of pattern lets us build an immensely large number of meaningful words out of only a handful of meaningless sounds. It is perhaps the chief characteristics that distinguishes true human language from the simpler communication system by all non human beings.

2. Language is vocal – auditory

Language is a system that can be expressed in many ways – by the marks on paper, or a computer screen that we call writing, by hand signals and gestures as in sign language, by coloured lights traffic lights, or moving flags, or by electronic clicks as in old fashioned telegraphy. However, the sign language is – its words end morphemes – are basically vocal, produced by the mouth and received by the ear.

The vocal-auditory channel means that the sender and receiver have a vocal tract for producing sound and an auditory mechanism to receive sounds.

3. Broadcast transmission and directional reception

This means that a signal travels in all directions. When you speak, anyone within earshot can hear you. The sounds of your voice are not narrowly beamed in the single direction. You have seen this at work if, you have ever been overheard by someone whom you did not intend to receive the message.

Speech is primary and writing is secondary to language. Human beings have been writing (as far as we can tell from the surviving evidence) for at least 5000 years, but they have been talking for much longer, ever since they were fully human. We cannot deny the fact that if speech makes human, writing makes us civilized.

4. Rapid fading

The sound of your voice goes away quickly. As soon as you utter something, the sound dissipates in a matter of milliseconds.

5. Interchangeability

A member of the species with this feature can be both sender and receiver.

6. Total feedback

Senders can monitor their signals. You can hear yourself speak and respond in the same way.

7. Specialization

The communication system serves no other function; it is specialized.

8. Semanticity

Expressions have meaning. Sounds or words in human language can have many meanings. They relate to ideas and information in the world. The chirping of a bird is part of the bird's signaling system but it has very limited meaning.

9. Arbitrariness

The world's many languages are conventional and generally arbitrary; that is to say there is usually no communication between the sounds we make and the phenomena of life. Any sound could be used to stand for the word 'house'. The fact that there are so many languages and different words for the same thing is a good example of arbitrariness.

10. Discreetness

This refers to the fact that signals are unique and discreet. There are many elements in the communication purposes. For example, the words 'tin' and 'fin' are distinguished by their initial sounds. Hence language is digital in that its basic elements (sounds) can be separated and recombined.

11. Displacement

Another aspect of the communicative function of the language is that it can be displaced. That is, you can talk about things not present – about rain when the weather is dry, about taxes even when they are not being collected, and about yeti even if no such creature exists. The characteristic of displacement means that human beings can abstract, lie, and talk about talk itself. Displaced language is a vehicle of memory and of imagination. A human can talk about something in the past, present, or future, in a real or imaginary world.

12. Traditional transmission

Human language is learned anew by each generation. It is taught to children and not genetically programmed. However, the ability to learn a language is genetic.

13. Productivity

Communication systems that are creative and allow for an unlimited supply of message are productive (such as fashion in clothing, hairstyles, cooking, and entertainment. Language is constantly being revised. It involves more slowly than do some other cultural activities but its change is continuous and inevitable.

When we have a new word, or a new pronunciation, or use of an old word, we may be catching the early stages of a change.

20.6 APPROPRIATE AND EFFECTIVE ENGLISH

As you have seen, English varies from situation to situation. To communicate effectively, you must learn to be skillful in adopting what you say and how you say it.

1. Language appropriate to each situation

Your remarks should be appropriate to each situation. You must try to decide what kind of language each situation calls for – how familiar or formal you should be; how open or how reserved. If you misinterpret a situation and use language that is too familiar you may offend some people.

2. Correct tone and style

If you use a tone of voice that seems impatient and unfriendly, you may antagonize them. Under either of these circumstances, you will have reduced your chances of receiving favourable consideration for what you have to say.

However the choice of correct tone and style is a matter of personal sensitivity and judgment. There is no formula which will define exactly what will be appropriate in various situations.

3. Courtesy and friendliness

In business dealings, it is important that you express yourself not only correctly but also positively and courteously. All employees work more harmoniously with co-workers who are not only competent but also cheerful and polite. Customers continue to do business with companies which offer efficient, positive and courteous service.

A friendly manner and courteous speech are even more important in dealing with people over the telephone than in meeting them face-to-face.

Always remember that courtesy towards others is the mark of a mature and considerate person. Courtesy and friendliness help you make a favourable impression. For example, an employee who uses a harsh or rude approach in requesting a favour stands little chance of obtaining the favour. If you approach your manager a letter of recommendation that will emphasize your desirable qualities, you will want to adopt a polite manner. You know that a respectful attitude will help you make a favourable impression. It can be a key factor influencing your success in the business world.

20.7 CORRECT BUSINESS ENGLISH

The English that is appropriate in business is different in important ways from the casual language used in daily life. Organizations cannot conduct business efficiently if they use ambiguous, imprecise and often careless English of daily conversation.

The language in business, therefore, must be more accurate in form and content than in everyday conversation. It must be better organized, more responsible in its use of evidence, and more logical in its reasoning and conclusions. It must give greater attention to the reactions of others and be much more sensitive about matters of tone. It should be unfailingly courteous because any lapse in courtesy introduces unnecessary complications.

English serves as an all-purpose tool for carrying out such tasks as the following.

1. For obtaining and presenting information as a basis for decisions at every level.
2. For making assignments, giving directions, posing questions providing answers, and evaluating results.
3. For analyzing the courses of action available, establishing priorities, and reaching decisions concerning which options offer the greatest advantages.
4. For conducting transactions and correspondence with customers, suppliers, contractors, stock holders, government agencies, and others.
5. For recording the exact terms involved in every contract, policy, regulation, agreement, order, proposal and transaction.
6. For advertising products and services and making their advantages known to potential customers and clients.
7. For establishing constructive relations that make it easier to reach agreements, that encourage cooperation, and that promote further business.

Therefore, the success of every organization is directly affected by the language used by its employees. For establishing constructive relations that make it easier to reach agreements, that encourage cooperation, and that promote further business.

REVIEW QUESTIONS

1. In your opinion, what would an interviewer learn about a job applicant from the sentences below? In what ways could the applicant change these sentences in order to make a more favourable impression?

(a) My experience don't include typing invoices.

(b) The supervisors did not permit no errors in business correspondences.

(c) The person whom I believe taught me most is Mr. Labroo.

(d) My summary of these points are contained in the letter.

2. Important changes in English have come about through the addition of new words related to inventions and technology. Name at least five new words which have resulted from developments in computers, space flight, or nuclear energy.
3. Name at least five countries that use English as their native language. Keep in mind that each of these countries includes a number of dialects of English, each with its own characteristics of pronunciation, vocabulary, and phrasing.
4. Following sentences contain mistakes that suggest that the speaker has not had an opportunity for much formal education. Such sentences would be out of place in a business setting. Classify each sentence as acceptable or unacceptable for business communication and suggest ways of changing the sentences that are unacceptable.

   (a) This here letter just come.

   (b) The invoice contained a complete record of the other.

   (c) Mrs. Paul has wrote for tickets.

   (d) Mr. David don't want no assistance from anybody.
5. For each sentence below, answer the following questions about the circumstances surrounding each sentence.

   (a) What kind of establishment is involved?

   (b) What kind of employee is being addressed?

   (c) Check my battery and oil too, David.

   (d) I want to deposit all but rupees thousand.

   (e) Please, let me know how you want me to proceed in returning 200 copies of this dictionary. My order was for 50 not 250 copies.

   (f) Make mine with extra onion and extra sausage.

   (g) How soon can you install network connections in our lab?
6. Revise the following sentences so that they would make a favourable impression on the reader and listener.

   (a) Notify us of your new address without further delay.

   (b) Do you want us to make an estimate or not?

   (c) This notice acknowledges that you finally returned our sample book.

   (d) Our records prove that your car is overdue for a checkup.

   (e) Fill out and return the enclosed form at once for a free specimen.

21
GRAMMAR: PARTS OF SPEECH

Chapter Objectives

This chapter will enable you to understand:

- ◇ Nouns
- ◇ Pronouns
- ◇ Verbs
- ◇ Adjectives
- ◇ Verbs
- ◇ Adverbs
- ◇ Prepositions
- ◇ Conjunctions
- ◇ Articles
- ◇ Interjections

Categorized by meaning, form and function, English fall into various parts of speech: nouns, pronouns, verbs, adjectives, adverbs, prepositions, conjunctions, articles, and interjections.

21.1 NOUNS

A noun is a word used to name a person, place, a thing or an idea (including objects, events, or concepts):

Persons	Places	Objects	Events	Concepts
secretary	lake	office	election	justice
principal	highway	computer	promotion	peace
typist	colony	bus	meeting	friendship

21.1.1 Characteristic Forms of Nouns

Nouns in English can have number and can show possession. Therefore most nouns have the following four distinct forms, and any word capable of having these forms is a noun:

1. Singular
2. Plural
3. Singular Possessive
4. Plural Possessive

In addition, the term 'case' refers to how nouns change form depending on their use in sentences. The following examples show that nouns have two basic cases: general and possessive.

General Case (Singular)	General Case (Plural)	Possessive Case (Singular)	Possessive Case (Plural)
Executive	Executives	Executive's	Executives'
Employee	Employees	Employee's	Employees'
Calculator	Calculators	Calculator's	Calculators'

Singular and plural nouns in the general case

Nouns can be either singular or plural. Singular nouns are formed in many different ways with many different spellings. (book, record, student, company)

The usual way to make a plural noun is to add 's' or 'es' to the singular form of the word:

Nouns adding 's' to form the plurals		Nouns adding 'es' to form the plurals	
Pen	Pens	Class	Classes
File	Files	Watch	Watches
Record	Records	Cargo	Cargoes
Map	Maps	Tax	Taxes

Many nouns have other ways of forming the plural:

1. Some plurals involve a change in a vowel. (mouse/mice, goose/geese, woman/women, tooth/teeth)

   The addition of 'en' or 'ren' (ox/oxen, child/children)

   The change from 'y' to 'ies' (city/cities, secretary/secretaries, speciality/specialities)

   The change from 'f' to 'v' (knife/knives, half/halves, life/lives); some exceptions: roofs, fifes
2. Some nouns which have been formed from foreign languages keep their foreign plural forms (datum/data)

   Some words of foreign origin offer a choice of purals (phenomenon/phenomena phenomenons, index/indexes or indices, antenna/antennas or antennae). It is always a good idea to consult a dictionary if you are in doubt about the proper plural form of any noun.

3. The plurals of compound nouns are usually formed by adding 's' or 'es' to the main word of the compound (fathers-in-law, editors-in-chief, attorneys-at law).
4. Some nouns are the same whether singular or plural (sheep, deer, mouse). Some nouns are plural in forms but singular in use (ethics, measles). Some nouns are used in the plural only (scissors, trousers).
5. Letters, numbers, and words used as words are sometimes made plural by adding an apostrophe and one 's' (A's, Ph.D's, I's). However, if no confusion would be created by leaving off the apostrophe, it is common practice to just add the 's' (1990s, RFPs, HODs, DVDs)

Possessive nouns

Nouns are either in the general case or the possessive case. The meaning of possessive case usually refers to possession or ownership. A noun becomes possessive when it is used to show the ownership of something. Then you add 's to the word:

The student's notebook = the notebook of the student
The manager's house = the house of the manager
The customer's credit card = the credit card of the customer
The company's asset = the asset of the company

In the above mentioned examples, the possessive refers to ownership. However, the possessive can also be used to express other relationships:

The president's concern = the concern of the president
The school's principal = the principal of the school
The teacher's satisfaction = the satisfaction of the teacher

Also, ownership may be nothing more than an automatic association. (a day's work, the job's profile)

An exception to the rule about adding 's to make a noun possessive has two 's' sounds at the end. In such cases, an apostrophe is all that is needed. (Crisis' dimensions)

When the noun has only one 's' sound at the end, however, retain the 's'. (Chris's application)

With compound nouns, add 's to the last word. (mother-in-law/mother-in-law's)

To form the possessive of plural nouns, just begin by following the same rule as with singular noun: add 's. However, if the plural noun already ends in an 's' , add only the apostrophe:

the authors recommendations = the authors' recommendations
the customers complaints = the customers' complaints
the judges decision = the judges' decision

For all nouns that form the plural in any way other than adding the suffix 's' or 'es', add 's to the plural in order to form the plural possessive:

children the children's books
alumnae the alumnae's record
women the women's college

21.1.2 Subclasses of Nouns

Nouns may be classified in a number of different ways.

1. Common and proper nouns

A common noun names something as a member of a class. All the members of a class have essential characteristics in common. For example, the word 'building' refers to a whole class of structures. The other examples of common noun are:

city

company

computer

desk

A proper noun is the name of a particular person, place, thing, or event. If you refer to one particular building, for example, 'Zee Building' you refer to a proper noun.

Proper nouns are capitalized; common nouns are not. Therefore, the distinction between common and proper nouns is vital in business writing. Following are the examples of common and proper nouns:

Common noun	Proper noun
City	Delhi
Automobile	Honda
State	Uttar Pradesh
Corporation	IBM
Holiday	Deepawali
Store	Loyal Book Depot

2. Collective nouns

Collective nouns encompass a group of people or objects:

Crowd	Jury	Committee
Team	Audience	Family
Herd	Class	

A collective noun can refer to a unit as a whole or to each individual in the unit. A collective noun referring to a unit as a whole takes a singular verb, and singular pronouns are used in referring to such a noun. A collective noun referring to the particular individuals in a unit takes a plural verb, and plural forms are used in referring to such a noun:

The team A <u>has been</u> selected for the final round.
(singular)

The staff <u>has</u> moved to <u>its</u> new quarters.
(singular) *(singular)*

The team A <u>have been</u> divided in <u>their</u> opinion.
(plural) *(plural)*

The staff have begun to compare their individual findings.
(plural) *(plural)*

The most important point to remember about collective noun is that you should be consistent in using them as either singular or plural nouns.

3. Concrete and abstract nouns

A concrete noun names one or more persons, place, things, or events:

beach computer promotion

In contrast, an abstract noun names an idea, a quality, or a condition:

friendship willingness courtesy independence accuracy

Many abstract nouns are formed from adjectives and have suffixes like 'ness', 'ty', 'dom', 'th', 'ence', 'ance':

Adjective	**Abstract Noun**
Effective	Effectiveness
Wise	Wisdom
True	Truth
Confident	Confidence
Secure	Security

A few noun, such as algorithm, software, and code are difficult to categorize as either abstract or concrete, but can reasonably be considered concrete even though they don't have a physical presence.

In business English, a writing style that uses many concrete nouns is likely to be concise and easy to understand. On the other hand, a style uses many abstract nouns and generalizations is likely to be wordy and confusing.

Nouns as subject and object

A noun which comes before the verb and determines whether a singular and plural verb should be used is a **subject**. A noun following a transitive verb (a verb that needs one object to complete its meaning) and telling who or what receives the verb's action is a **direct object.**

The secretary prepares the report.
(subject) *(d. object)*

The web designer created the homepage.
(subject) *(d.object)*

A noun following a sending type intransitive verb and referring to the receiver of what was sent is an **indirect object.**

The salesman delivered the carpet to the customer.
(subject) *(d.object)* *(ind.object)*

Mr. Burman gave the letter to the clerk.
(subject) *(d.object)* *(ind.object)*

Noun as appositive

If two nouns occur together and the second could substitute for the first, the second is appositive.

Henry Ford, father of the Ford Motor Corporation, developed production lines.
(noun) *(noun appositive)*

21.2 PRONOUN

A pronoun is a word that stands for a noun; it saves repeating the noun.

Ms Lisa typed the report after she received it.

The pronoun 'she' and 'it' stand in for the nouns 'Ms Lisa' and 'report' respectively. The noun that a pronoun stands for is called the **antecedent** of the pronoun. 'Ms. Lisa' is the antecedent of 'she' and 'report' is the antecedent of 'it'. When the antecedent is plural, the pronoun that stands in for it has to be plural. Likewise, when the antecedent is singular, the pronoun has to be singular.

Multiple antecedents

Sometimes a pronoun has a double (or even a triple) antecedents:

Katherine and Luis went beyond their sales quotas for March.

Unclear antecedents

In some sentences the pronoun antecedent is unclear:

Ms Sonal submitted her analysis and plan and was requested to revise it. (Was Ms Sonal requested to revise her analysis or her plan?)

Chapters 4 and 5 deal with tax matters, but it includes information on refunds. (Which chapter includes information on refunds-chapter 4 or chapter 5?)

The best way to clarify an ambiguous pronoun is usually to rewrite the sentence, repeating nouns when needed for clarity:

Ms Sonal submitted her analysis and plan and was requested to revise the plan.

Chapters 4 and 5 deal with tax matters, but chapter 5 includes information on refunds.

The noun needs to be repeated only when the antecedent is unclear.

Pronoun classes

Personal pronouns are classified by whether they refer to the person speaking, the person addressed, or the person or thing discussed.

1. First-person personal pronouns refer to the speaker or writer (I, me, my, mine, we, us, our, ours).
2. Second-person personal pronouns refer to the person being addressed (you, your, yours).
3. Third-person personal pronouns refer to the person or thing being discussed (he, him, his, she, her, hers, it, its, they, them, their, theirs).

While there are thousands of nouns in English, there are only thirty two personal pronoun forms. Many of these forms are closely related.

Compound Personal Pronouns are created by adding 'self' or 'selves' to simple personal pronouns (myself, ourselves, yourself, yourselves, himself, herself, itself, themselves).

Compound personal pronouns are used either **intensively**, to emphasize the identity of the noun or pronoun (I myself has seen the demonstration) or **reflexively**, to indicate that the subject is the receiver of his or her own action. (Me. Neel himself made the arguments). The 'intensive forms' are used for emphasis. (Ms. Reena revised the message herself.) The 'reflexive forms' are used to indicate that the person or thing designated by the subject of a verb is also designated by the object of the same verb. (The advocate criticized himself.)

Relative Pronouns refer to nouns in the main clause and are used to introduce clauses:

The four team leaders, whomever, the committee selects, will be at tomorrow's meeting.

The book, when it was finally returned, was torn and stained.

The relative pronouns are which, who, whom, whose, what. Other words used as relative pronouns include that, whoever, whomever, whatever, and whichever.

Interrogative pronouns are those used for asking questions: who, whom, whose, which, and what. There are just five **interrogative pronouns**. Each one is used to ask a very specific question or indirect question. Some, such as 'who' and 'whom', refer only to people. Others can be used to refer to objects or people:

What time are we supposed to be there?

Which colour do you prefer?

Demonstrative pronouns point out particular person, places, or things. The demonstrative pronouns are this, these, that, and those:

That was such an interesting experience.

This can't be correct.

Indefinite pronouns refer to persons or things not specifically identified. They include anyone, someone, everyone, everybody, somebody, either, neither, one, none, all, both, each, another, any, many, and similar words.

Case of pronouns

Personal pronouns have three cases: subjective or nominative case, objective case, and possessive case.

The case of a pronoun (nominative and objective) tells whether it is acting or acted upon:

She sells an average of six packages daily.

In this sentence, 'she' is doing the 'selling'. Because 'she' is acting 'she' is said to be in the **nominative case**.

After six months, Mr Gupta promoted her.

In this sentence, the pronoun 'her' is acted upon and is thus said to be in the **objective case**.

Possessive pronouns work like possessive nouns- they show ownership or automatic association:

her job his account their performances its equipment

Following is the list of nominative, objective, and possessive pronouns:

nominative	objective	possessive
i	me	my, mine
we	us	our, ours
you	you	your, yours
he	him	his
she	her	hers
they	them	their, theirs
it	it	its

Pronoun - antecedent agreement

Like nouns, pronouns can be singular or plural. Pronouns must agree in number with their antecedents:

1. A singular antecedent requires a singular pronoun:
   The team leader tendered his resignation.
2. Multiple antecedents require a plural pronoun:
   The team members tendered their resignations.
3. A pronoun referring to singular antecedents conneted by 'or' or 'nor' should be singular
   Neither Shree nor Tom made his quota.
   But a pronoun referring to a plural and a singular antecedent connected by 'or' or 'nor' should be plural:
   Neither Shree nor the twins made their quotas.
4. Formal English prefers the nominative case after the linking verb 'to be':
   It is I. That is he.
   However, for general usage it is perfectly acceptable to use the more natural "It's me" and "That's him."

21.3 VERBS

A **verb** indicates an action or state of being.

Verbs indicating action	Verbs indicating state of being
Suggest	Be
Verify	Seem
Deliver	Appear
Receive	Sound
Improve	Resemble

Auxiliary verb

Auxiliaries are function words that precede the main verb in verb phrases and signal certain grammatical meanings. The most important of these grammatical meanings are changes in voice or tense.

Auxiliary	Main verb
has	called
will	leave
shall	write
was	called
shall be	told

Verb phrases

Verb phrases are made up of one or more auxiliaries and one main verb. Each auxiliary verb has a distinct function and thus indicates a certain grammatical meaning. For example, some auxiliaries indicate that a verb refers to future action (The Company will refund its customers' money). Other auxiliaries signal that an action is complete (We have mailed the report). Still other auxiliaries indicate that a verb phrase is in passive voice (The letter was typed by the secretary).

Basic facts about verbs

1. Transitive and intransitive verbs

Verbs may be either **transitive** (those which need objects to complete their meaning) or **intransitive** (those which do not need objects to complete their meaning). For example:

Transitive	Intransitive
Mr Sen wrote the report.	The proposal arrived.

A special type of verb connects a subject with a word (adjective, noun, pronoun) which describes the subject and completes the meaning of the verb. Such a word is called a **linking verb.** Forms of such words as be, appear, become, and feel are linking verbs. For example:

It seemed a good plan at the time.

The sppeh was informative.

Simmi appeared tired after working six hours of overtime.

2. Voice of verbs

'Voice' is a technical term in grammar. Voice refers to the relation between a verb and its subject. Verbs have two voices, active and passive. If the subject of a sentence performs the action, the verb is in **active voice**. If the subject of the verb receives the action, the verb is in **passive voice**. For example:

Active	Passive
The reporter wrote the article.	The article was written by the reporter.
The customer paid a large amount.	A large amount was paid by the customer.

Uses of active voice and passive voice

- The active voice is usually preferable to active voice. The active voice is more direct and forceful. Usually it is more effective. However, passive voice is appropriate in certain circumstances. If you wish to refer to an action without drawing attention to the performer, use passive voice:

Active voice: Mr. Tim, the team leader, criticized the members severely. (Performer identified)

Passive voice: The members were criticized severely. (Performer omitted)

- Passive forms are found useful in describing processes:

  All relevant data is collected and analysed; then a suitable policy is formulated.

3. Verb tenses

Tense indicates the time of action of a verb. There are three **main verb tenses**: present, past, and future. For example:

Present	Past	Future
Sue takes notes.	Sue took notes.	Sue will take notes.

In addition to the three simple tenses, the three **perfect tenses** are created by adding forms of the auxiliary verb 'have'. The **present perfect tense** uses the past participle of the main verb, and adds the present 'have' or 'has' to the front of it:

(I, we, you, they) have offered 10% discount to clear the stock.

(He, she) has offered 10% discount to clear the stock.

The **past perfect tense** uses the past participle of the main verb, and adds the present 'had' to the front of it:

(I, we, you, they, he, she) had offered 10% discount to clear the stock.

The **future perfect tense** also uses the past participle of the main verb, but adds the future tense 'will have':

(I, we, you, they, he, she) will have offered 10% discount to clear the stock.

The Principal Parts of a Verb and Their Uses

A verb has three principal parts-its base form, its past tense and its past participle. All verb forms and phrases are built from these three parts:

1. The **base form** has three uses. It can be used as the present tense of the verb (except for the third person singular, which ends in 's' or 'es'). It can be used as the **infinitive,** which is preceded by 'to' or by the auxiliary function words – will/would, shall/should, may/might, can/could, or must. It can also be used as the **imperative** – the verb form used in commands. In addition, most verb suffixes are added to the base form.
2. The **past tense** has only one use – to express actions that occurred prior to the statement.
3. The **past participle** is used either as a verbal adjective (example: the written word) or as part of many verb phrases (example: is written, has written)

21.3.1 Ways of Forming the Past Tense

Verbs form their past tense in several different ways.

Type 1 – Regular verbs

Regular verbs add 'd' or 'ed' to their unchanged base to form the past tense. Most verbs belong to this class:

Base form	Past tense	Past participle
walk	walked	walked
paint	painted	painted
prepare	prepared	prepared
test	tested	tested
post	posted	posted

Type 2 – Irregular verbs

There are three main subtypes of irregular verbs:

1. The first subtype adds 'd', 'ed', or 't' to an altered base to form the past tense:

Base form	Past tense	Past participle
have	had	had
carry	carried	carried
sell	sold	sold
bring	brought	brought
sleep	slept	slept

2. The second subtype changes its base without adding 'd', 'ed', or 't' to form the past tense:

Base form	Past tense	Past participle
hold	held	held
lie	lay	lain
write	wrote	written
sit	sat	sat
get	got	got/gotten

3. The third type has no way of showing past tense:

Base form	Past tense	Past participle
burst	burst	burst
set	set	set
broadcast	broadcast	broadcast
hurt	hurt	hurt
cost	cost	cost

Type 3 – Left-over verbs

Three verbs (go, to, be) do not fit into Type 1 or Type 2. These verbs substitute a different word in their past tense or have other unique changes:

Base form	Past tense	Past participle
go	went	gone
do	did	done
be (present tense: am, are, is)	was/were	been

To be is the only verb which:

- has a base form (be) that is different from the present tense forms,
- has three different forms for the present tense (am/are/is)
- has two different forms for the past tense (was/were)

In addition to its use as a main verb, 'be' in all its forms also serves as an auxiliary function word. For example, it is often used to express passive voice: is praised, was promoted, will be rewarded. The forms of 'be', as main verbs or as auxiliary function words, occur frequently.

21.3.2 Subject-Verb Agreement

A verb must agree with its subject in various ways:

1. Agreement in person

A subject and verb must agree I person:

(a) The subject of a first-person verb is the person writing or speaking. Therefore, a first-person subject is always 'I' or 'we':

I plan.

We see.

(b) The subject of a second-person verb is always the person who is being addressed. Therefore, a second-person subject is always 'you':

You reported.

(c) The subject of a third-person verb is always the person or thing spoken about. Therefore, a third-person subject can be any noun or any third-person personal pronoun:

She sends the bills.

The management answers.

2. Agreement in number

A subject and verb must also agree in number. Thus, the singular form of a verb must be used when a singular noun or pronoun is the subject. The plural form of a verb must be used when a plural noun or pronoun is the subject.

Singular subject and verb	Plural subject and verb
The secretary keeps the records.	The secretaries keep the records.

3. Other matters involving subject-verb agreement

(a) Compound subjects: Compound subjects generally require plural verbs. For example:

Mr. Rohan and Ms. Neeti are excellent candidates and expect to be promoted soon.

Compound subjects are formed only by the coordinating conjunction 'and'. Such expressions as 'in addition to', 'together with', 'along with', 'as well as', 'and 'including' do not form compound subjects. Therefore, there occurrence does not require the use of plural verbs. For example:

Miss Kent, along with Ms Grover, plans the agenda.

Keep in mind that nouns occurring in prepositional phrases should not influence the form of the verb. For example:

A factory with many employees is a busy place.

Because the subject of the sentence is 'factory; it requires the singular verb 'is'. 'Employees' is the object of the preposition 'with' and does not influence the form of the verb.

There are, however, several situations in which compound subjects require singular verbs.

- Compound subjects modified limiting adjectives like 'each' and 'every' require singular verbs:

  Every member of the department was present at the meeting.

- Compound subjects which refer to a unit of some kind require singular verbs. For example:

  The secretary and accountant (if one person holds both titles) was present in the meeting.

- Quantities are sometimes considered singular and sometimes plural. If the quality refers to a total amount, it takes a singular verb; if the quantity refers to, countable units, it takes a plural verb.

  Six hours is a long time.

  Five thousand is the sales tax.

- Compound subjects which are joined by 'or' or 'nor' require singular verbs if the subject next to the verb is singular. However, if the subject next to the verb is plural, the sentence requires a plural verb. For example:

  Either the managers or the coordinator is responsible.

  Either the coordinator or the managers are responsible.

(b) Collective nouns: Plural verbs are used with collective nouns if used to emphasize the individual members of the group:

The staff are at their desks in the office.

However, singular verbs are used if you wish to emphasize the group as a unit:

The staff is ready to participate.

21.3.3 Verbals

Verbals are verbs that are modified to function as other parts of speech. They include infinitives, gerunds, and participles.

1. Infinitive

The infinitive is the verb form that can be preceded by 'to' (to go, to be, to teach). The infinitive has many uses. For example:

- As a noun: To succeed takes determination.
- As a descriptive objective: The way to improve is to practice.
- As part of a verb phrase: Mr. Wilson ought to attend the meeting.

2. Gerund and participles

The gerund and the present participle always end in the suffix 'ing'. However, they are distinguished from each other by their uses.

The **gerund** is used as a noun. Gerund and gerund phrases take a singular verb:

Proofreading takes concentration.
Walking is good for health.
Selling is an art.

The **present participle**, on the other hand, has two uses:

- As a descriptive objective: Coming events cast their shadow.
  An accommodating company
- As part of a verb phrase: The company is accommodating Ms. Leena's request.
  They are coming.

The present participle general describes action going on at the same time as other action. The **past participle** is usually the same form as the past tense and generally indicates completed action.

Mr. Murti has written the report.

The **perfect participle** is formed by adding 'having' to the past participle:
Having completed the report, Mr. Murti submitted his last invoice.

21.4 ADJECTIVES

An adjective modifies (tells something about) a noun or pronoun. For example:

brisk walk   a heavy discount   an efficient team   skillful workers

Adjectives modify nouns more often than they modify pronouns. When adjective do modify pronouns, however, the sentence usually has a linking verb. For example:

They were attentive.   He seems disappointed.

21.4.1 Types of Adjectives

1. Descriptive adjectives

Adjectives serve a variety of purpose. A **descriptive adjective** is a word which modifies a noun or pronoun by naming some quality or characteristic. Many descriptive adjectives are used to show comparison and thus have positive, comparative, and superlative forms to identify differing degrees of the quality or characteristic. For example:

Positive degree	Comparative degree	Superlative degree
large	larger	largest
tall	taller	tallest
attentive	more attentive	most attentive
observant	more observant	most observant

Patterns of comparison involving descriptive adjectives

Since persons, objects, and concepts possess qualities in varying degrees, you must have a way to express these differences. For this purpose, most descriptive adjectives use two kinds of signals to show degree of comparison. They either add the suffixes 'er' and 'est' or use the function words 'more' and 'most':

Base word	Adds suffix 'er'	Adds suffix 'est'
sweet	sweeter	sweetest
long	longer	longest
calm	calmer	calmest

Base word	Adds suffix 'more'	Adds suffix 'most'
careful	more careful	most careful
efficient	more efficient	most efficient
complex	more complex	most complex

Positive degree: The base form of descriptive adjectives is called the positive degree. This form is used in the following situations:

- when no comparison is involved
- when a comparison is introduced by 'as or 'not as'

a large order	as efficient as Suresh
a friendly attitude	not as complex as I imagined
a small problem	as energetic as Lucy

Comparative degree: When you are comparing two items, use the comparative form of the adjective. This form indicates that of the two items, one has a greater degree of a certain quality or characteristic than the other.

Larger	More efficient
Smaller	More complex
Stronger	More energetic

Superlative degree: When you are comparing more than two items, use the superlative form of the adjective. This form indicates that of a number of items, one has the greatest degree of the quality in question.

Largest	Most efficient
Smallest	Most complex
Strongest	Most energetic

A few adjectives do not follow the two regular methods for their comparative and superlative forms. Instead, these adjectives use entirely different words for the two forms:

Positive	Comparative	Superlative
Good	Better	Best
Bad	Worse	Worst
Little	Less/lesser	Least

Some adjectives like 'round', 'square', and 'perfect', 'unique', 'ultimate', have only positive forms because they themselves indicate the extreme. An item is either round or not round, perfect or not perfect.

2. Limiting adjectives

A **limiting adjective**, sometimes called a determiner, modifies the noun it precedes by identifying or numbering it. Limiting adjectives include:

- numeral adjectives : one, fifty, second
- articles : a, an, the
- Pronominal adjectives (pronouns used as adjectives) : my, his, your, her, its, their etc.
- demonstrative adjectives : this, these, that, those

Distinction between limiting adjectives and descriptive adjectives

One basic difference between the two types of adjectives is that limiting adjectives regularly precede descriptive adjectives when both modify a noun. (For example, all young and ambitious employees)

A second difference between limiting adjectives and descriptive adjectives is that limiting adjectives don't have forms for comparison (positive, comparative, and superlative) as do descriptive adjectives.

21.5 ADVERBS

An adverb modifies a verb, an adjective, or another adverb, answering such questions as when, where, how, and how much? Adverbs can thus indicate time, direction, place, manner, and extent of action.

Adverb		
modifying a verb	**modifying an adjective**	**modifying an adverb**
Our production line works efficiently.	The amazingly proficient secretary completed the report.	However reluctantly, Ms. prepared the report.
Ms. Sally quickly prepared the company report	She is highly intelligent.	Still upstairs, Rose picked up the telephone.

21.5.1 Types of Adverbs

1. **Simple adverbs** are simple modifiers: The door opened automatically.
2. **Interrogative adverbs** ask a question: Where have you been?
3. **Conjunctive adverbs** connect clauses: The company representative tried to explain how the new software works.

Words frequently used as conjunctive adverbs include where, wherever, when, whenever, while, as, how, why, before, after, until, and since.

4. **Negative adverbs** include not, never, seldom, rarely, scarcely, hardly etc.. Negative adverbs are powerful adverbs and therefore do not need any help in conveying a negative thought. For example:

   They could hardly read the report.

   I want no mistakes./I don't want any mistakes.

Adverb—Adjective confusion

Many adverbs are adjectives turned into adverbs by adding 'ly'. For example, 'highly', 'extremely', 'officially', 'really' etc. In addition, many words can be adjectives or adverbs, depending on their usage in a particular sentence:

Adjectives	Adverb
It was a hard decision.	He hit the ball hard
The traffic is slow.	The traffic moved slowly.

Comparative degree

Like adjectives, adverbs can also be used to compare items. Generally, the basic adverb is combined with 'more' or 'most', just as long adjectives are. However, some adverbs hae one-word comparative forms:

Positive (no comparison or equal comparison): Lee works faster.

Positive	Comparative	Superlative
No comparison or equal comparison	Two elements involved, one superior to the other	Three or more elements, one best of all
Lee works faster.	Lee works faster than her brother.	Lee works fastest of all the employees.
Lee works as courteously as her brother.	Lee works more courteously than her brother.	Lee works most courteously of all the employees.

21.6 PREPOSITIONS

A preposition is a word or group of words that describes a relationship between other words in a sentence. A preposition is always accompanied by its object. Also, prepositions frequently indicate such relationships such as position, direction, and time. For example:

to the auditorium	into the room	through the doorway
at that time	after the meeting	at 9 O' clock
on the table	in the drawer	on the corner

A **simple preposition** is made up of one word: of, in, by, above, beneath, beside, under, below. A **compound preposition** is made up of two prepositions: out of, from among, because of, instead of. **A prepositional** phrase is a group of words introduced by a group of prepositions that functions as an adjective or as an adverb. For example:

The parcel will be here by next Friday.

Exhausted from the game, the player walked away.

Here in the city, everything seems under control.

Some prepositions are closely linked with a verb. A prepositional phrase used as a verb modifier can sometimes occupy positions both preceding and following the verb. For example:

They ran into the room.

She answered in haste.

21.6.1 The Positioning of Prepositions

Prepositional phrase should be placed as close as possible to the element they are modifying:

Alice placed the report on the table.

Shopping on the internet can be confusing.

Although a preposition usually comes before its object, it does not always do so. In the following examples, preposition stands at the end of the construction:

What did you ask about?

Which equipment did the workers sent for?

Who/Whom did they enquire about?

What are you looking for?

21.6.2 Inappropriate Use of Prepositions

Certain prepositions are often used inappropriately:

- Avoid using unnecessary prepositions. For example:

  Incorrect : All of the staff members were happy.

  Correct : All the staff members were happy.

  Incorrect : Where are you going to?

  Correct : Where are you going?

  Incorrect : They could not help from wondering.

  Correct : They could not help wondering.

  Incorrect : Where are the accountants at?

  Correct : Where are the accountants?

In the above mentioned examples, the prepositions in parenthesis should be omitted.

- The other problem is failing to include a preposition when you should. Consider the following sentences:

  Incorrect : Sales were over for Lisa and Mill.

  Correct : Sales were over for Lisa and for Mill.

- When the same preposition can be used for two or more words in a sentence without affecting the meaning, only the last preposition is required:

  Incorrect : We are familiar with and satisfied with your company's policies.

  Correct : We are familiar and satisfied with your company's policies.

But when different prepositions are used with the words, all the prepositions must be included:

We are familiar with and interested with your company's policies.

- Some verb-preposition idioms vary depending on the situation. You **agree to** a proposal but **with** a person, **on a price** but **in principle**. You **agree about** something, **with** a person, and **for** or **against** a proposition. You compare one item **to** another to show their similarities; you compare one item **with** another to show differences.

21.7 CONJUNCTIONS

Conjunctions or connectors are function words that join parts of sentences: words, phrases, and clauses. There are three mail categories of these connectors: coordinating conjunctions, correlative conjunctions, and linking adverbs.

Coordinating conjunctions

The word 'coordinate' means equal in rank. A coordinating conjunction connects two words, phrases, or clauses of equal rank. The simple coordinating conjunctions include 'and', 'but', 'or', 'nor', 'for', 'yet', and 'so'. Coordinating conjunctions often join independent clauses. (A **clause** is a grammatically related group of words which contains a subject and a verb. **Independent** or **main clauses** are those which can stand by themselves: The manager left. **Subordinate** or **dependent clauses** are those which cannot stand alone; they would not make sense by themselves: After the office opens. Following are the examples of coordinating conjunctions:

Our sales have increased**, and** our prospects for next quarter seem excellent.

The report suggested a salary increase **or** a promotion.

The report is clear, **but** it does not contain the necessary details.

Correlative conjunctions

Correlative conjunctions are coordinating conjunctions used in pairs: 'both…and', 'either…or', 'neither…nor', 'not only…but also'. Constructions with correlative conjunctions should be parallel, with the same part of speech following each element of the conjunction. For example:

Neither the statistics **nor** the summaries provide the necessary information.

Both the employer **and** the employees were pleased.

Either Lisa **or** Mary will make the correction.

The stockholders **not only** held their shares **but also** bought more.

Linking adverbs

Linking adverbs are adverbs that are used to join one independent clause to another or one sentence to another. Linking verbs indicate how the ideas in the two clauses or sentences are related:

Linking adverbs		
indicate result	**indicate contrast**	**indicate continuation**
therefore, consequently, hence, thus, accordingly	however, nevertheless, yet, nonetheless	further, furthermore

Linking adverbs may occupy either of two positions in a sentence:

1. They may stand at the beginning of the second clause or sentence. In this case they are preceded by a semicolon or period and are usually followed by a comma:

The monthly report will be late; **nevertheless,** these changes must be made.

The books make the main idea clear; **however**, it does not provide enough details.

2. They may stand within the second clause or sentence. In this position, they are often set off by commas:

Mr. Allen left early; he was, **therefore,** unable to observe the proceedings.

The repairs on Route 34 are not completed; you should**, therefore**, plan to take Route 48.

Subordinating conjunctions

The word 'subordinate' means 'lower in rank'. A subordinate conjunction connects two clauses of unequal rank; it joins a dependent (subordinate) clause to the independent clause on which it depends. These introductory words also show the relationship of the subordinate clauses to main clauses. Common subordinate conjunctions include the following:

as	before
because	since
although	unless
while	that
when	where
whether	why

21.8 ARTICLES AND INTERJECTIONS

Only three **articles** exist in English: the 'a', 'an' and 'an'. These words are used, like adjectives, to specify which item you are talking about. 'The' is called the **definite article** because it indicates a specific noun, 'a' and 'an' are called the **indefinite articles** because they are less specific about what they are referring to.

If a word begins with a vowel sound, use 'an'; otherwise use 'a'. It's 'a history', not 'an history'. Use 'an' with an 'h' word only if it is a soft 'h', as in 'honour' and 'hour'. Use 'an' with words that are pronounced with a vowel soud even if they are spelled beginning with a consonant (usually in the case of abbreviations): an MP3 file, an NOC. Use 'a' with words that begin with vowels if they are pronounced with a consonant sound: a university, a union, a Usenet account.

Repeat an article if adjectives modify different nouns: The red pen and the blue pen are mine. Do not repeat an article if all adjectives modify the same noun: The red and blue shirt is mine.

Interjections are words that express only emotions. For example:

Wow! Oh, no! Alas! Well, well! Good!

Such purely emotional language has its place in private life and dvertising copy, but it only weakens the effect of most business writing.

22
AIDS TO CORRECT WRITING

Chapter Objectives

This chapter will enable you to understand:

- Tenses
- Auxiliaries and Modals
- Conditionals
- Verbal: Gerunds, Infinitives and Participles
- Active and Passive Voice
- Concord: Subject-Verb Agreement
- Analysis of Words with Prefixes and Suffixes

English grammar is the body of rules that describe the structure of expressions in the English language. This includes tenses, modals, conditionals, infinitives, gerunds and participles, active and passive voice, and subject-verb agreement. Right grammar and punctuation in your writing and speech allows you to present yourself in the best possible light.

22.1 TENSE

Tense may be defined as that form of a verb which shows the time of an action and its completeness or incompleteness. There are three main tenses:

1. Present tense: refers to present time
2. Past tense: refers to past time
3. Future tense: refers to future time

Examples

1. I love my colleagues. (Present)
   I loved my colleagues. (Past)
   I will always love my colleagues. (Future)

2. He attends a seminar today. (Present)

   He attended a seminar yesterday. (Past)

   He will attend a seminar tomorrow. (Future)

Since the tense of a verb not only shows the time of an action but also the state thus every tense is further divided into four parts, namely:

1. **The indefinite or simple form:** It simply states an action without anything whether the action is complete or not.
2. **The imperfect or continuous form:** It indicates that the action is in progress (continuing) and is not yet complete.
3. **The perfect form:** It indicates that the action has been completed or perfected.
4. **The perfect continuous form:** It shows that the action which began sometime before is still continuing.

Following chart presents the primary idea of all tenses and their divisions:

	Indefinite	Continuous	Perfect	Perfect continuous
PRESENT	I write a report now.	I am writing a report.	I have written a report.	I have been writing a report since 9 o'clock.
PAST	I wrote a report.	I was writing a report.	I had written a report.	I had been writing a report for three hours.
FUTURE	I shall write a report.	I shall be writing a report.	I shall have written a report.	I shall have been writing a report for three hours.

22.2 FORMATION AND USE OF THE TENSES

22.2.1 Present Tense

1. **Present indefinite (or Simple) tense**

   (a) Formation: Plural: Subject+ first form of the verb

   Singular: Subject+ first form of the verb+ s or es

Affirmative	Negative	Interrogative
I/we/you/they work.	I/we/you/they do not work.	Do I/we/you/they work?
He/she/ it works.	He/she/ it does not work.	Does he/she/ it work?

   (b) Uses: Use present indefinite tense when writing about:

   - ***an event taking place at the present moment***

     I live in Delhi.

     Here comes Mr. Kammath, the manager.

   - ***a regular activity, daily routine, a habit or custom***

     The manager usually visits the factory after lunch.

     I get up early in the morning.

     The director meets once a week.

- ***general facts***
  Volvo buses do not halt here.
  These private banks keep open on Saturdays.
- ***things that are always true***
  Two and two make four.
  Clarity makes communication effective.
- ***an action which must happen in the near future***
  Rohit goes to UK next year.
  We leave at 6 a.m. tomorrow.
- ***a subordinate clause, when main clause refers to future***
  If he works hard, he will pass.
  We will wait here until he comes.
- ***a quotation of someone***
  Shakespeare says, "What a piece of work is a man."
  Keats says, "A thing of beauty is a joy forever."
- ***Exclamation***
  How well he plays flute!
  Here comes the bird!

(c) Signal words: We often use the following words or phrases with this tense:
always, generally, frequently, often, usually, sometimes, regularly, every day, every week, every month, once a week, once in a while, twice a year, never, rarely, seldom, etc.

2. Present continuous tense

(a) Formation: Subject+ be (is, am, are) + first form of the verb+ing

Affirmative	Negative	Interrogative
I am working.	I am not working	Am I working?
We/you/they are working.	We/you/they are not working.	Are we/you/they working?
He/she/it is working.	He/she/it is not working.	Is he/she/it working?

(b) Uses: Use present continuous tense when writing about:

- ***things happening now***
  I am writing to thank you for the timely supply of goods.
  We are waiting for the call at the moment.
- ***temporary activities happening around the time of speaking***
  At present the world is facing global warming.
  Most of the buses are coming late these days.
- ***a scheduled programme in immediate future***
  I am returning his books by tomorrow evening.
  We are holding a meeting tomorrow.

(c) Signal words: We often use the following words or phrases with this tense:

Still, now, nowadays, today, at this moment, at present, presently, this morning, etc.

Note: The following verbs are not used in the present continuous tense even if they denote an action in progress at the time of speaking:

- *Verbs denoting mental states and processes:* agree, believe, know, differ, suppose, think, understand, etc.
- *Verbs denoting desires:* want, wish, desire, need.
- *Verbs denoting likes and dislikes:* love, hate, prefer, mind feel, etc.
- Verbs like appear, seem, resemble.

3. Present perfect tense

(a) Formation: Subject+ has/have + past participle form of the verb

Affirmative	Negative	Interrogative
I/we/you/they have already done the work.	I/we/you/they have not done the work till now.	Have I/we/you/they done the work so far?
He/she/ it has already done the work.	He/she/ it has not done the work till now.	Has he/she/ it done the work so far?

(b) Uses: Use present perfect tense when writing about:

- ***complete past actions with present results***

  The Government has liberalized the economy.

  The company has declared 25% dividend on its shares.

- ***life experiences***

  We have seen this trade fair before.

  I have known him for three years.

(c) Signal words: We often use the following words or phrases with this tense:

Yet, as yet, not yet, already, ever, ever since, just, just now, never, so far, till now, up to now, presently, once, twice, etc.

Note: In this tense we are not interested in when an action happened. We are interested only in its effect on the present.

4. Present perfect continuous tense

(a) Formation: Subject + has/have + been + first form of the verb + ing

Affirmative	Negative	Interrogative
I/we/you/they have been working here for two hours.	I/we/you/they have not been working here for two hours.	Have I/we/you/they been working here for two hours.
He/she/ it has been working here for two hours.	He/she/ it has not been working here for two hours.	Has he/she/ it been working here for two hours.

(b) Uses: Use present perfect continuous tense when writing about:

- ***an action that started in the past and is still continuing***

  She has been typing this report since morning.

  How long have you been working with this company?

- ***an action which began in the past and has been just completed, but whose result is still in the present***

  I have been preparing this report since morning, and I am very much tired now.

  My clothes are dirty because I have been repairing the machine.
- ***an action in a sentence which begins with ' how long' or 'since where'***

  Since when have you been waiting for her?

  How long have you been working her?

(c) **Signal words:** We often use the following words or phrases with this tense:

For, since, all day, for 4 years, since 1993, how long, the whole week, etc.

Note: 'Since' emphasises the point of view at which the action began. 'For' emphasises the period of time for which the action has been in progress.

22.2.2 Use of the Past Tense

1. Past indefinite tense

(a) **Formation:** Subject+ verb (past tense)

Affirmative	Negative	Interrogative
I/we/you/they/he/she/it worked yesterday.	I/we/you/they/he/she/it did not work yesterday.	Did I/we/you/they/he/she/it work yesterday?

(b) **Uses:** Use past indefinite tense when writing about:

- ***a past action or event***

  I went there.

  Newton laid the foundations for differential and integral calculus.
- ***Past showing time (yesterday, ago, last, etc.)***

  Toyota launched a new model last month.

  I received your letter yesterday.
- ***A habit or custom in the past***

  Gandhiji always spoke the truth.

  My father went for a walk every morning.
- ***An action going at the time stated***

  As we were walking along the sidewalk, we saw two cars crash.

  The manager was discussing with his colleagues when I went to his office.

(c) **Signal words:** We often use following words or phrases with this tense to define time:

Ago, back, past, yesterday, last night, last month, last year, a few years ago, a long time ago.

Note:

(a) Present perfect tense expresses past actions linked with the present. Past indefinite tense expresses past actions having no link with the present. Compare the following examples:

- Present perfect tense: We have offered a heavy discount to clear our stocks. (The discount is still available.)
- Past indefinite tense: We offered a heavy discount to clear our stocks. (The discount is probably no longer available.)

(b) We must not use present perfect tense with a time expression denoting past time. Consider the following examples:

- Incorrect: The company has announced modified rules and regulations yesterday.
- Correct: The company announced modified rules and regulations yesterday.

2. Past continuous tense

(a) Formation: Subject + be (was/were) + first form of the verb + ing

Affirmative	Negative	Interrogative
We/you/they were working yesterday.	I/we/you/they were not working yesterday.	Were we/you/they working yesterday?
I/he/she/it was working yesterday.	I/he/she/it was not working yesterday.	Was I/he/she/it working yesterday?

(b) Uses: Use past continuous tense when writing about:

- ***action in progress at a given moment of time in the past***

  We were attending a meeting yesterday at 2:00 pm.

  At 4 o'clock yesterday, Mr. Gupta was flying to UK.
- ***An incomplete or interrupted past action***

  I was evaluating the proposal when the Chairman called me to his room.

  We were discussing when he came.

(c) Signal words: We often use the following words or phrases with this tense to define time:

when, while, as long as.

3. Past perfect tense

(a) Formation: Subject + had + past participle form of the verb

Affirmative	Negative	Interrogative
I/we/you/they/he/she/it had worked all day.	I/we/you/they/he/she/it had not worked all day.	Had I/we/you/they/he/she/it worked all day?

(b) Uses: Use past perfect tense when writing about:

- ***A complete action at the given moment***

  The programme had finished peacefully.

  He had spoken to his manager.
- ***One action in the past happened before another***

  The meeting had been over before Mr. Gupta came.

  The train had left before I reached the station.

- ***To report what people thought or said in the past***

  She said she had just seen her old friend of hers.

  He said he had visited London twice.
- ***an unfulfilled wish in the past***

  I wish I had accepted the offer.

  I wish you had studied harder at school.

(c) **Signal words:** We often use the following words or phrases with this tense to define time:

Already, before, till, since, etc.

Note: We use past indefinite to describe one past event. We can also use it to describe two or more past events that followed one another. But we must use past perfect tense to emphasise that one action happened before the other. Consider the following examples:

- Past indefinite tense: We went to the office yesterday. (One past event)
- Past indefinite tense: We went to the office yesterday, attended the meeting and participated in the discussion. (Two or more past events)
- Past perfect tense: He had studied the proposal carefully before he came to the meeting. (One action happened before the other)

4. **Past perfect continuous tense**

(a) **Formation:** Subject + had + been + first form of the verb + ing

Affirmative	**Negative**	**Interrogative**
I/we/you/they/he/she/it had been working all day.	I/we/you/they/he/she/it had not been working all day.	Had I/we/you/they/he/she/it working all day?

(b) **Uses:** Use past perfect continuous tense when writing about:

- ***an action or activity in progress for some time and was yet incomplete at the time of making a reference to it.***

  The students had been studying for their examination since 5 o'clock.

  Ram had been waiting for two hours when I arrived.

(c) **Signal words:** We often use the following words or phrases with this tense to define time:

for, since, the whole day, all day.

22.2.3 Use of the Future Tense

1. **Future indefinite tense**

(a) **Formation:** Subject + will/shall + first form of the verb

Affirmative	**Negative**	**Interrogative**
I/we shall work.	I/we shall not work.	Shall I/we work?
You/they/he/she/it will work.	You/they/he/she/it will not work.	Will You/they/he/she/it work?

(b) Uses: Use future indefinite tense when writing about:

- ***future action or event***

  I shall submit this report tomorrow.

  We will see what we can do to help you.

- ***the principal clause of a conditional sentence***

  If we go by bus, it will be cheaper.

  If Ravi works hard, he will pass the examination.

2. Future continuous tense

(a) Formation: Subject + will/shall + be + first form of the verb + ing

Affirmative	Negative	Interrogative
I/we shall be working at that time.	I/we shall not be working at that time.	Shall I/we be working at that time?
You/they/he/she/it will be working at that time.	You/they/he/she/it will not be working at that time.	Will You/they/he/she/ be working at that time?

(b) Uses: Use future continuous tense when writing about:

- ***An action that will be going on at some time in the future***

  It will be raining when you reach home.

  We shall be playing tennis tomorrow evening.

3. Future perfect tense

(a) Formation: Subject + will/shall + have + past participle of the verb

Affirmative	Negative	Interrogative
I/we shall have finished the work before evening.	I/we shall not have finished the work before evening.	Shall I/we have finished the work before evening?
You/they/he/she/it will have finished the work before evening.	You/they/he/she/it will not have finished the work before evening.	Will You/they/he/she/ have finished the work before evening?

(b) Uses: Use future perfect tense when writing about:

- ***An action which is expected to be completed by a certain time in future***

  They will be tired when they arrive. They will not have slept for a long time.

  You can call me at work at 8 am. I shall have arrived at the office by 8.

4. Future perfect continuous tense

(a) Formation: Subject + will have been/shall have been + first form of the verb + ing

Affirmative	Negative	Interrogative
I/we shall have been working since morning.	I/we shall not have been working since morning.	Shall I/we have been working since morning?
You/they/he/she/it will have been working since morning.	You/they/he/she/it will not have been working since morning.	Will You/they/he/she/ have been working since morning?

(b) Uses: Use future perfect continuous tense when writing about:

- ***an action that will have been going on at or before some point of time in future***

  They will have been waiting for more than thirty minutes when the plane arrives.

  Jane will have been teaching at the university for more than a year by the time she leaves for abroad.

(c) Signal words: We often use the following words or phrases with this tense to define time:

by tomorrow, 8 o' clock, this year, this month, this week, next, next month, next week.

Note: If duration of an activity is unknown then the future continuous tense should be used instead of the perfect form. Consider the following examples:

- Correct: I will be taking a bath.
- Incorrect: I will have been taking a bath.

22.3 AUXILIARIES AND MODALS

Auxiliary verbs are those verbs which help other verbs to form their tense, mood or voice. An auxiliary verb is a helping verb because it helps the principal verb. The following chart presents a complete list of auxiliary verbs:

Be (is, am, are, was, were, being, been)	Will (would)
Have (has, had)	Must
Do (does, did)	Ought to
Can (could)	Used to
May (might)	Need
Shall (should)	Dare

Auxiliary verbs are divided into two categories:

22.3.1 Primary Auxiliaries

Primary auxiliaries are the form of the verb: be, have and do

Be:	Is, am, are, was, were, be, being, been
Have:	Has, have, had, having
Do:	Do, does, did, done, doing

Primary auxiliaries help to form the tenses, questions, voice, negative, etc., when they are combined, with the main verbs. These auxiliaries can be used alone and function as main verbs.

22.3.2 Modal Auxiliaries

Modal auxiliaries are: shall, should, will, would, can, could, may, might, must, dare, need, ought, need to, and used to.

Modal auxiliaries are used along with the main verbs. They are not used alone. Together with the main verbs that follow, the modal auxiliaries express ideas as ability, possibility, probability, permission, obligation, or duty, etc.

Correct use of some modal auxiliaries

1. **Asking for permission: may, can, could**

   'May' formal, 'can' informal and friendly, 'could' very polite

   May I leave the office early today? (seeking formal permission)

   Can I smoke here? (asking permission in a friendly way)

   Could you open the window please? (very polite)

2. **Asking for things: can, could, will**

   'Can' friendly, 'could' polite, 'will' slightly less polite

   Can I have this book please? (friendly)

   Could you send me a catalogue please? (polite)

   Will you pass on file please? (slightly less polite)

3. **Expressing ability to do something: can, could, be able to**

   'can' present ability, 'could' past ability, 'be able to' ability at any time

   John can speak French but he cannot write it very well. (present ability)

   He gave up his earlier job so that he could work for us. (past ability)

   He is/was/will be able to offer you the best price possible. (ability at any time)

4. **Expressing possibility: may, might, could**

   'may' a good possibility, 'might' a weak possibility, 'could' a very weak possibility

   We may sell our entire stock by the end of this month. (a good possibility)

   It might take more than a week. (a weak possibility)

   We could get this order in the next few days. (a very weak possibility)

5. **Expressing suggestion, advice, duty: should, ought to, could**

   We should open our branches in the rural areas. (suggestion; it carries the speaker's approval)

   You should answer his letter as soon as possible. (suggestion/advice)

   You ought to drive more carefully. (strong advice/that would be the right thing to do)

   We could write a proposal for additional staff. (suggestion put forward rather tentatively)

6. **Expressing necessity, obligation, compulsion, prohibition: must, has to, have to, have to, have got to, must not**

   You must provide proper identification in order to open your bank account. (necessity)

   She has to prepare this report in the next few days. (compulsion)

   You have to send a report to head office every week. (compulsion)

   I have to get permission from the manager before I can attend the seminar. (obligation)

   You must not leave the office before 6 o' clock. (prohibition)

   Note: 'must' suggests the desire/insistence of the speaker; 'have to' suggests external compulsion. Consider the following examples:

- You must carry all these documents with you. (the speaker insists)
- You have to carry all these documents with you. (It is a compulsion imposed by some external authority.)

22.4 CONDITIONALS

Conditional sentences have two parts: if-clause and main clause. For example:

If he comes I shall give him a lift. (if-clause: If he comes, main clause: I shall give him a lift.)

There are three kinds of conditional sentences. Each kind contains a different pair of tenses.

22.4.1 Conditional Sentences Type I: Probable

1. **Structure:** If + present + future

   This type of sentence implies that the action in the if-clause is quite probable.
2. **Uses:** If you hire a management consultant your business will go up.

   If he works in dim light he will ruin his eyes.

   She will be angry if she hears about this incident.

   Note: The meaning here is present or future, but the verb in the if-clause is in the present tense, not in the future tense.
3. **Possible variations of the basic structure**

   (a) Variations of the main clause
   - If + present + may/might (Possibility)

     If it rains the flight may/might be cancelled. (perhaps the flight will be cancelled)
   - If + present + may (permission) or can (permission or ability)

     If your files are in order you can leave at once. (permission)

     If it stops raining we can go out. (permission/ability)
   - If + present+ must, should or any expression of command, request, or advice.

     If you want to have a promising career, you should join a management course.

     If you visit the office tomorrow could you ask Tom to ring me?
   - If + present + another present tense

     If +two present tenses is used to express automatic and habitual results.

     If there is a shortage of any product prices of that product go up.

   (b) Variations of the if-clause
   - If + present continuous to indicate a present action or a future arrangement.

     If you are waiting for a bus you would better join the queue.

     If you are working in the late hours I shall ask the manager to give you better facilities.
   - If + present perfect

     If he has written the letter I shall post it.

22.4.2 Conditional Sentences Type II: Hypothetical

1. **Structure:** If + past + conditional tense

   The verb include if-clause in the past tense, the verb in the main clause is in the conditional tense.

2. **Uses:** If their evaluation were fair they would accept our proposal. (but it is not fair)

   If I were you I would go there. (but I am not you.)

   If they tried to bribe me I would cancel their offer. (but I don't expect that anyone will try to bribe me)

   If I lived near my office I would be in time for work. (but I don't live near my office)

   Note: The past tense in the if-clause is not a true past but a subjunctive which indicates unreality or improbability.

3. **Possible variations of the basic structure**

   (a) Variations of the main clause

   - 'Might' or 'could' may be used instead of 'would'.

     If I knew French I could tell you what this means. (ability)

     If he tried again he might succeed. (possible results)

   - If + past tense + past tense express automatic or habitual reactions in the past.

     If I asked him to work he got angry. (whenever I asked him to work)

   (b) Variations of the if-clause

   - If + past continuous

     If I were going by car I would/could drive you to the station.

   - If + past perfect

     If he had taken my suggestion he would be a successful man now.

22.4.3 Conditional Sentences Type III

1. **Structure:** If + past perfect tense + perfect conditional

   In this type of sentence the time is past and the condition cannot be fulfilled because action in the if-clause did not happen.

2. **Uses:** If I had known that you were coming I would have meet you at the station. (but I did not know so I did not come)

3. **Possible variations of the basic structure**

- 'Could' or 'might' may be used instead of 'would'.

  If you had arrived ten minutes earlier you could have got a seat. (ability)

  If you had arrived ten minutes earlier you might have got a seat. (possibility)

- 'If' can be replaced by certain other words.

  Had you informed us earlier, we would have attended the workshop. (if you had informed)

  I'll come tomorrow in case you need my help. (If you need my help)

22.5 VERBALS: INFINITIVES, GERUNDS, AND PARTICIPLES

As you learned earlier in Chapter 21, infinitives, gerunds and participles are called 'verbals.'

An infinitive is the 'to form' of a verb. For example:

to work	Present infinitive
to be working	Present continuous infinitive
to have worked	perfect infinitive
to have been working	Perfect continuous infinitive

An infinitive is split when one or more words separate the 'to' and the verb. As:

- Below standard: He was wrong to suddenly leave the country.
  Correction: He was wrong to leave the country suddenly.
- Below standard: I have tried to consciously stop worrying about it.
  Correction: I have consciously tried to stop worrying about it.
- Below standard: He wanted me to finally make an announcement.
  Correction: He finally wanted me to make an announcement.

There is nothing ungrammatical about splitting an infinitive, but sometimes a split results in clumsiness or ambiguity in the sentence. Therefore, we should avoid placing a modifier between the 'to' and 'the verb form' in an infinitive for the sake of clarity and right emphasis.

A gerund is a noun made by adding '—ing' to a verb. The gerund being a verb -- noun, may be used as

1. subject of a sentence:
   Seeing is believing.
   Painting is my hobby.
2. object of a transitive verb
   Stop shouting.
   He likes reading poetry.
3. complement of a verb
   Seeing is believing.
   My hobby is painting.
4. after preposition
   I am fond of dancing.

A participle is a form of a verb used as an adjective to modify a noun or a pronoun. It is made by adding '—ing' to a verb. For example:

- She is a working woman.
- Her living conditions are good.
- A participle, though it is derived from a verb, can never be used as an adverb and cannot make a statement about a subject.

Note:

1. A verb + -ing, like, reading, is not always a participle. It is a participle only when it is used as an adjective. When it is used as a noun, it is a gerund. For example:

   Reading is beneficial. (Here the word 'reading' is used as a noun, therefore it is a gerund.)

   The boy, reading the paper, is my senior. (Here the word 'reading' is used as an adjective, therefore it is a participle.)

   There was a sound of matching feet. (Here the word 'matching' is used as an adjective, therefore it is a participle.)

2. A participle should clearly refer to the noun. A single participle is generally placed just before the noun that it modifies. For example:

   The foaming water poured from the broken pipe.

3. A participle phrase usually follows the noun. For example:

   The boy carrying the banner rode in a wagon drawn by four horses.

4. Following verbs are followed by infinitives and not by gerunds:

   agree, decide, fail, forget, hope, want learn, offer, plan, promise, refuge, manage, choose

   Examples:

   - He promised me to go there.
   - I failed to turn up for the meeting.

5. Following verbs are followed by gerunds and not by infinitives:

   avoid, continue, suggest, mind, deny, finish, keep, miss, dislike, enjoy, delay, do on, give up, put off, can't help

   Examples:

   - I denied working late.
   - I don't mind waiting.

6. Following verbs are followed both by an infinitive and by a gerund but with a different meaning:

   agree, forget, hate, like, love, mean, propose, prefer, regret, remember, stop, try, used to

   Examples:

   - I stopped writing the proposal. (I was writing the proposal, and then I stopped.)
   - I stopped to write the proposal. (I stopped whatever I was doing and wrote the proposal.)

7. Following verbs are followed both by an infinitive and by a gerund but without change of meaning:

   begin, start, continue, cease, advise, allow, intend, permit, recommend, require, want, need

   Examples:

   - I began writing. / I began to write.
   - He continued working. / He continued to work near the shop.
   - I intend calling him. / I intend to call him.

22.6 ACTIVE AND PASSIVE VOICE

As you learned in Chapter 21, there are two ways of expressing an action by using a transitive verb. A transitive verb may be used in two voices: active voice and passive voice.

The active voice is that form of the verb, which shows that the subject is the doer of the action. For example:

Mr. Kamath is writing a letter.

The passive voice is that form of the verb, which shows that something is done to the subject. For example:

The letter is being written by Mr. Kamath.

Transformation from the Active Voice to the Passive Voice

- When a verb is changed from the active into the passive voice, the object of the active voice becomes the subject and vice versa.

Subject		Object
I	is changed into	me
we	is changed into	us
you	is changed into	you
he	is changed into	him
she	is changed into	her
it	is changed into	it
they	is changed into	them

- Change the verb into past participle (III form). Put proper form of the verb 'to be' before it according to the tense of the main verb in active voice and the number (singular/plural) of the new subject.
- Tense of the verb is not changed. Only its form is changed.
- 'By' is used with the doer of action when it helps to complete sense.

  Note: Such indefinite and vague subjects as 'someone', 'somebody', 'everybody', 'they', 'people', etc. are dropped. For example:

Someone has broken this pen.	(active)	This pen has been broken.	(passive)
People always admire this book.	(active)	This book is always admired.	(passive)

1. When a verb in the active voice takes two objects, a direct one and an indirect one, either of them may be used as the subject in the passive voice. For example:

Sita gave me a book. (active) — I was given a book by Sita. (passive)
OR
A book was given to me by Sita. (passive)

2. Prepositions must not be left out with verbs requiring them.

She must look after the girl. (active) — The girl must be looked after. (passive)

The forms of a verb in the present indefinite tense

Active Voice	Passive Voice
First Form + s/es	**is/am/are + Third Form**
Harish sells computers. They like you. We admire him. I seldom keep him waiting. She manages the office. What do you want? Why do you tell a lie? Whom do you want?	Computers are sold by Harish. You are liked by them. He is admired by us. He is seldom kept waiting by me. The office is managed by her. What is wanted by you? Why is a lie told by you? Who is wanted by you?

The forms of a verb in the past indefinite tense

Active Voice	Passive Voice
Second Form	**was/were + Third Form**
He kept us waiting. They did not proclaim him leader. What did he speak to you? Who wrote this report? Why did your secretary write such a letter? Where did you buy it?	We were kept waiting by him. He was not proclaimed leader by them. What was spoken to you by him? By whom was this report written? Why was such a letter written by your secretary? Where was it bought by you?

The forms of a verb in the future indefinite tense

Active Voice	Passive Voice
will/shall + First Form	**will/shall + be + Third Form**
Everybody will blame us. My mother will look after you. I shall not speak a word to you. Shall I ever forget those happy days? When will she give up her studies? Where will she keep her files?	We shall be blamed by everybody. You will be looked after by my mother. Not a word will be spoken to you by me. Will those happy days be ever forgotten by me? When will her studies be given up by her? Where will her files be kept by her?

The forms of a verb in the present continuous tense

Active Voice	Passive Voice
is/am/are + Present Participle (First Form of Verb + ing)	**is/am/are + being + Past Participle (Third Form of Verb)**
Tapesh is building a house. He is running a race. I am writing a proposal. Are you writing a letter? What is she doing? Why are you helping him?	A house is being built by Tapesh. A race is being run by him. A proposal is being written by me. Is a letter being written by you? What is being done by her? Why is he being helped by you?

The forms of a verb in the past continuous tense

Active Voice	Passive Voice
Was/were + Present Participle (First Form of Verb + ing)	**was + being + Past Participle (Third Form of Verb)**
I was writing a letter. We were preparing a report. I was not laughing at my colleague. Was the peon knocking at the door? What was she doing? Why were you wasting my time?	A letter was being written by me. A report was being prepared by us. My colleague was not being laughed at by me. Was the door being knocked by the peon? What was being done by her? Why was my time being wasted by you?

The forms of a verb in the present perfect tense

Active Voice	Passive Voice
Has/have + Past Participle	**Has/have+been+ Past Participle**
I have completed the work. We have locked our rooms. I have not invited all the friends. Has he invited you? Have you dispatched letters? Why have you missed the lecture?	The work has been completed by me. Our rooms have been locked by us. All the friends have not been invited by me. Have you been invited by him? Have letters been dispatched by you? Why has the lecture been missed by you?

The forms of a verb in the past perfect tense

Active Voice	Passive Voice
Had + Past Participle	**Had + been + Past Participle**
I had completed the work. He had already seen the machine. She had already missed the bus. She had never read this book before. Had they seen us before? Why had he sold his house?	The work had been completed by me. The machine had already been seen by him. The bus had already been missed by her. This book had never been read by her before. Had we been seen by them before? Why had his house been sold by him?

The forms of a verb in the future perfect tense

Active Voice	Passive Voice
will/shall+have+III form	**will/shall+have+been+III form**
The peon will have rung the bell. He will have posted the letter. I shall have finished the work in a fortnight. You will have won a prize by then. They will not have done this work. They will have purchased all the goods by 2 p.m.	The bell will have been rung by the peon. The letter will have been posted by him. The work will have been finished by me in a fortnight. The prize will have been won by her by then. This work will not have been done by them. All the goods will have been sold by 2 p.m.

Change of voice in interrogative sentences which begin with a modal auxiliary

Active Voice	Passive Voice
May I take this file?	May this file be taken by me?
May I have your pen for five minutes?	May your pen be had by me for five minutes?
Can we send our goods by train?	Can our goods be sent by train?
Will you help me?	Shall I be helped by you?
Must I reveal the secret?	Must the secret be revealed by me?
Why should I read this paper?	Why should this paper be read by me?
How could I help you?	How could you be helped by me?

Change of voice in imperative sentences (command, order, request, advice)

Active Voice	Passive Voice
Do it.	Let it be done.
Let him sell this mobile.	Let this mobile be sold by him.
Work hard.	You are advised to work hard.
Switch off the lights.	Let the lights be switched off.
Please help me.	You are requested to help me.
May I go out?	Am I allowed to go out?
Kindly go through this report.	You are requested to go through this report.
Shut the windows.	You are ordered to shut the windows.
God helps those who help themselves.	Those who are helped by themselves are helped by God.

22.7 CONCORD: AGREEMENT OF THE VERB WITH ITS SUBJECT

A verb must agree with its subject in number or person. Such agreement is called concord. There are certain rules to make the verb agree with its subject:

1. In English, number concord only affects present tense verbs plus the past tense of 'be'.
   I work.
   He works.
   They work.
2. Usually, singular subjects take singular verbs and plural subjects take plural verb.
   They read fast.
   He reads fast.
3. Two or more singular subjects joined by 'and' take a plural verb.
   Fog, smoke and heavy rain cancel scheduled flight.
   He and I were entrusted with the job.
   But if the mind suggests one idea or refers to the same person or thing, the verb is singular.
   Honour and glory is his reward.
   The owner and CEO of this company is going on a tour.
   Note: The use of the article is very important in these cases. 'The owner and CEO' refers to one person only; 'The owner and the CEO' refers to two persons.

4. Words connected to a singular subject by 'with', 'together with', 'along with', 'in addition to', 'as well as' etc., (are parenthetical) do not affect the number of the verb.
   I as well as they am tired of this job.
   The Chairperson, with all the members of the Board, has arrived.
5. When two subjects are connected with 'not only...but also', the verb agrees with the latter subject.
   Not only the supervisor but his workers also are hard at work.
   Not only the workers but their supervisor also is hard at work.
6. Singular subjects separated by 'or', 'nor', 'neither...nor', or 'either...or' take a singular verb.
   Either the television or the newspaper is a good source for news.
   Neither the driver nor the cleaner feels sleepy.
   - Plural subjects separated by 'or', 'nor', 'neither...nor', or 'either...or' take a plural verb.
     Neither the section officer nor the subordinates are to blame.
   - When two noun phrases are joined by 'or', 'nor', 'neither...nor', or 'either...or' and one has a plural subject, the verb must be plural, and the plural subject should be placed nearest the verb.
     Neither the chairman nor the directors are present.
     Neither the inspector nor the officers were able to help us.
   - When the subjects joined by 'or', 'nor', 'neither...nor', or 'either...or' are of different persons, the verb agrees with the nearer.
     Either he or I am mistaken.
     Either you or he is mistaken.
     Neither my friend nor I am mistaken.
7. Phrases separating the subject and verb do not influence the number of the subject. A subject following the verb still agrees in number with the verb.
   Here come Mr. Rai and his secretary now.
   Here comes Mr. Rai now.
8. Context determines the number of collective nouns. (For example: group, team, crowd, audience, army, family, committee.
   - When the collective noun acts as an individual the verb is plural.
     The team are discussing next year's schedule.
     The audience were taking turns to give donations to the trust.
     The committee were divided on one minor point.
     The staff vote on every issue.
   - When the collective noun acts as a unit (when the collection is thought of as one unit) the verb is singular.
     The team wins every game it plays.
     The audience was cheering the band.
     The committee has issued its report.
     The staff is adequate.

9. When a plural noun denoting distance, weight, height or amount of money is illustrated as a single unit, it takes a singular verb.
   Ten kilometers is a long walk.
   Fourteen minutes is allowed to each speaker.
   Hundred rupees is a lot of money for a poor fellow.
   The government is doing well.
10. Phrases like 'a lot of', 'many a', 'a great deal of', 'some of', 'some of', 'most of', 'plenty of', are singular when they refer to amount or quantity and are plural when they refer to number.
    A lot of money is needed.
    A lot of books have been purchased.
    Plenty of books are available on this subject.
    Plenty of information was given to me at the reception.
11. 'Either', 'neither', 'each', 'every', 'one of the' take a singular verb.
    Each of these boys is doing good business.
    Either of these resumes is fit for the job.
    Neither of the two proposals was found practicable.
    One of these students is sure to win gold medal.
    - Two nouns qualified by 'each', 'every' or 'even though' connected by 'and' require a singular verb.
      Every gentlemen and every lady in this industry works sincerely.
12. 'None' can take either a singular or a plural verb; it often doesn't matter whether you use a singular or a plural verb — unless something else in the sentence determines its number. For example:
    None of you claims responsibility for this incident?
    None of you claim responsibility for this incident?
    None of the students have done their homework. (The word 'their' precludes the use of the singular verb.
    - When 'none' refers to amount or quality, it takes a singular verb.
      None of the food is fresh.
      None of the food was wasted.
13. 'Pains' and 'means' take either the singular or the plural verb, but the construction must be consistent. (Not varying)
    Great pains have been taken.
    Much pains has been taken.
    Unfair means were employed by the management.
    Wealth is only a means, the end is happiness.
14. When the word 'means' is used in the sense of income or wealth, it always takes a plural verb.
    My means are ample/sufficient.
    His means are small, but being resourceful, he will be able to run his business successfully.

15. Words, plural in form and singular in meaning, take a singular verb.

    The news is true.

    Linguistics is the study of a language.

    The wages is meager in this factory.

16. When 'number' is preceded by 'the' it takes a singular verb and when by 'a', plural verb.

    The number of crimes in Delhi is increasing.

    A number of meetings were held to discuss the issue.

    The number of people who reported for work this morning is small.

    A number of books are missing from the library.

17. 'It' always takes a singular verb, irrespective of whether the subject is plural or singular.

    It is the people who matter in a democracy.

    It is the fundamental principle that matters.

18. In sentences, beginning with 'there' the number of the verb is determined by the true subject, which generally follows the verb.

    There are various methods of collecting data.

    There is no need for typing this report.

19. A 'pair of' when applied to things where the two components are always thought together ('scissors', shears', 'shoes', 'gloves', 'trousers',) takes a singular verb.

    A pair of trousers is all I need.

    A pair of scissors is kept in the drawer.

    A pair of spectacles is lying on the table.

    - But if we omit the words 'a pair of' and only use the plural words, then, it must take a plural verb.

      The scissors are very sharp.

      His shoes are very expensive.

      My spectacles have been lost.

20. Certain nouns are used in singular so they take singular verb.

    The scenery of Kashmir attracts the tourists.

    The furniture of my office is old fashioned.

    No information has been received so far.

22.8 ANALYSING WORDS WITH PREFIXES AND SUFFIXES

All words have a base word or root word. A base word stands on its own as a word. In addition there are parts which come before and after the base word. These are called affixes. If you come across an unfamiliar word in your reading, you can figure out the meaning of the word by dividing it into its base word and affixes.

A base word is the main part of the word, i.e., the part that contains its primary meaning. Affixes which come before the base word are called prefixes (pre=before + fix=make firm or attach). A prefix, therefore, is a group of letters, that is attached to the beginning of the base word to modify or change its meaning. Affixes which come after the base word are called suffixes (suf or sub=under or after + fix=make firm or attach). A suffix, therefore, is a group of letters, that is attached to the end of the base word to make a new word. A suffix can make a new word in one of two ways:

Inflectional suffixes (grammatical): Inflectional suffixes do not change the meaning of the original word. For example, changing singular to plural (dog > dogs), or changing present tense to past tense (walk > walk**ed**). In this case, the basic meaning of the base word does not change. Compare the following list of words:

Base word	Word with suffix
Car	Cars
Computer	Computers
Record	Records
Walked	Walked
Work	Worked

The words 'car' and 'cars' have the same basic meaning. Similarly, the basic meaning of the words 'walk' and 'walked' is exactly the same. In these cases, the suffix is added simply for grammatical correctness.

Derivational suffixes: With derivational suffixes, the new word has a new meaning, and is usually a different part of speech. But the new meaning is related to the old meaning, i.e., it is derived from the original word. For example, compare the following list of words:

Base word	Word with suffix
Teach	Teacher
Record	Recorder
Diction	Dictionary
Treat	Treatment

In this case, suffixes do not alter meaning of the base word, but change the way in which it can be used.

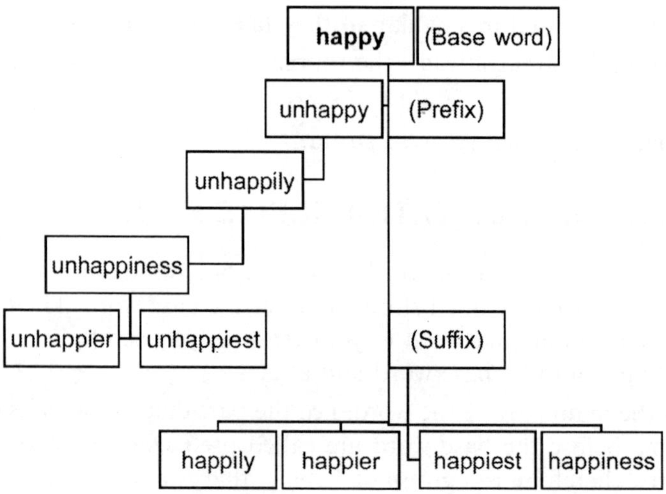

Figure 22.1: Family tree of 'happy'

There are many prefixes and suffixes in English that are often used. The following section contains prefixes and suffixes, together with meanings and examples that are particularly important in business.

22.9 PREFIXES

Note that the same prefix can sometimes have more than one meaning and that the same meaning can sometimes be indicated by more than one prefix.

Prefix	Meaning	Examples with brief explanation	
a-	a. in a certain manner, in a particular state or condition, in the process of b. not, without, not affected by	aloud: asleep: askew: aside: apolitical:	in a speaking tone in a state of sleep in a twisted position to one side having no involvement in politics
ab-	away, from, off	abolish: abhor: abstain: abduct:	to do away with to reject with fear or scorn to hold back from to carry off by force
ad-	to, towards	adhere: admonish: attract:	to support or stick to to give warning or disapproval to to draw toward oneself
ante-	prior, before	antecedent: anteroom:	prior in time or order, a word later referred to by a pronoun an outer room leading to a more important room
anti-	opposite, against	antipollution: antisocial :	designed to eliminate pollution harmful or adverse to society
bi-	two	biennial: bilingual:	occurring every two years; lasting for two years knowing two languages
circum-	around	circumspect: circumscribe:	careful to look around and consider all circumstances to draw a line around
con- **com-** **co-**	with, together	concur: communicate: cooperate:	to come to an agreement to share information with others to act or work together
contra- **counter-**	opposite, against	contradict: counter-clockwise:	to say the opposite opposite to the direction in which the hands of a clock move
de-	down, away from	demoralize: dethrone: deviate:	to weaken the morale of to remove from a throne or other place of power to stray from a principle or topic

Prefix	Meaning	Examples with brief explanation	
dis-	away, opposite	dismiss: discomfort: disagree	to send away uneasiness to hold a different opinion
ex-	a. outside b. former	exclude: exterior: exception: ex-president:	to omit, to keep something out the outside part or surface something outside a general rule a former president
fore-	before, preceding	forecast: forewarn: foreclose:	to predict something to warn beforehand to close or stop something beforehand
in- **il-** **im-** **ir-**	not	indefinite: illegible: improbable: irrational:	not precise not capable of being read not probable, not likely not reasonable
inter-	between, among, within	intercede: interrupt: international:	to go between those who disagree to break into others' conversation between two nations, or among more than two nations
mis-	wrong, opposite	misplace: misinterpret: misfortune: mistrust:	to put something in the wrong place to interpret wrongly opposite of good fortune opposite of trust
non-	not	nonsense: nonrestrictive:	something that does not make sense not restricting or limiting
out-	to be superior in some sense	outperform: outweigh: outmaneuver:	to surpass in performance to surpass in value, weight, or significance to defeat by using superior tactics
over-	beyond what is expected or necessary	overachieve: overcharge: overwork:	to achieve success beyond what was expected to charge an excessive amount to work excessively
per-	completely, thoroughly	perforate: perfect: perceptive:	to bore completely through brought to completion without omission or flow able to understand thoroughly
post-	after, following	postpone: postdate: postscript:	to put off until afterwards to assign a date later than the actual one a note following the main part of a message
pre-	before	precede: preliminary: preface:	to go before before the main part remarks before the main text

Prefix	Meaning	Examples with brief explanation	
pro-	forward, in support of	proceed: promote: pro-business	to move forward to support something or advance someone in rank being favourable to business interests
re-	again, anew, back	reappear: reform: retrieve:	to appear again to form something again and approve it to get something back
semi-	half, partly	semicircle: semiannual: semimonthly: semiliterate:	half of a circle occurring every half year occurring every half month partly able to read
sub-	under, below	subsection: submerge: subconscious: substandard: subway:	a section included in a large unit to put under water below the level of consciousness below standard a way under the ground
super-	above, over, beyond	superhuman: supervise: superimpose: superintendent:	beyond normal human abilities to oversee to place above or ever something one who has charge over others
trans-	across, through, beyond	transmit: transport: transparent: transcend:	to send from one person to another to carry from one place to another sheer enough to be seen through to go beyond the limits of
tri-	three	triangle: triennial: trimonthly: triplicate:	having three angles and sides lasting three years, occurring every three years occurring every three months in three copies
un-	not	unproductive: unpaid: unable: uncovered: unhurt:	not productive not paid not capable not covered not hurt
under-	beneath, less	underground: underwater: underpaid:	beneath the ground beneath water paid less than a sufficient amount
with-	against: back:	withstand: withdraw: withhold:	to stand up against to take back to hold back

22.10 SUFFIXES

Suffix	Meaning	Examples with brief explanation	
-able **-ible**	capable or worthy of, subject to	profitable: credible: creditable: perishable: promotable: portable: legible:	capable of producing profits worthy of belief worthy of receiving praise or credit subject to decaying worthy of being promoted able to be carried able to be read
-ac **- ic**	like, pertaining to	cardiac: aquatic:	pertaining to heart pertaining to water
-age	the condition of, relationship to, or amount for	average: percentage: postage: marriage:	the relationship of the mean among different numbers the relationship of some amount to 100 the amount paid for sending something by post the condition of being married
-al	a. relating to b. the act of	annual: national: procedural: natural: appraisal:	relating to one year relating to a nation relating to a certain procedure relating to nature the act of evaluating
-an **-ian** **-ean**	related to, skilled in	utilitarian: urban: suburban: electrician:	relating to usefulness relating to a city relating to a suburb one skilled in working with electrical circuits
-ar	resembling, relating to	popular: circular: popular:	relating to the people resembling a circle relating to a regular practice
-ary **-ory**	relating to, connected with	elementary: auditory: honorary: dictionary:	relating to elements or fundamentals relating to hearing a person connected with honour book connected with words
-ate	a. person(s) with a certain authority b. having a certain characteristic c. to cause something to happen	electorate: isolate: accurate:	persons who have the authority to elect someone to cause something to be isolated having the characteristic of being accurate
-cy	the quality, state of being, or condition of	obstinacy: democracy: consistency:	the state of being stubborn the state of rule by the people the condition of being consistence

Suffix	Meaning	Examples with brief explanation	
-dom	a quality or condition of, a geographic area	wisdom: freedom: kingdom:	the quality of being wise the condition of being free the area governed by a king
-ee	recipient of an action	addressee: lessee: payee employee:	a person to whom something is addressed a person to whom a lease is granted a person to whom payment is granted a person to whom employment is granted
-en	a. made or consisting of b. to change in some way c. to come to be	wooden: widen: brighten:	made of wood to make longer; to become longer to make brighter; to become brighter
-er **-or**	a. someone or something that performs action b. a person who lives in a certain place or associated with a certain activity	builder: investor: author: supervisor	a person who builds something a person who makes investments a person who writes articles or books a person who gives supervision
-ful	a. characterized by a certain quality b. containing a certain amount	helpful: peaceful: handful:	characterized by giving help characterized by peace the amount necessary to fill one's hand
-fy **-ify**	to bring about a certain condition	simplify: falsify: solidify:	to make something simple to make something false to make something solid
-hood	a. the quality, state of being, or condition of b. an instance of a quality, state, or condition c. a group of individuals sharing a certain state d. a period of time	sisterhood: falsehood: childhood:	the state of relating to one another as sisters an instance of untruthfulness the state of being a child; the time when one was a child
-ical **-ics** **-ic**	a. relating to, characteristic of b. the science of	logical: logic: mathematical: mathematics:	related to careful reasoning the science of careful reasoning related to numbers the science of numbers
-ine	relating to, characteristic of	feminine: masculine: marine:	characteristic of a woman characteristic of a man relating to the sea

Suffix	Meaning	Examples with brief explanation	
-ing ings	an action or process, something associated with an action or process	inquiring: housing: earnings:	the action of making inquiries a structure built to provide shelter that which is earned
-ion	the action of	completion: competition: repetition:	the action of completing the action of competing the action of repeating`
-ish	a. relating to, characteristic of b. the approximate age or time of	bluish: childish: fiftyish:	related to the colour blue characteristic of a child being approximately fifty years old
-ism	a. system of belief or attitude b. the action of	capitalism: individualism: plagiarism:	a system of belief emphasizing the value of free enterprise and competition an attitude emphasizing the value of the needs and actions of individuals the action of plagiarizing
-ist	one who holds certain views, acts in certain ways, or possesses certain training	capitalist: individualist: dentist:	one who believes in the theory of capitalism one who behaves in a very independent manner one trained in the professional care of teeth
-ity -ty	the quality, state of being, or condition of	flexibility: liberty: sanity:	the quality of being flexible the state of being free the condition of being sane
-ive	tending toward an action	attractive: aggressive: lucrative:	tending to attract tending to take the initiative tending to produce wealth
-ize -ise	a. to change or modify something b. to feel a certain emotion	advertise: crystallize: sympathize:	to cause an advertisement to appear to cause something to form crystals to feel sympathy
-less	without	tireless: debtless: senseless:	without becoming tired free of debt without sense
-ly	characterized by a certain quality, manner, or time interval	friendly: efficiently: hourly:	acting in a cheerful pleasant manner acting in an efficient, productive manner occurring at or during every hour
-ment	the result of a certain action	agreement: settlement: enlargement:	the result of agreeing the result of settling something the result of increasing something

Suffix	Meaning	Examples with brief explanation	
-ness	the quality, state of being, or condition of	cooperativeness: preparedness: nervousness: kindness:	the quality of being cooperative the condition of being prepared the state of being nervous the quality of being kind
-ous	characterized by	continuous: famous: dangerous:	characterized by being interrupted characterized by fame characterized by danger
-osis	condition	psychosis: hypnosis:	diseased mental condition induced sleep
-ship	a relationship, position, condition, or skill associated with something	partnership: friendship: salesmanship:	the relationship between partners the relationship between friends the skills associated with selling
-tude	the quality, condition, state of being, measure of	magnitude: gratitude:	the quality of being large the state of being grateful
-ure	an action or result of an action; a group performing an action	capture: legislature:	to seize something a group that makes law
-ward	in the direction of	upward toward northward	from lower to higher in a direction indicated by the next word in the direction of the north
-y	characterized by	guilty angry risky	characterized by guilt characterized by anger characterized by risk

23
DEVELOPING EFFECTIVE SENTENCES

Chapter Objectives

This chapter will enable you to understand:

- Sentence Unity
- Forming Coherent Sentences
- Forming Emphatic Sentences

In communication, the ideas are transmitted from one person to another person. The primary concern of language is to communicate meaning to achieve clarity in writing reports, memorandum or a business letter. The construction of clear, correct and well-balanced sentences is essential to successful writing. In order to compose a good sentence, the most important thing is to master the art of arranging words, phrases and clauses in their most effective setting. A paragraph is only as good as the individual sentences within it. Effective sentences—those which achieve their purposes—are unified, coherent, and clear. Furthermore, they place emphasis upon appropriate elements.

23.1 SENTENCE UNITY

23.1.1 Sentences as Building Blocks

Sentences are the building blocks of written communication. Thus, sentences are the basic units of thought which you can phrase and arrange in various ways to present information and reach other objectives. To be effective, however, sentences must meet certain requirements. For instances, sentences must be correct, and to be correct, they must be unified and coherent. In other words, a sentence must be a clearly marked unit of thought that is grammatically complete and independent.

23.1.2 Sentences as Separate Unit

Each sentence is a separate, clearly marked unit means each sentence begins with a capital letter and ends with some form of sentence-end punctuation (period, question mark, or exclamation point). The advantage of setting off each sentence in this way is that you can present your idea in an easy-to-follow orderly fashion. You can conveniently make revisions in your sentences by adding, taking out, changing, or rearranging words. From reader's point of view, the meaning of each individual sentence becomes clear first as a separate unit of thought. Then the meaning resulting from the relationships among these units emerges. In this way the reader is able to follow writer's sequence of thoughts unit by unit and step by step.

23.1.3 Identifying True Sentences

Thus, a sentence can be defined as a grammatically related group of words which presents a unit of thought and is both 'complete' and 'independent'. A complete ***sentence*** needs only two elements: **a subject—predicate unit** and **a complete thought.**

According to this basic definition a sentence must fulfill the following two conditions: completeness and independence.

1. **Completeness:** Is the group of words a complete clause?

   That is, does the construction contain both a subject and a predicate (verb or verb phrasing)? If the group of words does not have both a subject and a predicate, it is a phrase, and thus cannot be a sentence.

2. **Independence:** Is the clause a grammatically independent unit?

   That is, does the construction stand by itself without being subordinate to any other element in the sentence?

   If the group of words is made subordinate to another element by such words as 'because', 'if', 'when', or 'until', it is a dependent clause. As you know a dependent clause cannot stand as a sentence.

   Also keep in mind that a sentence must also begin with a capital and end with some type of sentence-end punctuation.

23.1.4 Identifying Mistakes in Sentence Unity

Sentence fragments, run-on sentences, and comma faults are among the most basic grammatical errors found in business writing.

1. Sentence fragments

Sentence fragment is a group of words that appear to be a sentence but does not make a complete thought. Fragments make no sense by themselves and leave important questions unanswered. All speakers of English use sentence fragments freely in informal conversations. Sometimes, conversational language does not follow the usual sentence pattern. In oral interaction a sentence consists of one word. For example:

'Go.'

'Really?'

'Yes.'

'Today.'

'The sooner the better.'

You use and hear these oral fragments repeatedly in conversation. This practice is so common it attracts little attention. The usual written sentence pattern consists of two parts—a subject and a predicate, or a subject and a verb. They may have their extensions—verbs, phrases, and objects, etc. As you know, any group of words, having a subject and a verb is a clause. There are two kinds of clauses: independent and dependent clauses. Independent clause is able to stand alone while dependent clause is unable to stand alone. Sometimes a dependent clause has a subject and a verb just like an independent clause, but it cannot stand alone because it begins with a dependent word, such as: after, although, before, even if, since, that, etc., for example, "We finished the game". It is an independent clause. If we put one dependent word in front of it, it becomes dependent,

After
As
While } we finished the game.
When
If

It is a fragment and must not be punctuated as a sentence.

Improved sentence: After we finished the game, we went to the college.

You should use complete sentences in written messages because such sentences are much more likely to be clear and easy for your reader to understand. Besides complete sentences are required forms of courtesy in written communication. For these reasons, sentence fragments are not appropriate in written business messages.

There are two very common types of sentence fragments—phrases and dependent clauses.

Phrases: As you learned earlier, a group of words, punctuated as a sentence, contains both a subject and a predicate. If it does not, the word group is a type of sentence fragment called a phrase. It is not a sentence, for example, following sentences lack the subject and predicate required as the nucleus of a sentence:

1. The brochure having been sent to the printer.
2. Each application to be considered by the committee.
3. The newsletter requiring extensive checking before being released.
4. The manager having prepared a complete list.
5. Many of the best ideas being offered by junior executives.

You can use either of the following methods to change these types of ineffective sentence fragments into complete sentences:

(a) Change the participial or infinitive construction into an appropriate verb form.

(b) Attach the fragment to an independent clause or make it part of an independent clause.

Method 1

1. The brochure had been sent to the printer.
2. Each application will be considered by the committee.
3. The newsletter requires extensive checking before being released.

4. The manager has prepared a complete list.
5. Many of the best ideas are being offered by junior executives.

Method 2

1. The brochure having been sent to the printer, Ms. Anisha notified her supervisor.
2. The procedures required each application to be considered by the committee.
3. The newsletter requiring extensive checking before being released, Mr. Shah postponed the announcement.
4. The manager having prepared a complete list, the president directed that the full order be placed at once.
5. Many of the best ideas being offered by junior executives, the committee reached to a conclusion.

Dependent clauses: As you know, if a group of words contains a subject-predicate nucleus and is punctuated as a sentence but is made independent by an introductory function word, it is not a sentence. It is instead a type of sentence fragment called a dependent clause. Listed below are five examples of sentence fragments that are dependent clauses:

1. When the repairs have been completed on the generator.
2. Because the visitors were prospective customers.
3. After Mr. Varshney returned from Shimla.
4. If the conference could develop a workable plan.
5. Since prices have been rising each month.
6. Because there was no other way of escaping the fire.

You can change each of these sentence fragments into complete sentences by either of the following methods:

(a) Remove the subordinating element (the introductory function word), but leave the rest of the clause intact.

(b) Attach the dependent clause to an independent clause.

Method 1

1. The repairs have been completed on the generator.
2. The visitors were prospective customers.
3. Mr. Varshney returned from Shimla.
4. The conference could develop a workable plan.
5. Prices have been rising each month.
6. There was no other way of escaping the fire.

Method 2

1. Operations will begin when the repairs have been completed on the generator.
2. Because the visitors were prospective customers, they received special courtesies.
3. After Mr. Varshney returned from Shimla, he saw the record.
4. If the conference could develop a workable plan, Ms. Kamath would adopt it.
5. Since prices have been rising each month, our operating costs have increased greatly.
6. Because there was no other way of escaping the fire, he leaped through the window with a crash.

2. The run-on sentences

A run-on is two independent clauses without punctuation between them. This mistake happens when phrases or dependent clauses come between two sentences. In such situations, the reader has no way of knowing whether the phrases or dependent clauses belong to the first or second sentence. The following are the examples of the run-on sentences:

1. Tim bought a wristwatch he gave shopkeeper Rs.1000 a month for three years.
2. Catherine is the head cheerleader she is often coaching the other girls who need extra help.
3. The consignment was found to be correct when it was examined the invoice was found to contain a serious mistake.
4. The university issued the announcement the following week the number of inquiries increased greatly.
5. The first half of the meeting had already been held in the afternoon attendance was better than had been expected.
6. Many improvements were suggested by the employees without checking on the availability of space management responded that the matter would be studied.

You can correct a run-on sentence in either of the following ways:

(a) Divide the run-on sentence into two separate sentences.

(b) Join the independent clauses into a compound sentence.

Method 1

1. Tim bought a wristwatch. He gave shopkeeper Rs.1000 a month for three years.
2. Catherine is the head cheerleader. She is often coaching the other girls who need extra help.
3. The consignment was found to be correct when it was examined. The invoice was found to contain a serious mistake.
4. The university issued the announcement. The following week the number of inquiries increased greatly.
5. The first half of the meeting had already been held in the afternoon. Attendance was better than had been expected.
6. Many improvements were suggested by the employees without checking on the availability of space. Management responded that the matter would be studied.

Method 2

1. Tim bought a computer; therefore, he gave shopkeeper Rs.1000 a month for three years.
2. Catherine is the head cheerleader, and she is often coaching the other girls who need extra help.
3. The consignment was found to be correct when it was examined, but the invoice was found to contain a serious mistake.
4. The university issued the announcement, and the following week the number of inquiries increased greatly.
5. The first half of the meeting had already been held in the afternoon; therefore, attendance was better than had been expected.

6. Many improvements were suggested by the employees without checking on the availability of space; management responded that the matter would be studied.

Thus run-on sentences do more than cause confusion. They also waste time. Many business persons will not take the time required to speculate about such matters. They are likely to discard the message without giving it further attention. In addition, they receive a negative impression of the person and the company sending messages with such obvious mistakes.

3. The comma fault

The comma fault is two independent clauses with only a comma and no coordinating conjunction between them. The following are the examples of the comma fault:

1. Tommy runs away from the bully each day, the bully wants his lunch money.
2. The tax had been paid before the deadline, the documents had previously been completed and filed.
3. The last paragraph requires revision, I believe the summary is also inaccurate.
4. It is nearly half past five, we cannot reach home before dark.
5. Nancy read the information about commas carefully, she earned a perfect score on the practice quiz.
6. He was late to office again, his bus got caught in heavy traffic.

You can correct a comma fault in the same ways that you can correct a run-on sentence:

(a) Divide the original sentence into two separate sentences.

(b) Join the original sentence into a compound sentence.

Method 1

1. Tommy runs away from the bully each day. The bully wants his lunch money.
2. The tax had been paid before the deadline. The documents had previously been completed and filed.
3. The last paragraph requires revision. I believe the summary is also inaccurate.
4. It is nearly half past five. We cannot reach home before dark.
5. Nancy read the information about commas carefully. She earned a perfect score on the practice quiz.
6. He was late to office again. His bus got caught in heavy traffic.

Method 2

1. Tommy runs away from the bully each day because the bully wants his lunch money.

   Or

   Tommy runs away from the bully each day; the bully wants his lunch money.
2. The tax had been paid before the deadline, but the documents had previously been completed and filed.

   Or

   The tax had been paid before the deadline; the documents had previously been completed and filed.
3. The last paragraph requires revision and I believe the summary is also inaccurate.

   Or

   The last paragraph requires revision; I believe the summary is also inaccurate.

4. It is nearly half past five; we cannot reach home before dark.

   Or

   It is nearly half past five; therefore, we cannot reach home before dark.
5. Nancy read the information about commas carefully; she earned a perfect score on the practice quiz.

   Or

   Nancy read the information about commas carefully, and she earned a perfect score on the practice quiz.
6. He was late to office again because his bus got caught in heavy traffic.

23.2 FORMING COHERENT SENTENCES

To be correct, a sentence must also be coherent. A sentence is coherent when all its parts relate to one another in a clear and straightforward way. For example, consider the following sentence:

- Preparing the report, an error occurred.

The sentence begins to say something about the person preparing a report. Without completing the statement, at midpoint the sentence moves towards a different direction. Here are two sentences which present the same information in coherent form:

1. Preparing the report, Karan made an error.
2. An error occurred while Karan was preparing a report.

23.2.1 Identifying Mistakes in Coherence

Following are the kinds of mistakes in coherence that are the most likely to cause confusion in business messages:

1. Errors in word choice
2. Dangling infinitives, participles, and gerunds
3. Misplaced modifiers
4. Squinting modifiers
5. Faulty parallelism
6. Split infinitives
7. Faulty agreement
8. Faulty pronoun reference
9. Careless use of connectives
10. Illogical sequence of sentences
11. Unwarranted shift in point of view

1. Errors in word choice

The first requirement for writing coherent sentences is to use words that express meaning accurately. Many words look alike but have different meanings and uses. Other words sound the same or much the same but are spelled differently. Here are some examples of such words that occur frequently in business writing:

there/their/they're
to/too/two
its/it's
are/our/hour
your/you're
sight/site/cite
principle/principal
write/right/rite
affect/effect
assistants/assistance
whether/weather
correspondents/correspondence
advise/advice
access/excess
devise/device
appraise/apprise
adapt/adept
counsel/council
dependent/dependant
later/latter
lose/loose
practice/practise
stationary/stationery

Since there are many words in English which are similar in sound or appearance, you must concentrate fully when you are writing.

2. Dangling infinitives, participles, and gerunds

An infinitive is the 'to form' of the verb. For example:

To go, to write, to walk, etc.

A gerund is a noun made by adding '–ing' to verb. For example:

Selling is an art.

Working is a pleasure.

A participle is an adjective made by adding '-ing' to a verb. For example:

Working women lead an active life.

Our living conditions need to be improved.

A verb + -ing, like, reading, is not always a participle. It is a participle only when it is used as an adjective. When it is used as a noun, it is a gerund. For example:

- Reading is beneficial. (Here the word 'reading' is used as a noun, therefore it is a gerund.)
- The boy, reading the paper, is my senior. (Here the word 'reading' is used as an adjective, therefore it is a participle.)

- There was a sound of matching feet. (Here the word 'matching' is used as an adjective, therefore it is a participle.)

A dangling construction is a phrase or a clause that either modifies nothing in the sentence or that seems to modify a word to which it is not logically related. A dangling construction often begins a sentence and then fails to relate logically to what follows. It is the result of carelessness in writing or thinking. For example, consider the following sentences:

1. Studying the contract carefully, a mistake was found. (dangling participial phrase)
2. Driving home that night, the road seemed endless. (dangling participial phrase)
3. On receiving words on her husband's return, her eyes filled with tears. (dangling gerund)
4. In reviewing the account, three mistakes were discovered. (dangling gerund)
5. Riding my bicycle, a dog chased me.
6. To write effectively, practice is necessary. (dangling infinitive)
7. To use words accurately, a dictionary should be consulted. (dangling infinitive)

You can correct a dangling construction by one of the following two methods:

(a) Changing the subject so that the dangling phrase modifies the new subject.

(b) By expanding the dangling phrase into a subordinate clause.

Following sentences illustrate both the methods of correcting the dangling constructions in the preceding list:

1. Studying the contract carefully, Sania found a mistake.

   Or,

   When Sania studied the contract carefully, she found a mistake.
2. Driving home that night, he thought that the road was endless.

   Or,

   As he drove home that night, the road seemed endless.
3. Driving home that night, he thought that the road was endless.

   Or,

   On receiving words on her husband's return, Hina filled her eyes filled with tears.
4. In reviewing the account, the manager discovered three mistakes.

   Or

   When the manager Studied the contract carefully, he found a mistake.
5. Riding my bicycle, I was chased by a dog.

   Or,

   When I was riding my bicycle, a dog chased me.
6. To write effectively, one must practice. ('To write' logically refers to 'one', the subject of the main clause.
7. To use words accurately, one should consult a dictionary.

While a dangling construction often occurs at the beginning of a sentence, it can also occur at the end or in the middle of a sentence. For example:

- A fragment was discovered proofreading the message.

The sentence seems to say that the fragment was doing the proofreading. You can correct the sentence in the following ways:

- A fragment was discovered while the typist was proofreading the message.

Or

- A fragment was discovered while the message was being proofread.

3. Misplaced modifiers

In a broad sense, words and phrases, which change or restrict the meaning of other words, are called modifiers. A modifier is generally placed nearest the word it modifies. Its position in the sentence should be such that it clearly indicates what it modifies. If you do not phrase sentences carefully, with modifiers as close as possible to the terms they modify, the resulting sentences will be weak and may sound awkward. For example:

1. He barely kicked that ball twenty yards.
2. I only gave him three dollars.
3. John mailed an order to the company with the check enclosed.
4. The lady wearing green saree that greeted me is Mrs. Suman Gupta.
5. Elizabeth came over while I was playing the piano with a piece of chocolate cake.

Sentences of this kind give the impression that the writer does not really care about making a favourable impression on the reader. The following sentences illustrate various ways of correcting the misplaced modifiers in the preceding list:

1. He kicked that ball barely twenty yards.
2. I gave him only three dollars.
3. John mailed an order, with the check enclosed, to the company.
4. The lady who was wearing green saree and who greeted me is Mrs. Suman Gupta.
5. Elizabeth came over with a piece of chocolate cake while I was playing the piano.

4. Squinting modifiers

A squinting modifier is one that may modify either a preceding word or a following word. It squints at the words on its right and left and leaves the reader confused. For example, consider the following sentences:

1. Students who seek their instructor's advice often can improve their grades.
2. His physician told him frequently to exercise.
3. The instructor told his student when the class was over they could ask their questions.
4. The president said after the election he would raise taxes.
5. The new employees only had to file the form.

In business writing, therefore, where inaccuracy can lead to misunderstanding you should use particular care to clearly indicate which term the modifier is intended to modify. You can correct the preceding list of sentences in the following ways:

1. Students who seek their instructor's advice can often improve their grades.

   Or

   Students who seek their instructor's advice often can improve their grades.

2. His physician told him to exercise frequently.
   Or
   His physician frequently told him to exercise.
3. When the class was over, the instructor told his student they could ask their questions.
   Or
   The instructor told his student they could ask their questions when the class was over.
4. The president said he would raise taxes after the election.
   Or
   After the election, the president said he would raise taxes.
5. Only the new employees had to file the form.
   Or
   The new employees had only to file the form.

5. Faulty parallelism

Parallel structure is an important device for organizing sentences, so as to emphasize their close relation in thought. As we know the connectives are used to express the logical relationship between the sentences. Sometimes the same thoughts are expressed in sentences, but sometimes we have change thoughts. Parts of a sentence, that express equal thoughts, should be parallel (the same) in grammatical form. Parallel comparison is, one should express equal thoughts in a parallel or equal grammatical form. Thus, parallel structure puts similar ideas into the same kinds of grammatical constructions. Parallel constructions must be logically connected by the coordinating conjunctions 'and', 'but', 'or'... etc.

It should be ensured that the sentence element connected by these conjunctions of the same grammatical type. If one idea in a sentence is expressed by a phrase, other equal ideas should be expressed by phrases. If one idea in a sentence is expressed by a gerund or a clause, other equal ideas should be expressed by duplicate grammatical construction. Parallelism helps make sentences grammatically clear and also produces an agreeable rhythm, which is an essential quality in good writing.

Listed below are examples of sentences in which the coherence is weakened by a lack of parallelism.

1. The supervisor either made the telephone call or his assistant did.
2. Jim not only has been outstanding in athletics, but also in his studies.
3. The policeman told us to drive very slowly and that we should not put on our bright lights.
4. The company objectives for the coming year are to match last year's production, higher sales and improving consumer relations.
5. The questionnaire asks for this information: number of employees; what is our union status; and how much do we pay.

You can easily strengthen the coherence of these sentences through revision. Note the following revisions of the defective sentences given above:

1. Either the supervisor made the telephone call or his assistant did.
2. Jim has been outstanding not only in athletics, but also in his studies.

3. The policeman told us to drive very slowly and not to put on our bright lights.
4. The company objectives for the coming year are to match last year's production, to increase sales and to improve consumer relations.
5. The questionnaire asks for this information: number of employees, union affiliation and pay scale.

6. Split infinitives

An infinitive is the 'to' form of a verb. For example: 'to sell', 'to go', etc. An infinitive is split when one or more words separate the 'to' form of the verb. In other words, a split infinitive occurs when one or more words separate the 'to' and the verb. For example:

1. I would like you to just sit down and keep quiet.
2. Jai's instructor told him to never look back.
3. She told me I had to quickly finish this work.
4. He decided to completely re-write his proposal.
5. It is advisable for you to at least to send a small deposit with order.

There is nothing ungrammatical about splitting an infinitive, but sometimes a split results in clumsiness or ambiguity in the sentence. Therefore, we should avoid placing a modifier between the 'to' and the verb form in an infinitive for the sake of clarity and right emphasis. You can correct the preceding list of sentences in the following ways:

1. I would like you just to sit down and keep quiet. (You could also say: I would just like you to sit down and keep quiet.)
2. Jai's instructor told him never to look back.
3. She told me that I had to finish this work quickly.
4. He decided to re-write his proposal completely.
5. It is advisable for you to send at least a small deposit with order.

7. Faulty agreement

Agreement is the grammatical relationship between a subject and a verb, or a pronoun and its antecedent. While writing business messages, you should see that subject and verb in a sentence agree with each other. Similarly throughout your writing, you should make sure that a pronoun agrees with its antecedent in number, gender and person.

A verb and its subject should agree in number and person. (Such agreement is called concord.) Usually, singular subjects take singular verbs and plural subjects take plural verb.

More often, writers use a singular subject with a plural verb or a plural subject with a singular verb, because they are uncertain of the number of the subject. There are certain rules to make the verb agree with its subject:

(a) Making verb and its subject agree

- *Make every verb agree in number with its subject.*

Errors in agreement frequently arise when other words intervene between the subject and verb. Do not be confused by words or phrases that intervene between the subject and verb. Do not make the verb agree with the nearest noun instead of the real noun. Find the subject and make the verb agree with it. For example:

1. A careful study of these two reports reveal the truth. (the verb 'reveal' agrees with the subject 'reports' not with the actual subject 'study')

2. The first two chapters of the book is worth reading. (the verb 'is' agrees with the subject 'book' not with the actual subject 'chapters')

The correct sentences are as follows:

1. A careful study of these two reports reveals the truth.
2. The first two chapters of the book are worth reading.

Remember that words connected to a singular subject by 'with', 'together with', 'along with', 'accompanied by', 'in addition to', and 'as well as' take singular verbs. Following are some examples of faulty concord:

1. The manager, along with his team members, have arrived.
2. He, as well as you, are mistaken.
3. The boss, as well as his colleagues, have been robbed by the robber.
4. The president, accompanied by his wife, are travelling to India.
5. The woman, with her children, walk down the street.
6. The chairman, together with his wife, greet the press cordially.

The phrases introduced by such expressions are not part of the subject, even though they do suggest a plural meaning. Following are the revised sentences:

1. The manager, along with his team members, has arrived.
2. He, as well as you, is mistaken.
3. The boss, as well as his colleagues, has been robbed by the robber.
4. The president, accompanied by his wife, is travelling to India.
5. The woman, with her children, walks down the street.
6. The chairman, together with his wife, greets the press cordially.

- Two or more singular subjects joined by 'and' take a plural verb. For example:
    1. Fog, smoke and heavy rain cancel scheduled flight.
    2. Are your father and mother at home?

But if the mind suggests one idea or refers to the same person or thing, the verb is singular:

1. The novelist and poet is dead.
2. Bread and butter is my favourite food.
3. The horse and carriage is at the door.
4. Honour and glory is his reward.
5. Slow and steady wins the race.
6. Time and tide waits for none.

- *Singular subjects separated by 'or', 'nor', 'neither...nor', or 'either...or' take a singular verb,* as in
    1. Either the television or the newspaper is a good source for news.
    2. Our happiness or our sorrow is due to our own action.
    3. Neither the driver nor the cleaner feels sleepy.
    4. Either answer is acceptable.

- *Plural subjects separated by 'or', 'nor', 'neither…nor', or 'either…or' take a Plural verb, as in*
    1. Neither the teachers nor the parent are to blame.
    2. Either the colours or the papers are defective.

When two noun phrases are joined by 'or 'nor', 'neither…nor', or 'either…or' and one has a plural subject, the verb must be plural, and the plural subject should be placed nearest the verb.

1. Neither the chairman nor the directors are present.
2. Neither the inspector nor the officers were able to help us.

When the subjects joined by 'or', 'nor', 'neither…nor', or 'either…or' are of different persons, the verb agrees with the nearer.

1. Either he or I am mistaken.
2. Either you or he is mistaken.
3. Neither my friend nor I am mistaken.

- *Use a singular verb with collective nouns to indicate that the group is considered as one unit. Use a plural verb to indicate that the individual members of the group are acting separately.*
    1. The team wins every game it plays.
    2. The team are discussing next year's schedule.
    3. The audience was cheering the band.
    4. The audience were taking turns to give donations to the trust.
    5. The committee is meeting today.
    6. The committee are divided on one minor point.
    7. The committee has issued its report.
    8. The staff is adequate.
    9. The staff vote on every issue.
- *When a plural noun denoting distance, weight, height, amount of money, or period of time is illustrated as a single unit, it takes a singular verb.*
    1. Ten kilometers is a long walk.
    2. Fourteen minutes is allowed to each speaker.
    3. Hundred rupees is a lot of money for a poor fellow.
    4. The government is doing well.
    5. Bread and butter is a good diet.
    6. Five years is the maximum sentence for that offence.
- *Phrases like 'a lot of', 'many a', 'a great deal of', 'some of', 'most of', 'plenty of', 'none of' are singular when they refer to quantity and are plural when they refer to number.*
    1. A lot of money is needed.
    2. A lot of books have been purchased.
    3. None of you claims responsibility for this incident?

- *Two nouns qualified by 'each', 'every' or 'even though' connected by 'and' require a singular verb.*
    1. Every boy and every girl was given a packet of sweets.
    2. Each of the girls sings well.
    3. Every one of the cakes is gone
- *'Pains' and 'means' take either the singular or the plural verb, but the construction must be consistent.* However, in the sense of 'income', the word 'means' always takes a plural verb.
    1. Great pains have been taken.
    2. Much pains has been taken.
    3. My means are ample/sufficient.
- *Words, plural in form and singular in meaning, take a singular verb.*
    1. The news is true.
    2. Linguistics is the study of a language.
    3. The wages is meager in this factory.
- *When 'number' is preceded by 'the' it takes a singular verb and when by 'a', a plural verb.*
    1. The number of people we need to hire is thirteen.
    2. A number of meetings were held to discuss the issue.
    3. The number of people who reported for work this morning is small.
    4. A number of books are missing from the library.
    5. A number of people have written in about this subject.
- *'It' always takes a singular verb, irrespective of whether the subject is plural or singular.*
    1. It is the people who matter in a democracy.
    2. It is the fundamental that matter.
- *In sentences, beginning with 'there' the number of the verb is determined by the true subject, which generally follows the verb.*
    1. There are various methods of collecting data.
    2. There is no need for typing this report.
    3. There are four hurdles to jump.
    4. There is a high hurdle to jump.
- *'A pair of' when applied to things where the two components are always thought together ('scissors', shears', 'shoes', 'gloves', 'trousers',) takes a singular verb.*
    1. A pair of trousers is hanging on the peg.
    2. A pair of scissors is kept in the drawer.
    3. A pair of spectacles is lying on the table.

But if we omit the words 'a pair of' and only use the plural words, then, it must take a plural verb.

1. The scissors are very sharp.
2. His shoes are very expensive.

- *Certain nouns are used in singular so they take singular verb.*
    1. The scenery of Kashmir attracts the tourists.
    2. The furniture of my drawing room is old fashioned.
    3. No information has been received so far.
- *If a sentence compounds a positive and a negative subject and one is plural, the other singular, the verb should agree with the positive subject.*
    1. The department members but not the chair have decided not to teach on Valentine's Day.
    2. It is not the faculty members but the president who decides this issue.
    3. It was the speaker, not his ideas, that has provoked the students to riot.

(b) Making pronoun and its antecedent agree

As pronouns are words used in place of nouns, they agree in person, number, gender and case with the nouns for which they are used. (The word or phrase, which a pronoun refers back to or replaces, is called the antecedent.)

- *The number of the pronoun should agree with the number of its antecedent.*

If the antecedent is singular, its pronoun must be singular. If the antecedent is plural, pronoun must be plural. For example:

1. Taxes and insurance are necessary evils in any business, and they must be considered carefully in anticipating profits.
2. The secretary put his contribution in the collection box.
3. The boys lost their way in the crowd.

When two or more singular nouns are joined by 'and' (and refer to different persons or things), the pronoun used for them is in the plural.

1. Mohan and Shyam are good boys.
2. Jack and Jill have finished their work.

When two or more singular nouns are joined by 'and' but refer to one person or thing, the pronoun is in the singular:

1. The soldier and statesman was honored for his services.
2. The scholar and poet has won his award.

- *A singular pronoun must be used with each, everybody anybody, some body, etc.*
    1. When the meeting began, everybody took his or her seat at the desk assigned to him or her.

       Or

    When the meeting began, all the members took their seats at the desks assigned to them.

    2. Every dentist and physician in the city will ask to give some of his time to the children's clinic.
    3. Everybody should make plans for his or her retirement.
    4. The aim of the commission is to stimulate the physical growth of the children and to improve their morale.

- *When two nouns are joined by either...or..., neither...nor, the pronoun is in the singular. But in the case of difference of gender the pronoun is in the plural.*

    1. Either Jyoti or Rina is to blame for her fault.
    2. Neither Mohan nor Mira have neglected their work.

    In the case where one is singular and the other is plural, the pronoun agrees with the noun nearer to it.

    3. Neither the teacher nor the students have finished their work.

8. Faulty pronoun reference

As you know pronouns make it possible for you to avoid the monotony of repeating the same nouns. Therefore, every pronoun must have a clearly stated or clearly implied antecedent.

Some sentences are structured in such a way that pronouns are not clear; lacking clear or appropriate antecedents, such pronouns must be replaced by clear words and phrases. In addition, some pronouns are separated from their antecedents; in such cases, repetition of the antecedent provides necessary clarity. Otherwise it will create confusion. Here are some suggestions that will help you use pronouns to conduct coherent sentences.

(a) Do not use a pronoun to replace one among several possible antecedents.

In business writing, you must assure that each pronoun has no more than one noun (or antecedent) to which it could reasonably refer. If there are two possible antecedents in a sentence and the pronoun does not refer to the right one, it will be known as 'faulty reference of pronoun'. Following are examples of sentences that are incoherent because each pronoun could refer to either of the two possible antecedents:

1. The directors instructed the staff to bring their copies. ('their' could refer either to 'directors' or to 'staff'.)
2. Jane told Clara she would be held responsible. ('she' could refer either to 'Jane' or to 'Clara'.)
3. Jane took Joan and her mother shopping. (Whose mother did Jane take, Jane's or Joan's?)
4. When the president objected to Mr. Carter, he told him to mind his own business. (Who told whom?)
5. Each damaged article is marked in such a way that it cannot be erased. (What does 'it' refer to? To the article or to the mark?)
6. When a student hands in a theme to the teacher, he is not always satisfied with it. (Who? Teacher or student?)
7. The hive is constructed so that the bee may work all around each frame and so that it may be removed when full without disturbing the others. (Is the bee removed?)

The fault may be corrected by dropping the pronoun and repeating the noun or by using a synonym for the noun or by changing the construction of the sentences. In order to make pronoun antecedents clear and obvious, we should place pronouns as close to their antecedents as possible. The following revisions illustrate ways of avoiding such ambiguity:

1. The directors instructed the staff to bring the directors' copies, or

    The directors instructed the staff to bring the staff's copies.

2. Jane told Clara that Clara would be held responsible, or
   Jane told Clara, "I would be held responsible."
3. Jane took Joan and Joan's mother shopping, or
   Jane took her mother and Joan shopping, or
   Jane's mother went shopping with Jane and Joan.
4. When the president objected to Mr. Carter, Mr. Carter told him to mind his own business.
5. Each damaged article is marked in such a way that the mark cannot be erased.
6. A student is not always satisfied with a theme when he hands it in to the teacher.
7. The hive is constructed so that the bee may work all around each frame and so that the latter, when full, may be removed without disturbing the other frames.

(b) Avoid implied reference for a pronoun:

When the antecedent of pronoun is not expressed in the sentence, but is implied in some word or group of words, it creates confusion. Consider these examples:

1. We took the oranges out of the boxes, and threw them on to the floor.
2. There are several inconsistencies in the new football rules, and the coaches say that these must be changed before they are adopted.
3. Girls, sitting at both sides of a table, wrap the magazine in thin paper and then put them in pasteboard cartons.
4. If a person sees an advertisement for help and thinks it worth applying for, he must do so.
5. Our employees are enjoying the sunny lunch hour breaks while they last.

The following revisions illustrate ways of avoiding such ambiguity:

1. We took out the oranges, and threw the boxes on to the floor.
2. There are several inconsistencies in the new football rules, and the coaches say that these inconsistencies must be changed before the revised code is adopted
3. Girls, sitting at both sides of a table, wrap the magazine in thin paper and then put the packages in pasteboard cartons.
4. If a person sees an advertisement for help and thinks the position worth applying for, he must do so.
5. Our employees are enjoying their sunny lunch breaks while the good weather lasts.

(c) A pronoun cannot usually represent an entire thought or a group of words.

You should be especially careful to avoid a broad or vague 'this', 'who', or 'which' reference. Here are the examples:

1. Pat blamed the teacher for the unclear lesson, which was foolish. (What was foolish? Blaming the teacher? The lesson? The lesson's being unclear?)
2. My parents decided to move to Florida after retirement. This upsets me. (My parents' decision upsets me or my parents' move to Florida upsets me?)
3. The accountant of Mr. Williams, who is a skilled communicator, is on leave. (The antecedent of 'who' is 'the supervisor' or Mr. Williams?
4. The observation in the report, which you should consider, is reliable. (The antecedent of 'which' is 'the suggestions' or 'these reports'?

Thus, mistakes involving unclear pronoun reference lead to incoherent sentences. These sentences can be improved in the following ways:

1. Foolishly, Pat blamed the teacher for the unclear lesson, or
   Pat was foolish to blame the teacher for the unclear lesson, or
   Confused about the lesson, Pat was foolish to blame the teacher.
2. My parents decided to move to Florida after retirement. Their decision upsets me.
3. Mr. William's accountant, who is a skilled communicator, is on leave.
4. The report's observation, which you should consider, is reliable.

(d) Do not use a pronoun to refer to an unidentified or vague antecedent.

Another suggestion for strengthening the coherence of your sentences is to avoid using pronouns in vague reference to an idea expressed in a preceding construction. Consider the ambiguity in the following sentences:

1. Kelly dropped out of school because they emphasized sports too much.
2. It was a shame that it couldn't find the road leading home.
3. In India, they have many curious customs.
4. He was always friendly, which made everybody like him.
5. He completed his report in time, which pleased the directors.
6. He once lost his money that he had invested in share market and this made him suspicious of all investments.
7. The report has been typed late, which explains why the effort failed.

In these sentences pronoun may refer to a preceding noun or to the idea in the preceding clause. To avoid such confusion, provide a definite antecedent whenever you use a definite pronoun. Here are revisions of the above sentences:

1. Kelly dropped out of school because the teachers emphasized sports too much, or
   Kelly dropped out of school because the students emphasized sports too much.
2. It was a shame that the baby couldn't find the road leading home.
3. In India there are many curious customs.
4. His friendliness made everybody like him.
5. His completion of the report in time pleased the directors, or
   By completing the report in time he pleased the directors, or
   The directors were pleased by his early completion of the report.
6. He once lost his money that he had invested in share market and this experience made him suspicious of all investments.
7. The report has been typed late, a fact which explains why the effort failed.

(e) Avoid using pronouns to refer to antecedents in the possessive case:

The following sentences illustrate the loose relationship that results when an antecedent is a possessive form:

1. In Somaya's report, he emphasizes the need for greater efficiency and more manpower.
2. On the basis of Mr. Anil Srivastava's analysis, he identified two possible causes.

These sentences can be improved in the following ways:

1. In his report, Somaya emphasizes the need for greater efficiency and more manpower.
2. On the basis of his analysis, Mr. Anil Srivastava identified two possible causes.

9. Careless use of connectives

Care must be taken to choose the connective that accurately represents the logical relation between the sentences or thoughts. Following are the most frequently used connectives, classified according to their meaning:

- **Continuation of the same line of thought:** and, moreover, too, again, also, in like manner, likewise, furthermore.
- **Contrast or change in line of thought:** but, however, yet, on the contrary, on the other hand, nevertheless.
- **Result or consequence:** therefore, thus, consequently, accordingly, as a result, hence.
- **Miscellaneous relations:** for example, then here, fortunately, in fact, etc.

Careless use of such conjunctions as 'and', 'as', 'but', and 'while' conceals the exact relationship of meaning that one intends to convey. Here are some suggestions that will help you use pronouns to conduct coherent sentences.

(a) ***Do not use the conjunction 'as' in sentences where it could imply either time or cause.*** For example consider the following examples:

1. As the river rose to flood stage, many people fled to higher ground.
2. As the furnace broke down, the superintendent closed the office.

Here are revisions of the above sentences:

1. When the river rose to flood stage, many people fled to higher ground. (Time intended)
   Because the river rose to flood stage, many people fled to higher ground. (Cause intended)
2. Because the furnace broke down, the superintendent closed the office. (Time intended)
   When the furnace broke down, the superintendent closed the office. (Cause intended)

(b) ***Do not use the conjunction 'as' in the sentence of 'whether' or 'that'.*** For example:

1. I do not know as I want to go tomorrow.
2. I don't know if I could paint, as I have never tried.

Following are the revised sentences:

1. I do not know whether/that I want to go tomorrow.
2. I don't know if I could paint, because I have never tried.

(c) ***Use the conjunction 'but' to connect contrasted sentences.*** Consider the following examples:

1. He was an all American in college, and today he is in poor physical condition.
2. The office is very old, and is well preserved.
3. I argued with him for a long time, and I could not bring him to my point of view.

Following are the improved sentences:

1. He was an all American in college but today he is in poor physical condition.
2. The office is very old but is well preserved.
3. I argued with him for a long time but I could not bring him to my point of view.

(d) ***Do not use the preposition 'like' as a substitute for the conjunctions 'as if' or 'as though' in formal writing.*** For example:

1. He looks like he were exhausted.
2. I really don't feel like I should take the risk of going out in this weather—not with the cold I have.

These sentences can be improved in the following ways:

1. He looks as if (or as though) he were exhausted. (formal)
2. I really don't feel as if I should take the risk of going out in this weather—not with the cold I have.

(e) ***Do not use the conjunction 'while' in the sense of 'and' and 'but'.*** For example:

1. John is a doctor, while Ray is an engineer.
2. Monday was a good day, while Tuesday was warmer.

The following revisions illustrate ways of avoiding such ambiguity:

1. John is a doctor, and Ray is an engineer.
2. Monday was a good day, but Tuesday was warmer.

(f) ***Do not use the conjunction 'while' in cases where it is not clear whether time or concession is intended.*** For example:

1. While I was working at night in the library, I saw John often.
2. While it was very cold, I continued to study.

The sentence can be revised in the following ways.

1. When I was working at night in the library, I saw John often. (Time intended)
   Although I was working at night in the library, I saw John often. (Concession intended)
2. When it was very cold, I continued to study. (Time intended)
   Although it was very cold, I continued to study. (Concession intended)

(g) ***Unless it is essential, place the formal connectives such as, however, therefore, nevertheless, etc., within the sentence rather than in the beginning.*** For example:

1. Therefore, the committee decided to postpone the meeting.
2. However, we realized that the case was hopeless.

Following are the revised sentences:

1. The committee, therefore, decided to postpone the meeting.
2. We, however, realized that the case was hopeless.

10. Illogical sequence of sentences

In the context of language, a sequence of sentences implies some logical order in terms of grammatical correctness. You will weaken the coherence of a sentence if you shift from one point of view to another for no good reason. Unless there is a logical reason for a shift, you should be sure that all items in a sentence are in logical order as well as in parallel form. Logical order means using a natural and chorological sequence for the events, you want to relate. Here are some suggestions for strengthening the coherence of a sentence.

(a) All related parts of a sentence are not unnecessarily separated by other elements.

To write a correct sentence, you need to have a good understanding of what a sentence is. Students who do not have this understanding, or do not take care, often weaken the coherence of a sentence in their writing. Consider the following examples:

1. The fire was put out before any serious damage was done by the fireman.
2. As the car wound up the narrow road we found the trees becoming more scattered as we reared the top of the mountain.
3. The workers were arrested by the police carrying the banner.

These sentences can be improved in the following ways:

1. The fire was put out by the fireman (or the fireman put out the fire) before any serious damage was done.
2. As the car wound up the narrow road and reared the top of the mountain, we found the trees becoming more scattered.
3. The workers, carrying the banner, were arrested by the police.

(b) Logical order may sometimes refer to climatic order

In a series of words and phrases which vary considerably in relative importance, the elements should be arranged in rising order of importance; that is with the weakest first and the strongest last. For example:

1. The play closed after the first week and received terrible reviews.
2. His life was tragic and brief.
3. The earthquake caused 100 deaths and toppled several buildings in the area.
4. He opened the envelope, made a note of its contents and read the proposal.

You can rewrite the above-mentioned sentences by arranging ideas in more logical order. Following are the improved sentences:

1. The play received terrible reviews and closed after the first week.
2. His life was brief and tragic.
3. The earthquake toppled several of the buildings in the area and caused 100 deaths.
4. He opened the envelope, read the proposal, and made a note of its contents.

(c) The shorter elements before a longer are kept in a series

As a general rule the shorter number of a series should precede the longer number. For example:

1. The book is beautifully illustrated in colours and interesting.
2. We went to a cafeteria after the meeting.

These sentences are effectively revised in the sentences below:

1. The book is interesting and is beautifully illustrated in colours.
2. After the meeting, we went to a cafeteria.

(d) Negative statement should be kept before a contrasted affirmative statement makes a more emphatic sentence. For example:

1. He failed because he was overconfident, not because he was over trained.
2. His actions were guided by a desire for power, not by the love of humanity.

3. He accepted the position because he felt it was his duty not because he wanted the money.

Following are the improved sentences:

1. He failed not because he was over trained but because he was overconfident.
2. His actions were guided not by love of humanity but by a desire for power,
3. He accepted the position not because he wanted the money but because he felt it was his duty.

11. Unwarranted shifts in the point of view

The most effective writing normally sticks to one subject, one tense (past, present or future), one person (first, second or third), and to one voice (active or passive). You should be consistent within the sentence about matters such as the following:

(a) Do not shift the subject of a sentence or the voice of the verb.
(b) Do not shift person or number.
(c) Do not shift tense or mood.

Therefore, if you start writing in the present tense, you should continue to use verbs in the present tense. If you start writing with pronouns in the second person, you should continue using pronouns in the second person. And if you start with active voice, you should use active voice till the end. Needless derivations in any of these elements will impair the effectiveness of your sentence and may confuse the reader. Here are the examples of improper shifts in point of view:

1. When you have good health, one should feel fortunate. (a shift from second to third person)
2. He was a scholar and he loves to read. (the verb shifts from past tense to present tense)
3. If a person practices diligently, they can become an expert technician. (a shift from singular to plural number)
4. Ellen stayed at a beach resort, and much of her time was spent in writing. (the verb shifts from active to passive voice)
5. The manager told me he would have my car for me as soon as he can get the service garage. (a shift in verb tense in indirect quotation)

Following are the revised sentences by eliminating all needless shifts point of view:

1. When you have good health, you should feel fortunate, or

   When one has good health, one should feel fortunate.
2. He was a scholar and he loved to read. Or

   He is a scholar and he loves to read.
3. If a person practices diligently, he or she can become an expert technician.
4. Ellen stayed at a beach resort, and spent much of her time in writing.
5. The manager told me he would have my car for me as soon as he could get the service garage.

23.3 FORMING CLEAR AND EMPHATIC SENTENCES

As you know, to be effective a sentence must be correct. That is, it must be grammatically complete (unified) and logically organized (coherent). However, an effective sentence should also be clear with appropriate emphasis. Following are some guidelines for writing effective sentences:

1. Using active and passive voice
2. Eliminating redundant words and phrases
3. Variation in sentence length and structure
4. Using positive statements
5. Eliminating needless qualifiers
6. Emphasizing key points

23.3.1 Using Active and Passive Voice

Active voice is more direct and forceful than passive voice. In the active voice, the sentence is directly identified, the subject acts, and the action is presented concisely. Conversely, in the passive voice, the doer is obscured and the action is indirectly presented using more words. Therefore, use active voice for concise, emphatic sentences. Consider the following examples which contrast the effects of passive voice and active voice:

Passive voice: indirect, weak, and wordy

1. A letter was written to Mr. Sam by Luis in which an opportunity was requested so that his proposal could be explained by him.
2. The bill was sent to the general manager by the appropriation committee.
3. Each candidate was introduced to the interviewer by Ms. Etta.
4. The circular has been sent to all members by the secretary.

Active voice: direct, strong, and concise

1. Luis wrote a letter to Mr. Sam requesting an opportunity to explain his proposal.
2. Appropriation committee sent the bill to the general manager.
3. Ms. Etta introduced each candidate to the interviewer.
4. The secretary sent the circular to all members.

However, there are certain circumstances when passive voice may be advantageous. For example, you should use passive voice for any of the following reasons:

1. You wish to emphasize the recipient of the action rather than the performer.
   Example: John was awarded a prize.
   Cheques written in Hindi are also accepted here.
2. When you prefer not to mention the performer.
   Example: The report was completed two weeks late.
   No decision has been made.
3. When you don't know who performed the action.
   Example: The store was robbed.

4. When the agent is irrelevant.
   Example: The paragraphs will be numbered.
5. When you describe a process.
   Example: All relevant data is collected and analysed; then a suitable policy is performed.

23.3.2 Eliminating Redundant Words and Phrases

Proper selection of precise and forceful words and phrases will make your writing more effective. If writing contains unnecessary, pompous, or long words or phrases, it will be hard to read. Remember, the longer it takes to read, the weaker it comes across. Following are some guidelines for writing effective sentences and eliminating wordy expressions.

(a) Pompous diction

Some writers choose words to impress, rather than to express. Big words and pompous phrases make sentences laborious to read. Most wordy expressions have much shorter common synonyms far easier to read, write, say, and hear. For example, consider the following list of words and phrases. On the left are the wordy, roundabout phrases and on the right are the corresponding concise and specific expressions.

Vague, wordy, roundabout phrasing	Concise, specific phrasing
consideration be given to	Consider
Made an announcement	Announced
for the purpose of	To
In view of the fact that	Because
forwarded under separate cover	sent separately
pursuant to authority contained in	Per
prioritized list	priority list
at the conclusion of	After
which is aimed at improving things	for improving efficiency
which is adopted by the organization	the company adopts
despite the fact that	Although
on a daily basis	Daily
in the final analysis	Finally

(b) Overuse of 'the', 'that', or 'which'

Overuse of 'the', 'that', or 'which' will make your writing ineffective and hinder meaning. Use these words to clarify meaning; otherwise, leave them out. Consider the following sentences:

1. The regulations won't allow it.
2. I feel that it's a good decision.
3. The report which I'm writing is nearly finished.

Following are the concise, specific sentences by eliminating all needless 'the', 'that', or 'which':

1. Regulations won't allow it.
2. I feel it's a good decision.
3. The report I'm writing is nearly finished.

(c) Dummy subjects

Delete the dummy subject and move the real subject to the front. Dummy subjects are empty expressions that

obscure the real subject.	**Examples:** Beginning a sentence 'with'
make the sentence longer	It is
delay the point	It appears
encourage passive voice	There is (are)
hide responsibility	It will be

Instead of saying	**Say**
The use of this method	This method
There is no alternative for our company	We have no alternative for our company
It is my intention to	I intend to
There is one thing bothering me	One thing bothers me
It appears that	I think
It is essential that	You must

The real subject should be highlighted. Also, try to avoid beginning sentences with 'there is' or 'it is. For example:

However, beginning a sentence with 'It' is permissible when the pronoun refers to its antecedent in the previous sentence. For example:

- In spite of efforts to eradicate it, poor writing still survives. It is embedded in the bureaucracy.

(d) Smothered verbs

A smothered verb is a verb converted to a noun, so it needs a helping verb and prepositions or articles to express action. This lengthens a sentence and weakens its strength. It also encourages use of the passive voice. In communicating a message action verb should be prominent. An action verb is one that expresses meaning without helping verbs or other modifiers. Technical writing can be very weighted down if the writer uses nouns where verbs would do far better. For example; consider the following sentence:

We are in agreement with the decision.

In this sentence, the writer has smothered the main verb 'agree' with a noun 'agreement'. The noun now requires a helping verb 'are' and a preposition 'in' to show action. Following is the revised sentence with action verb 'agree':

We agree with the decision.

Most smothered verbs have distinct endings:

- ance
- ant
- ence
- ity

- mant
- ment
- ness
- sion
- tion.

To make your sentences more effective, find the smothered verb and convert it into an action verb. This eliminates the need for a helping verb and other modifiers.

Instead of writing	Write
We held a meeting	We met
I made a choice	I chose
They conducted an investigation	They investigated
Consideration was given to	We considered
We are in support of the plan	We support the plan
He made an attempt to escape.	He attempted to escape.

(e) Needless repetition of words and phrases

Needless repetition of words or phrases also creates redundancy and makes writing appear not fully formed. If two ideas are slightly different, eliminate one and retain the one that expresses meaning more precisely. Examples:

1. The manager's function and role . . .
2. The diplomats engaged in a frank and candid dialogue.
3. The staff provides guidance and assistance.
4. First and foremost, we must focus on priorities.

Following are the examples of redundant modifiers:

- Basic fundamentals
- Actual facts
- Really glad
- Honest truth
- End result
- Separate out
- Start over again
- Symmetrical in form
- Narrow down
- Seldom or ever.

23.3.3 Variation in Sentence Length and Structure

Emphatic sentences use a variety of patterns. In using different word orders and sentence lengths, fluent sentences make clear connections between major and minor points. The sentences you write in technical documents ought to have some variety in length and word order. These variations will make ideas clear and emphatic.

You should try to vary your sentences in both length and type. While sentences should *average* about 15 words, they need not all be the same length. If written clearly, an occasional long sentence is fine. However, after writing a long sentence, keep the next one short.

Though short sentences can be used to emphasize a point, often a string of short sentences is monotonous, choppy, and most importantly, unclear. **Similarly, long sentences may make your writing** dense and hard to read. Consider the following examples:

1. **Short sentences:** Brisk walking can be healthy. You need good shoes and guidance about how to walk properly.
2. **Long sentence:** I learned I was selected for the job, so I called Jane immediately, and I told her the good news, and that evening we celebrated by going out to dinner.

Monotony results from too much of the same thing, whether it is too many short, simple sentences or too many long, complicated sentences. In both the sentences we are not sure which point the writer is emphasizing. The solution to the problem is variety. Following are the revised sentences:

1. Walking can be healthy, but you need good shoes and guidance about how to walk properly.
2. Upon hearing I was selected for the job, I called Jane and told her the good news. That evening we celebrated by going out to dinner.

23.3.4 Using Positive Statements

Positive statements are more easily understood than negative ones, because they are direct. In addition, positive statements are more concise and clear. Consider the following example:

Negative statement: I did not gain anything from the lecture.

Positive statement: I gained nothing from the lecture.

23.3.5 Eliminating Needless Qualifiers

Many qualifiers--I feel, I believe, in my opinion—are unnecessary. For example:

1. In my opinion, you have completed this project.
2. I think this proposal can be approved.

In these sentences, the 'I' referred to is the writer and it is obvious that he or she is the one expressing beliefs or feelings. We can revise the sentence in the following way:

1. You have completed this project.
2. This proposal can be approved.

23.3.6 Emphasizing Key Points

Arrange words and phrases in sentences to emphasize key points. Here are some guidelines for writing sentences that underscore the most important information.

(a) Connect ideas using coordination

To connect ideas that require equal emphasis, use coordinating conjunctions (and, or, nor) or conjunctive adverbs (however, therefore) for example:

Two simple sentences: This course is difficult. It is packed with useful information.

Revised coordinated sentence: This course is difficult, but it is packed with useful information.

(b) Connect ideas using subordination

Subordination demonstrates that a less important idea is related or dependent upon a more important idea. To demonstrate that one idea is less important than another, you can combine two simple sentences and deemphasize the less important idea by putting it in a dependent or subordinate clause. A dependent clause is signalled by a subordinating conjunction (because, so that, if, after, until, since, while, as, unless, and although) For example:

Two sentences: Jean tries to get her work done on time in the factory. She has a physical disability.

Combined: Although she has a physical disability, Jean tried to get her work done on time in the factory.

(c) Use parallel structure

Using parallel structure in presenting items of similar importance ensures that sentences will have greater clarity, better flow and appropriate emphasis on key ideas.

Parallelism is used when presenting aspects of a problem, steps in a process or a series of results, conclusions or recommendations. For example:

The store is 100 feet in length, 80 feet wide, and has a height of six stories.

Revised: The store is 100 feet in length, 80 feet wide, and six stories high.

24

DEVELOPING EFFECTIVE PARAGRAPHS

Chapter Objectives

This chapter will enable you to understand:

- The need for clear paragraphing
- Developing Unified, Orderly Paragraphs
- Variety in Paragraphs
- Methods of Paragraph Development
- Strengthening Coherence in Paragraph
- Emphasizing Key Points

The effectiveness of each sentence in a paragraph directly influences the effectiveness of the paragraph as a whole. As you know, a sentence is an independent unit requiring grammatical completeness. In contrast, the paragraph is not a unit of grammar but of rhetoric. (Rhetoric is the art of speaking or writing effectively.) The paragraph is a unit of writing set off by spacing or by indentation of its first line. It is made up of one or more sentences that pertain to a particular topic. That topic is the unifying idea of the paragraph. You will need to use paragraphs in preparing almost every kind of business message.

24.1 THE NEED FOR CLEAR PARAGRAPHING

Paragraphs are useful because they make messages much easier to interpret. However, it is important that paragraphs should be carefully constructed and the sequence of sentences in every paragraph is logical. Good paragraphing is important in business communication. Business people prefer to deal with messages which are concise and easy to follow, yet which do not omit necessary details.

Sentences and paragraphs can be regarded as small and medium size containers for packaging information. Sentences are the small containers; they present some statement, request, or question as a unit. Paragraphs, the medium size containers, can hold a number of sentences.

Each paragraph container should have a label indicating its contents. The label is the topic sentence. Any sentence not covered by the label should be omitted from that paragraph. Thus, each paragraph container is a complete unit containing sentences that develop a single topic.

24.2 DEVELOPING UNIFIED, ORDERLY PARAGRAPHS

24.2.1 The Topic Sentence: Key to Paragraph Unity

The topic sentence can be regarded as the label on the paragraph container. All sentences in the paragraph are unified around the idea presented in this sentence. Usually, the topic sentence stands first in a paragraph, just as a label is the most noticeable part of a container. The topic sentence is the key to the unity of the paragraph. It is the point of reference around which the other sentences are organized.

A topic sentence can be valuable to both—the writer and the reader. You as a writer try to unify your paragraphs and as a reader try to identify the key idea in each paragraph. Once you decide topic sentence of a paragraph, you can then use rest of the sentences in the paragraph to develop that topic. However, remember that your main goal is always to present information clearly. If sentences in a paragraph follow a logical sequence, readers find it much easier to understand the information in the paragraph.

Another important use for a topic sentence is to serve as a bridge between paragraphs. A topic sentence that usually occurs early in a paragraph acts as a transitional statement. It draws the reader's attention to an important shift in topic or the next phase of your presentation.

Thus, to be unified, your paragraphs must contain only the sentences that are logically developed around a central idea. This unifying idea is usually expressed in the topic sentence, which can also provide the link between paragraphs in messages. The following guidelines will help you develop unifying paragraphs:

1. State the topic clearly in the paragraph preferably in an opening topic sentence.
2. Check that each sentence in a paragraph is related closely to that topic.
3. Organize the paragraph in a logical sequence that makes it easy for the reader to follow your presentation.
4. Provide enough detail to meet the needs of the reader.
5. Keep the paragraph short enough so that the reader will be able to understand it readily.
6. Make clear the relationships between paragraphs.

24.3 VARIETY IN PARAGRAPHING

Variety is important in designing effective paragraphs as it is in designing effective sentences. The main reason for providing variety in writing is to keep your reader's interest. If your reader loses interest and stops reading, your carefully unified paragraphs will not have any effect. There are various ways to achieve variety in designing an effective paragraph.

1. Length of the paragraphs

One way to achieve variety is in the length of the paragraphs you use. Do not use paragraphs of equal length. Your paragraphs should not contain the same number of sentences. The length of your paragraph should be decided by the amount of detail you wish to include. To write with clarity, write your sentences that are neither too long nor too short.

In a business message, your paragraph should vary in length from about three to eight (or even ten) sentences. If a paragraph is getting too long, (more than twelve or fourteen lines) your reader will probably find it hard to follow. In this case, you can divide the topic into two parts. You may occasionally use a one-sentence paragraph to get maximum attention to the idea in that sentence. However, this technique works only if used sparingly.

2. Variation in sentences

The second way to add variety to your writing is to vary the sentences within each paragraph. If you use sentences of contrasting type (some statement, request, or question) within your paragraphs, your writing will become more interesting. Similarly, you can sometimes shift from a positive to negative approach.

3. Pace in writing

The third way to add variety is to change the pace in your writing. For example, after writing a general statement, give examples to illustrate your points. The shift from the general to the specific, from the abstract to the concrete, will clarify your messages and help business people for making decisions. By listing points with little or no discussion, particularly as an introduction to new material, you can speed the pace of your writing.

4. Summarization of discussion

Summarize your discussion at frequent intervals. A summary restates all earlier points in general terms, giving readers a chance to review and consider what you have said.

24.4 METHODS OF PARAGRAPH DEVELOPMENT

Another requirement for effective paragraphs is the logical arrangement of sentences. Following are the various methods of developing effective paragraphs:

(a) to organize the sentences within a paragraph

(b) to organize the paragraph within a message.

At times, you may combine various patterns in order to bring flexibility and variety. However, remember that choice of method depends upon purpose, subject, and audience.

1. Time sequence

There are two types of time arrangement—narration of something that has happened and instructions for doing something. In presenting a narration, for example, narrating reports, the sequence of sentences should correspond to the sequence of actions or events you are presenting. In presenting instructions, for example, preparing instruction manuals, the sequence of sentences should correspond step-by-step with the procedures you are describing. However, in the description of a procedure, it is essential that the sentences are in proper order.

2. Space arrangement

This method is useful when you wish to write about the location of a place or the description of a particular object. For example, when you describe something like the layout of an office or you write out directions of a route, in both situations, the sequence of your sentences should take your reader step-by-step from one location to the next.

Time and space arrangements have their special purposes and their usefulness is limited to these purposes.

3. Logical analysis

The method based on logical analysis is especially important for business purposes. There are two kinds of logical analysis: partitioning and classification. One kind of logical analysis, called partitioning, divides a unit into its parts. For example, following are the parts of a single organization:

(a) The manufacturing division
(b) The accounting division
(c) The marketing division
(d) The personnel division
(e) The R&D division

You might then write sentences about each part and thus develop your paragraph in a logical way. In the same way, if you devote one or more paragraphs to each part, you might prepare a message.

The type of analysis in which a class of things is divided into its subclasses is called classification. In other words, partitioning refers to dividing up one thing into its parts; classification refers to dividing up a group of related things into subgroups. For example, the class printer may be divided into various types of printers:

(a) Inkjet
(b) Desk jet
(c) Solid ink
(d) Laser
(e) Black and white laser
(f) Color laser
(g) Dedicated photo

Thus, you might develop an orderly paragraph by writing sentences to each kind of machine. Likewise, you might also develop an orderly message by writing one or more paragraphs to each type.

4. Comparison and contrast

Comparison is another form of paragraph writing that is flexible and widely used in business communication. It is mostly used in combination with other paragraph arrangements. Broadly speaking, the term 'comparison' means to draw attention to similarities or to differences. If you are emphasizing only differences, the method of paragraph development is called 'contrast'. In business writing, for example, in presenting the advantages of one brand, style or service over another you might use this devise of contrast. On the other hand, if you are emphasizing similarities, the general term 'comparison' is used to refer to the method of development. The method of comparison is one of the best effective ways of clarifying any point. For example, you might use this method in preparing your sales brochure. By comparing the unfamiliar object or service with something that is unfamiliar to your reader, you can clarify the matter simply and concisely.

At times comparison and contrast can take place within a single paragraph where every sentence compares or contrasts one subject with another. Comparison and contrast can also be developed in different paragraphs, where one paragraph takes up one subject while in the other paragraph the writer compares and contrasts the other subject with the first.

5. Argumentation

In business, argumentation provides a method for considering the reasons for preferring one course of action or one policy to others. The process of argumentation gives you the most effective method for decision making since it allows you to examine the available options systematically. When argumentation is used as a method for organizing a paragraph, you present the reasons that have led you to some conclusion or proposal.

There are two types of argumentation that correspondent to two types of reasoning: deductive and inductive.

(a) **Deductive reasoning:** In deductive reasoning you apply a general principle to a specific case. You use deductive order for the following two reasons: the relationships are known accurately and reasoning is valid. In deductive order topic sentence is the first sentence in the paragraph. You start with known relationships and reach a conclusion that is completely reliable.

(b) **Inductive reasoning:** In inductive reasoning, you start with one or more specific cases and reach a general conclusion or explanation. You give details, arguments or illustrations, which lead finally to the conclusion. In this order, the topic sentence comes at the end of the paragraph.

Inductive order is used for the following two purposes: to reach a generalization about a situation in which you cannot check all the evidence and to predict what will happen in the future. Thus inductive method is a tool for making predictions, understanding complex events, and reaching generalizations about cases which cannot be examined.

6. General to specific

Paragraph development moves from general to the specific or from abstract statements to concrete examples. In a sense, it is the most obvious and natural form of paragraph development. In business writing, where clarity and accuracy are essential, you can use this form of paragraph development. For example, in a job application letter, it is not enough to make a general statement about your experience. In this situation, you can develop an effective paragraph by devoting sentences to the kind of responsibilities you have had and kinds of machines you can operate. In addition, you can provide details about the length of your experience, the places you have worked or any special recognition you have received. A paragraph developed in this way will provide the necessary information about you and make a favourable impression.

7. Exposition

In exposition method, the topic sentence occurs in the beginning of the paragraph. You devote the entire paragraph to an explanation of the topic sentence. You can try to explain the idea in simpler words and give your comments on it in order to make it more intelligible. You might also use exposition order to explain how to perform an operation, or how to operate a machine. In this situation, you give more emphasis on definition, explanation, comments rather than on illustration, though occasionally you may find that exposition and the deductive order have been mixed in one paragraph.

8. Question to answer

In question to answer method you develop the paragraph by beginning it with a question which is answered within the same paragraph. Such a paragraph has no explicit topic sentence, but the opening question announces the purpose of the paragraph.

24.5 STRENGTHENING COHERENCE IN PARAGRAPHS

An effective sentence must be coherent. As you know, in order to interpret the meaning of a sentence as a whole, the reader must understand the relationships between modifiers and modified elements, pronouns and antecedents, and subjects and verbs. Like sentences, paragraphs must be coherent in order to be effective. The relationships among the parts of the paragraph must be logical and clear to the reader. Following methods are used for achieving coherence within the paragraphs:

1. Inclusion of linking words and phrases
2. Repetition of key terms
3. Introduction of headings
4. Introduction of enumerations
5. Use of questions

1. Linking words and phrases

Special linking words and phrases, (for example: thus, therefore, in addition, similarly) draw attention to the relationship between ideas within a paragraph. Use of these expressions enables a reader to follow writer's thoughts more easily. Following chart shows the relationships represented by the words. Most of the words listed are frequently used in nearly all business messages. Linking words and phrases used to show relationships between ideas

1.	**signifying cause or purpose**	in order to so that with this in view to+infinitive because for the purpose of
2.	**signifying effect or result**	so that with the result that hence consequently accordingly so therefore thus as a result
3.	**signifying examples**	for example for instance to illustrate
4.	**signifying emphasis**	certainly of course indeed really above all truly

5.	**signifying sequence or addition**	in adition and furthermore besides also again further finally as well as both...and
6.	**signifying exclusion**	all except all but not that but not neither...nor
7.	**signifying condition**	if whether provided that
8.	**signifying alternatives**	or either...or whether...nor
9.	**signifying similarity**	similarly likewise
10.	**signifying contrast**	but however nevertheless contrastingly on the other hand in spite of in contrast still yet
11.	**signifying details**	including namely especially in particular in detail to list to enumerate
12.	**signifying concession**	although at least still though even though at any rate

2. Repetition of key terms

Another way to establish coherence between sentences and paragraphs is to repeat key expressions or ideas. Through such repetition, the writer indicates that the discussion will continue to focus on that point.

(a) **Use of adjectives:** The use of adjectives such as this/these, that/those, such, some, or many provides a means of tying two sentences together through the repetition of some key word.

(b) **Use of nouns and pronouns:** Careful use of nouns and pronouns increases coherence. However, pronouns can be repeated more often than nouns without causing awkwardness or monotony. The most common and useful pronouns are: he, she, it, they (and their other case forms—him, his, her, hers, its, them, their, theirs) who (when, whose), which, that, those, this, these, and one.

3. Headings

In certain situations headings are used to introduce various parts of a message. These headings act as road signs for the reader by drawing attention to and separating certain sections.

Headings use visual effects to catch the readers' eye. These effects include spacing, capital letters, italics, boldface type, and different coloured ink. You can use headings primarily to identify important parts of reports, proposals, agreements, or other documents.

4. Enumerations

Enumerations, used as a device of increasing coherence, enable writers to present a great deal of information in a small space and prepare the reader for the material to follow. Through enumerations, you can present an overview of your main points and then add as much additional information and as many examples as you wish. Enumerations can also be used for summarizing major points in the conclusion of a paragraph.

5. Questions

Another device to increase the coherence of a paragraph is to design a series of questions that relate to the major points of your writing. Arrange your questions in a logical sequence. After each question, you may provide the answer, including details and examples. This question-answer method offers a concise way for presenting paragraphs in clear and distinct units.

24.6 EMPHASIZING KEY POINTS

In order to use emphasis properly, you must first decide what to emphasize. If you try to emphasize everything in your message, nothing will stand out. In making such decisions, you must keep your objectives clearly in mind.

The secret of effective emphasis is contrast. Contrast between important points. The greater the contrast, the greater the emphasis. Following are the suggestions for emphasizing important points in a paragraph.

(a) State directly that such and such point is the most important point in your message. This approach is the most straightforward and can be very effective if used selectively.

(b) Present major points in emphatic positions. The most attention-getting positions are the beginning and the end of a paragraph.

(c) Elaborate the important points. If you present a point with little or no elaboration, you are implying that the point does not deserve much attention.

(d) Phrase an important point in a striking way. It is essential to find exactly the right word to convey a key point. Use a phrase or slogan that readers will remember.

(e) Repeat key words and ideas in the paragraph. Repetition can be a powerful tool if used selectively. If you repeat something too often, you may bore your readers.

(f) Use visual techniques. You can emphasize key points through visual effects, such as headings, colours, and distinctive type. However, these visual effects should be used sparingly.

25
PUNCTUATION AND MECHANICS OF BUSINESS WRITING

Chapter Objectives

This chapter will enable you to understand:

- Sentence-End Punctuation
- Internal Punctuation
- Capitalization in Business Writing
- The Expression of Numbers

25.1 SENTENCE-END PUNCTUATION

Sentence-end punctuation marks are used to end sentences. These marks can be thought of as stop signs in the traffic of ideas indicating that readers should make a full pause before proceeding to the next unit/sentence.

There are three types of sentence-end punctuation – the period, the question mark, and the exclamation point.

25.1.1 The Period

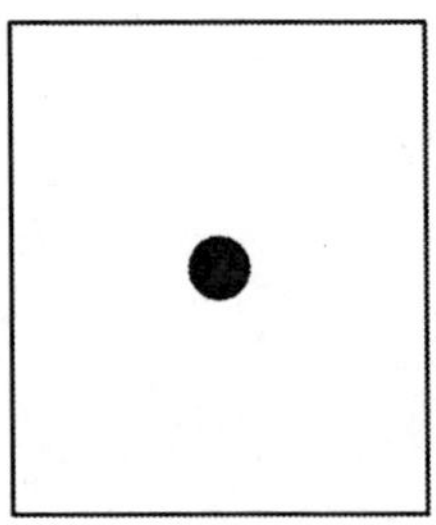

Of the three types of sentence-end punctuation, the period is the most common and the most important. Most sentences within almost every paragraph end with periods.

The period at the end of a sentence corresponds to a full pause in speech.

1. Use the period after every declarative sentence.
   - The workers are happy.
   - The chairperson adjourned the meeting, and the audience left the room.
2. Use the period at the end of most imperative sentences.
   - Please check the date on your tickets.
   - Mail the enclosed report by next week.
3. Use the period at the end of interrogative sentences that are really requests.
   - Will you please examine this report.
   - Would you kindly send your quotation at once.
4. Use the period after initials and after most abbreviations.
   - Lucknow, U.P.
   - Sharnam Software Ltd.
   - Ph.D.
   - a.m.

Note, however, that many abbreviations composed of several capitalized initial letters are written without periods and without spacing. (For example: IGNOU – Indira Gandhi Nehru Open University).

25.1.2 The Question Mark

The question mark alerts your readers that you are asking a question. Often the purpose of questions in technical communication is to get information through the reader's reply. Therefore, it is important to phrase such operations clearly and courteously. Use question marks appropriately.

- What arrangements did you make?
- What deadline do you suggest?

Note that the question mark is not used after a question referred to but not quoted word for word. Such an indirect question is actually a declarative sentence and should be followed by a period.

- Mr. Sunil asked whether we would help him.

Use a question mark after each question in a series of questions within an interrogative sentence. In such situations, the question mark should be followed by a lowercase letter.

Please answer the following questions: What is your age? Height? Weight? Condition of health? Level of education?

Note also that in business messages do not use repeated question marks (???) for emphasis.

25.1.3 The Exclamation Point

Use the exclamation point to indicate strong emotion, urgency, or emphasis. Excessive use will reduce the effectiveness of the exclamation point.

- Look out! The bus is backing up!
- Hurry up! We are late.

25.2 INTERNAL PUNCTUATION

Internal punctuation marks tell readers certain things about the relationships within each sentence and show how the writer's thoughts are organized within each sentence. These marks can be regarded as slow signs alerting readers to special constructions with in sentences. Different marks draw attention to different relationships and situations.

There are three most common and important marks of internal punctuation: **the comma, the semicolon, and the colon**. Accurate use of these three marks communicates your thoughts more clearly and helps your readers better understand the presentation of your ideas within your sentences.

The three other internal punctuation marks—**parentheses, dashes, and quotation marks** are used to enclose one or more words within a sentence. These marks all have the purpose of showing that the material set off has a special relationship to the rest of the sentence.

Italics (underlining), hyphens, omission marks, and apostrophes draw attention to unusual circumstances. Accurate use of these marks communicates your thoughts more clearly and helps your readers better understand the presentation of your ideas within your sentences.

25.2.1 The Comma

The comma is the most frequently used and most important internal punctuation mark. Comma indicate pauses and thus set off certain subunits within sentences.

1. Use a comma before a coordinating conjunction (such as and, but, or,) to join independent clauses in a compound sentence.
   - The data have been collected, and the graphs are now being prepared.

   Since commas are used so frequently, there are many opportunities for them to be misused. For example,

   Comma fault: The secretary brought the reports to the meeting, each member received a copy.

   Correction: The secretary brought the reports to the meeting, and each member received a copy.
2. Use a comma to separate three or more elements in a series. For example, you should use a comma to separate:
   (a) Three or more dependent or independent clauses in a series.
   - The chairperson called the meeting, the committee member took their places, and the hearing began.

   (b) Three or more words or phrases in a series.
   - In drafting a message, in revising it, and in proofreading, cultivate the ability to concentrate.
   - The material may now be sent by road, by rail, or by sea.
3. Use a comma to separate certain introductory elements from the main clause. Use comma to set off:
   (a) Introductory subordinate clauses.
   - Because these laptops are so reliable, the company bought a supply of them.

   (b) Other introductory elements containing a verb form (such as infinite, participal, or gerund phrases).
   - In summarizing, the report omitted the quotation.

   (c) Introductory transitional words and phrases or expressions that might otherwise be confusing.
   - However, few customers read the instructions carefully.
4. Use the comma to set off words in direct address, whether they come at the beginning or within the sentence.

- We shall call for an appointment, Mr. Singh, to demonstrate our new machine.

5. Use the comma to set off non-restrictive or parenthetical elements within a sentence. Commas should be used to set off:
   (a) Non restrictive adjective clauses (clauses which can be expressed in a separate sentence without changing the meaning of the original sentence).
   - My new printer, which is a portable model, is easy to use.

   Remember that comma should not be used with restrictive adjective clauses. (Clauses which cannot be omitted. Without changing the meaning of the original sentence).

   For example:

   Comma fault: Anyone, who works hard, deserves to succeed.

   Correction: Anyone who works hard deserves to succeed.

   (b) Nonrestrictive appositive words or phrases.
   - DLF Tower, a tall office building, is located in New Delhi.

   (c) Parenthetical words, phrases, and clauses (transitional emphatic, and other expressions that interrupt the development of a sentence).
   - That model, on the other hand, is a wise choice.

6. Use a comma to separate coordinate adjectives (adjectives which can be joined be 'and').
   - The smart, efficient girl got the job.
   - The sales representative gave a long, informative presentation.

Note: Do not use a comma if the adjectives cannot be joined by 'and'.

- Mr. S.K. Rao is an honest public official.

7. Use a comma as a means of introducing short quotations in an informal way.
   - The secretary said, "the customers will be mailed tomorrow>"

8. Use a comma to mark the omission of a word or phrase in a series of parallel constructions or to increase the clarity of any sentence.
   - Ever since, the company has had excellent health benefits.

25.2.2 The Semicolon

Semicolons are used mainly to join the independent clauses of a compound sentence. Semicolons sometimes substitute for commas when other commas occur in the same sentence.

In addition, semicolons are used before same kinds of examples and lists occurring late in a sentence. Here are the guidelines concerning the semicolon:

1. Use a semicolon to join independent clauses in a compound sentence if you do not employ a coordinating conjunction (and, but, or, nor). For example, use a semicolon:
   (a) By itself between the independent clauses
   - The plant opens at 7:30 a.m.; it closes at 5:00 p.m.
   - The application form calls for information about the candidate's education; the form also calls for the names of all prior employees.

   (b) With a linking adverb or phrase between the independent clauses.
   - Mr. Anand's payment arrived late; as a result, the company sent a reminder.
   - The annual sales conference will take place in June; therefore, most of our sales representatives will be able to attend.
2. Substitute a semicolon for a comma within a sentence if the elements being separated contain commas.
   - The committee, which was composed of volunteers, prepared a list of grievances; they made an appointment with the CEO; and, on the appointment day, they travelled to the head office.
3. Use a semicolon before expressions as 'namely' and 'for example' when they are used to introduce a series of items at the end of a sentence.
   - The board members considered many proposals from the administrative officer; for example, to repair boundary wall, to build a new lab, and to remodel the director's office.
   - Four faculty members were appointed to the discipline committee; namely J.S. Dubey, Sunil Kumar, R.A. Verma, and Ramanuj.

25.2.3 The Colon

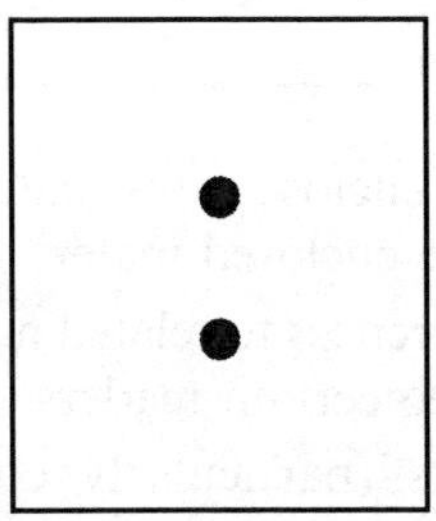

A colon indicates the end of an independent clause and points strongly to the rest of the sentence. Here are the guidelines concerning the colon:

1. Use a colon after a main clause to point to the rest of the sentence.
   (a) When a second independent clause provides an explanation or example clarifying a general statement contained in the first independent clause.
   - The company plans a major expansion: it will acquire a site and build a large office and employees' apartments in Gujarat.

(b) When a series of details or examples gives specific information clarifying a general statement contained in the preceding independent clause.

- Mr. Bose prefers three kinds of reading material: historical novels, science fiction and technical journals.
- The secretary presented his report in four parts: background, evidence, findings, and recommendations.

2. Use a colon as a means of introducing quotations in a more formal way.

(a) When a introductory clause contains such expressions as 'the following', 'this', or a number.

- Mr. Dave made the following statement: our staff will be expanded as soon as we move into our new office.

(b) When the quotation is long or particularly significant.

- Pg.151

3. Use a colon to separate hours from minutes when times are expressed in numerals.

- 1:30 a.m.
- 6:00 p.m.
- 2:20 this afternoon

Pg.152

25.2.4 Parentheses

Parentheses occur only in pairs and enclose extra material provided for the convenience of readers. Parentheses indicate that the enclosed material is secondary or supplemental.

1. Use parentheses to set off references to related materials, as well as details or examples likely to be of concern only to certain readers.
   - Some punctuation marks (particularly comma and dash) tend to be used inaccurately.
   - Our cost-benefit ratio (see especially the data on page 123) is improving.
2. Use parentheses around figures or signs which are used to eliminate the possibility of error.
   - Place a slash (/) at the end of each line.
3. Use parentheses to enclose numbers or letters in enumerations within the text.
   - The consultant presented his report in for parts: (1) background, (2) evidence, (3) findings, and (4) recommendations.

- Ms. Nancy advanced three primary arguments for the plan: (a) reasonable cost, (b) wide public support, and (c) community benefits.

25.2.5 The Dash

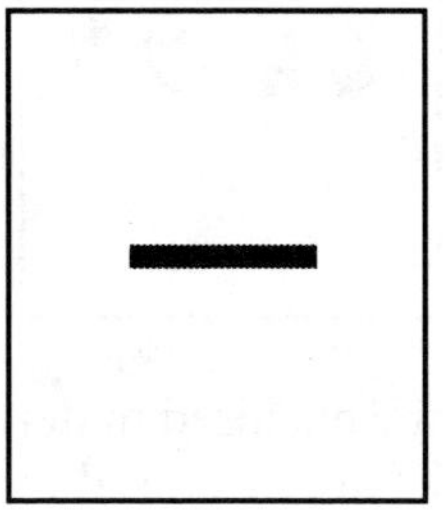

The dash can be used alone or in pairs. The dash is a substitute for certain other punctuation marks, i.e., for example, parenthesis, the comma, the colon, and the semicolon.

1. Use the dash to set off supplementary material.
   - The key element of the proposal – that all agreements should be in writing – will minimize the danger of later misunderstandings.
   - All of Juan's morning classes – Chemistry, Mathematics, and Business Communication – were cancelled because of the seminar.
2. Use the dash to mark a break in thought.
   - My colleague – you met her last week – will be going with us.
   - Ethnocentrism – being fond of your own way of life and condensing or even hostile toward other cultures – is a normal human action.
3. Use the dash as an informal substitute for a colon preceding one or more examples at the end of a sentence.
   - There are two main points to be considered – the benefits to be derived from the change and the cost of making the change.
4. Use the dash as an informal substitute for a semicolon preceding one or more examples at the end of a sentence.
   - Ms. Shalley has many skills – for example, she is an engineer as well as an MBA.
   - The consultant suggested two ideas – namely, shortening the vacation period and hiring additional employees.
5. Use the dash as an informal substitute for a period after figures or letters enumerating items in a list.
   - Here are the rules:

     1 – Complete every assignment.
     2 – Submit every assignment on time.
     3 – Prepare every assignment as accurately and neatly as possible.
6. Use a dash between a quotation and the name of the author.
   - Gladly would he learn and gladly teach. – Chaucer
   - The reward of a thing well done is to have done it. – Emerson

25.2.6 Quotation Marks

“ ”

Quotation marks tell the readers that the enclosed material was written or spoken by someone other than the writer. Quotation marks are also used to set off certain titles and cited words.

1\.
   (a) Use quotation marks to enclose every direct quotation.
   - Ms. Fletcher said, “Competition among manufacturers leads to improvements in the design and quality of products.”
   - “The development of this shopping centre,” said Mayor Kent, “will stimulate building in this area.”

   (b) With a long quotation (a quarter-page or more), omit the quotation marks but use extra spacing before and after the quotation and wider margins.
2. Use quotation marks to enclose the titles of published works.
   - Prof. Dubey’s second lecture, “New Methods in Data Processing,” will soon be published.
3. Use quotation marks as an informal substitute for italics to identify cited words and other kinds of examples.
   - The word “parallel” is frequently misspelled.

25.2.7 Italics (Underlining)

Italics

Italics in printed material correspond to underling in typed material. The main uses of italics (underlining) are to draw attention to the titles of certain publications or to words, expressions, or sentences being used in special ways.

- The *Wall Street Journal* provides the most complete stock market coverage.
- The word *misspelling* is often misspelled.
- Unnecessary repetition is called *redundancy.*

25.2.8 The Hyphen

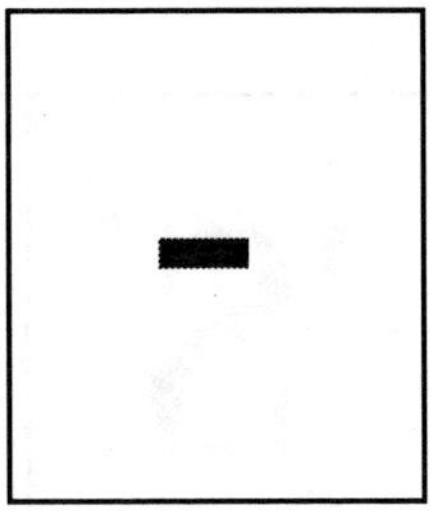

Hyphen has two main purposes: (1) to indicate the division of a word at the end of a line and (2) to join the parts of certain compound words.

- Self-made
- All-encompassing
- Vice-president
- Pre-1930
- Low-cost housing
- Up-to-date theory
- State-of-the-art
- Twenty-three employees
- A one-third state

25.2.9 The Omission Mark

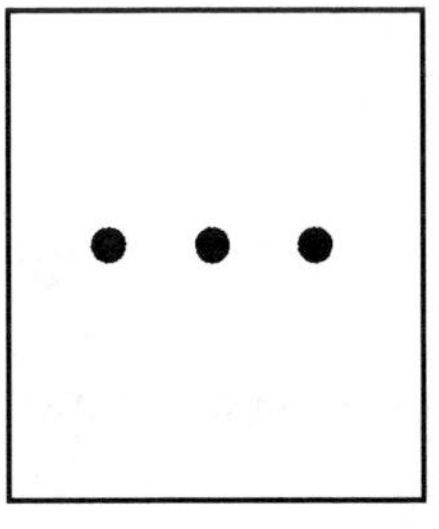

The omission mark consists of three periods ordinarily typed without spacing before, between, or after the periods. It is used to signify that words, sentences, or longer passages have been omitted from quoted material: If the omission occurs at the end of a sentence, a fourth period is added.

- The regulations contain this statement: "All persons who are using these facilities... must have had a recent medical checkup."
- The chairperson's report concluded as follows: "The public deserves the principal credit for the improvements... ."

25.2.10 The Apostrophe

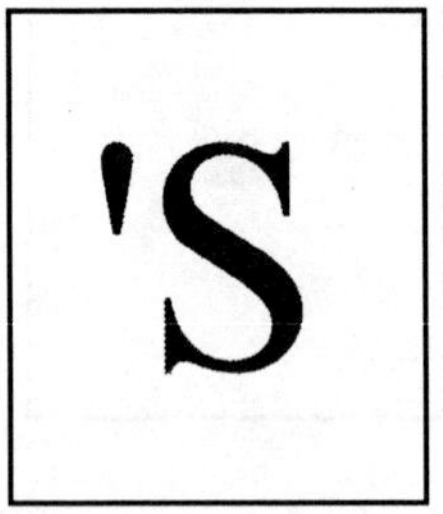

The apostrophe has three main purposes:

- To form possessive noun, for example: *Ms. Potter's house, the house of Ms. Potter.*
- In contractions, for example: *I'm, she's, you'll.*
- With the plural of abbreviations, letters, figures, signs, and cited words, for example: *M.D.'s, e's, 30's, $'s, and's.*

1. Use the apostrophe to form the possessive of nouns.
   (a) Singular noun
   - The attorney's secretary.
   - Conscience' sake
   - Ulysses' first speech
   - The class's tests

   (b) Plural nouns
   - Corporation's annual reports
   - Children's television programs
   - Men's efforts

   (c) Joint ownership
   - Stine and Woodward's stores (stores owned jointly by Stine and Woodward)

   (d) Separate ownership
   - Stine's and Woodward's stores (stores owned separately by stine and woodward)

   (e) Compound nouns
   - The daughter-in-law's encouragement
   - The editor-in-chief's decision

2. Use the apostrophe to form contractions
   - I'm I am
   - it's it is
   - don't do not
   - won't will not

   Note: Contractions may be used in informal messages, such as memorandums, sales presentations, and advertisements. However, they should be avoided in business reports, policy statements, regulations, and other more formal business messages.

3. Use the apostrophe to form the plural of abbreviations, letters, figures, signs, and cited words.
   - The 10's, 20's, and 50's have not been counted.
   - You may use *'s to indicate footnotes.
   - Too many *and's*, *but's*, and *for's* make sentences clumsy.

25.3 CAPITALIZATION IN BUSINESS WRITING

Capital letters are obvious and important features of business writing. Correct use of capitals will make it easier for readers to interpret your messages.

25.3.1 Persons, Titles and Academic degrees

1. Capitalize a person's name exactly as the person capitalizes it.
   - M. K. Srivastava
   - Pamela L. Jordan
2.
   (a) Capitalize all titles that precede a name.
   - Dr. A. K. Mathur
     Professor of English
   - Dear Dr. Holbrooke

   (b) In general, do not capitalize titles used after a person's name and a part of a proper noun. However, capitalize the official names of government departments, the titles of high-ranking officials that precede or follow a name or that stand alone, and names of legislative bills and acts.
   - Mr. Dutt, our mayor, spoke at the dinner.
   - Elizabeth II, Queen of England
   - the Secretary of State
   - the Prime Minister,
   - Dr. Rajendra Prasad, President of India
   - the Department of Inland Revenue
3. Capitalize academic degrees and their abbreviations.
   - M.D.
   - Ph.D.
   - M. B. A.

25.3.2 Nationalities, Languages, and Other Words Based on Proper Nouns

1. Capitalize all adjectives derived from the names of all countries, nationalities, races, and languages.
   - India—Indian
   - China—Chinese

- Sweden—Swedish—Swedes
- Great Britain—British—English
- America—American

2. Do not capitalize words based on proper nouns if those words have acquired specialized meanings.
   - pasteurize—based on the name Louise Pasteur
   - bycott—based on the name Charles Boycott
3. Capitalize the titles of specific courses taught in the college but not the names of general areas of study.
   - Susan's favourite subjects are history, Spanish, and social studies.
   - In his first year of university he took three subjects: Biology, Chemistry and Physics. He also had to take a foreign language.

25.3.3 Places, Organizations, and Certain Man-Made Objects

1. Capitalize the proper names of geographic areas and features, such as continents, oceans, lake, rivers, islands.
   - the Mekong Delta
   - the Sahara Desert
   - the Atlantic Ocean
   - Cameron Highlands
2. Capitalize north, south, east and west and their derivatives (e.g. northern, southwest) when they refer to sections of a country or the world. Do not capitalize these words to indicate direction only.
   - President Narayanan is going on a tour of the Far East.
   - Turn east at the next corner.
   - The West and the Northwest
3. Capitalize the proper names of towns, cities, states, nations, alliances, international organizations, and other political entities.
   - New Delhi
   - Uttar Pradesh
   - New York City
4. Capitalize the proper names of buildings, bridges, centers, airports, dams, streets, tunnels, mountains, and other special man-made product, including brand or trade names.
   - The Asoka Hotel
   - The Gandhi Memorial
   - Hoover Dam
   - Straits Times Building, Suleiman Court,
   - Indian Embassy

- Indian Airlines
- Campbell Road Police Station

5. Capitalize the proper names of churches, mosques, temples, schools, businesses, companies, agencies, and other institutions, as well as their major departments and divisions.
   - Hindu College
   - Rotary Club
   - Forge and Piston Company
   - The University of Michigan
   - Uttar Pradesh Technical University
   - Leaders of the Republican Party
6. Capitalize the proper name of a train, ship, or airplane; capitalize the proper name of a product but not a common noun referring to the product.
   - Tide detergent
   - Johnson & Johnson's Spic and Span
   - Ford Granada
   - Chevrolet automobile
   - Kellog's cereals
   - General Mill's Total
7. Capitalize the names of stars, planets, and constellations; however, the nouns *earth, sun* and *moon* are capitalized only in association with other astronomical names that are capitalized.
   - the North Star
   - the Southern Cross
   - the planet Mars and Earth

25.3.4 Calendar Terms, Holidays, Historical Periods, and Events

1. Capitalize the names of the days of the week and the months of the year, but not the names of the seasons.
   - Ruchi said, "Last year school opened on the first Monday in January."
   - The store will open on May 23, 20… .
   - Rainfall has been higher than average during this spring and summer.
2. Capitalize the names of holidays, holy days, and other special days.
   - Children's Day
   - Labour Day
   - Republic Day celebrations
   - Independence Day
   - Christmas Day
   - New Year's Day

3. Capitalize the names of historic periods and important events, but ordinarily not references to centuries. For decades, use figures.
   - the Atomic Age
   - the Industrial Age
   - the French Revolution
   - World War II
   - the twentieth century
   - the 1980's or the 1980s

25.3.5 Documents, Treaties, and Published Materials

1. Capitalize the first and all important words in the titles of charters, treatise, declarations, and other official documents.
   - in the Indian Constitution
   - by the Bill of Rights
   - from the Fourteenth Amendment
   - to the United Nations Charter
2. Capitalize the first and all important words in the titles of books, sets of books, newspapers, musical compositions, movies, and theatrical productions, as well as the titles of chapters and articles in the books and magazines.
   - the Month of Ramzan
   - The English Language Encyclopedia
   - Star Wars
   - Chapter 3, "The process of Business Communication"

25.3.6 Other Situations Calling for Capitals

1. Capitalize the first word of every new sentence.
   - Accuracy is essential in business messages.
   - You can find people in leadership roles almost everywhere you look.
2. If you wish to emphasize the separate status of an independent clause following a colon, capitalize the first word after the colon.
   - The value of advertising to the public is obvious: No one can buy a product without knowing its name.
   - Ms. Pamela's reason for joining the company is obvious: The possibilities for advancement are excellent.
3. Capitalize the first word of a direct quotation.
   - Confucius wrote: "Not to alter one's faults is to be faulty indeed."
   - Mr. Goyal insisted, "standards must be kept high in our correspondence."
4. In letters, capitalize the first word and all titles and nouns in the salutation and the first word in the complimentary close.

- Dear Ms. Helen
- Dear Dr. S.B. Bhardwaj
- Yours sincerely
- Yours faithfully

5. Capitalize the pronoun I and its contractions.
   - I, I'm, I'll, I'd, I've
   - It was I who authorized the payment.
6. Capitalize words referring to the deity, to sacred books, and to their parts.
   - Bhagwad Gita
   - the Bible
   - The Koran
   - God
   - the Creator
   - the Scriptures
7. Capitalize a noun or abbreviation designating the formal parts of a written work when the designation comes before a figure.
   - Volume III or Vol. III
   - Book X
   - Chapter 14
   - Act II, Scene 2
   - Paragraph 5
   - Section 3
   - Unit VII
8. A poet may capitalize the first word of each line of poetry if he wishes (including rhymes and limericks).
   - "Apartment house
A filing-cabinet of human lives
Where people swarm like bees in tunneled hives,
Each to his own cell in the towered comb,
Identical and cramped—we call it home."
9. Capitalize the titles of literary, musical and art works. In such titles, capitalize prepositions, conjunctions and the articles:
   - My favourite poem is Carl Sandburg's Lost, my favourite novel is Paul Gallico's Matilda, and my favourite painting is William Dobell's The Billy Boy.
   - 'Sport,
that wrinkled Care derides, And Laughter holding both his sides'—Milton
10. Capitalize initials and abbreviations of words that themselves would be capitalized if written in full.
    - P.T.A. (Parents'-Teachers' Association)

- Letterite Co. Ltd. (Company Limited)
- Capt. Ashad.

25.4 THE EXPRESSION OF NUMBERS

25.4.1 General Guidelines

1. Use words for a number that begins with a sentence. However, it is often better to revise the sentence so that the number does not come first.
   - Forty-seven reams of bond papers were ordered, or we ordered 47 reams of bond paper.
   - Rs. fifteen hundred was the cost of the book.
   - The cost of the book was Rs. 1500.
2. Use figures for numbers greater than ten, except for large round numbers.
   - The newspaper reported that 2286 people attended the rally.
   - The company has three million consumers.
   - There are nine pages of data in the proposal.
3. Use figures for all numbers used in similar constructions within a sentence.
   - The order called for 52 monitors, 52 keyboards, 100 CD boxes, and 30 pen drives.
     (a) Use words for small numbers and figures for large numbers in the same sentence if the two are used in different ways.
   - Over a period of ten years, the three investors received dividends and capital gains totaling $534,220.
     (b) If the first word is a number, it may be written out even though the other numbers appear as figures.
   - Seventy-two secretaries, 147 typists, and 23 clerks attended the session.
4. Use a comma between two unrelated numbers that stand together.
   - In 1949, 127 new automobile agencies opened in this state.
   - In 2009, 8000 students attended the college.
   - 27 secretaries are participating in the workshop.

25.4.2 Dates

1. Use figures in both of the current styles of dating: (a) when the month comes before the day and the year (July 22, 19--) and (b) when the month comes between the day and the year (22 July 19--). The same style of dating should be used throughout any message or document.
   - After October 11, 20--, our rater will increase.
   - The deadline for applications is May 7, 20--.
2. Use words (or figures with d, st, or th) for the day when it occurs alone and when the month is expressed in a prepositional phrase.
   - On the eleventh of October, the conference will begin.

- On the 11th of October, the conference will begin.

3. Use words for references to centuries and for decades when the century is omitted. Use figures for decades when the century is given.
   - Nineteenth century
   - During the twenties

25.4.3 Addresses

Express house numbers in figures, except for the number one.

- 2734 MacArthur Street
- 9 Wilson Lane
- 246 Nehru Road
- 9 Firozshah Road
- One Park Avenue

25.4.4 Amounts of Money

1. Use figures for sums of money (whether in dollars or foreign denominations).
   - The total cost came to Rs. 10,896.98.
   - She spent Rs. 1248 for groceries.
2. Use words to express small sums of money used as adjectives.
   - Marvin has a five rupees pen.
   - There is a 3-dollar parking fee.

25.5 FRACTIONS, DECIMALS, AND PERCENTAGES

1. Use words for simple fractions. Use a hyphen between the parts of a fraction if the fraction is used as an objective. Otherwise, omit the hyphen.
   - Ms. Geeta gives one tenth of her income to charities.
   - We collected two thirds of the money.
   - Dr. Shuman receives a three-eighths of share of the state.
2. Use figures for mixed fractions and decimals.
   - The length of the garage is 20 ¾ feet.
   - The length of the garage is 20.75 feet.
   - The answer to the problem is 0.552.
3. Use figures plus the word percent for percentages. (However, use the symbol % in statistical copy.)
   - Almost 90 per cent of the loan has been repaid.
   - The interest rate will be 8.5 per cent a year.

25.5.1 Quantities and Measurements

1. Use figures to express exact age.
   - Amanda Kiminski is 15 years and 7 months old.
   - I think he is about thirty years old.
2. Use figures for measurements, weights, distances. Note: Only in technical writing *x* is substituted for *by* in giving dimensions.
   - The brochure is 8 ½-by-11 inches.
   - It is 450 miles to Lucknow.
3. Use figures and the degree sign to express temperature, and indicate the scale you are using.
   - The temperature is 20° Celsius.
4. Except in combination with the word o'clock, use figures with the designations a.m., p.m., m. (=noon), or other modifiers, to express time.
   - 6:30 a.m.
   - 12:00 p.m. (=midnight)
   - 7:15 at night
   - 9:45 in the morning
   - Three o'clock

25.5.2 Book Divisions and Official Titles or Designations

1. Use figures for page numbers of books. Usually, capitalized Roman numerals are used for major divisions and Arabic numerals for minor divisions.
   - The test will cover all of Division II.
   - The definition is given in Chapter 6, page 251.
2. In general, use words for numbers in official titles or designations. However, always follow the official style of the particular organization.
   - Fifth Ward
   - Third Naval District

APPENDICES

1
GUIDELINES FOR TYPING BUSINESS LETTERS

In business communication, your aim should be to produce the most effective letters possible. In a message produced by a skilful business staff, the following qualities stand out:

1. Attractive design
2. Thoughtful content and organization
3. Accurate use of language and punctuation

When typing a business letter, plan a layout that has a balanced look. Visualize the appearance of each page, paying particular attention to the balance between white space and typed matter.

The following commonly used guidelines provide straightforward answers to the most frequently asked questions about the preparation of business letters.

- If a company has an official format for its correspondence, follow that format in every detail. Use letterhead for only the first page of the letter.
- Select margins appropriate for the length of the letter, so that each page will have an attractive, balanced appearance. Usually, the side margins are approximately equal, and the bottom margin is somewhat larger.
- Position the dateline according to the letter style and letterhead. Begin the dateline in one of the following positions: (a) at the left margin – block style, (b) at the horizontal centre of the page – modified block style, or (c) at a point which will make the dateline end at the right margin – modified block style. Allow some space between the letterhead and the dateline if the letter is brief and a better balanced page results.
- Spell out the names of months, both in the dateline and in the body of the message.
- Do not use *d, st,* and *th* after the number of the day in the dateline. Use such forms (or words) for the day in the body of the message only if you omit the name of the month.
- Use a comma between the day of the month and the year in the dateline and in the body of the message.
- Omit punctuation after the year in a dateline.

- Type the inside address in block form on the fourth line below the dateline, beginning at the left margin.
- Make the lines of the address as equal in length as possible. In order to do so, place the addressee's title in one of the following positions: (a) on the same line as the addressee's name, (b) on the next line, preceding the company name, or (c) on a separate line between the addressee's name and the company name.
- In the addressee's name and the title or title and company name appear on the same line, use a comma to separate the two elements.
- In the inside address, type the addressee's name exactly as that person types it. Capitalize the important words in titles and in the names of departments and divisions of a company.
- Omit end-of-line punctuation in the inside address, except for a period after an appropriate abbreviation.
- Type the company's name exactly as it appears on the company's letterhead.
- In a company name, use the abbreviations *Inc.* for *Incorporated and Ltd.* for *Limited* if the company does so, and use a comma before these words and abbreviations if the company does so.
- Type the ZIP/PIN code one space after the state designation, without punctuation between them. Type the inside address and the envelope address in exactly the same style.
- Include the attention line only if you address the message to the company, using a situation such as *Dear Sir or Madam.* Use no punctuation after the attention line. Place the attention line on the second line below the last line of the inside address, beginning at the left margin.
- Types of salutation on the second line below the last line of the inside address (or the attention line), beginning at the left margin. Capitalize the first word as well as names and titles.
- If you address a letter to a company rather than to a person by name, use one of the following modern salutations: *Ladies and Gentlemen* or *Dear Sir* or *Madam.* These salutations are proper because in the modern world of business, both men and women hold decision-making positions.
- Use a colon after the salutation if you are using mixed punctuation (with Modified Block Style). Omit the colon if you are using open punctuation (with Block Style Or Modified Block Style).
- Begin the first line of the body of the message on the second line below the salutation, either at the left margin (Block Style or Modified Block Style) or with an indentation of five to ten spaces (Modified Block Style).
- Begin each new paragraph on the second line below the last line of the preceding paragraph.
- Maintain as even a right margin as possible. To do so, you will have to hyphenate words occasionally.
- A dash or hyphen should always be typed at the end of a line, never at the beginning of the next line.

- Use commas to separate three or more elements in a series.
- Use a colon (or, informally, a dash) to introduce an enumeration. Use a colon to introduce a quotation formally; use a comma to introduce a quotation informally.
- Type the complementary close on the second line below the last line of the body. The placement of the dateline and the complementary close should correspond; that is, both should begin or end at the same horizontal point.
- Type the name and official title of the originator on the fourth line below the preceding line. However, to lengthen a short letter for better appearance, allow up to six blank lines above the typed name. Align the name and the title with the complementary close. The title of the originator may be typed on the next line below the name of the originator.
- Type the typist's reference initials (in lowercase letters) on the second line below the title (or name and title) at the left margin.
- If you are enclosing any material with the letter, type the word *Enclosure* on the second line below the signature identification and the left margin. Indicate more than one enclosure by adding the appropriate figure after the word *Enclosures.*
- If copies are being sent to others, type *Copy to, Copies to*, or *cc* followed by the name or names of those receiving copies of the letter.

LAYOUT OF A BUSINESS LETTER

As computer literacy has gripped the world, according to the latest format of letter writing (formal or informal) every detail begins very close to the margin i.e., to the left. Do not write 'To', 'From', 'Date', etc. as they may undermine the sensibility of the reader.

Vimal Kumar Kaushik

Regional Sales Manager
The Hindustan Watch Company
36, Munirka
Mumbai-1

29.1.20...........

Mr. Ashutosh Sinha
Manager (Purchase)
A.B.C. Co. Ltd.
24, South Patel Nagar
New Delhi-8
Dear Sir

Sub: ....

Ref:..

Body (para1)..
....
....
(para2) ....
....
....
(para3) ....
....
....
Yours faithfully

(Signature)

(Vimal Kumar)

2

FOREIGN WORDS AND PHRASES USED IN BUSINESS COMMUNICATION

Nowadays, with the emergence of multinational companies, foreign words and phrases have become part and parcel of English speech and writing. It is necessary, therefore, to be acquainted with them so that if you come across them anywhere, you may not have any difficulty in understanding their meaning.

As a general rule, one should avoid using words and phrases of foreign origin in order to bring clarity in writing. The words and phrases given below are mostly of Latin and French origin.

- ab initio — From the beginning
- addenda — List of additions, to a book, report etc.
- Ad hoc — For a particular purpose
- Ad valorem — According to value
- Ad infinitum — Endlessly
- Apropos — Connected with, relevant to
- Bona fide — Genuine or real
- Bizarre — Whimsically add or unusual
- Corrigenda — A list of errors
- De facto — Actual, even though not planned or intended
- De jure — By right
- Detente — A state of friendly relations
- Elite — A group of the most powerful or talented people
- Entrepreneur — A person who sets up business
- En masse — As a group
- Esprit de corps — Feeling of loyalty shared by members of a group
- Bon-homie — Easy friendliness
- Ex officio — Because of one's position
- Ex parte — One sided

• Faux pas	A mistake or socially embarrassing action
• In memoriam	In memory of
• In toto	Totally, as a whole
• Ipso facto	By the fact itself
• Inter alia	Among other things
• Locus standi	Right to reference
• Mala fide	In bad faith
• Modus operandi	A particular way of doing something, especially criminal's way of committing a crime
• Par excellence	Pre-eminently
• Per se	By itself
• Post mortem	Examination after death
• Prima facie	On first consideration
• Pro rata	According to rate or proportion
• Per capita	Per head
• Per annum	Per year
• Nouveau riche	A person with new wealth, not modest in spending it
• Millenium	A period of 1000 years
• Resume	Curriculum vitae
• Sine die	Without fixing a date
• Status quo	Existing state of affairs
• Sub judice	Being considered in law
• In camera	In secret
• Ultra vires	Beyond legal powers
• Verbatim	Word by word
• Vice versa	In the opposite way
• Vis-a-vis	When compared to
• Viva voice	By means of speaking
• Via media	A means to carry a point
• Magnum opus	Greatest work
• Incognito	Hiding one's identity
• Ditto	The same
• Cliche	Worn out expression or idea
• Proviso	Requirement, clause modifying a contact
• Infra dig	Below one's dignity
• Infrastructure	The system supporting the operation of an organization
• Ex gratia	Payment made as a favour
• Communique	Official report
• En route	On the way

- Rapport — Close agreement and understanding
- Lingua franca — Any language widely used as a means of communication among speakers of other languages
- Volte face — A change to a completely different position
- Finesse — Delicate skill in guiding relations between people
- Decor — Style of decoration

3

IDIOMATIC EXPRESSIONS WITH PREPOSITIONS

Below is a list of the "Idiomatic Use of Prepositions." It is impossible to list all of the prepositional combinations, but several of the most troublesome are given below. When in doubt about the appropriate preposition for a particular word or expression, consult a dictionary.

- **a need for:** All babies have a need for constant attention.
- **abide by:** I promise to abide by your decision.
- **abstain from:** If you do not know anything about the candidates, abstain from voting.
- **accord with:** The two rival companies finally reached accord with each other.
- **according to:** According to my grammar teacher, *whom* is never a subject.
- **accuse of:** Tim has been accused of stealing watermelons.
- **accustomed to:** I am not accustomed to this kind of weather.
- **acquiesce in:** I did not acquiesce in the unjustified suppression of evidence.
- **acquitted of:** The accused man was finally acquitted of the crime.
- **adapted for:** This program is especially adapted for television. (prepared for)
- **adapted to:** I have not adapted to this climate. (become accustomed to)
- **adhere to:** You must adhere to the contract you signed.
- **admit of:** This document admits of conflicting interpretations. (to give the possibility of something)
- **admit to:** He admitted to his part in the robbery. (to confess or tell the truth about)
- **adverse to:** The decision of the court is adverse to our interests.
- **agree on/upon:** The committee members could not agree on a course of action. (to decide on; to have the same opinion about)
- **agree to:** We will agree to your proposal if you postpone action. (to promise to follow something)
- **agree with:** In all matters of importance, I promise to agree with you. (to have the same opinion about)

- **aim to prove:** I aim to prove that your accusation is unjust.
- **alarmed at:** Beach residents are alarmed at the news of the hurricane's approach.
- **amazed at *or* by:** I am amazed at your audacity.
- **amendment to:** The first amendment to the Constitution guarantees the freedom of the press.
- **annoyed at:** The clerk was very annoyed at the customer's condescending tone. (not annoyed *with*)
- **answerable to:** You are answerable to your supervisor.
- **apologize for:** You should apologize for starting the erroneous rumour. (apologize *for* doing something)
- **apologize to:** He apologized to me for that rude remark. (apologize *to* a person)
- **as far as:** As far as that goes, I've never seen him before in my life.
- **angry about:** I was angry about the missing jewels. (angry *about*, not angry *at*, a fact or situation)
- **angry with:** I get the impression that you are angry with me. (angry *with* a person)
- **aspire to:** He is a quiet man who does not aspire to distinction.
- **as regards:** As regards the subject of capital punishment, I am against it.
- **assent to:** Please remember that I did not assent to your proposal.
- **attend to:** We must stop talking and attend to the business at hand.
- **avail oneself of:** One should avail oneself of every opportunity to learn something new.
- **blames him for it:** As witness to the accident, I cannot blame him for it.
- **can't help feeling:** I can't help feeling guilty about not going last night. (NOT can't help but)
- **capable of:** I wonder if Jim is capable of rational thinking.
- **censorship of:** Does he believe in the censorship of books?
- **charge with:** The police are going to charge him with assault and battery.
- **coincide with:** Mark Twain's death coincided with the appearance of Halley's comet.
- **collide with:** Drive carefully or you might collide with another car.
- **compare to:** use compare *to* for similarities.
- **compare with:** use compare *with* to show differences or similarities.
- **compatible with:** His actions are not compatible with our standards of conduct.
- **comply with:** I shall make every effort to comply with your request.
- **concern about:** I am concerned about your poor eating habits. (to give attention or worry to)
- **concern with:** I am rather concerned with the publication of this book. (to busy oneself; to take interest or part in something)
- **conclude from:** He concluded from her expression that his mother was not happy.
- **concur with:** I concur with you in your estimate of the damage.
- **confer with . . . about:** The supervisor conferred with the committee about the proposal.
- **confide in:** Please feel free to confide in me when you have a problem.

- **confide (something) to:** He did not confide his problem to me.
- **conform to:** The new building must conform to the specifications of the building code.
- **consist of:** His diet consisted of potato chips, pretzels and soda.
- **consistent with:** My actions were consistent with your recommendations.
- **convince (someone) of:** It is often difficult to convince him of anything.
- **critical of:** She is very critical of my efforts.
- **deficient in:** The food is good, but it is deficient in vitamins.
- **deprive of:** Because of poor grades, Sue will be deprived of all privileges.
- **derived from:** Resin is derived from the pine tree.
- **die of/or from:** Many people die from heart attacks, but many others die of old age.
- **differ with:** He differs with me on every issue.
- **different from:** Every person is different from every other person.
- **disappointed in:** I was disappointed in the performance of our glee club.
- **disaprove of:** I disapprove of your choice of words.
- **dissent from:** Frequently one court justice will dissent from the majority opinion.
- **dissuade from:** I will certainly try to dissuade you from doing something foolish.
- **divest of:** The governor has decided to divest the sheriff of all responsibility.
- **doubt that:** I doubt that he even noticed our absence.
- **eager to:** He was eager to start the trip.
- **engrossed in:** The little boy was engrossed in the monster movie.
- **enter into:** We entered into a lengthy political discussion.
- **emphasis on:** Try to put the emphasis on the positive points.
- **familiar to:** Your face is not familiar to me. (familiar *to* someone)
- **familiar with:** I am familiar with the campaign issues. (familiar *with* something)
- **find fault with:** Lately you seem to find fault with everything I do.
- **free from:** They are never entirely free from doubt and fear.
- **graduated from:** Every one of the ten children graduated from college.
- **identical with:** Try to find a costume identical with mine.
- **ignorant of:** He was arrested because he was ignorant of the law.
- **impervious to:** He is impervious to subtle reminders.
- **importance of:** Don't you understand the importance of being on time?
- **impressed with:** She was not impressed with his efforts to get her attention.
- **in accordance with:** In accordance with your request, I have the book with me.
- **in need of:** He is in need of transportation.
- **in proportion to:** Price increases in proportion to demand.
- **in search of:** The immigrants who came to America in the nineteenth century were in search of a better way of life.
- **inconsistent with:** His latest business deal was inconsistent with his usual code of ethics.
- **independent of:** They decided to proceed, independent of outside help.

- **indifferent to:** Some people seem indifferent to heat, cold, and pain.
- **infer from:** I infer from your remark that you have never been here before.
- **infected with:** Mr Jones is infected with AIDS.
- **inferior to:** This new car is inferior to last year's model.
- **in search of:** John spent many heartbreaking years in search of success.
- **insist on:** Newspaper editors should insist on accuracy in reporting.
- **interfere with:** Police promised not to interfere with the demonstration.
- **interfere in:** You should not interfere in your neighbour's affairs.
- **jealous of:** That man is jealous of every man who speaks to his wife.
- **kind of:** I have never liked that kind of jelly. (*kind of = type of*)
- **long for:** Every man longs for some type of recognition in life.
- **married to:** He is married to a millionaire.
- **necessity for:** The necessity for action is clearly understated.
- **object to:** I do not object to your going with us.
- **obliged to (+ verb):** He felt obliged to say something nice to her.
- **oblivious of:** She was oblivious of everything around her.
- **overcome by:** She was overcome by his statement. (overcome *by* a fact)
- **overcome with:** She was overcome with joy when her grandchild was born. (overcome *with* an emotion)
- **part with:** I cannot bear to part with any of my books.
- **partial to:** You seem to be partial to the color blue.
- **participate in:** Freshers are not permitted to participate in some activities.
- **persevere in:** He was tired, but he continued to persevere in his effort to win.
- **persist in:** If you persist in bothering your sister, she may kick you.
- **pertain to:** Your comment does not pertain to the subject we are discussing.
- **pleased with:** I am pleased with your suggestion.
- **preferable to:** Even a simple game is preferable to inactivity.
- **prevail on:** Perhaps you can prevail on your father to take your friend to the race.
- **prevent someone from:** Try to prevent them from leaving today.
- **prior to:** Prior to leaving for the beach, Cindy gathered her towel and sunscreen. (*prior to = before*)
- **provide for:** Be sure to provide for all possible emergencies.
- **provide someone with:** He did not provide me with enough money for the trip.
- **reason with . . . on:** Try to reason with your mother on the issue. (reason *with* someone *on* an issue)
- **refrain from:** Everyone should refrain from repeating malicious gossip.
- **regardless of:** Regardless of your desire to have your test score immediately, your score will not be ready till tomorrow.
- **rejoice at:** The whole country rejoiced at the news of the prince's marriage.

- **required of:** An oath of allegiance is required of all members.
- **replace with:** We will need to replace these curtains with blinds.
- **responsible to . . . for:** I am responsible to your mother for your safety. (responsible *to* someone *for* something)
- **result in:** Tardiness may result in suspension. (a cause *results in* an effect)
- **result from:** Obesity may result from overeating and lack of exercise. (an effect *results from* a cause)
- **rich in:** This country is rich in many natural resources.
- **short of:** Just before payday, we are all a little short of cash.
- **secede from:** I hope that no state will ever secede from the Union again.
- **similar to:** Your taste in clothes is similiar to mine.
- **speak to . . . about:** I must speak to you about your grades. (speak *to* someone *about* something)
- **substitute for:** This class may substitute for your thesis.
- **succeed in:** The prisoner did not succeed in his attempt to escape. (not succeed *at*)
- **superior to:** A pipe organ is superior to an electronic organ.
- **surprised at:** I am surprised at your sudden interest in chemistry. (not surprised *with*)
- **take charge of:** You must take charge of your own affairs
- **transfer to/onto:** Transfer your answers onto your answer sheet.
- **threatened with:** His actions have been so obnoxious that he has been threatened with legal action.
- **unmindful of:** The children raced down the beach, unmindful of my warning.
- **wait for:** Let's just sit quietly and wait for developments.
- **wait on:** We left the restaurant because we could not get anyone to wait on us.
- **worthy of:** This paper is worthy of a passing grade.

4
CONFUSABLES

This section contains some of the commonest groups of words that are sometimes confused. It does not include words that are confused because of their spelling (like 'curb' and 'kerb').

- **Ability/Capacity**
  Ability is a skill that you have gained, through practice, study, or in some other way. Capacity refers to talent you were born with.
- **Abnormal/Subnormal**
  If something is abnormal it is outside the range of normal events. If a thing is subnormal it is below the normal level. If a person is of subnormal intelligence his intelligence is below the average; if he is abnormally intelligent, his intelligence is extraordinary (usually extraordinarily high).
- **Actuate/Activate**
  If something actuates you it provides you with your drive or motivation. To activate something is to make it active.
- **Adduce/Deduce**
  If you are making a case, or presenting an argument, you can adduce evidence to support it. When you read or hear something you may use reasoning to deduce other information or ideas from it.
- **Adherence/Adhesion**
  Adherence means holding to or supporting a belief or opinion. Adhesion refers to the physical sticking of one thing to another.
- **Affect/Effect**
  If something affects you, it has an effect on you. To effect something, on the other hand, is to make it happen.
- **Affront/Effrontery**
  An affront is an insult. Effrontery is impudence.

- **Amoral/Immoral**

  If someone or something is amoral, they are without a set of moral values. If a person or action is immoral, then they are breaking the moral code.
- **Apprehend/Comprehend**

  If you apprehend an idea you have grasped it in your mind. This meaning is also carried by comprehend with the added meaning of 'understand'.
- **Astrology/Astronomy**

  Astronomy is the scientific study of heavenly bodies. Astrology uses the stars to foretell people's futures.
- **Bail/Bale**

  Bails are used in cricket, and someone who is arrested by the police is often allowed to go home on bail. A bale is a bundle of something, such a straw or paper.
- **Bathos/Pathos**

  Bathos means 'anti-climax'. If something has pathos it inspires pity.
- **Between/Among/Through**

  'Between' means to refer to something that stands or moves with things on either side of it. 'Among' implies that something is in or moves through the middle of a group of scattered items. 'Through' implies a movement which actually enters something and exits from it.
- **Capital/Corporal**

  Capital punishment is the death penalty; corporal punishment means physical punishment, such as beating.
- **Childish/Childlike**

  'Childlike' is an emotionally neutral term, implying neither praise nor blame. 'Childish, on the other hand, implies that the person concerned was old enough to have known better.
- **Climactic/Climatic/Climacteric**

  'Climactic' is the adjective that comes from 'climax', while climatic comes from 'climate'. 'Climacteric' is a noun and an adjective referring to critical point or stage in a person's life.
- **Collage/Montage**

  Anything which involves superimposing two or more items on top of each other to a composite whole can be called a montage – whether the things are physical, like photographs, or computer images. If the things superimposed are stuck onto a base with glue, then the whole is properly a collage, from the French for 'glue'.
- **Commissionaire/Commissioner**

  A commissioner is a person who has been made a member or head of a team who have been assigned a particular duty. A commissionaire is a uniformed doorman.
- **Complaisant/Complacent**

  A complacent person is self-satisfied. If someone is complaisant he accepts a situation and is willing to go along with it. Complaisant lover is aware of being two-timed, and condones.

- **Compliment/ Complement/Complimentary**

  If you pay someone a compliment, you commend him on something. A complement is what makes something complete, so a ship's complement is its crew. If something is described in a sales catalogue as 'complimentary'. It means that it is free.

- **Compose/Compile**

  To compose a letter or piece of music means to make it up. To compile a list, for example, is to bring together the different elements required for a particular purpose.

- **Comprise/Consist/Compose**

  'Comprise' is a straightforward verb taking an object. 'Consist' and 'Compose' are the verbs normally followed by a preposition.

- **Compulsive/Compulsory**

  If an activity is compulsive, you may find it difficult or impossible to give it up. If an activity is compulsory, then you are obliged by law or by some other external authority to do it.

- **Consistently/Persistently**

  'Consistently' merely records the facts; 'persistently' states or implies that the repetition is deliberate.

- **Contagious/Infectious**

  If a disease is contagious, it is transmitted by physical contact. An infectious disease can be communicated through bacteria in the air or in water.

- **Contiguous/Contagious**

  A contagious disease is one spread by physical contact. If two objects are contiguous they are touching.

- **Continual/Continuous**

  Something that is continuous goes on without interruption. If it is continual it keeps on happening.

- **Councillor/Counsellor**

  A councillor is a member of a council; a counsellor is someone who provides advice.

- **Credence/Credibility**

  If you believe something to be true you can be said to give it credence. The features that make something believable give it credence. The features that make something believable give it credibility.

- **Credible/Credulous**

  Something that is credible is believable. A person who is credulous is willing to believe things.

- **Deceitful/Deceptive**

  People are deceitful when they set out to deceive (and they perform deceitful actions). Something that is deceptive can easily deceive you, but there isn't necessarily any intention involved.

- **Defective/Deficient**

  Something that is defective has got something wrong with it. Something that is deficient is lacking something.

- **Delusion/Illusion**

  An illusion is either already known to be false or will be at some point be thus known in the future. A delusion is an illusion that someone holds to in the face of all reason.

- **Deprecate/Depreciate**

  If you deprecate something you show disapproval of it. If something depreciates its value falls.

- **Discreet/Discrete**

  Discreet is used to refer to a person who can keep a secret. Discrete means separate and distinct.

- **Discrepancy/Disparity**

  Disparity means inequality between two things. Discrepancy means that something which occurs in one and should also occur in the other, doesn't.

- **Dispose of/Dispense with**

  If you dispose of something, you throw it away; if you dispense with it, you do without it.

- **Dominate/Domineer**

  Both words mean to be in control of or to have considerable power over people and situations. Dominate is neutral in tone, however, whereas domineer is critical and implies that the person involved is behaving like a tyrant.

- **Effective/Effectual/Efficient/Efficacious**

  If something is effective it has the desired effect. The same can be said of people. Effectual applies to actions not to people and means 'having the effect of'. Something is efficient if it achieves results promptly and economically, and the adjectives can also be applied to people. Only things can be efficacious—when they have the desired effect.

- **Emigrant/Immigrant/Migrant**

  Migrants are people or other creatures that move from one territory to another. Immigrants are those coming into a territory; emigrants are those departing from a territory.

- **Empathy/Sympathy**

  If you have sympathy for someone, then you have fellow-feeling for them. Empathy is the ability to imagine yourself in their position.

- **Endemic/Epidemic/Pandemic**

  All refer to diseases. If a disease is endemic it is common in an area or population and people are likely to be exposed to it. An epidemic refers to a widespread occurrence of a disease in a region. A pandemic is an epidemic that is even more widespread.

- **Envy/Envious/Jealousy/Jealous**

  Envy is a longing for something that belongs to someone else. Jealousy is the consuming emotion that you do not trust another person to be faithful to you. It can also mean that you are determined to guard your own belongings or rights.

- **Equable/Equitable**

  An equable person is easy going; an equitable settlement is fair to both sides.

- **Expedient/Expeditious**
  If a thing is expedient it is convenient or advantageous; if it is expeditious it is speedy.
- **Explicit/Implicit**
  Explicit means stated directly; implicit means stated indirectly.
- **Factious/Fractious**
  A group that is factious is likely to split into smaller groups; a person or a group that is fractious is argumentative or quarrelsome.
- **Factitious/Fictitious**
  While factitious means artificially achieved, fictitious means invented.
- **Fewer/Less/Fewest/Least**
  Few, fewer, and fewest should be used with nouns that can have a plural ('countable' or 'count' nouns). Less and least should be used with nouns that cannot be counted ('uncountable' or 'non-count' nouns).
- **Flaunt/Flout**
  To flaunt something is to show it off in a shameless or outrageous way. To flout is deliberately to ignore a rule or accepted standard.
- **Gesticulate/Gesture**
  A person who gesticulates waves their arms about, probably fairly wildly. A gesture is a more restrained action, usually with a meaning.
- **Glance/Glimpse**
  To glance is to take quick look. To glimpse is to get a brief sight of something.
- **Graceful/Gracious**
  Graceful describes a person's attractive bearing and ease of movement. Gracious implies kindness or courtesy from a superior, and can sound condescending.
- **Illegible/Unreadable**
  If something is illegible, it is impossible to read because it is badly written or printed. If a text is unreadable, readers give up, because it is not to their taste, is badly composed, is too difficult to understand, or for some other reason.
- **Imply/Infer**
  If you imply something, you hint at it through the words you use, without stating it directly. Your audience can then infer it from your words.
- **Inapt/Inept**
  Both words derive from the word apt. Inapt has the sense of 'inappropriate, unsuitable'. Inept means 'foolish, ineffectual'.
- **Ingenious/Ingenuous**
  Someone or something that is ingenious is clever, possibly in a fairly intricate way. Someone who is ingenuous, on the other hand, is naïve.
- **Into/In to**
  Into indicates 'the intention of being inside': 'They drove into the town.' Separated as in to, the word to indicates the purpose of going in: 'The parent came in to see the headmaster.'

- **Intolerable/Intolerant**

  Intolerable means 'unbearable', 'impossible to put up with'. 'Intolerant' means 'unable to tolerate' and so possibly 'narrow-minded'.

- **Judicial/Judicious**

  Judicial applies to the administration of justice, the judicial process through courts of law. 'Judicious' means 'of sound judgment, sensible, discreet'.

- **Lawful/Legal/Legitimate/Licit**

  All four mean 'permitted by law' with different shades of meaning. Lawful indicates 'entitlement' and therefore 'rightful' will often express the meaning. Legal has the force of 'the law of the land' and also 'connected with the law' and in 'the legal profession'. Legitimate means 'sanctioned by legal authority' and is applied particularly to children born to a married couple. Licit, which is rarely used, means 'not forbidden by law', 'permissible'. Its opposite, illicit, is far more common.

- **Legible/Readable**

  Legible applies to writing or print which is physically capable of being read. Readable applies to a text which can be read with some enjoyment.

- **Libel/Slander**

  Both words refer to defaming a person's character. Libel is written, or published in some other form; slander is spoken.

- **Loathe/Loath/Loth**

  To loathe something is to hate it. Loath and loth are different spellings of the same adjective expressing reluctance.

- **Meantime/Meanwhile**

  The word conveys the same meaning, although meantime is commonly used as a noun and meanwhile as an adverb.

- **Momentary/Momentous**

  Momentary is 'lasting only a moment', 'brief'. Momentous is 'of great significance'.

- **Passed/Past**

  Passed is the past tense and past participle of the verb 'to pass'. 'We passed their house yesterday. We have passed it several times'. Past has several functions:

  Adjective: During the past year

  Adverb: The seagull glided past.

  Noun: Let us put the past behind us.

  Preposition: We drove past their house.

- **Perpetrate/Perpetuate**

  Perpetrate means 'to commit (something bad). Perpetrator is often used to mean 'criminal'. To perpetuate is to cause something to continue.

- **Perquisite/Prerequisite**

  Informally shortened to 'perk', a perquisite is an extra benefit attached to some jobs. A prerequisite is a condition which must be satisfied in advance.

- **Precede/Proceed**

  Precede means to go first, to go in front. Proceed means to go further, to carry on, to continue.

- **Precipitate/Precipitous**

  A precipitate action would be sudden and possibly ill-advised. Precipitous means very steep.

- **Prescribe/Proscribe**

  Prescribe is to recommend, to advise or specify. Proscribe is to advise against, to prohibit.

- **Prevaricate/Procrastinate**

  To prevaricate is to speak evasively and deceitfully. To procrastinate is to delay.

- **Principal/Principle**

  As an adjective principal means 'main' or 'chief'. As a noun it may mean the person at the head of an institution—the principal of the college. Principle means personal code of conduct.

- **Psychiatry/Psychology**

  Psychiatry is the treatment of mental disorders. Psychology is the study of the mind.

- **Rare/Scarce**

  Rare means 'uncommon', 'seldom seen'. Rare can also carry the sense of 'valuable'. Scarce indicates a shortage of a particular commodity which may be plentiful elsewhere.

- **Remittance/Remission/Remittal/Remit**

  Remittance means payment which is to be sent for goods ordered. Remission provides relief from pain or disease, or from the guilt of sins. Remittal is a legal term meaning the removal of a case to another court of justice. Remit is the verb for all the preceding meanings. The word remit is also used as a noun to mean 'area of responsibility'.

- **Temerity/Timidity**

  Temerity means boldness and daring. Timidity applies to someone who is anxious, hesitant, and fearful.

- **Unconscious/Subconscious**

  The subconscious is that part of the mind which lies just below the surface, or whose workings we are from time to time partially aware. The unconscious is deeper below the surface and we are never directly aware of it.

- **Uneatable/Inedible**

  If you find something uneatable, you think that it is not palatable to eat; if it is inedible it is impossible to eat it without great difficulty or even harm.

- **Venal/Venial**

  Venal means 'capable of being bought' and is now commonly applied to officials in positions which should have been conferred for merit and not for favours or money. Venial means pardonable, and is applied to an error or fault which can be excused or overlooked.

5

COMMONLY MISSPELLED WORDS

Below is a list of commonly misspelled words. Use this list to help you avoid common spelling mistakes when writing letters and documents.

A lot
Absence
Abundance
Acceptable
Accessible
Accidentally
Acclaim
Accommodate
Accomplish
Accordion
Accumulate
Achievement
Acquaintance
Acquire/Descend
Acquitted
Across
Advertisement
Aggravate
Alleged
Amateur
Analysis
Analyze
Annoy
Annual
Apparatus
Apparent
Appearance
Arctic
Arithmetic
Ascend
Atheist
Attendance
Auxiliary
Balloon
Barbecue
Barbiturate
Bargain
Basically
Battalion
Beginning
Benefited
Biscuit
Boundary
Bourgeois
Britain
Business
Calendar
Camouflage
Cantaloupe
Category
Cemetery
Changeable
Characteristic
Chauffeur
Chief
Cigarette
Collectible
Colonel
Colossal
Commitment
Committee
Comparative
Competent
Completely
Concede
Conceivable
Condemn
Condescend
Conscience
Conscientious
Conscious
Consensus
Consistent
Continuous
Controversial
Controversy
Convenient
Correlate
Correspondence
Counselor
Criticize
Deceive
Defendant
Deferred
Definitely
Dependent
Desperate
Development
Develop
Dilemma
Disappearance
Disappoint

Discipline
Dispensable
Dissatisfied
Dominant
Dormitory
Drawer
Ecstasy
Eighth
Eligible
Eliminate
Embarrass
Eminent
Endeavour
Entirely
Equipped
Equivalent
Exaggerate
Excellence
Exhaust
Exhilarate
Existence
Expense
Experience
Experiment
Explanation
Exuberance
Fahrenheit
Familiar
Fascinate
Feasible
Fictitious
Financially
Fluorescent
Forcibly
Foreign
Foresee
Forty

Fulfill
Gauge
Government
Grammar
Guarantee
Guerrilla
Handkerchief
Harass
Hemorrhage
Heroes
Hoarse
Hypocrisy
Hypocrite
Ideally
Idiosyncrasy
Ignorance
Immediately
Incredible
Independence
Indicted
Indispensable
Inevitable
Insurance
Intellectual
Intelligence
Interesting
Interference
Interrupt
Irrelevant
Irresistible
Irritate
Jealousy
Judgment
Knowledge
Laboratory
Legitimate
Length

Liaison
License
Lieutenant
Maintenance
Manageable
Maneuver
Manufacture
Mathematics
Millennium
Millionaire
Miniature
Mischievous
Misspell
Mortgage
Narrative
Nauseous
Necessary
Ninety
Noticeable
Nuisance
Obedience
Obstacle
Occurred
Occurrence
Official
Opponent
Opportunity
Ordinarily
Origin
Panicky
Parallel
Paralysis
Paralyze
Particular
Particularly
Pastime
Peculiar

Permissible
Perseverance
Persistence
Personnel
Perspiration
Picnicking
Pilgrimage
Playwright
Pleasant
Possession
Possibility
Potato
Practically
Precede
Precedence
Preference
Preferred
Prejudice
Preparation
Prescription
Prevalent
Primitive
Principal
Principle
Privilege
Probably
Proceed
Profession
Professional
Prominent
Pronunciation
Propaganda
Psychology
Publicly
Quarantine
Questionnaire
Realistically

Recede
Receipt
Receive
Recommend
Reference
Referring
Relevant
Remembrance
Repetition
Representative
Reservoir
Resistance
Rhyme
Rhythm
Ridiculous
Sacrifice
Sacrilegious
Salary
Savvy
Secretary
Seize
Separate
Sergeant
Shining
Similar
Sincerely
Skiing
Sophomore
Specifically
Specimen
Spontaneous
Strength
Subtle
Succeed
Succession
Susceptible
Suspicious
Technique
Temperamental
Temperature
Therefore
Thursday
Tomorrow
Transferring
twelfth
Tyranny
Unanimous
Undoubtedly
Unnecessarily
Until
Vacuum
Villain
Visible
Whether
Wholly

6
DISTINCTION BETWEEN SIMILAR EXPRESSIONS

1. (a) **Go to sea** (become a sailor)
   (b) **Go to the sea** (go on a voyage)
2. (a) **Go to school** (attend school for lessons)
   (b) **Go to the school** (for any other purpose)
3. (a) **Go to market** (for making purchases)
   (b) **Go to the market** (for any other purpose)
4. (a) **Go to bed** (go to sleep)
   (b) **Go to the bed** (go to the place where bed is)
5. (a) **Go to play** (for the purpose of taking part in the game)
   (b) **Go to a or the play** (go to the theatre for seeing the acting)
6. (a) **Work in hand** (work in which engaged)
   (b) **Work on hand** (work not yet done)
7. (a) **At no time** (never)
   (b) **In no time** (very soon)
8. (a) **In an hour** (just after an hour)
   (b) **Within an hour** (before the hour is over)
9. (a) **In the North** (North but inside; e.g., Kashmir is in the North of India)
   (b) **To the North** (North but outside; e.g., Kabul is to the North of India)
10. (a) **Work hard** (diligently)
    (b) **Work hardly** (scarcely)
11. (a) **Little hope of success** (no hope)
    (b) **A little hope of success** (some hope at least)
12. (a) **Few persons** (none)
    (b) **A few persons** (some at least)

13. (a) **Shot the bird** (killed)
    (b) **Shot at the bird** (aimed at the killing of bird)
14. (a) **To search a man** (to examine his body and clothes)
    (b) **To search for a man** (to find out a man)
15. (a) **Believe a man** (believe his statement)
    (b) **Believe in a man** (have faith in his honesty)
16. (a) **Meet a man** (knowingly)
    (b) **Meet with a man** (by chance)
17. (a) **Wait for a man** (expect him)
    (b) **Wait upon a man** (serve him)
18. (a) **A black horse and cow** (a black horse and a cow which is not black)
    (b) **A black horse and a black cow** (a black horse and a black cow)
19. (a) **A neighbour to one** (living near one)
    (b) **Neighbour** to one (kind to one)
20. (a) **Kalidas** (Kalidas himself)
    (b) **A Kalidas** (a poet like Kalidas)
21. (a) **Suffer from a headache** (suffer from an occasional attack of headache)
    (b) **Suffer from headache** (suffer from a disease, namely headache)
22. (a) **The poet and scholar** (one person)
    (b) **The poet and the scholar** (two persons)
23. (a) **Picture of Ram** (that is, picture of Ram)
    (b) **Picture of Ram's** (picture of which Ram is owner)
24. (a) **English** (English language)
    (b) **The English** (the English people)
25. (a) **Set the book on fire** (burn the book)
    (b) **Set the book on the fire** (place the book on the fire)
26. (a) **Think little** (to have a poor opinion)
    (b) **Little think** (think scarcely)
27. (a) **Come late** (come after fixed time)
    (b) **Come lately** (come recently)
28. (a) **Go home direct** (go home without stopping anywhere)
    (b) **Go home directly** (go home at once)
29. (a) **Has come** (coming is finished)
    (b) **Is come** (in the state of having come)
30. (a) **Is to go** (decided to go)
    (b) **Has to go** (under obligation to go)
31. (a) **Who is he?** (What is the name of the person?)
    (b) **What is he?** (What is the occupation of the person?)
    (c) **Which is he?** (Which is he among a group of person?)

32. (a) **The greatest poet** (the greatest poet of the male and female poets)
    (b) **The greatest poetess** (the greatest poet of all the female poets)
33. (a) **The eldest son** (the first born son)
    (b) **The oldest son** (the oldest of living sons)
34. (a) **Well** (in good health)
    (b) **Well off** (quite rich)
35. (a) **A garden flower** (a flower which grows only in gardens)
    (b) **A flower garden** (a garden of flowers)
36. (a) **Dead in sin** (great sinner)
    (b) **Dead to sin** (free from sin)
37. (a) **Go before Monday** (go up to Monday)
    (b) **Go by Monday** (go up to Monday)
38. (a) **Live at Aligarh** (live in the city of Aligarh)
    (b) **Live in Aligarh** (live in the district of Aligarh)
39. (a) **Eat the fruit** (eat the hole of the fruit)
    (b) **Eat of the fruit** (eat a part of the fruit)
40. (a) **Live on grass** (feed on grass)
    (b) **Live in grass** (live inside the grass)
41. (a) **Deal the cards** (distribute the cards)
    (b) **Deal in cards** (sell cards)
42. (a) **Take heart** (acquire courage)
    (b) **Take to heart** (to be deeply affected)
43. (a) **Enquire of one** (ask one something)
    (b) **Enquire for one** (desire to know one's whereabouts)
44. (a) **Stop at Agra** (for some time while going to another place)
    (b) **Stop in Agra** (live in Agra temporarily)
45. (a) **Want of one** (expect from one)
    (b) **Want with one** (to have business with one)
46. (a) **At fault** (puzzled)
    (b) **In fault** (to blame)
47. (a) **Lose one's only son** (to lose one son whom one had)
    (b) **Lose one's son only** (to lose one's son and none else)
48. (a) **Look sick** (appear to be sick just now)
    (b) **Look sickly** (appear to be unhealthy)
49. (a) **I have done the work** (I myself have done the work)
    (b) **I have the work done** (I have got the work done by somebody else)
50. (a) **I can do it** (I can do it without the help of anybody)
    (b) **I alone can do it** (I and nobody else can do it)

51. (a) **Was to come** (decided to come)
    (b) **Had to come** (obliged to come)
52. (a) **Arrive home safe** (to be safe when arriving home)
    (b) **Arrive home safely** (to have no difficulty on the way)
53. (a) **As you are poor** (because you are poor)
    (b) **Poor as you are** (although you are poor, yet ....)
54. (a) **Seem to be poor** (appear to be poor)
    (b) **Seem to have been poor** (appear to have been poor before)
55. (a) **Shall die** (destined to die)
    (b) **Will die** (determined to die)
56. (a) **Be honest** (it implies determination)
    (b) **May be honest** (it implies a mere wish)
57. (a) **A most interesting play** (interesting in a high degree)
    (b) **The most interesting play** (no other is more interesting)
58. (a) **May I do this work** (I want to do this work but I seek your permission to do it)
    (b) **Shall I do this work** (I want to know if you wish me to do this work)
59. (a) **The jury was** (the members of the jury taken as a whole)
    (b) **The jury were** (the members of the jury taken individually)
60. (a) **I would help you if I would** (I would help you if I had the power to help you. I had the will to help you but not the power)
    (b) **I could help you if I would** (I could help you if I had a will to help you. I had the power to help you but not the will or intention)
61. (a) **A member of society** (one of the human beings who constitute society)
    (b) **A member of a society** (a member of a particular association)
62. (a) **You love me more than he** (you love me more than he loves me)
    (b) **You love me more than him** (you love me more than you love him)
63. (a) **Find easy** (find no difficulty in understanding)
    (b) **Find easily** (find with no difficulty)
64. (a) **Complain to the man** (bring a complain against the man)
    (b) **Complain of the man** (bring a complain against the man before somebody)
65. (a) **Proceed to the work** (begin the work)
    (b) **Proceed with the work** (resume the work, which had been postponed for a time)
66. (a) **See one go** (see one leave the place)
    (b) **See one going** (see one when one was on the way)
67. (a) **He teaches English as well as writes it** (he teaches English and also writes it)
    (b) **He teaches English as well as he writes it** (he teaches and writes English with equal proficiency)
68. (a) **Tell me briefly** (tell me in few words)
    (b) **Tell me shortly** (tell me in a short time)

69. (a) **Are you going?** (the speaker wants to know whether you are going)
    (b) **Are you coming?** (it implies that the speaker is also going)
70. (a) **Get drunk** (to become drunk)
    (b) **Get drink** (to bring wine)
71. (a) **To have regard for** (to have respect for)
    (b) **To be regardful of** (to be careful about)
72. (a) **Called me** (shouted my name and asked me to come)
    (b) **Called on me** (visited me at my house)
73. (a) **Begin this book** (commence to read this book)
    (b) **Begin with this book** (begin this book before beginning any other)
74. (a) **Close the bargain** (finish the bargain)
    (b) **Close with the bargain** (accept the bargain)
75. (a) **Dispense the books** (distribute the books)
    (b) **Dispense with the books** (do away with the books)
76. (a) **Grasp the chain** (hold the chain tightly)
    (b) **Grasp at the chain** (attempt to catch the chain)
77. (a) **Guard this man** (protect this man)
    (b) **Guard against this man** (take every precaution against this man)
78. (a) **Inquire the matter** (ask what the matter is)
    (b) **Inquire into the matter** (investigate the matter by careful examination)
79. (a) **Repair the house** (put the house in good order)
    (b) **Repair to the house** (go to the house)
80. (a) **Work the machine** (manage the machine)
    (b) **Work at the machine** (be engaged with the machine)
81. (a) **Attend the meeting** (to be present in the meeting)
    (b) **Attend to the meeting** (to pay attention to the business of the meeting)
82. (a) **Come soon** (refer to the time taken in coming and means to come in as short a time as possible)
    (b) **Come quickly** (refer to the manner of coming and means, come on as rapid a pace a possible)
83. (a) **To have business** (to have a particular affair which demands attention and settlement)
    (b) **To have a business** (to have some occupation as a merchant or a shopkeeper)
84. (a) **To have enough food** (to have sufficient food)
    (b) **To have enough of food** (to have overeaten oneself)
85. (a) **Nothing like a battle** (nothing resembling a battle, meaning that the struggle is a trivial affair)
    (b) **Nothing like the battle** (meaning that no such battle has occurred before, in other words, the struggle is the most serious)

INDEX

A

Accent 55
  in compound words 57
Active listening 101
Active voice 397, 435
Adjectives 376
Adverbs 378
Apostrophe 460
Appraisal interview 340
Aristotle's art of persuasion 160
Articles 382
Artifacts 51
Auxiliary verbs 391

B

Bank correspondence 240
Better listening 105
Body language 117
Brainstorming 185
  benefits of 187
  limitations of 187
  rules of 186
Business communicators 4
Business etiquette 144
Business letter 190
  characteristics of 195
  examples of 204
  functions of 191
  importance of 191
  layout of 195
  parts of 199
  planning of 197
  purposes of 191
  typing guidelines for 471, 474
Business meetings 137
  conducting 140
  follow up 143
  planning 138
  purpose 138
Business presentations
  organization of 113
  planning of 111
  role of 108
  types of 109
  visual aids for 114
Business proposal 288
  designing of 295
  evaluation of 293
  feasibility of 293
  parts of 291
  revision of 296
  types of 289
Business reports 253
  characteristics of 254
  meaning and definition of 253
  significance of 255
  types of 255
  writing style of 269
Business writing
  drafting of 155
  evaluation of 159
  persuasion in 160
  revision of 157
  steps in 152-160

C

Capitalization 461
Career search 318
Casual listening 100
Chain communication 27
Chairperson, responsibilities of 138
Chromatics 50

Chronemics 50
Circular communication 27
Circular letters 232
Closed gesture 46
Closed questions 342
Cluster chain 31
Coherent sentences 418
Collectivism culture 131
Colon 455
Comma 453
Communication
  barriers in 75-79
  definition of 5
  directions of 21
  in business 4, 71
  in life 3
  in workplace 4
  meaning of 5
  media of 36
  nature of 6
  role of 3
Communication environment 14
Communication process
  components of 10-14
  levels of 15
  models of 7
Compound words, accent in 57
Concord 400
Conditional sentences 393
Conditionals 393
Confirmation letter 214
Conflict resolution 124
Conjunctions 381
Consensus 33
  advantages of 34
  limitations of 34
Correct business English 361
Counselling interviews 340
Covering letter 333
Creativity 163, 170
  and mind mapping 181
  blocking of 169
  definitions of 164
  in workplace 170
  situations and 164
  stages of 168
Credit information 227
Culture 128-129
Curriculum vitae 329

D

Dash 457
Decimals 467
Defective order 214
Diagonal communication 27
Downward communication 25
  essentials of 25
  importance of 25
  limitations of 25
Dyadic communication 71

E

Edward de Bono's creative techniques 172
Edward de Bono's problem-solving techniques 172
Effective communication, principles of 88-94
Effective English 360
Electronic information 309
  quality of 310
  sharing of 311
Electronic resume 330
  benefits of 330
  tips for 331
Emphatic sentences 435
Employment interview 339
English, different forms of 357
Ethical communication, significance of 85
Ethical decisions 135
Exclamation point 452
External proposal 290
External-operational communication 16
Extrapersonal communication 17

F

Feasibility report 260
Foreign words 475
Formal communication 22, 34
  advantages of 23
  characteristics of 22

limitations of 23
types of 23
Formal proposals 296
Formal report 257
Fractions 467
Frame of reference barriers 76
Free flow communication 28
Future tense 389

G

Goal setting 68
Gossip chain 30
Grapevine activity 30
advantages of 32
limitations of 32
Grapevine network 30
Group brainstorming 185
Group communication 15, 71
Growth career areas 320

H

Hearing-listening distinction 99
Hierarchical noise 14
High-context culture 130
Horizontal communication 24
importance of 24
limitations of 24
techniques for 24
Human brain
capacity of 175
hemispheres of 176
working of 175
Hyphen 459

I

Idiomatic expressions 478
Individual brainstorming 185
Individualism 131
Informal communication 29, 34
Informal report 256
Informational interview 338
Informational report 258
Innovation 170
Interjections 382
Internal proposal 290, 294
Internal punctuation 452
Internal-operational communication 15
Internet 309
Interpersonal communication 17
Interpretive report 258
Interview 335
definition of 336
myths about 336
nature of 338
parts of 346
relevant factors for 341
types of 338
Interview questions 347
Interviewee's preparation 344
Interviewer's preparation 342
Intrapersonal communication 17
Intuitive space 167
Inverted 'V' communication 28
Italics 458

J

Job application letters 331

L

Laboratory report 259
Language
background of 356
characteristics of 358
definition of 356
Letter of enquiry 204
Letters 257
Letters to the editor 245
Listening
in business 97
in a conference setting 102
in a small group 102
in specific situations 101
types of 100
Listening process 99-105
Low-context culture 130

M

Mass communication 16
Memorandums 257
Mind mapping
advantages of 180
and genius 178

creativity and 181
for essays 182
for lectures, seminars, workshops and tutorials 184
for report writing and proposal writing 184
for self-analysis 184
for summarizing reading 183
learning process and 178
note taking and 182
principles in 179
uses of 180
Miscellaneous reports 260
Modal auxiliaries 391
Modals 391
Modern communication devices 308
Multicultural audiences, communication with 133
Murphy's model of communication process 8

N

Negative team behavior 124
Noise 14
Non-berbal barriers 79
Non-verbal communication 42
advantages of 58
forms of 43
kinesics (body language) 44
limitations of 59
Nouns 363-366

O

Offers 206
Official letters 193
Olfactics 50
Omission mark 459
Open gesture 46
Open questions 342
Oral communication 37
advantages of 39
characteristics of 38
forms of 38
limitations of 40
utility of 40
Oral presentation 111
advantages of 109
disadvantages of 109
Oral report 256
Order form 213
Order, drafting of 212
Organizational communication 15-16
external dimension of 18
internal dimension of 18
scope of 18
Organizations
communication in 66, 71
functions of 65
macro approaches in 67
purposes of communication in 73
things common in 63.
understanding of 61

P

Panel interview 347
Paragraphing 441
coherence in 446
development in 443
variety in 442
Paragraphs, construction and length of 274
Paralanguage 51
elements of 52
Parentheses 456
Passive voice 397, 435
Past tense 387
Percentages 467
Performance appraisal report 259
Period 450
Periodic report 258
Personal communication 16
Phrases 436
Physical noise 14
Poor listening 102
Positive statements 439
Positive team behaviour 124
Prefixes 403, 405
Prepositions 379
Present tense 384
Presentation environment 120
Primary audience 153
Primary auxiliaries 391
Probability chain 31

Problem solving skills 162
  alternative approaches to 163
Problem, types of 162
Project report 258
Pronouns 368
Proxemics 48
Public communication 17, 72
Public relations letters 248
Purchase order 213

Q

Question mark 451
Quotation marks 458
Quotations 206

R

Radiant thinking 177
Redundant words 436
Replies 215
Resume
  elements of 321
  format of 321
  functional format of 328
  length of 321
  preparation of 320
  types of 327
Routine/progress report 258
Rumour, characteristics and control of 33

S

Sales letters 234
  characteristics of 235
  drafting of 236
Secondary audience 153
Semantic noise 14
Semicolon 454
Sentence stress 56
Sentence, unity in 412
  as separate unit 413
Sentence-end punctuations 450-467
Sentences, construction and length of 273
Shannon and Weaver's model of communication process 7
Single-strand chain 30
Solicited proposal 290
Spatial relationship 48
Stress 55
  importance of 57
Stress-shift 57
Structured interviews 337
Subject-verb agreement 374
Successful groups/teams, characteristics of 125
Suffixes 403

T

Team development, phases of 123
Teamwork 171
Teleconferencing 313
Thill and Bovee's model of communication process 9
Topic sentence 442
True sentences 413

U

Unsolicited proposal 290
Unstructured interviews 337
Upward communication 25
  importance of 26
  limitations of 26
  techniques for 26

V

Verbal barriers 77
Verbal communication 37
Verbals 375, 395
Verbs 370
Vertical communication 24
Videoconferencing 313
Virtual teams 126

W

Wheel communication 27
Word stress 56
Work-team communication, ethical dimension of 127
Written communication 40
  advantages of 41
  characteristics of 41
  forms of 41
  limitations of 42
  utility of 42
Written report 256

Portfolio [illegible] 194
[illegible] 188
[illegible] 195
Presentation [illegible]
[illegible] 188
[illegible] 48
Public relations [illegible]
Public relations officers 248
[illegible]
Q
Question [illegible] 81
[illegible]
R
[illegible]
[illegible]
S
Sales [illegible]
[illegible]
Semantic noise 16
[illegible]
Shannon and Weaver's model of communication 6
[illegible]
Structured interviews 37
Subject-verb agreement 4[illegible]
T
Team development, stages of 30
[illegible]
Telecommuting [illegible]
[illegible]
U
[illegible]
V
Visual communication 3[illegible]
W
Written communication 41
advantages of 41
characteristics of 41
forms of 41
limitations of 42
[illegible]